4000
99185

Advances in Behavioral Economics
Volume 1

Contributors

RICHARD A. BAUMAN
Walter Reed Army Institute of Research
Washington, D.C. 20307

GARY BECKER
Department of Economics
The University of Chicago
Chicago, Illinois 60637

ALAN P. COVICH
Department of Zoology
University of Oklahoma
Norman, Oklahoma 73017
    and
Center for Energy and Environment
    Research
University of Puerto Rico
Marine Ecology Division
College Station,
Mayaguez, Puerto Rico 00708

LEONARD GREEN
Department of Psychology
Washington University
St. Louis, Missouri 63130

R.J. HERRNSTEIN
Department of Psychology
Harvard University
Cambridge, Massachusetts 02138

STEVEN R. HURSH
Department of Medical Neuroscience
Walter Reed Army Institute of Research
Washington, D.C. 20307

F. THOMAS JUSTER
Institute for Social Research
The University of Michigan
Ann Arbor, Michigan 48106

JOHN H. KAGEL
Department of Economics
University of Houston
Houston, Texas 77004

S.E.G. LEA
Department of Psychology
Washington Singer Laboratories
University of Exeter
Exeter, England
EX4 4QG

HOWARD RACHLIN
Department of Psychology
State University of New York
    at Stony Brook
Stony Brook, New York 11794

HERBERT A. SIMON
Department of Psychology
Carnegie-Mellon University
Pittsburgh, Pennsylvania 15213

WILLIAM VAUGHAN, JR.
Department of Psychology
Harvard University
Cambridge, Massachusetts 02138

LOUIS L. WILDE
California Institute of Technology
Division of the Humanities and
    Social Sciences
Pasadena, California 91125

ADVANCES IN
BEHAVIORAL ECONOMICS
VOLUME 1

Edited by

Leonard Green
Washington University

John H. Kagel
University of Houston

Ablex Publishing Corporation
Norwood, N.J. 07648

ISBN 0-89391-218-2

ISSN 0890-0159

Ablex Publishing Corporation
355 Chestnut Street
Norwood, N.J. 07648

Contents

Introduction

For most of their respective histories, psychology and economics have remained relatively insulated from one another. In economics, the concept of rational man, whether explicitly stated or not, has been an overriding assumption. When behavior failed to conform to economic theory, the causes were often seen as noneconomic and thus relegated to the psychological, by which was meant irrational behavior. The economist's view of behavior was little influenced by the work being conducted by psychologists. This may appear somewhat surprising, given that psychology is often defined as "the science of behavior." Should not the psychological work, then, benefit economic theory?

Psychologists, for their part, have ignored the wealth of theory that economics had to offer. Since microeconomics deals with individual consumer behavior, would not such work be of value in evaluating and interpreting psychological theories of behavior, behavior which takes place within an economic arena? Should not the economic work, then, benefit psychological theory?

In 1953, B.F. Skinner noted the parallel between ratio schedules of reinforcement studies in the operant psychology laboratory and piece-rate wages and commission selling. Under a ratio schedule of reinforcement, the subject is presented with an outcome (reinforcer) after a given number of responses. For example, under a fixed ratio of 50 schedule of reinforcement, the subject would receive an outcome following every fiftieth response. Notice the similarity to piece-rate wages, in which a worker receives a payoff for every fixed number of work units. The study of ratio schedules, pursued for years by operant psychologists, would, one might suppose, provide economists with valuable information on how such schedules influence behavior. The analysis of such schedules would, one might also suppose, be aided by economic models. Yet only recently has any significant interaction between economic and psychological theory been evident.

The reasons for the lack of interaction between the two disciplines are several, and not difficult to appreciate. Within academic disciplines, lines demarcating intellectual areas are strict and often unyielding. Historical antecedents define areas of study. Methods within disciplines develop along different paths, thus providing different approaches to the study of behavior, as well as markedly different vocabularies.

The methods of inquiry between the two disciplines have been noticeably different. Economists traditionally use macro-data, compiled from large populations and relating to aggregate economic variables, while experimental psychologists use data generated by considerably fewer subjects and relating to individual subject behavior. Nonhuman organisms are frequently studied by psychologists in an attempt to better control extraneous and confounding variables and previous, extra-experimental histories. The study of nonhuman animals has a long history in psychology. However, such research was without precedent within economics. After all, how could the study of rational man be advanced by the use of such lowly creatures as rats, pigeons, or even monkeys? Further, the use of highly-controlled, laboratory environments of any sort has been seen by many economists as artificial, and thus not relevant to "real" economic problems.

This traditional insularity between the fields has been dramatically changing over the past decade. Economists have begun to enter the laboratory, and conduct smaller-scale experiments on delimited samples of subjects under controlled environments. Psychologists have begun to incorporate economic theory into their designs of experiments and analyses of results. In addition, behavioral biology has drawn upon the theories and research of psychology and economics while, concomitantly, the latter two disciplines have incorporated biological and evolutionary concepts into their analyses.

Thus the area of behavioral economics has emerged. While a strict definition of the field will not be attempted—it is still too soon to delimit the field of inquiry and interaction—we are much encouraged by a transdisciplinary approach to the understanding of behavior. Behavioral economics, by emphasizing experimental and laboratory research to test hypotheses bearing on the various tenets and theories of psychology, economics, and behavioral biology, holds promise of providing new insights and valuable contributions to these fields of study. Whether these fields will benefit from this transdisciplinary approach, whether their insights and contributions will prove to be richer than if the fields were to remain insulated and separate, remains to be seen. However, we already see some signs that augur well for the future of behavioral economics.

The present series, *Advances in Behavioral Economics,* will provide a forum for research and theory, with this, the first volume of the series, to provide an introduction to the field. Because the theoretical scope and approach to be taken within the field will vary, the value of any one to be determined by its success in prediction and comprehensiveness, we present three proposals for research programs in Part I (Proposed Research Programs in Behavioral Economics) by Gary Becker, Herbert A. Simon, and Howard Rachlin. Behavioral economics, as an experimental science, requires the generation of data which can be valuably used to test among competing theories. In Part II (A Call for Data), F. Thomas Juster describes some of the problems associated with the more traditional economic approaches to data collection while describing types of data seen as necessary in order for substantially new contributions to emerge. The work of experimental psychologists and biologists who use nonhuman animal subjects is highlighted in Part III (Animal Models in Behavioral Economics). Here the importance of such nonhuman research for investigating demand theory (chapters by S.E.G. Lea and by Steven R. Hursh and Richard A. Bauman) and intertemporal choice (John H. Kagel and Leonard Green) becomes evident. In addition, the interrelations of psychology, economics, and evolutionary biology are made explicit in William Vaughan, Jr. and R.J. Herrnstein's contribution. Finally, two reviews of research, the first by Louis L. Wilde based on work with humans in the area of consumer search behavior, and the other by Alan P. Covich based upon animal foraging and behavioral responses to surplus resources, appear in Part IV (Research Reviews). We hope through this arrangement of the volume to provide an overview of some of the questions and approaches subsumed under the heading of behavioral economics.

Leonard Green
John H. Kagel

PART I

PROPOSED RESEARCH PROGRAMS IN BEHAVIORAL ECONOMICS

Gary Becker ("Economic Analysis and Human Behavior") and Herbert A. Simon ("Rational Decision Making in Business Organizations") present contrasting research strategies, or scientific paradigms, for behavioral economics. Both have as their goals descriptive/predictive models of behavior. The conflict between the research strategies is clear, however:

> The combined assumptions of maximizing behavior, market equilibrium and stable preferences, used relentlessly and unflinchingly, form the heart of the economic approach as I see it. (Becker)

> Human behavior, even rational human behavior, is not to be accounted for by a handful of invariants. It is certainly not to be accounted for by assuming perfect adaptation to the environment. (Simon)

In the case of conflict between the model's prediction and the agent's behavior, Becker's research strategy calls for respecification of the constraints, and identification of relevant characteristics of the objective function which agents are presumably maximizing. Simon, on the other hand, would weaken assumptions about the decision maker's capabilities and incorporate notions of bounded rationality into the objective function, replacing optimization with satisficing, and emphasizing learning and adaptation mechanisms. These differences in approach are neatly summarized in Simon's characterization of the neoclassical approach to search and information transfer:

> In none of these theories—any more than in statistical decision theory or the theory of games—is the assumption of perfect maximization abandoned. Limits and costs of information are introduced, not as psychological charac-

teristics of the decision maker, but as part of his technological environment. Hence, the new theories do nothing to alleviate the computational complexities facing the decision maker—do not see him coping with them by heroic approximation, simplifying and satisficing, but simply magnify and multiply them. (Simon)

One will find adherents to both of these research paradigms within the field of behavioral economics as operationally defined here. The common theme that we would hope to employ to tie such divergent approaches together is the use of replicable and verifiable experimental analyses of behavior. In advocating experimental methods as a common underlying theme of inquiry, we are not committed exclusively to human vs. animal experiments or to laboratory vs. naturally-occurring experiments (what Campbell and Stanley, 1966, call quasi-experimental designs). Further, we are fully committed to the use of theory to analyze experimental outcomes and to identify the observational implications of behavioral assumptions. Finally, we are convinced that the different behavioral disciplines—economics, psychology, ecology, political science, and sociology—have something to learn from each other, and that to do so we must maintain a dialogue that is intelligible to all.

The contrasting research approaches of Becker and Simon are reflected in the two strands of "objective functional psychology" that Howard Rachlin discusses in "Animal Choice and Human Choice." Rachlin argues that the difference between these two branches of psychology which he classifies as "cognitivist vs. behaviorist," is often a difference "more of tone than substance."[1] Rachlin suggests that developing ways to study choice situations in the laboratory with meaningful, nonverbal problems, irrespective of whether the subjects are humans or other animals, is of critical importance to reconciling these two strands of psychology. Certainly, such studies are an essential element of the field of behavioral economics as we see it.

REFERENCES

Campbell, D.T., & Stanley, J.C. (1966). *Experimental and quasi-experimental designs for research*. Chicago: Rand-McNally.

---

[1] Indeed, one might make a similar argument for differences between neoclassical (Becker) and bounded rationality approaches (Simon) to a number of situations. For example, in discussing satisficing theories of business firm behavior, Simon notes "...a number of these (satisficing) theories assume that organizational learning takes place, so that if the environment were stationary for a sufficient length of time, the system equilibrium would approach closer and closer to the classical profit-maximizing equilibrium." At this level, the argument reduces to whether environmental disturbances are generally large enough and frequent enough to prevent the neoclassical solution from being an adequate approximation.

Chapter 1

Economic Analysis and Human Behavior*

Gary Becker

Department of Economics
University of Chicago

Economy is the art of making the most of life. (George Bernard Shaw, *Maxims for Revolutionaries*)

Although few persons would dispute the distinctiveness of an 'economic' approach to human behavior, it is not easy to state exactly what distinguishes the economic approach from social, psychological, anthropological, political, or even genetical approaches. In this essay I attempt to spell out the principal attributes of the economic approach.

Let us turn for guidance first to the definitions of different fields. At least three conflicting definitions of economics are still common. Economics is said to be the study of (a) the allocation of material goods to satisfy material wants,[1] (b) the market sector,[2] and (c) the allocation of scarce means to satisfy competing ends.[3]

---

* *For valuable comments* I am indebted to Joseph Ben-David, Milton Friedman, Victor Fuchs, Robert T. Michael, Jacob Mincer, Richard Posner, and T.W. Schultz. I am especially indebted to George J. Stigler for many discussions, comments, and much needed encouragement, and to Robert K. Merton for a helpful and lengthy response to an earlier draft that provided a sociologist's perspective on the issues covered in this essay. The usual disclaimer to the effect that none of these persons should be held responsible for the arguments made in this essay is especially appropriate, since several disagreed with the central theme.

This chapter is a revised version of Gary Becker's Introduction to his book *The Economic Approach to Human Behavior* (copyright ©1976, The University of Chicago Press), and is published here by permission of The University of Chicago Press.

[1] "[Economics] is the social science that deals with the ways in which men and societies seek to satisfy their material needs and desires," Albert Rees (1968); "[Economics is the] study of the supplying of man's physical needs and wants," "Economics," *The Columbia Encyclopedia,* 3rd edn, p. 624; and see the many earlier references to Marshall, Cannan, and others in Robbins (1962).

[2] Pigou (1962, p. 11) said "[Economic welfare is] that part of social welfare that can be brought directly or indirectly into relation with the measuring rod of money."

[3] Economics is the science which studies human behavior as a relationship between ends and scarce means which have alternative uses," Robbins (1962, p. 16); "Economics...is the study of the allocation of scarce resources among unlimited and competing uses," Rees (1968), and many other references.

The definition of economics in terms of material goods is the narrowest and the least satisfactory. It does not describe adequately either the market sector or what economists "do." For the production of tangible goods now provides less than half of all the market employment in the United States, and the intangible outputs of the service sector are now larger in value than the outputs of the goods sector (see Fuchs, 1968). Moreover, economists are as successful in understanding the production and demand for retail trade, films, or education as they are for autos or meat. The persistence of definitions which tie economics to material goods is perhaps due to a reluctance to submit certain kinds of human behavior to the "frigid" calculus of economics.

The definition of economics in terms of scarce means and competing ends is the most general of all. It defines economics by the nature of the problem to be solved, and encompasses far more than the market sector or "what economists do."[4] Scarcity and choice characterize all resources allocated by the political process (including which industries to tax, how fast to increase the money supply, and whether to go to war); by the family including decisions about a marriage mate, family size, the frequency of church attendance, and the allocation of time between sleeping and waking hours); by scientists (including decisions about allocating their thinking time and mental energy to different research problems); and so on in endless variety. This definition of economics is so broad that it often is a source of embarrassment rather than of pride to many economists, and usually is immediately qualified to exclude most nonmarket behavior.[5]

All of these definitions of economics simply define the scope, and none tells us one iota about what the "economic" approach is. It could stress tradition and duty, impulsive behavior, maximizing behavior, or any other behavior in analyzing the market sector or the allocation of scarce means to competing ends.

Similarly, definitions of sociology and other social sciences are of equally little help in distinguishing their approaches from others. For example, the statement that sociology "is the study of social aggregates and groups in their institutional organization, of institutions and their organization, and of causes and consequences of changes in institutions and social organization" Reiss, 1968) does not distinguish the subject matter, let alone the approach, of sociology from, say, economics. Or the statement that "comparative psychology is concerned with the behavior of different species of living organisms" (Waters & Bunnell, 1968) is as general as the definitions of economics and sociology, and as uninformative.

---

[4] Boulding (1966) attributes this definition of economics to Jacob Viner.

[5] Almost immediately after giving the broad definition of economics, Rees (1968) gives one in terms of material needs, without explaining why he so greatly reduced the scope of economics. Even Robbins, after an excellent discussion of what an economic problem is in the first chapter of his classic work on the nature and scope of economics (1962), basically restricts his analysis in later chapters to the market sector.

Let us turn away from definitions, therefore, because I believe that what most distinguishes economics as a discipline from other disciplines in the social sciences is not its subject matter but its approach. Indeed, many kinds of behavior fall within the subject matter of several disciplines: for example, fertility behavior is considered part of sociology, anthropology, economics, history, human biology, and perhaps even politics. I contend that the economic approach is uniquely powerful because it can integrate a wide range of human behavior.

Everyone recognizes that the economic approach assumes maximizing behavior more explicitly and extensively than do other approaches, be it the utility or wealth function of the household, firm, union, or government bureau that is maximized. Moreover, the economic approach assumes the existence of markets that with varying degrees of efficiency coordinate the actions of different participants—individuals, firms, even nations—so that their behavior becomes mutually consistent. Preferences are assumed not to change substantially over time, nor to be very different between wealthy and poor persons, or even between persons in different societies and cultures.

Prices and other market instruments allocate the scarce resources within a society and thereby constrain the desires of participants and coordinate their actions. In the economic approach, these market instruments perform most, if not all, of the functions assigned to "structure" in sociological theories.[6]

The preferences that are assumed to be stable do not refer to market goods and services, like oranges, automobiles, or medical care, but to underlying objects of choice that are produced by each household using market goods and services, their own time, and other inputs. These underlying preferences are defined over fundamental aspects of life—such as health, prestige, sensual pleasure, benevolence, or envy—that do not always bear a stable relation to market goods and services (see Michael & Becker, 1973). The assumption of stable preferences provides a stable foundation for generating predictions about responses to various changes, and prevents the analyst from succumbing to the temptation of simply postulating the required shift in preferences to "explain" all apparent contradictions to his predictions.

Maximizing behavior and stable preferences are not simply primitive assumptions, but can be derived from arguments about natural selection of suitable behavior as humans evolved over time (see Wilson, 1975; Dawkins, 1976; and Becker, 1976). Indeed, the economic approach and the modern biological theory of natural selection are closely related (recall that both Darwin and Wallace stated that they were greatly influenced by Malthusian population theory), and are perhaps different aspects of the same more basic theory (see the discussion in Hirshleifer, 1977; also see Tullock, 1971).

---

[6] An excellent statement of structural analysis can be found in Merton (1975).

The combined assumptions of maximizing behavior, market equilibrium, and stable preferences, used relentlessly and unflinchingly, form the heart of the economic approach as I see it. They are responsible for the many theorems associated with this approach. For example, that (a) a rise in price reduces quantity demanded,[7] be it a rise in the market price of eggs reducing the demand for eggs, a rise in the "shadow" price of children reducing the demand for children, or a rise in the office waiting time for physicians, which is one component of the full price of physician services, reducing the demand for their services; (b) a rise in price increases the quantity supplied, be it a rise in the market price of beef increasing the number of cattle raised and slaughtered, a rise in the wage rate offered to married women increasing their labor force participation, or a reduction in "cruising" time raising the effective price received by taxicab drivers and thereby increasing the supply of taxicabs; (c) competitive markets satisfy consumer preferences more effectively than monopolistic markets, be it the market for aluminium or the market for ideas; or (d) a tax on the output of a market reduced that output, be it an excise tax on gasoline that reduces the use of gasoline, punishment of criminals (which is a "tax" on crime) that reduces the amount of crime, or a tax on wages that reduces the labor supplied to the market sector.

The economic approach is clearly not restricted to material goods and wants, nor even to the market sector. Prices, be they the money prices of the market sector or the shadow imputed prices of the nonmarket sector, measure the opportunity cost of using scarce resources, and the economic approach predicts the same kind of response to shadow prices as to market prices. Consider, for example, a person whose only scarce resource is his or her limited amount of time. This time is used to produce various commodities that enter his or her preference function, the aim being to maximize utility. Even without a market sector, either directly or indirectly, each commodity has a relevant marginal shadow price, namely, the time required to produce a unit change in that commodity; in equilibrium, the ratio of these prices must equal the ratio of the marginal utilities.[8] Most importantly, an increase in the relative price of any commodity—i.e., an increase in the time required to produce a unit of that commodity—would tend to reduce the consumption of that commodity.

The economic approach does not assume that all participants in any market necessarily have complete information or engage in costless transac-

---

[7] That maximizing behavior is not necessary to reach this conclusion is shown in Becker (1962).

[8] He maximizes $U = U(Z_1 \ldots Z_m)$ subject to $Z_i = f_i(t_i)$ and $\sum_{i=1}^{m} t_i = t$, where Z_i is the ith commodity, f_i the production function for Z_i, and t_i is the time input into Z_i. The well-known first-order equilibrium conditions for the allocation of his scarce resource, time, are $\partial U/\partial Z_i = \lambda(\partial t_i)/(\partial Z_i) = (\lambda)/(\partial Z_i/\partial t_i) = \lambda/MP_{t_i}$, where λ is his marginal utility of time.

tions. Incomplete information or costly transactions should not, however, be confused with irrational or volatile behavior.[9] The economic approach has developed a theory of the optimal or rational accumulation of costly information[10] that implies, for example, greater investment in information when undertaking major rather than minor decisions—the purchase of a house or entrance into marriage versus the purchase of a sofa or bread. The assumption that information is often seriously incomplete because it is costly to acquire is used in the economic approach to explain the same kind of behavior that is explained by irrational and volatile behavior, or traditional behavior, or "nonrational" behavior in other discussions.

When an apparently profitable opportunity to a firm, worker, or household is not exploited, the economic approach does not take refuge in assertions about irrationality, contentment with wealth already acquired, or convenient ad hoc shifts in values (i.e., preferences). Rather, it postulates the existence of costs, monetary or psychic, of taking advantage of these opportunities that eliminate their profitability—costs that may not be easily "seen" by outside observers. Of course, postulating the existence of costs closes or "completes" the economic approach in the same, almost tautological, way that postulating the existence of (sometimes unobserved) uses of energy completes the energy system, and preserves the law of the conservation of energy. Systems of analysis in chemistry, genetics, and other fields are completed in a related manner. The critical question is whether a system is completed in a useful way; the important theorems derived from the economic approach indicate that it has been completed in a way that yields much more than a bundle of empty tautologies in good part because, as I indicated earlier, the assumption of stable preferences provides a foundation for predicting the responses to various changes.

Moreover, the economic approach does not assume that decision units are necessarily conscious of their efforts to maximize or can verbalize or otherwise describe in an informative way reasons for the systematic patterns in their behavior.[11] Thus, it is consistent with the emphasis on the subconscious in modern psychology and with the distinction between manifest and latent functions in sociology (Merton, 1968). In addition, the economic approach does not draw conceptual distinctions between major and minor decisions, such as those involving life and death[12] in contrast to the choice of a brand of coffee; or between decisions said to involve strong emotions

---

[9] Schumpeter appears to confuse them, although with considerable modification (1950, ch. 21, section "Human Nature in Politics").

[10] The pioneering paper is Stigler's "The Economics of Information" (1961).

[11] This point is stressed in Milton Friedman's seminal article, "The Methodology of Positive Economics" (1953).

[12] The length of life itself is a decision variable in the important study by Grossman (1972).

and those with little emotional involvement,[13] such as in choosing a mate or the number of children in contrast to buying paint; or between decisions by persons with different incomes, education, or family backgrounds.

Indeed, I have come to the position that the economic approach is a comprehensive one that is applicable to all human behavior, be it behavior involving money prices or imputed shadow prices, repeated or infrequent decisions, large or minor decisions, emotional or mechanical ends, rich or poor persons, patients or therapists, businessmen or politicians, teachers or students. The applications of the economic approach so conceived are as extensive as the scope of economics in the definition given earlier that emphasizes scarce means and competing ends. It is an appropriate approach to go with such a broad and unqualified definition, and with the statement by Shaw which begins this essay.

The economic approach to human behavior is not new, even outside the market sector. Adam Smith often (but not always!) used this approach to understand political behavior. Jeremy Bentham was explicit about his belief that the pleasure–pain calculus is applicable to all human behavior: "Nature has placed mankind under the governance of two sovereign masters, *pain and pleasure*. It is for them alone to point out what we ought to do as well as to determine what we shall do... They govern us in all we do, in all we say, in all we think" (1963). The pleasure–pain calculus is said to be applicable to *all* we do, say, and think, without restriction to monetary decisions, repetitive choices, unimportant decisions, etc. Bentham did apply his calculus to an extremely wide range of human behavior, including criminal sanctions, prison reform, legislation, usury laws, and jurisprudence, as well as the markets for goods and services. Although Bentham explicitly states that the pleasure-pain calculus is applicable to what we "shall" do as well as to what we "ought" to do, he was primarily interested in "ought"—he was first and foremost a reformer—and did not develop a theory of actual human behavior with many testable implications. He often became bogged down in tautologies because he did not maintain the assumption of stable preferences, and because he was more concerned about making his calculus consistent with all behavior than about deriving the restrictions it imposed on behavior.

Marx and his followers have applied what is usually called an "economic" approach to politics, marriage, and other nonmarket behavior as well as to market behavior. But to the Marxist, the economic approach means that the organization of production is decisive in determining social and political

---

[13] Jeremy Bentham said, "As to the proposition that passion does not calculate, this, like most of these very general and oracular propositions is not true... I would not say that even a madman does not calculate. Passion calculates, more or less, in every man" (1963). He does add, however, that "of all passions, the most given to calculation... [is] the motive of pecuniary interest."

structure, and he places much emphasis upon material goods, processes, and ends, conflict between capitalists and workers, and general subjugation of one class by another. What I have called the "economic approach" has little in common with this view. Moreover, the Marxist, like the Benthamite, has concentrated on what ought to be, and has often emptied his approach of much predictive content in the effort to make it consistent with all events.

Needless to say, the economic approach has not provided equal insight into and understanding of all kinds of behavior: for example, the determinants of war and of many other political decisions have not yet been much illuminated by this approach (or by any other approach). I believe, however, that the limited success is mainly the result of limited effort and not lack of relevance. For, on the one hand, the economic approach has not been systematically applied to war, and its application to other kinds of political behavior is quite recent; on the other hand, much apparently equally intractable behavior—such as fertility, child-rearing, labor force participation, and other decisions of families—has been greatly illuminated in recent years by the systematic application of the economic approach.

Support for the wide applicability of the economic approach is provided by the extensive literature developed in the last 20 years that uses the economic approach to analyze an almost endlessly varied set of problems, including the evolution of language (Marschak, 1965), church attendance (Azzi & Ehrenberg, 1975), political behavior (Buchanan & Tullock, 1962; Stigler, 1975), the legal system (Posner, 1973; Becker & Landes, 1974), the extinction of animals (Smith, 1975), the incidence of suicide (Hamermesh & Soss, 1974), altruism and social interactions (Becker, 1974, 1976, Hirshleifer, 1977), and marriage, fertility, and divorce (Schultz, 1974; Becker, Landes, & Michael, 1977). To convey dramatically the flavor of the economic approach, I briefly discuss several of the more unusual and controversial applications.

Good health and a long life are important aims of most persons, but surely no more than a moment's reflection is necessary to convince anyone that they are not the only aims: somewhat better health or a longer life may be sacrificed because they conflict with other aims. The economic approach implies that there is an "optimal" expected length of life, where the value in utility of an additional year is less than the utility forgone by using time and other resources to obtain that year. Therefore, a person may be a heavy smoker or so committed to work as to omit all exercise, not necessarily because he is ignorant of the consequences or "incapable" of using the information he possesses, but because the lifespan forfeited is not worth the cost to him of quitting smoking or working less intensively. These would be unwise decisions if a long life were the only aim, but as long as other aims exist, they could be informed and in this sense "wise."

According to the economic approach, therefore, *most* (if not all!) deaths are to some extent "suicides" in the sense that they could have been postponed if more resources had been invested in prolonging life. This not only has implications for the analysis of what are ordinarily called suicides,[14] but also calls into question the common distinction between suicides and "natural" deaths. Once again, the economic approach and modern psychology come to similar conclusions, since the latter emphasizes that a "death wish" lies behind many "accidental" deaths and others allegedly due to "natural" causes.

The economic approach does not merely restate in language familiar to economists different behavior with regard to health, removing all possibility of error by a series of tautologies. The approach implies, for example, that both health and medical care would rise as a person's wage rate rose, that ageing would bring declining health although expenditures on medical care would rise, and that more education would induce an increase in health even though expenditures on medical care would fall. None of these or other implications are necessarily true, but all appear to be consistent with the available evidence.[15]

According to the economic approach, a person decides to marry when the utility expected from marriage exceeds that expected from remaining single or from additional search for a more suitable mate. Similarly, a married person terminates his (or her) marriage when the utility anticipated from becoming single or marrying someone else exceeds the loss in utility from separation, including losses due to physical separation from one's children, division of joint assets, legal fees, and so forth. Since many persons are looking for mates, a *market* in marriages can be said to exist: each person tries to do the best he or she can, given that everyone else in the market is trying to do the best they can. A sorting of persons into different marriages is said to be an equilibrium sorting if persons not married to each other in this sorting could not marry and make each other better off.

Again, the economic approach has numerous implications about behavior that could be falsified. For example, it implies that "likes" tend to marry each other, when measured by intelligence, education, race, family background, height, and many other variables, and that "unlikes" marry when measured by wage rates and some other variables. The implication that men with relatively high wage rates marry women with relatively low wage rates (other variables being held constant) surprises many, but appears consistent with the available data when they are adjusted for the large fraction of married women who do not work (see Becker, 1973). The economic approach also implies that higher-income persons marry younger and divorce less frequently than others, implications consistent with the available evidence (see Keeley, 1977) but not with common beliefs. Still another

---

[14] Some of these implications are developed in Hammermesh and Soss (1974).

[15] These implications are derived, and the evidence is examined, in Grossman (1972).

implication is that an increase in the relative earnings of wives increases the likelihood of marital dissolution, which partly explains the greater dissolution rate among black than white families.

According to the Heisenberg indeterminacy principle, the phenomena analyzed by physical scientists cannot be observed in a "natural" state because their observations change these phenomena. An even stronger principle has been suggested for social scientists, since they are participants as well as analysts and, therefore, are supposed to be incapable of objective observation. The economic approach makes a very different but distantly related point: namely, that persons only choose to follow scholarly or other intellectual or artistic pursuits if they expect the benefits, both monetary and psychic, to exceed those available in alternative occupations. Since the criterion is the same as in the choice of more commonplace occupations, there is no obvious reason why intellectuals would be less concerned with personal rewards, more concerned with social well-being, or more intrinsically honest than others.[16]

It then follows from the economic approach that an increased demand by different interest groups or constituencies for particular intellectual arguments and conclusions would stimulate an increased supply of these arguments, by the theorem cited earlier on the effect of a rise in "price" on quantity supplied. Similarly, a flow of foundation or government funds into particular research topics, even "ill-advised" topics, would have no difficulty generating proposals for research on those topics. What the economic approach calls normal responses of supply to changes in demand, others may call intellectual or artistic "prostitution" when applied to intellectual or artistic pursuits. Perhaps, but attempts to distinguish sharply the market for intellectual and artistic services from the market for "ordinary" goods have been the source of confusion and inconsistency (see Director, 1964; Coase, 1974).

The economic approach assumes that crime is a part-time or full-time occupation like carpentry, engineering, or teaching. Persons choose to become criminals for the same reason that others choose to become carpenters or teachers; namely, because they expect the "profit" from becoming a criminal—the present value of the series of differences between returns and costs, both nonmonetary and monetary returns and costs—to exceed the "profit" from other occupations. An increase in return or a decrease in costs from criminal activity increases the number of persons becoming criminals by increasing the "profit" from crime relative to other occupations.

Therefore, this approach implies that felonies like robbery and theft are committed mainly by poorer persons, not because of anomie or alienation,

---

[16] This example is taken from Stigler (1976). Also see the discussion of the reward system in science and of related issues in Merton (1973, esp. part 4).

but because their deficiencies in education and other training reduce the "profit" to them from legal occupations. Similarly, unemployment in the legal sector increases the number of crimes against property (see Ehrlich, 1973), not because of restlessness and bitterness, but because unemployment reduces the "profit" from legal occupations. The number and severity of the crimes committed by women have been growing relative to those committed by men (see Bartel, 1976) because it has become more "profitable" for women to participate in market occupations, including crime (see Mincer, 1963).

The most controversial implication of the economic approach to crime is that punishment "works" in the sense that an increased probability of conviction of criminals or punishment when convicted reduces the amount of crime because returns from crime are reduced. If criminals correctly anticipated the probability and magnitude of punishments, a high rate of recidivism would be no more surprising and no more indicative of the failure of punishments than would the return to carpentry of a large fraction of unemployed or injured carpenters be indicative that the number of carpenters is unaffected by the frequency of their unemployment and injury. Similarly, rehabilitation programs have generally failed (see Martinson, 1974) for the same reason that retraining persons in the legal sector has generally failed: when people have chosen their "occupations," including crime, wisely, their choices would not be much affected by exhortation or by minor changes in their prospects in other occupations.

Punishments deter crimes of "passion"[17] like rape or terrorism (see Landes, 1977) as much as "economic" crimes like bank robbery (Ozenne, 1974) and embezzlement; among other things, this conclusion raises doubts about the insanity plea, premeditation, and other distinctions made in the conviction and sentencing of criminals. The economic approach implies that capital punishment would significantly deter murder and other crimes *if the alternative is the usual punishment for these crimes* in the United States and many other Western countries (see Ehrlich, 1975, 1977; National Academy of Science, 1977).

I am not suggesting that the economic approach is used by all economists for all human behavior, or even by most economists for most human behavior. Indeed, many economists cannot resist the temptation to hide their own lack of understanding behind allegations of irrational behavior, unnecessary ignorance, folly, ad hoc shifts in values, and the like, which is simply acknowledging defeat in the guise of considered judgement. For example, if some Broadway theater-owners charge prices that result in long delays before seats are available, the owners are alleged to be ignorant of the profit-maximizing price structure rather than the analyst ignorant of why actual prices do maximize profits. When only a portion of the variation in

---

[17] Even passion calculates; see the quotation from Bentham in note 13.

earnings is explained, the unexplained portion is attributed to luck or chance,[18] not to ignorance of or inability to measure additional systematic components. The coal industry is called inefficient because certain cost and output calculations point in that direction (see Henderson, 1958), although an attractive alternative hypothesis is that the calculations are seriously in error.

War is said to be caused by madmen, and political behavior, more generally, dominated by folly and ignorance. Recall Keynes's remark about "madmen in authority, who hear voices in the air" (1962, p. 383), and, although Adam Smith, the principal founder of the economic approach, interpreted some laws and legislation in the same way that he interpreted market behavior, even he, without much discussion, lamely dismissed others as a result of folly and ignorance.[19]

Examples abound in the economic literature of changes in preferences conveniently introduced ad hoc to explain puzzling behavior. Education is said to change preferences—about different goods and services, political candidates, or family size—rather than real income or the relative cost of different choices.[20] Businessmen talk about the social responsibilities of business because their attitudes are said to be influenced by public discussions of this question rather than because such talk is necessary to maximize their profits, given the climate of public intervention. Or advertisers are alleged to take advantage of the fragility of consumer preferences, with little explanation of why, for example, advertising is heavier in some industries than others, changes in importance in a given industry over time, and occurs in quite competitive industries as well as in monopolistic ones.[21]

Naturally, what is tempting to economists nominally committed to the economic approach becomes irresistible to others without this commitment, and without a commitment to the scientific study of sociology, psychology, or anthropology. With an ingenuity worthy of admiration if put to better use, almost any conceivable behavior is alleged to be dominated by ignorance and irrationality, values and their frequent unexplained shifts, custom and tradition, the compliance somehow induced by social norms, or the ego and the id.

---

[18] An extreme example is Jencks (1972). Jencks even grossly understates the portion that can be explained, because he neglects the important work by Mincer and others (see especially Mincer, 1974).

[19] See Stigler (1971). Smith does not indicate why ignorance is dominant in the passage of certain laws and not others.

[20] For an interpretation of the effects of education on consumption entirely in terms of income and price effects, see Michael (1972).

[21] For an analysis of advertising that is consistent with stable preferences and implies that advertising might even be more important in competitive than monopolistic industries, see Stigler and Becker (1977). For a good discussion of advertising that also does not rely on shifts in preferences, see Nelson (1975).

I do not mean to suggest that concepts like the ego and the id, or social norms, are without any scientific content. Only that they are tempting materials, as are concepts in the economic literature, for ad hoc and useless explanations of behavior. There is no apparent embarrassment in arguing, for example, both that the sharp rise in fertility during the late 1940s and early 1950s resulted from a renewed desire for large families, and that the prolonged decline starting just a few years later resulted from a reluctance to be tied down with many children. Or developing countries are supposed simply to copy the American's "compulsiveness" about time, whereas the growing value of their own time is a more fruitful explanation of their increased effort to economize on their use of time (see Becker, 1965). More generally, custom and tradition are said to be abandoned in developing countries because their young people are seduced by Western ways; it is not recognized that while custom and tradition are quite useful in a relatively stationary environment, they are often a hindrance in a dynamic world, especially for young people (see Stigler & Becker, 1977).

Even those who believe that the economic approach is applicable to all human behavior recognize that many noneconomic variables also significantly effect human behavior. Obviously, the laws of mathematics, chemistry, physics, and biology have a tremendous influence on behavior through their influence on preferences and production possibilities. That the human body ages, that the rate of population growth equals the birth rate plus the migration rate minus the death rate, that children of more intelligent parents tend to be more intelligent than children of less intelligent parents, that people need to breathe to live, that a hybrid plant has a particular yield under one set of environmental conditions and a very different yield under another set, that gold and oil are located only in certain parts of the world and cannot be made from wood, or that an assembly line operates according to certain physical laws—all these and more influence choices, the production of people and goods, and the evolution of societies.

To say this, however, is not the same as saying that, for example, the rate of population growth is itself "noneconomic" in the sense that birth, migration, and death rates cannot be illuminated by the economic approach, or that the rate of adoption of new hybrids is noneconomic because it cannot be explained by the economic approach. Indeed, useful implications about the number of children in different families have been obtained by assuming that families maximize their utility from stable preferences subject to a constraint on their resources and prices, with resources and prices partly determined by the gestation period for pregnancies, the abilities of children, and other noneconomic variables (see Becker, 1960; Becker & Lewis, 1973; Schultz, 1974). Similarly, the rate of adoption of hybrid corn in different parts of the United States has been neatly explained by assuming that farmers maximize profits: new hybrids were more profitable, and thus adopted earlier, in some parts because weather, soil, and other physical conditions were more favorable (Griliches, 1957).

Just as many noneconomic variables are necessary for understanding human behavior, so too are the contributions of sociologists, psychologists, sociobiologists, historians, anthropologists, political scientists, lawyers, and others. Although I am arguing that the economic approach provides a useful framework for understanding all human behavior, I am not trying to downgrade the contributions of other disciplines, or even to suggest that the economists' are more important. For example, the preferences that are given and stable in the economic approach, and that determine the predictions from this approach, are analyzed by sociologists, psychologists, and potentially most successfully in judgement by the sociobiologist (see Wilson, 1975). How preferences have become what they are, and their perhaps slow evolution over time, are obviously relevant in predicting and understanding behavior. The value of some other disciplines is not diminished even by an enthusiastic and complete acceptance of the economic approach.

At the same time, however, I do not want to soften the impact of what I am saying in the interest of increasing its acceptability in the short run. I am saying that the economic approach provides a valuable unified framework for understanding all human behavior, although I recognize, of course, that much behavior is not yet understood, and that noneconomic variables and the techniques and findings from other fields contribute to the understanding of human behavior. A comprehensive *framework* is provided by the economic approach, although some of the important concepts and techniques are provided and will continue to be provided by other disciplines.

The heart of my argument is that human behavior is not compartmentalized, sometimes based on maximizing, sometimes not, sometimes motivated by stable preferences, sometimes by volatile ones, sometimes resulting in an optimal accumulation of information, sometimes not. Rather, all human behavior can be viewed as involving participants who maximize their utility from a stable set of preferences and accumulate an optimal amount of information and other inputs in a variety of markets.

If this argument is correct, the economic approach provides a unified framework for understanding behavior that has long been sought by and eluded Bentham, Comte, Marx, and others.

REFERENCES

Azzi, C., & Ehrenberg, R. (1975). Household allocation of time and church attendance. *Journal of Political Economy, 83,* 27–56.

Bartel, A.P. (1976). *Women and crime: An economic analysis.* Graduate School of Business, Columbia University Research Paper No. 143.

Becker, G.S. (1960). An economic analysis of fertility. In *Demographic and economic change in developed countries,* a Conference of the Universities-National Bureau Committee for Economic Research. Princeton University Press for the National Bureau of Economic Research.

Becker, G.S. (1962). Irrational behavior and economic theory. *Journal of Political Economy, 70,* 1–14.

Becker, G.S. (1964). (1st ed.); (1975). (2nd ed.). *Human capital: A theoretical and empirical analysis.* New York: Columbia University Press for the National Bureau of Economic Research.

Becker, G.S. (1965). A theory of the allocation of time. *Economic Journal, 75,* 493–517.

Becker, G.S. (1973). *A theory of marriage, Part 1. Journal of Political Economy, 81,* 813–846.

Becker, G.S. (1974). *A theory of social interactions. Journal of Political Economy, 82,* 1063–1093.

Becker, G.S. (1976). Altruism, egoism, and genetic fitness: Economics and sociobiology. *Journal of Economic Literature, 14,* 817–826.

Becker, G.S., & Landes, W.M. (Eds.). (1974). *Essays in the economics of crime and punishment.* New York: Columbia University Press for the National Bureau of Economic Research.

Becker, G.S., & Lewis, H.G. (1973). On the interaction between the quantity and quality of children. *Journal of Political Economy, 81* (2), S279–S288.

Becker, G.S., Landes, E.M., & Michael R.T. (1977). An economic analysis of marital instability. *Journal of Political Economy, 85,* 1141–1187.

Bentham, J. (1963). *An introduction to the principles of morals and legislation.* New York: Hafner.

Boulding, K. (1966). *Economic analysis.* New York: Harper & Row.

Buchanan, J.M., & Tullock, G. (1962). *The calculus of consent.* Ann Arbor: University of Michigan Press.

Coase, R.H. (1974). The market for goods and the market for ideas. *American Economic Review, 64,* 384–391.

Dawkins, R. (1976). *The selfish gene.* New York: Oxford University Press.

Director, A. (1964). The parity of the economic market place. *Journal of Law and Economics, 7,* 1–10.

Ehrlich, I. (1973). Participation in illegitimate activities: A theoretical and empirical investigation. *Journal of Political Economy, 81,* 521–565.

Ehrlich, I. (1975). The deterrent effect of capital punishment: A question of life and death. *American Economic Review, 65,* 397–417.

Ehrlich, I. (1977). Capital punishment and deterrence: Some further thoughts and additional evidence. *Journal of Political Economy, 85,* 741–788.

Friedman, M. (1953). The methodology of positive economics. In *Essays in positive economics.* Chicago: University of Chicago Press.

Fuchs, V. (1968). *The service economy.* New York: Columbia University Press for the National Bureau of Economic Research.

Griliches, Z. (1957). Hybrid corn: An exploration in the economics of technological change. *Econometrica, 25,* 501–522.

Grossman, M. (1972). *The demand for health: A theoretical and empirical investigation.* New York: Columbia University Press for the National Bureau of Economic Research.

Hamermesh, D., & Soss, N.M. (1974). An economic theory of suicide. *Journal of Political Economy, 82,* 83–98.

Henderson, J.M. (1958). *The efficiency of the coal industry: An application of linear programming.* Cambridge, MA: Harvard University Press.

Hirshleifer, J. (1977). Economics from a biological viewpoint. *Journal of Law and Economics, 20,* 1–52.

Jencks, C. (1972). *Inequality.* New York: Basic Books.

Keeley, M.C. (1977). The economics of family formation. *Economic Inquiry, 15,* 238–250.

Keynes, J.M. (1962). *The general theory of employment, interest, and money.* New York: Harcourt, Brace and World.

Landes, W. (1977). Fear of flying: An economic study of U.S. aircraft hijacking. Mimeographed. University of Chicago.

Marschak, J. (1965). Economics of language. *Behavioral Science, 10,* 135–140.

Martinson, R. (1974). What works?—questions and answers about prison reform. *Public Interest, 35,* 22–54.

Merton, R.K. (1968). *Social theory and social structure.* New York: Free Press.

Merton, R.K. (1973). *The sociology of science.* University of Chicago Press.

Merton, R.K. (1975). Structural analysis in sociology. In P.M. Blau (Ed.), *Approaches to the study of social structure.* New York: Free Press.

Michael, R.T. (1972). *The effect of education on efficiency in consumption.* New York: National Bureau of Economic Research.

Michael, R.T., & Becker, G.S. (1973). On the new theory of consumer behavior. *The Swedish Journal of Economics, 75,* 378–396.

Mincer, J. (1963). Labor force participation of married women. In *Aspects of labor economics.* New York: National Bureau of Economic Research.

Mincer, J. (1974). *Schooling, experience, and earnings.* New York: Columbia University Press for the National Bureau of Economic Research.

National Academy of Science (National Research Council) (1977). *Report of the panel on research on deterrent and incapacitative effects.* Mimeo.

Nelson, P.J. (1975). The economic consequence of advertising. *Journal of Business, 48,* 213–241.

Ozenne, T. (1974). The economics of bank robbery. *Journal of Legal Studies, 3,* 19–51.

Pigou, A. (1962). *The economics of welfare* (4th ed.). New York: St. Martin's Press.

Posner, R. (1973). *Economic analysis of law.* Boston: Little, Brown.

Rees, A. (1968). Economics. In D.L. Sills (Ed.), *International encyclopedia of the social sciences.* New York: Macmillan and Free Press.

Reiss, A.J. (1968). Sociology. In D.L. Sills (Ed.), *International encyclopedia of the social sciences.* New York: Macmillan and Free Press.

Robbins, L. (1962). *The nature and significance of economic science.* London: Macmillan.

Schultz, T.W. (Ed.). (1974). *Economics of the family: Marriage, children, and human capital.* University of Chicago Press for the National Bureau of Economic Research.

Schumpeter, J. (1942). *Capitalism, socialism, and democracy.* Reprinted in New York: Harper, 1950.

Smith, V.L. (1975). The primitive hunter culture, pleistocene extinction, and the rise of agriculture. *Journal of Political Economy, 83,* 727–755.

Stigler, G.J. (1961). The economics of information. *Journal of Political Economy, 69,* 213–225.

Stigler, G.J (1971). Smith's travels on the ship of state. *History of Political Economy, 3,* 265–277.

Stigler, G.J. (1975). *The citizen and the state.* Chicago: University of Chicago Press.

Stigler, G.J. (1976). Do economists matter?. *Southern Economic Journal, 42,* 347–354.

Stigler, G.J., & Becker, G.S. (1977). De gustibus non est disputandum. *American Economic Review, 67,* 76–90.

Tullock, G. (1971). The coal tit as a careful shopper. *American Naturalist, 105,* 77–80.

Waters, R.H., & Bunnell, B.N. (1968). Comparative psychology. In D.L. Sills (Ed.), *International encyclopedia of the social sciences.* New York: Macmillan and Free Press.

Wilson, E.O. (1975). *Sociobiology.* Cambridge, MA: Harvard University Press.

Chapter 2

Rational Decision Making in Business Organizations

*Herbert A. Simon**

Department of Psychology
Carnegie-Mellon University

In the opening words of his *Principles,* Alfred Marshall (1920) proclaimed economics to be a psychological science:

> Political Economy or Economics is a study of mankind in the ordinary busi-
> ness of life; it examines that part of individual and social action which is most
> closely connected with the attainment and with the use of the material re-
> quisites of wellbeing.
>
> Thus it is on the one side a study of wealth; and, on the other, and more
> important side, a part of the study of man. For man's character has been
> moulded by his every-day work, and the material resources which he thereby
> procures, more than by any other influence unless it be that of his religious
> ideals. (p. 1)

In its actual development, however, economic science has focused on just one aspect of man's character, his reason, and particularly on the application of that reason to problems of allocation in the face of scarcity. Still, modern definitions of the economic sciences, whether phrased in terms of allocating scarce resources or in terms of rational decision making, mark out a vast domain for conquest and settlement. In recent years there has been considerable exploration by economists even of parts of this domain that were thought traditionally to belong to the disciplines of political science, sociology, and psychology.

I. DECISION THEORY AS ECONOMIC SCIENCE

The density of settlement of economists over the whole empire of economic science is very uneven, with a few areas of modest size holding the bulk of

* This article is the lecture Herbert Simon delivered in Stockholm, Sweden, December 8, 1978, when he received the Nobel Prize in Economic Science. The article is copyright © the Nobel Foundation 1978. It is published here with the permission of the Nobel Foundation.

The author is indebted to Albert Ando, Otto A. Davis, and Benjamin M. Friedman for valuable comments on an earlier draft of this paper.

the population. The economic Heartland is the normative study of the international and national economies and their markets, with its triple main concerns of full employment of resources, the efficient allocation of resources, and equity in distribution of the economic product. Instead of the ambiguous and over-general term "economics," I will use "political economy" to designate this Heartland, and "economic sciences" to denote the whole empire, including its most remote colonies. Our principal concern in this paper will be with the important colonial territory known as decision theory. I will have something to say about its normative and descriptive aspects, and particularly about its applications to the theory of the firm. It is through the latter topic that the discussion will be linked back to the Heartland of political economy.

Underpinning the corpus of policy-oriented normative economics, there is, of course, an impressive body of descriptive or "positive" theory which rivals in its mathematical beauty and elegance some of the finest theories in the physical sciences. As examples I need only remind you of Walrasian general equilibrium theories and their modern descendants in the works of Henry Schultz (1938), Samuelson (1963), Hicks, and others; or the subtle and impressive body of theory created by Arrow, Hurwicz, Debreu, Malinvaud, and their colleagues showing the equivalence, under certain conditions, of competitive equilibrium with Pareto optimality.

The relevance of some of the more refined parts of this work to the real world can be, and has been, questioned. Perhaps some of these intellectual mountains have been climbed simply because they were there—because of the sheer challenge and joy of scaling them. That is as it should be in any human scientific or artistic effort. But regardless of the motives of the climbers, regardless of real world veridicality, there is no question but that positive political economy has been strongly shaped by the demands of economic policy for advice on basic public issues.

This too is as it should be. It is a vulgar fallacy to suppose that scientific inquiry cannot be fundamental if it threatens to become useful, or if it arises in response to problems posed by the everyday world. The real world, in fact, is perhaps the most fertile of all sources of good research questions calling for basic scientific inquiry.

A. Decision Theory in the Service of Political Economy

There is, however, a converse fallacy that deserves equal condemnation: the fallacy of supposing that fundamental inquiry is worth pursuing only if its relevance to questions of policy is immediate and obvious. In the contemporary world, this fallacy is perhaps not widely accepted, at least as far as the natural sciences are concerned. We have now lived through three centuries or more of vigorous and highly successful inquiry into the laws of nature. Much of that inquiry has been driven by the simple urge to understand, to find the beauty of order hidden in complexity. Time and again, we have found the "idle" truths arrived at through the process of inquiry to be of the greatest moment for practical human affairs. I need not take time here to argue the point. Scientists know it, engineers and physicians know it, congressmen and members of parliaments know it, the man on the street knows it.

But I am not sure that this truth is as widely known in economics as it ought to be. I cannot otherwise explain the rather weak and backward development of the descriptive theory of decision making including the theory of the firm, the sparse and scattered settlement of its terrain, and the fact that many, if not most, of its investigators are drawn from outside economics —from sociology, from psychology, and from political science. Respected and distinguished figures in economics—Edward Mason, Fritz Machlup, and Milton Friedman, for example—have placed it outside the Pale (more accurately, have placed economics outside *its* Pale), and have offered it full autonomy provided that it did not claim close kinship with genuine economic inquiry.

Thus, Mason (1952), commenting on Papandreou's 1952 survey of research on the behavioral theory of the firm, mused aloud:

> has the contribution of this literature to economic analysis really been a large one?...The writer of this critique must confess a lack of confidence in the marked superiority, *for purposes of economic analysis,* of this newer concept of the firm, over the older conception of the entrepreneur. (pp. 221–22)

And, in a similar vein, Friedman (1953) sums up his celebrated polemic against realism in theory:

> Complete "realism" is clearly unattainable, and the question whether a theory is realistic "enough" can be settled only by seeing whether it yields predictions that are good enough *for the purpose in hand* or that are better than predictions from alternative theories. (p. 41, emphasis added)

The "purpose in hand" that is implicit in both of these quotations is providing decision-theoretic foundations for positive, and then for normative, political economy. In the views of Mason and Friedman, fundamental inquiry into rational human behavior in the context of business organizations is simply not (by definition) economics—that is to say, political economy— unless it contributes in a major way to that purpose. This is sometimes even interpreted to mean that economic theories of decision making are not falsified in any interesting or relevant sense when their empirical predictions of *microphenomena* are found to be grossly incompatible with the observed data. Such theories, we are told, are still realistic "enough" provided that they do not contradict aggregate observations of concern to political economy. Thus economists who are zealous in insisting that economic actors maximize turn around and become satisficers when the evaluation of their own theories is concerned. They believe that businessmen maximize, but they know that economic theorists satisfice.

The application of the principle of satisficing to theories is sometimes defended as an application of Occam's Razor: accept the simplest theory that works.[1] But Occam's Razor has a double edge. Succinctness of statement is not the only measure of a theory's simplicity. Occam understood his rule as recommending theories that make no more assumptions than necessary to account for the phenomena (*Essentia non sunt multiplicanda praeter necessitatem*). A theory of profit or utility maximization can be stated more briefly than a satisficing theory of the sort I shall discuss later. But the former makes much stronger assumptions than the latter about the human cognitive system. Hence, in the case before us, the two edges of the razor cut in opposite directions.

In whichever way we interpret Occam's principle, parsimony can be only a secondary consideration in choosing between theories, unless those theories make identical predictions. Hence, we must come back to a consideration of the phenomena that positive decision theory is supposed to handle. These may include both phenomena at the microscopic level of the decision-making agents, or aggregative phenomena of concern to policial economy.

B. Decision Theory Pursued for its Intrinsic Interest

Of course the definition of the word "economics" is not important. Like Humpty Dumpty, we can make words mean anything we want them to mean. But the professional training and range of concern of economists does have importance. Acceptance of the narrow view that economics is concerned only with the aggregative phenomena of political economy defines away a whole rich domain of rational human behavior as inappropriate for economic research.

I do not wish to appear to be admitting that the behavioral theory of the firm *has been* irrelevant to the construction of political economy. I will have more to say about its relevance in a moment. My present argument is counterfactual in form: *even if* there were no present evidence of such relevance, human behavior in business firms constitutes a highly interesting body of empirical phenomena that calls out for explanation as do all bodies of phe-

---

[1] The phrase "that works" refutes, out of hand, Friedman's celebrated paean of praise for lack of realism in assumptions. Consider his example of falling bodies (1953, pp. 16–19). His valid point is that it is advantageous to use the simple law, ignoring air resistance, when it gives a "good enough" approximation. But of course the conditions under which it gives a good approximation are not at all the conditions under which it is unrealistic or a "wildly inaccurate descriptive representation of reality." We can use it to predict the path of a body falling in a vacuum, but not the path of one falling through the Earth's atmosphere. I cannot in this brief space mention, much less discuss, all of the numerous logical fallacies that can be found in Friedman's 40-page essay. For additional criticism, see Simon (1963) and Samuelson (1963).

nomena. And if we may extrapolate from the history of the other sciences, there is every reason to expect that as explanations emerge, relevance for important areas of practical application will not be long delayed.

It has sometimes been implied (Friedman, 1953, p. 14) that the correctness of the assumptions of rational behavior underlying the classical theory of the firm is not merely irrelevant, but is not even empirically testable in any direct way, the only valid test being whether these assumptions lead to tolerably correct predictions at the macroscopic level. That would be true, of course, if we had no microscopes, so that the micro-level behavior was not directly observable. But we do have microscopes. There are many techniques for observing decision-making behavior, even at second-by-second intervals if that is wanted. In testing our economic theories, we do not have to depend on the rough aggregate time-series that are the main grist for the econometric mill, or even upon company financial statements.

The classical theories of economic decision making and of the business firm make very specific testable predictions about the concrete behavior of decision-making agents. Behavioral theories make quite different predictions. Since these predictions can be tested directly by observation, either theory (or both) may be falsified as readily when such predictions fail as when predictions about aggregate phenomena are in error.

C. Aggregative Tests of Decision Theory: Marginalism

If some economists have erroneously supposed that micro-economic theory can only be tested by its predictions of aggregate phenomena, we should avoid the converse error of supposing that aggregate phenomena are irrelevant to testing decision theory. In particular, are there important, *empirically verified,* aggregate predictions that follow from the theory of perfect rationality but that do not follow from behavioral theories of rationality?

The classical theory of omniscient rationality is strikingly simple and beautiful. Moreover, it allows us to predict (correctly or not) human behavior without stirring out of our armchairs to observe what such behavior is like. All the predictive power comes from characterizing the shape of the environment in which the behavior takes place. The environment, combined with the assumptions of perfect rationality, fully determines the behavior. Behavioral theories of rational choice—theories of bounded rationality—do not have this kind of simplicity. But, by way of compensation, their assumptions about human capabilities are far weaker than those of the classical theory. Thus, they make modest and realistic demands on the knowledge and computational abilities of the human agents, but they also fail to predict that those agents will equate costs and returns at the margin.

D. Have the Marginalist Predictions Been Tested?

A number of empirical phenomena have been cited as providing more or less conclusive support for the classical theory of the firm as against its behavioral competitors (see Jorgensen & Siebert, 1968). But there are no direct observations that individuals or firms do actually equate marginal costs and revenues. The empirically verified consequences of the classical theory are almost always weaker than this. Let us look at four of the most important of them: the fact that demand curves generally have negative slopes; the fact that fitted Cobb-Douglas functions are approximately homogeneous of the first degree; the fact of decreasing returns to scale; and the fact that executive salaries vary with the logarithm of company size. Are these indeed facts? And does the evidence support a maximizing theory against a satisficing theory?

Negatively Sloping Demand Curves. Evidence that consumers actually distribute their purchases in such a way as to maximize their utilities, and hence to equate marginal utilities, is nonexistent. What the empirical data do confirm is that demand curves generally have negative slopes. (Even this "obvious" fact is tricky to verify, as Henry Schultz showed long years ago.) But, negatively sloping demand curves could result from a wide range of behaviors satisfying the assumptions of bounded rationality rather than those of utility maximization. Gary Becker (1962), who can scarcely be regarded as a hostile witness for the classical theory, states the case very well:

> Economists have long been aware that some changes in the feasible or opportunity sets of households would lead to the same response *regardless of the decision rule used*. For example, a decrease in real income necessarily decreases the amount spent on at least one commodity...It has seldom been realized, however, that the change in opportunities resulting from a change in relative prices also tends to produce a systematic response, regardless of the decision rule. In particular, the fundamental theorem of traditional theory—that demand curves are negatively inclined—largely results from the change in opportunities alone and is largely independent of the decision rule. (p. 4)

Later, Becker is even more explicit, saying, "Not only utility maximization but also many other decision rules, incorporating a wide variety of irrational behavior, lead to negatively inclined demand curves because of the effect of a change in prices on opportunities" (p. 5).[2]

First-Degree Homogeneity of Production Functions. Another example of an observed phenomenon for which the classical assumptions provide sufficient, but not necessary, conditions is the equality between labor's share of product and the exponent of the labor factor in fitted Cobb-Douglas production functions (see Simon & Levy, 1963). Fitted Cobb-Douglas func-

---

[2] In a footnote, Becker indicates that he denotes as irrational "[A]ny deviation from utility maximization." Thus, what I have called "bounded rationality" is "irrationality" in Becker's terminology.

tions are homogeneous, generally of degree close to unity and with a labor exponent of about the right magnitude. These findings, however, cannot be taken as strong evidence for the classical theory, for the identical results can readily be produced by mistakenly fitting a Cobb-Douglas function to data that were in fact generated by a linear accounting identity (value of goods equals labor cost plus capital cost), (see Phelps-Brown, 1957). The same comment applies to the SMAC production function (see Cyert & Simon, 1971). Hence, the empirical findings do not allow us to draw any particular conclusions about the relative plausibility of classical and behavioral theories, both of which are equally compatible with the data.

The Long-Run Cost Curve. Somewhat different is the case of the firm's long-run cost curve, which classical theory requires to be U shaped if competitive equilibrium is to be stable. Theories of bounded rationality do not predict this—fortunately, for the observed data make it exceedingly doubtful that the cost curves are in fact generally U shaped. The evidence for many industries shows costs at the high-scale ends of the curves to be essentially constant or even declining (see Walters, 1963). This finding is compatible with stochastic models of business firm growth and size (see Y. Ijiri & Simon, 1977), but not with the static equilibrium model of classical theory.

Executive Salaries. Average salaries of top corporate executives grow with the logarithm of corporate size (see Roberts, 1959). This finding has been derived from the assumptions of the classical theory of profit maximization only with the help of very particular *ad hoc* assumptions about the distribution of managerial ability (see Lucas, 1978). The observed relation is implied by a simple behavioral theory that assumes only that there is a single, culturally determined, parameter which fixes the average ratio of the salaries of managers to the salaries of their immediate subordinates (see Simon, 1957b). In the case of the executive salary data, the behavioral model that explains the observations is substantially more parsimonious (in terms of assumptions about exogenous variables) than the classical model that explains the same observations.

Summary: Phenomena that Fail to Discriminate. It would take a much more extensive review than is provided here to establish the point conclusively, but I believe it is the case that specific phenomena requiring a theory of utility or profit maximization for their explanation rather than a theory of bounded rationality simply have not been observed in aggregate data. In fact, as my last two examples indicate, it is the classical rather than the behavioral form of the theory that faces real difficulties in handling some of the empirical observations.

Failures of Classical Theory. It may well be that classical theory can be patched up sufficiently to handle a wide range of situations where uncertainty and outguessing phenomena do not play a central role—that is, to handle the behavior of economies that are relatively stable and not too distant from a competitive equilibrium. However, a strong positive case for replacing the classical theory by a model of bounded rationality begins to emerge when we examine situations involving decision making under uncertainty and imperfect competition. These situations the classical theory was never designed to handle, and has never handled satisfactorily. Statistical decision theory employing the idea of subjective expected utility, on the one hand, and game theory, on the other, have contributed enormous conceptual clarification to these kinds of situations without providing satisfactory descriptions of actual human behavior, or even, for most cases, normative theories that are actually usable in the face of the limited computational powers of men and computers.

I shall have more to say later about the positive case for a descriptive theory of bounded rationality, but I would like to turn first to another territory within economic science that has gained rapidly in population since World War II, the domain of normative decision theory.

E. Normative Decision Theory

Decision theory can be pursued not only for the purposes of building foundations for political economy, or of understanding and explaining phenomena that are in themselves intrinsically interesting, but also for the purpose of offering direct advice to business and governmental decision makers. For reasons not clear to me, this territory was very sparsely settled prior to World War II. Such inhabitants as it had were mainly industrial engineers, students of public administration, and specialists in business functions, none of whom especially identified themselves with the economic sciences. Prominent pioneers included the mathematician Charles Babbage, inventor of the digital computer, the engineer Frederick Taylor, and the administrator Henri Fayol.

During World War II, this territory, almost abandoned, was rediscovered by scientists, mathematicians, and statisticians concerned with military management and logistics, and was renamed "operations research" or "operations analysis." So remote were the operations researchers from the social science community that economists wishing to enter the territory had to establish their own colony, which they called "management science." The two professional organizations thus engendered still retain their separate identities, though they are now amicably federated in a number of common endeavors.

Optimization techniques were transported into management science from economics, and new optimization techniques, notably linear programming, were invented and developed, the names of Dantzig, Kantorovich, and Koopmans being prominent in the early development of that tool.

Now the salient characteristic of the decision tools employed in management science is that they have to be capable of actually making or recommending decisions, taking as their inputs the kinds of empirical data that are available in the real world, and performing only such computations as can reasonably be performed by existing desk calculators or, a little later, electronic computers. For these domains, idealized models of optimizing entrepreneurs, equipped with complete certainty about the world—or, at worst, having full probability distributions for uncertain events—are of little use. Models have to be fashioned with an eye to practical computability, no matter how severe the approximations and simplifications that are thereby imposed on them.

Model construction under these stringent conditions has taken two directions. The first is to retain optimization, but to simplify sufficiently so that the optimum (in the simplified world!) is computable. The second is to construct satisficing models that provide good enough decisions with reasonable costs of computation. By giving up optimization, a richer set of properties of the real world can be retained in the models. Stated otherwise, decision makers can satisfice either by finding optimum solutions for a simplified world, or by finding satisfactory solutions for a more realistic world. Neither approach, in general, dominates the other, and both have continued to coexist in the world of management science.

Thus, the body of theory that has developed in management science shares with the body of theory in descriptive decision theory a central concern with the *ways* in which decisions are made, and not just with the decision outcomes. As I have suggested elsewhere (1978b), these are theories of *how* to decide rather than theories of *what* to decide.

Let me cite one example, from work in which I participated, of how model building in normative economics is shaped by computational considerations (see Holt, Modigliani, Muth, & Simon, 1960). In face of uncertain and fluctuating production demands, a company can smooth and stabilize its production and employment levels at the cost of holding buffer inventories. What kind of decision rule will secure a reasonable balance of costs? Formally, we are faced with a dynamic programming problem, and these generally pose formidable and often intolerable computational burdens for their solution.

One way out of this difficulty is to seek a special case of the problem that will be computationally tractable. If we assume the cost functions facing the company all to be quadratic in form, the optimal decision rule will then be a linear function of the decision variables, which can readily be computed in terms of the cost parameters. Equally important, under uncertainty about future sales, only the expected values, and not the higher moments, of the probability distributions enter into the decision rule (Simon, 1956b). Hence the assumption of quadratic costs reduces the original problem to one that is readily solved. Of course the solution, though it provides optimal decisions for the simplified world of our assumptions, provides, at best, satisfactory solutions for the real-world decision problem that the quadratic function approximates. In-principle, unattainable optimization is sacrificed for in-practice, attainable satisfaction.

If human decision makers are as rational as their limited computational capabilities and their incomplete information permit them to be, then there will be a close relation between normative and descriptive decision theory. Both areas of inquiry are concerned primarily with procedural rather than substantive rationality (Simon, 1978a). As new mathematical tools for computing optimal and satisfactory decisions are discovered, and as computers become more and more powerful, the recommendations of normative decision theory will change. But as the new recommendations are diffused, the actual, observed, practice of decision making in business firms will change also. And these changes may have macro-economic consequences. For example, there is some agreement that average inventory holdings of American firms have been reduced significantly by the introduction of formal procedures for calculating reorder points and quantities.

II. CHARACTERIZING BOUNDED RATIONALITY

The principal forerunner of a behavioral theory of the firm is the tradition usually called Institutionalism. It is not clear that all of the writings, European and American, usually lumped under this rubric have much in common, or that their authors would agree with each other's views. At best, they share a conviction that economic theory must be reformulated to take account of the social and legal structures amidst which market transactions are carried out. Today, we even find a vigorous development within economics that seeks to achieve institutionalist goals within the context of neoclassical price theory. I will have more to say about that a little later.

The name of John R. Commons is prominent—perhaps the most prominent—among American Institutionalists. Commons' difficult writings (for example, *Institutional Economics,* 1934) borrow their language heavily from the law, and seek to use the *transaction* as their basic unit of behavior. I will not undertake to review Commons' ideas here, but simply remark that they provided me with many insights in my initial studies of organizational decision making (see my *Administrative Behavior,* 1947, p. 136).

Commons also had a substantial influence on the thinking of Chester I. Barnard, an intellectually curious business executive who distilled from his experience as president of the New Jersey Bell Telephone Company, and as executive of other business, governmental, and nonprofit organizations, a profound book on decision making titled *The Functions of the Executive* (1938). Barnard proposed original theories, which have stood up well under empirical scrutiny, of the nature of the authority mechanism in organizations, and of the motivational bases for employee acceptance of organizational goals (the so-called "inducements-contributions" theory); and he provided a realistic description of organizational decision making, which he characterized as "opportunistic." The numerous references to Barnard's work in *Administrative Behavior* attest, though inadequately, to the impact he had on my own thinking about organizations.

A. In Search of a Descriptive Theory

In 1934–35, in the course of a field study of the administration of public recreational facilities in Milwaukee, which were managed jointly by the school board and the city public works department, I encountered a puzzling phenomenon. Although the heads of the two agencies appeared to agree as to the objectives of the recreation program, and did not appear to be competing for empire, there was continual disagreement and tension between them with respect to the allocation of funds between physical maintenance, on the one hand, and play supervision on the other. Why did they not, as my economics books suggested, simply balance off the marginal return of the one activity against that of the other?

Further exploration made it apparent that they didn't equate expenditures at the margin because, intellectually, they couldn't. There was no measurable production function from which quantitative inferences about marginal productivities could be drawn; and such qualitative notions of a production function as the two managers possessed were mutually incompatible. To the public works administrator, a playground was a physical facility, serving as a green oasis in the crowded gray city. To the recreation administrator, a playground was a social facility, where children could play together with adult help and guidance.

How can human beings make rational decisions in circumstances like these? How are they to apply the marginal calculus? Or, if it does not apply, what do they substitute for it?

The phenomenon observed in Milwaukee is ubiquitous in human decision making. In organization theory it is usually referred to as *subgoal identification*. When the goals of an organization cannot be connected operationally with actions (when the production function can't be formulated in concrete terms), then decisions will be judged against subordinate goals that can be so connected. There is no unique determination of these subordinate goals. Their formulation will depend on the knowledge, experience, and organizational environment of the decision maker. In the face of this ambiguity, the formulation can also be influenced in subtle, and not so subtle, ways by his self-interest and power drives.

The phenomenon arises as frequently in individual as in social decision making and problem solving. Today, under the rubric of *problem representation,* it is a central research interest of cognitive psychology. Given a particular environment of stimuli, and a particular background of previous knowledge, how will a person organize this complex mass of information into a problem formulation that will facilitate his solution efforts? How did Newton's experience of the apple, if he had one, get represented as an instance of attraction of apple by Earth?

Phenomena like these provided the central theme for *Administrative Behavior.* That study represented "an attempt to construct tools useful in my own research in the field of public administration." The product was actually not so much a theory as prolegomena to a theory, stemming from the conviction "that decision making is the heart of administration, and that the vocabulary of administrative theory must be derived from the logic and psychology of human choice." It was, if you please, an exercise in problem representation.

On examination, the phenomena of subgoal identification proved to be the visible tip of a very large iceberg. The shape of the iceberg is best appreciated by contrasting it with classical models of rational choice. The classical model calls for knowledge of all the alternatives that are open to choice. It calls for complete knowledge of, or ability to compute, the consequences that will follow on each of the alternatives. It calls for certainty in the decision maker's present and future evaluation of these consequences. It calls for the ability to compare consequences, no matter how diverse and heterogeneous, in terms of some consistent measure of utility. The task, then, was to replace the classical model with one that would describe how decisions could be (and probably actually were) made when the alternatives of search had to be sought out, the consequences of choosing particular alternatives were only very imperfectly known both because of limited computational power and because of uncertainty in the external world, and the decision maker did not possess a general and consistent utility function for comparing heterogeneous alternatives.

Several procedures of rather general applicability and wide use have been discovered that transform intractable decision problems into tractable ones. One procedure already mentioned is to look for satisfactory choices instead of optimal ones. Another is to replace abstract, global goals with tangible subgoals, whose achievement can be observed and measured. A third is to divide up the decision-making task among many specialists, coordinating their work by means of a structure of communications and authority relations. All of these, and others, fit the general rubric of "bounded rationality," and it is now clear that the elaborate organizations that human beings have constructed in the modern world to carry out the work of production and government can only be understood as machinery for coping with the limits of man's abilities to comprehend and compute in the face of complexity and uncertainty.

This rather vague and general initial formulation of the idea of bounded rationality called for elaboration in two directions: greater formalization of the theory, and empirical verification of its main claims. During the decade that followed the publication of *Administrative Behavior,* substantial progress was made in both directions, some of it through the efforts of my colleagues and myself, much of it by other research groups that shared the same Zeitgeist.

B. Empirical Studies

The principal source of empirical data about organizational decision making has been straightforward "anthropological" field study, eliciting descriptions of decision-making procedures and observing the course of specific decision-making episodes. Examples are my study, with Guetzkow, Kozmetsky, and Tyndall (1954/1978), of the ways in which accounting data were used in decision making in large corporations; and a series of studies, with Richard Cyert, James March, and others, of specific nonprogrammed policy decisions in a number of different companies (see Cyert, Simon, & Trow, 1956). The latter line of work was greatly developed and expanded by Cyert and March and its theoretical implications for economics explored in their important work, *A Behavioral Theory of the Firm* (1963).

At about the same time, the fortuitous availability of some data on businessmen's perceptions of a problem situation described in a business policy casebook enabled DeWitt Dearborn and me to demonstrate empirically the cognitive basis for identification with subgoals, the phenomenon that had so impressed me in the Milwaukee recreation study (Dearborn & Simon, 1958). The businessmen's perceptions of the principal problems facing the company described in the case were mostly determined by their own business experiences—sales and accounting executives identified a sales problem, manufacturing executives, a problem of internal organization.

Of course there is vastly more to be learned and tested about organizational decision making than can be dealt with in a handful of studies. Although many subsequent studies have been carried out in Europe and the United States, this domain is still grossly undercultivated (for references, see March, 1965; Johnsen, 1968; Eliasson, 1976). Among the reasons for the relative neglect of such studies, as contrasted, say, with laboratory experiments in social psychology, is that they are extremely costly and time consuming, with a high grist-to-grain ratio, the methodology for carrying them out is primitive, and satisfactory access to decision-making behavior is hard to secure. This part of economics has not yet acquired the habits of patience and persistence in the pursuit of facts that is exemplified in other domains by the work, say, of Simon Kuznets or of the architects of the MIT-SSRC-Penn econometric models.

C. Theoretical Inquiries

On the theoretical side, three questions seemed especially to call for clarification: what are the circumstances under which an employment relation will be preferred to some other form of contract as the arrangement for securing the performance of work; what is the relation between the classical theory of the firm and theories of organizational equilibrium first proposed by Chester Barnard; and what are the main characteristics of human rational choice in situations where complexity precludes omniscience?

The Employment Relation. A fundamental characteristic of modern industrial society is that most work is performed, not by individuals who produce products for sale, nor by individual contractors, but by persons who have accepted employment in a business firm and the authority relation with the employer that employment entails. Acceptance of authority means willingness to permit one's behavior to be determined by the employer, at least within some zone of indifference or acceptance. What is the advantage of this arrangement over a contract for specified goods or services? Why is so much of the world's work performed in large, hierarchic organizations?

Analysis showed (Simon, 1951) that a combination of two factors could account for preference for the employment contract over other forms of contracts: uncertainty as to which future behaviors would be advantageous to the employer, and a greater indifference of the employee as compared with the employer (within the former's area of acceptance) as to which of these behaviors he carried out. When the secretary is hired, the employer does not know what letters he will want her to type, and the secretary has no great preference for typing one letter rather than another. The employment contract permits the choice to be postponed until the uncertainty is resolved, with little cost to the employee and great advantage to the employer. The explanation is closely analogous to one Jacob Marschak (1949) had proposed for liquidity preference. Under conditions of uncertainty, it is advantageous to hold resources in liquid, flexible form.

Organizational Equilibrium. Barnard had described the survival of organizations in terms of the motivations that make their participants (employees, investors, customers, suppliers) willing to remain in the system. In *Administrative Behavior,* I had developed this notion further into a motivational theory of balance between the inducements that were provided by organizations to their participants, and the contributions those participants made to the organizations' resources.

A formalization of this theory (Simon, 1951, 1952) showed its close affinity to the classical theory of the firm, but with an important and instructive difference. In comparing the two theories, each inducement-contribution relation became a supply schedule for the firm. The survival conditions became the conditions for positive profit. But while the classical theory of the firm assumes that all profits accrue to a particular set of participants, the owners, the organization theory treats the surplus more symmetrically, and does not predict how it will be distributed. Hence the latter theory leaves room, under conditions of monopoly and imperfect competition, for bargaining among the participants (for example, between labor and owners) for the surplus. The survival conditions—positive profits rather than maximum profits—also permit a departure from the assumptions of perfect rationality.

Mechanisms of Bounded Rationality. In *Administrative Behavior,* bounded rationality is largely characterized as a residual category—rationality is bounded when it falls short of omniscience. And the failures of omniscience are largely failures of knowing all the alternatives, uncertainty about relevant exogenous events, and inability to calculate consequences. There was needed a more positive and formal characterization of the mechanisms of choice under conditions of bounded rationality. Two papers (Simon, 1955; 1956a) undertook first steps in that direction.

Two concepts are central to the characterization: *search* and *satisficing.* If the alternatives for choice are not given initially to the decision maker, then he must search for them. Hence, a theory of bounded rationality must incorporate a theory of search. This idea was later developed independently by George Stigler (1961) in a very influential paper that took as its example of a decision situation the purchase of a second-hand automobile. Stigler poured the search theory back into the old bottle of classical utility maximization, the cost of search being equated with its marginal return. In my 1956 paper, I had demonstrated the same formal equivalence, using as my example a dynamic programming formulation of the process of selling a house.

But utility maximization, as I showed, was not essential to the search scheme—fortunately, for it would have required the decision maker to be able to estimate the marginal costs and returns of search in a decision situation that was already too complex for the exercise of global rationality. As an alternative, one could postulate that the decision maker had formed some *aspiration* as to how good an alternative he should find. As soon as he discovered an alternative for choice meeting his level of aspiration, he would terminate the search and choose that alternative. I called this mode of selection *satisficing.* It had its roots in the empirically based psychological theories, due to Lewin and others, of aspiration levels. As psychological inquiry had shown, aspiration levels are not static, but tend to rise and fall in consonance with changing experiences. In a benign environment that provides many good alternatives, aspirations rise; in a harsher environment, they fall.

In long-run equilibrium it might even be the case that choice with dynamically adapting aspiration levels would be equivalent to optimal choice, taking the costs of search into account. But the important thing about the search and satisficing theory is that it showed how choice could actually be made with reasonable amounts of calculation, and using very incomplete information, without the need of performing the impossible—of carrying out this optimizing procedure.

D. Summary

Thus, by the middle 1950s, a theory of bounded rationality had been proposed as an alternative to classical omniscient rationality, a significant number of empirical studies had been carried out that showed actual business decision making to conform reasonably well with the assumptions of bounded rationality but not with the assumptions of perfect rationality, and key components of the theory—the nature of the authority and employment relations, organizational equilibrium, and the mechanisms of search and satisficing—had been elucidated formally. In the remaining parts of this paper, I should like to trace subsequent developments of decision-making theory, including developments competitive with the theory of bounded rationality, and then to comment on the implications (and potential implications) of the new descriptive theory of decision for political economy.

III. THE NEOCLASSICAL REVIVAL

Peering forward from the late 1950s, it would not have been unreasonable to predict that theories of bounded rationality would soon find a large place in the mainstream of economic thought. Substantial progress had been made in providing the theories with some formal structure, and an increasing body of empirical evidence showed them to provide a far more veridical picture of decision making in business organizations than did the classical concepts of perfect rationality.

History has not followed any such simple course, even though many aspects of the Zeitgeist were favorable to movement in this direction. During and after World War II, a large number of academic economists were exposed directly to business life, and had more or less extensive opportunities to observe how decisions were actually made in business organizations. Moreover, those who became active in the development of the new management science were faced with the necessity of developing decision-making procedures that could actually be applied in practical situations. Surely these trends would be conducive to moving the basic assumptions of economic rationality in the direction of greater realism.

But these were not the only things that were happening in economics in the postwar period. First, there was a vigorous reaction that sought to defend classical theory from behavioralism on methodological grounds. I have already commented on these methodological arguments in the first part of my talk. However deeply one may disagree with them, they were stated persuasively and are still influential among academic economists.

Second, the rapid spread of mathematical knowledge and competence in the economics profession permitted the classical theory, especially when combined with statistical decision theory and the theory of games due to von Neumann and Morgenstern (1944), to develop to new heights of sophistication and elegance, and to expand to embrace, albeit in highly stylized form, some of the phenomena of uncertainty and imperfect information. The flowering of mathematical economics and econometrics has provided two generations of economic theorists with a vast garden of formal and technical problems that have absorbed their energies and postponed encounters with the inelegancies of the real world.

If I sound mildly critical of these developments, I should confess that I have also been a part of them, admire them, and would be decidedly unhappy to return to the premathematical world they have replaced. My concern is that the economics profession has exhibited some of the serial one-thing-at-a-time character of human rationality, and has seemed sometimes to be unable to distribute its attention in a balanced fashion among neoclassical theory, macroeconometrics, and descriptive decision theory. As a result, not as much professional effort has been devoted to the latter two, and especially the third, as one might have hoped and expected. The Heartland is more overpopulated than ever, while rich lands in other parts of the empire go untilled.

A. Search and Information Transfer

Let me allude to just three of the ways in which classical theory has sought to cope with some of its traditional limitations, and has even sought to make the development of a behavioral theory, incorporating psychological assumptions, unnecessary. The first was to introduce search and information transfer explicitly as economic activities, with associated costs and outputs, that could be inserted into the classical production function. I have already referred to Stigler's 1961 paper on the economics of information, and my own venture in the same direction in the 1956 essay cited earlier.

In theory of this genre, the decision maker is still an individual. A very important new direction, in which decisions are made by groups of individuals, in teams or organizations, is the economic theory of teams developed by Jacob Marschak and Roy Radner (1972). Here we see genuine organizational phenomena—specialization of decision making as a consequence of the costs of transmitting information—emerge from the rational calculus. Because the mathematical difficulties are formidable, the theory remains largely illustrative and limited to very simple situations in miniature organizations. Nevertheless, it has greatly broadened our understanding of the economics of information.

In none of these theories—any more than in statistical decision theory or the theory of games—is the assumption of perfect maximization abandoned.

Limits and costs of information are introduced, not as psychological characteristics of the decision maker, but as part of his technological environment. Hence, the new theories do nothing to alleviate the computational complexities facing the decision maker—do not see him coping with them by heroic approximation, simplifying and satisficing, but simply magnify and multiply them. Now he needs to compute, not merely the shapes of his supply and demand curves, but, in addition, the costs and benefits of computing those shapes to greater accuracy as well. Hence, to some extent, the impression that these new theories deal with the hitherto ignored phenomena of uncertainty and information transmission is illusory. For many economists, however, the illusion has been persuasive.

B. Rational Expectations Theory

A second development in neoclassical theory on which I wish to comment is the so-called "rational expectations" theory. There is a bit of historical irony surrounding its origins. I have already described the management science inquiry of Holt, Modigliani, Muth, and myself (1960) that developed a dynamic programming algorithm for the special (and easily computed) case of quadratic cost functions. In this case, the decision rules are linear, and the probability distributions of future events can be replaced by their expected values, which serve as certainty equivalents (see Simon, 1956b; Theil, 1957).

Muth imaginatively saw in this special case a paradigm for rational behavior under uncertainty. What to some of us in the HMMS research team was an approximating, satisficing simplification, served for him as a major line of defense for perfect rationality. He said in his seminal 1961 *Econometrica* article, "It is sometimes argued that the assumption of rationality in economics leads to theories inconsistent with, or inadequate to explain, observed phenomena, especially changes over time....Our hypothesis is based on exactly the opposite point of view: that dynamic economic models do not assume enough rationality" (p. 316).

The new increment of rationality that Muth proposed was that "expectations, since they are informed predictions of future events, are essentially the same as the predictions of the relevant economic theory" (p. 316). He would cut the Gordian knot. Instead of dealing with uncertainty by elaborating the model of the decision process, he would once and for all—if his hypothesis were correct—make process irrelevant. The subsequent vigorous development of rational expectations theory, in the hands of Sargent, Lucas, Prescott, and others, is well known to most readers (see, for example, Lucas, 1975).

It is too early to render a final verdict on the rational expectations theory. The issue will ultimately be decided, as all scientific debates should be, by a gradual winnowing of the empirical evidence, and that winnowing process has just begun. Meanwhile, certain grave theoretical difficulties have already been noticed. As Muth himself has pointed out, it is rational (i.e., profit maximizing) to use the "rational expectations" decision rule if the relevant cost equations are in fact quadratic. I have suggested elsewhere (1978a) that it might therefore be less misleading to call the rule a "consistent expectations" rule.

Perhaps even more important, Albert Ando (1978) and Benjamin Friedman (1978, 1979) have shown that the policy implications of the rational expectations rule are quite different under conditions where new information continually becomes available to the system, structural changes occur, and the decision maker learns, than they are under steady-state conditions. For example, under the more dynamic conditions, monetary neutrality—which in general holds for the static consistent expectations models—is no longer guaranteed for any finite time horizon.

In the recent "revisionist" versions of consistent expectations theory, moreover, where account is taken of a changing environment of information, various behavioral assumptions reappear to explain how expectations are formed—what information decision makers will consider, and what they will ignore. But unless these assumptions are to be made on a wholly ad hoc and arbitrary basis, they create again the need for an explicit and valid theory of the decision-making *process* (see Simon, 1978a; Friedman, 1979).

C. Statistical Decision Theory and Game Theory
Statistical decision theory and game theory are two other important components of the neoclassical revival. The former addresses itself to the question of incorporating uncertainty (or more properly, risk) into the decision-making models. It requires heroic assumptions about the information the decision maker has concerning the probability distributions of the relevant variables, and simply increases by orders of magnitude the computational problems he faces.

Game theory addresses itself to the "outguessing" problem that arises whenever an economic actor takes into account the possible reactions to his own decision of the other actors. To my mind, the main product of the very elegant apparatus of game theory has been to demonstrate quite clearly that it is virtually impossible to define an unambiguous criterion of rationality for this class of situations (or, what amounts to the same thing, a definitive definition of the "solution" of a game). Hence, game theory has not brought to the theories of oligopoly and imperfect competition the relief from their contradictions and complexities that was originally hoped for it. Rather, it has shown that these difficulties are ineradicable. We may be able to reach consensus that a certain criterion of rationality is appropriate to a particular game, but if someone challenges the consensus, preferring a different criterion, we will have no logical basis for persuading him that he is wrong.

D. Conclusion

Perhaps, I have said enough about the neoclassical revival to suggest why it has been a highly attractive commodity in competition with the behavioral theories. To some economists at least, it has held open the possibility and hope that important questions that had been troublesome for classical economics could now be addressed without sacrifice of the central assumption of perfect rationality, and hence also with a maximum of a priori inference and a minimum of tiresome grubbing with empirical data. I have perhaps said enough also with respect to the limitations of these new constructs to indicate why I do not believe that they solve the problems that motivated their development.

IV. ADVANCES IN THE BEHAVIORAL THEORY

Although they have played a muted role in the total economic research activity during the past two decades, theories of bounded rationality and the behavioral theory of the business firm have undergone steady development during that period. Since surveying the whole body of work would be a major undertaking, I shall have to be satisfied here with suggesting the flavor of the whole by citing a few samples of different kinds of important research falling in this domain. Where surveys on particular topics have been published, I will limit myself to references to them.

First, there has been work in the psychological laboratory and the field to test whether people in relatively simple choice situations behave as statistical decision theory (maximization of expected utilities) say they do. Second, there has been extensive psychological research, in which Allen Newell and I (1972, 1976) have been heavily involved, to discover the actual microprocesses of human decision making and problem solving. Third, there have been numerous empirical observations—most of them in the form of "case studies"—of the actual processes of decision making in organizational and business contexts. Fourth, there have been reformulations and extensions of the theory of the firm replacing classical maximization with behavioral decision postulates.

A. Utility Theory and Human Choice

The axiomatization of utility and probability after World War II and the revival of Bayesian statistics opened the way to testing empirically whether people behaved in choice situations so as to maximize subjective expected utility (*SEU*). In early studies, using extremely simple choice situations, it appeared that perhaps they did. When even small complications were introduced into the situations, wide departures of behavior from the predictions of *SEU* theory soon became evident. Some of the most dramatic and convincing empirical refutations of the theory have been reported by Kahneman and Tversky (1973), who showed that, under one set of circumstances, decision makers gave far too little weight to prior knowledge and based their choices almost entirely on new evidence, while in other circumstances new evidence had little influence on opinions already formed. Equally large and striking departures from the behavior predicted by the *SEU* theories were found by Howard Kunreuther and his colleagues (1978) in their studies of individual decisions to purchase or not to purchase flood insurance. On the basis of these and other pieces of evidence, the conclusion seems unavoidable that the *SEU* theory does not provide a good prediction—not even a good approximation—of actual behavior.

Notice that the refutation of the theory has to do with the *substance* of the decisions, and not just the process by which they are reached. It is not that people do not go through the calculations that would be required to reach the *SEU* decision—neoclassical thought has never claimed that they did. What has been shown is that they do not even behave *as if* they had carried out those calculations, and that result is a direct refutation of the neoclassical assumptions.

B. Psychology of Problem Solving

The evidence on rational decision making is largely negative evidence, evidence of what people do *not* do. In the past 20 years, a large body of positive evidence has also accumulated about the processes that people use to make difficult decisions and solve complex problems. The body of theory that has been built up around this evidence is called information processing psychology, and is usually expressed formally in computer programming languages. Newell and I have summed up our own version of this theory in our book, *Human Problem Solving* (1972), which is part of a large and rapidly growing literature that assumes an information processing framework and makes use of computer simulation as a central tool for expressing and testing theories.

Information processing theories envisage problem solving as involving very selective search through problem spaces that are often immense. Selectivity, based on rules of thumb or "heuristics," tends to guide the search into promising regions, so that solutions will generally be found after search of only a tiny part of the total space. Satisficing criteria terminate search when satisfactory problem solutions have been found. Thus, these theories of problem solving clearly fit within the framework of bounded rationality that I have been expounding here.

By now the empirical evidence for this general picture of the problem solving process is extensive. Most of the evidence pertains to relatively simple, puzzle-like situations of the sort that can be brought into the psychological laboratory for controlled study, but a great deal has been learned, also, about professional level human tasks like making medical diagnoses, investing in portfolios of stocks and bonds, and playing chess. In tasks of these kinds, the general search mechanisms operate in a rich context of information stored in human long-term memory, but the general organization of the process is substantially the same as for the simpler, more specific tasks.

At the present time, research in information processing psychology is proceeding in several directions. Exploration of professional level skills continues. A good deal of effort is now being devoted also to determining how initial representations for new problems are acquired. Even in simple problem domains, the problem solver has much latitude in the way he formulates the problem space in which he will search, a finding that underlies again how far the actual process is from a search for a uniquely determined optimum (see Hayes & Simon, 1974).

The main import for economic theory of the research in information processing psychology is to provide rather conclusive empirical evidence that the decision-making process in problem situations conforms closely to the models of bounded rationality described earlier. This finding implies, in turn, that choice is not determined uniquely by the objective characteristics of the problem situation, but depends also on the particular heuristic process that is used to reach the decision. It would appear, therefore, that a model of process is an essential component in any positive theory of decision making that purports to describe the real world, and that the neoclassical ambition of avoiding the necessity for such a model is unrealizable (Simon, 1978a).

C. Organizational Decision Making

It would be desirable to have, in addition to the evidence from the psychological research just described, empirical studies of the process of decision making in organizational contexts. The studies of individual problem solving and decision making do not touch on the many social-psychological factors that enter into the decision process in organizations. A substantial number of investigations have been carried out in the past 20 years of the decision-making process in organizations, but they are not easily summarized. The difficulty is that most of these investigations have taken the form of case studies of specific decisions or particular classes of decisions in individual organizations. To the best of my knowledge, no good review of this literature has been published, so that it is difficult even to locate and identify the studies that have been carried out.[3] Nor have any systematic methods been

---

[3] For leads into the literature, see March and Simon (1958); March (1965); Johnsen (1968); Dutton and Starbuck (1971). However, there are large numbers of specific case studies, some of them carried out as thesis projects, some concerned with particular fields of business application, which have never been recorded in these reference sources (for example, Eliasson, 1976).

developed and tested for distilling out from these individual case studies their implications for the general theory of the decision-making process.

The case studies of organizational decision making, therefore, represent the natural history stage of scientific inquiry. They provide us with a multitude of facts about the decision-making process—facts that are almost uniformly consistent with the kind of behavioral model that has been proposed here. But we do not yet know how to use these facts to test the model in any formal way. Nor do we quite know what to do with the observation that the specific decision-making procedures used by organizations differ from one organization to another, and within each organization, even from one situation to another. We must not expect from these data generalizations as neat and precise as those incorporated in neoclassical theory.

Perhaps the closest approach to a method for extracting theoretically relevant information from case studies is computer simulation. By converting empirical evidence about a decision-making process into a computer program, a path is opened both for testing the adequacy of the program mechanisms for explaining the data, and for discovering the key features of the program that account, qualitatively, for the interesting and important characteristics of its behavior. Examples of the use of this technique are G.P.E. Clarkson's (1963) simulation of the decision making of an investment trust officer, Cyert, Feigenbaum, and March's (1959) simulation of the history of a duopoly, and C.P. Bonini's (1963) model of the effects of accounting information and supervisory pressures in altering employee motivations in a business firm. The simulation methodology is discussed from a variety of viewpoints in Dutton and Starbuck (1971).[4]

D. Theories of the Business Firm

The general features of bounded rationality—selective search, satisficing, and so on—have been taken as the starting points for a number of attempts to build theories of the business firm incorporating behavioral assumptions. Examples of such theories would include the theory of Cyert and March (1963), already mentioned; William Baumol's (1959) theory of sales maximization subject to minimum profit constraints; Robin Marris' (1964) models of firms whose goals are stated in terms of rates of growth; Harvey Leibenstein's (1976) theory of "X-inefficiency" that depresses production below the theoretically attainable; Janos Kornai's (1971) dichotomy between supply-driven and demand-driven management; Oliver Williamson's (1975) theory of transactional costs; the evolutionary models of Richard Nelson and Sidney Winter (1973); Cyert and DeGroot's (1974) models incorporating adaptive learning; Radner's (1975a,b) explicit satisficing models; and others.

---

[4] In addition to simulations of the firm, there are very interesting and potentially important efforts to use simulation to build bridges directly from decision theory to political economy. See Orcutt, Caldwell, & Wertheimer (1976), and Eliasson (1978).

Characterized in this way, there seems to be little commonality among all of these theories and models, except that they depart in one way or another from the classical assumption of perfect rationality in firm decision making. A closer look, however, and a more abstract description of their assumptions, shows that they share several basic characteristics. Most of them depart from the assumption of profit maximization in the short run, and replace it with an assumption of goals defined in terms of targets—that is, they are to greater or lesser degree satisficing theories. If they do retain maximizing assumptions, they contain some kind of mechanism that prevents the maximum from being attained, at least in the short run. In the Cyert-March theory, and that of Leibenstein, this mechanism can be viewed as producing "organizational slack," the magnitude of which may itself be a function of motivational and environmental variables.

Finally, a number of these theories assume that organizational learning takes place, so that if the environment were stationary for a sufficient length of time, the system equilibrium would approach closer and closer to the classical profit-maximizing equilibrium. Of course they generally also assume that the environmental disturbances will generally be large enough to prevent the classical solution from being an adequate approximation to the actual behavior.

The presence of something like organizational slack in a model of the business firm introduces complexity in the firm's behavior in the short run. Since the firm may operate very far from any optimum, the slack serves as a buffer between the environment and the firm's decisions. Responses to environmental events can no longer be predicted simply by analyzing the "requirements of the situation," but depend on the specific decision processes that the firm employs. However well this characteristic of a business firm model corresponds to reality, it reduces the attractiveness of the model for many economists, who are reluctant to give up the process-independent predictions of classical theory, and who do not feel at home with the kind of empirical investigation that is required for disclosing actual real world decision processes.

But there is another side to the matter. If, in the face of identical environmental conditions, different decision mechanisms can produce different firm behaviors, this sensitivity of outcomes to process can have important consequences for analysis at the level of markets and the economy. Political economy, whether descriptive or normative, cannot remain indifferent to this source of variability in response. At the very least it demands that—before we draw policy conclusions from our theories, and particularly before we act on those policy conclusions—we carry out sensitivity analyses to test how far our conclusions would be changed if we made different assumptions about the decision mechanisms at the micro level.

If our conclusions are robust—if they are not changed materially by substituting one or another variant of the behavioral model for the classical model—we will gain confidence in our predictions and recommendations; if the conclusions are sensitive to such substitutions, we will use them warily until we can determine which micro theory is the correct one.

As reference to the literature cited earlier in this section will verify, our predictions of the operations of markets and of the economy *are* sensitive to our assumptions about mechanisms at the level of decision processes. Moreover, the assumptions of the behavioral theories are almost certainly closer to reality than those of the classical theory. These two facts, in combination, constitute a direct refutation of the argument that the unrealism of the assumptions of the classical theory is harmless. We cannot use the in vacua version of the law of falling bodies to predict the sinking of a heavy body in molasses. The predictions of the classical and neoclassical theories and the policy recommendations derived from them must be treated with the greatest caution.

V. CONCLUSION

There is a saying in politics that "you can't beat something with nothing." You can't defeat a measure or a candidate simply by pointing to defects and inadequacies. You must offer an alternative.

The same principle applies to scientific theory. Once a theory is well entrenched, it will survive many assaults of empirical evidence that purports to refute it unless an alternative theory, consistent with the evidence, stands ready to replace it. Such conservative protectiveness of established beliefs is, indeed, not unreasonable. In the first place, in empirical science we aspire only to approximate truths; we are under no illusion that we can find a single formula, or even a moderately complex one, that captures the whole truth and nothing else. We are committed to a strategy of successive approximations, and when we find discrepancies between theory and data, our first impulse is to patch rather than to rebuild from the foundations.

In the second place, when discrepancies appear, it is seldom immediately obvious where the trouble lies. It may be located in the fundamental assumptions of the theory, but it may as well be merely a defect in the auxiliary hypotheses and measurement postulates we have had to assume in order to connect theory with observations. Revisions in these latter parts of the structure may be sufficient to save the remainder.

What then is the present status of the classical theory of the firm? There can no longer be any doubt that the micro assumptions of the theory—the assumptions of perfect rationality—are contrary to fact. It is not a question of approximation; they do not even remotely describe the processes that human beings use for making decisions in complex situations.

Moreover, there is an alternative. If anything, there is an embarrassing richness of alternatives. Today, we have a large mass of descriptive data, from both laboratory and field, that show how human problem solving and decision making actually take place in a wide variety of situations. A number of theories have been constructed to account for these data, and while these theories certainly do not yet constitute a single coherent whole, there is much in common among them. In one way or another, they incorporate the notions of bounded rationality: the need to search for decision alternatives, the replacement of optimization by targets and satisficing goals, and mechanisms of learning and adaptation. If our interest lies in descriptive decision theory (or even normative decision theory), it is now entirely clear that the classical and neoclassical theories have been replaced by a superior alternative that provides us with a much closer approximation to what is actually going on.

But what if our interest lies primarily in normative political economy rather than in the more remote regions of the economic sciences? Is there then any reason why we should give up the familiar theories? Have the newer concepts of decision making and the firm shown their superiority "for purposes of economic analysis"?

If the classical and neoclassical theories were, as is sometimes argued, simply powerful tools for deriving aggregative consequences that held alike for both perfect and bounded rationality, we would have every reason to retain them for this purpose. But we have seen, on the contrary, that neoclassical theory does not always lead to the same conclusions at the level of aggregate phenomena and policy as are implied by the postulate of bounded rationality, in any of its variants. Hence, we cannot defend an uncritical use of these contrary-to-fact assumptions by the argument that their veridicality is unimportant. In many cases, in fact, this veridicality may be crucial to reaching correct conclusions about the central questions of political economy. Only a comparison of predictions can tell us whether a case before us is one of these.

The social sciences have been accustomed to look for models in the most spectacular successes of the natural sciences. There is no harm in that, provided that it is not done in a spirit of slavish imitation. In economics, it has been common enough to admire Newtonian mechanics (or, as we have seen, the Law of Falling Bodies), and to search for the economic equivalent of the laws of motion. But this is not the only model for a science, and it seems, indeed, not to be the right one for our purposes.

Human behavior, even rational human behavior, is not to be accounted for by a handful of invariants. It is certainly not to be accounted for by assuming perfect adaptation to the environment. Its basic mechanisms may be relatively simple, and I believe they are, but that simplicity operates in interaction with extremely complex boundary conditions imposed by the environment and by the very facts of human long-term memory and of the capacity of human beings, individually and collectively, to learn.

If we wish to be guided by a natural science metaphor, I suggest one drawn from biology rather than physics (see Newell & Simon, 1976). Obvious lessons are to be learned from evolutionary biology, and rather less obvious ones from molecular biology. From molecular biology, in particular, we can glimpse a picture of how a few basic mechanisms—the DNA of the Double Helix, for example, or the energy transfer mechanisms elucidated so elegantly by Peter Mitchell—can account for a wide range of complex phenomena. We can see the role in science of laws of qualitative structure, and the power of qualitative as well as quantitative explanation.

I am always reluctant to end a talk about the sciences of man in the future tense. It conveys too much the impression that these are potential sciences which may some day be actualized, but that do not really exist at the present time. Of course that is not the case at all. However much our knowledge of human behavior falls short of our need for such knowledge, still it is enormous. Sometimes we tend to discount it because so many of the phenomena are accessible to us in the very activity of living as human beings among human beings that it seems commonplace to us. Moreover, it does not always answer the questions for which we need answers. We cannot predict very well the course of the business cycle nor manage the employment rate. (We cannot, it might be added, predict very well the time of the next thunderstorm in Stockholm, or manage the earth's climates.)

With all these qualifications and reservations, we do understand today many of the mechanisms of human rational choice. We do know how the information processing system called Man, faced with complexity beyond his ken, uses his information processing capacities to seek out alternatives, to calculate consequences, to resolve uncertainties, and thereby—sometimes, not always—to find ways of action that are sufficient unto the day, that satisfice.

REFERENCES

Alchian, A.A. (1950). Uncertainty, evolution, and economic theory. *Journal of Political Economy, 58,* 211–221.

Ando, A. (1978, October). *On a theoretical and empirical basis of macroeconometric models.* Paper presented to the NSF-NBER conference on macroeconomic modeling, Ann Arbor, MI.

Barnard, C.I. (1938). *The functions of the executive.* Cambridge, MA: Harvard University Press.

Baumol, W. (1959). *Business behavior, value and growth.* New York: Macmillan.

Becker, G.S. (1962). Irrational behavior and economic theory. *Journal of Political Economy, 70,* 1–13.

Bonini, C.P. (1963). *Simulation of information and decision systems in the firm.* Englewood-Cliffs, NJ: Prentice-Hall.

Chandler, A. (1962). *Strategy and structure.* Cambridge, MA: M.I.T. Press.

Churchill, N.C., Cooper, W.W., & Sainsbury, T. (1964). Laboratory and field studies of the behavioral effects of audits. In C.P. Bonini, R.K. Jaedicke, & H.M. Wagner (Eds.), *Management controls: New directions in basic research.* New York: McGraw-Hill.

Clarkson, G.P.E. (1963). A model of the trust investment process. In E.A. Feigenbaum & J. Feldman (Eds.), *Computers and thought.* New York: McGraw-Hill.

Commons, J.R. (1934). *Institutional economics: Its place in political economy.* Madison: University of Wisconsin Press.

Cyert, R.M., Feigenbaum, E.A., & March, J.G. (1959). Models in a behavioral theory of the firm. *Behavioral Science, 4,* 81–95.

Cyert, R.M., & De Groot, M.H. (1974). Rational expectations and Bayesian analysis. *Journal of Political Economy, 82,* 521–536.

Cyert, R.M., & De Groot, M.H. (1975). Adaptive utility. In R.H. Day & T. Groves (Eds.), *Adaptive economic models.* New York: Academic Press.

Cyert, R.M., & March, J.G. (1963). *A behavioral theory of the firm.* Englewood Cliffs, NJ: Prentice-Hall.

Cyert, R.M., & Simon, H.A. (1971). *Theory of the firm: Behavioralism and marginalism.* Unpublished working paper, Carnegie-Mellon University, Pittsburgh, PA.

Cyert, R.M., Simon, H.A., & Trow, D.B. (1956). Observation of a business decision. *Journal of Business, 29,* 237–248.

Dearborn, D.C., & Simon, H.A. (1958). Selective perception: A note on the departmental identifications of executives. *Sociometry, 21,* 140–144 (Reprinted in Simon, H.A. (1976). *Administrative behavior* (Ch. 15) (3rd ed.). New York: Free Press.)

Dutton, J.M., & Starbuck, W.H. (1971). *Computer simulation of human behavior.* New York: Wiley.

Eliasson, G. (1976). *Business economic planning.* London: Wiley.

Eliasson, G. (1978). *A micro-to-micro model of the Swedish economy* (IUI conference reports). Stockholm.

Friedman, B.M. (1978). A discussion of the methodological premises of Professors Lucas and Sargent. In *After the Phillips curve: Persistence of high inflation and high unemployment* (Conference Series No. 19). Boston: Federal Reserve Board of Boston.

Friedman, B.M. (1979). Optimal expectations and the extreme information assumptions of "rational expectations" macromodels. *Journal of Monetary Economics, 5,* 23–41.

Friedman, M. (1953). *Essays in positive economics.* Chicago: University of Chicago Press.

Hayes, J.R., & Simon, H.A. (1974). Understanding written problem instructions. In L.W. Gregg (Ed.), *Knowledge and cognition* (pp. 167–200). Potomac, MD: Erlbaum.

Hirschman, A.O. (1970). *Exit, voice and loyalty.* Cambridge, MA: Harvard University Press.

Holt, C.C., Modigliani, F., Muth, J.F., & Simon, H.A. (1960). *Planning production, inventories, and work force.* Englewood Cliffs, NJ: Prentice-Hall.

Ijiri, Y., & Simon, H.A. (1977). *Skew distributions and the sizes of business firms.* Amsterdam: North-Holland.

Johnsen, E. (1968). *Studies in multiobjective decision models.* Lund, Sweden: Studentlitteratur.

Jorgenson, D.W., & Siebert, C.D. (1968). A comparison of alternative theories of corporate investment behavior. *American Economic Review, 58,* 681–712.

Kahneman, D., & Tversky, A. (1973). On the psychology of prediction. *Psychological Review, 80,* 237–251.

Kornai, J. (1971). *Anti-equilibrium.* Amsterdam: North-Holland.

Kunreuther, H. (1978). *Disaster insurance protection: Public policy lessons.* New York: Wiley.

Leibenstein, H. (1976). *Beyond economic man.* Cambridge, MA: Harvard University Press.

Lesourne, H. (1977). *A theory of the individual for economic analysis.* Amsterdam: North-Holland.

Lucas, R.E., Jr. (1975). An equilibrium model of the business cycle. *Journal of Political Economy, 83,* 1113–1114.

Lucas, R.E., Jr. (1978). On the size distribution of business firms. *Bell Journal of Economics, 9,* 508–523.

March, J.G. (Ed.) (1965). *Handbook of organizations.* Chicago: Rand McNally.

March, J.G., & Simon, H.A. (1958). *Organizations.* New York: Wiley.

Marris, R. (1964). *The economic theory of "managerial" capitalism.* New York: Free Press of Glencoe.

Marschak, J. (1949). Role of liquidity under complete and incomplete information. *American Economic Review, 39,* 182-195.

Marschak, J., & Radner, R. (1972). *Economic theory of teams.* New Haven, CT: Yale University Press.

Marshall, A. (1920). *Principles of economics* (8th ed.). London: Macmillan.

Mason, E.S. (1952). Comment. In B.F. Haley (Ed.), *A survey of contemporary economics* (Vol II). Homewood, IL: R.D. Irwin.

Montias, J.M. (1976). *The structure of economic systems.* New Haven, CT: Yale University Press.

Muth, J.F. (1960). Optimal properties of exponentially weighted forecasts. *Journal of the American Statistical Association, 55,* 299-306.

Muth, J.F. (1961). Rational expectations and the theory of price movements. *Econometrica, 29,* 315-353.

Nelson, R.R., & Winter, S. (1973). Toward an evolutionary theory of economic capabilities. *American Economic Review, 63,* 440-449.

Nelson, R.R., & Winter, S. (1974). Neoclassical vs. evolutionary theories of economic growth. *Economic Journal, 84,* 886-905.

Newell, A., & Simon, H.A. (1972). *Human problem solving.* Englewood Cliffs, NJ: Prentice-Hall.

Newell, A., & Simon, H.A. (1976). Computer science as empirical inquiry: Symbols and search. *Communications of the ACM, 19,* 113-126.

Orcutt, G., Caldwell, S., & Wertheimer, R., II. (1976). *Policy exploration through microanalytic simulation.* Washington, DC: Urban Institute.

Papandreou, A. (1952). Some basic problems in the theory of the firm. In B.F. Haley (Ed.), *A survey of contemporary economics* (Vol. II). Homewood, IL: R.D. Irwin.

Phelps-Brown, E.H. (1957). The meaning of the fitted Cobb-Douglas function. *Quarterly Journal of Economics, 71,* 546-560.

Radner, R. (1975a). A behavioral model of cost reduction. *Bell Journal of Economics, 6,* 196-215.

Radner, R. (1975b). Satisficing. *Journal of Mathematical Economics, 2,* 253-262.

Roberts, D.R. (1959). *Executive compensation.* Glencoe, IL: Free Press.

Samuelson, P.A. (1963). Discussion: Problems of methodology. *American Economic Review, 53,* 231-236.

Schultz, H. (1938). *The theory and measurement of demand.* Chicago: University of Chicago Press.

Simon, H.A. (1947). *Administrative behavior.* New York: Macmillan.

Simon, H.A. (1951). A formal theory of the employment relation. *Econometrica, 19,* 293-305.

Simon, H.A. (1952). A comparison of organisation theories. *Review of Economic Studies, 20,* 40-48.

Simon, H.A. (1955). A behavioral model of rational choice. *Quarterly Journal of Economics, 69,* 99-118.

Simon, H.A. (1956a). Rational choice and the structure of the environment. *Psychological Review, 63,* 129-138.

Simon, H.A. (1956b). Dynamic programming under uncertainty with a quadratic criterion function. *Econometrica, 24,* 74-81.

Simon, H.A. (1957a). *Models of man.* New York: Wiley.

Simon, H.A. (1957b). The compensation of executives. *Sociometry, 20,* 32-35.

Simon, H.A. (1959). Theories of decision making in economics and behavioral science. *American Economic Review, 49,* 223-283.

Simon, H.A. (1963). Discussion: Problems of methodology. *American Economic Review, 53,* 229–231.

Simon, H.A. (1976). From substantive to procedural rationality. In S.J. Latsis (Ed.), *Method and appraisal in economics.* Cambridge, England: Cambridge University Press.

Simon, H.A. (1978a). Rationality as process and as product of thought. *American Economic Review, 68,* 1–16.

Simon, H.A. (1978b). On how to decide what to do. *Bell Journal of Economics, 9,* 494–507.

Simon, H.A., Guetzkow, H., Kozmetsky, G., & Tyndall, G. (1978). *Centralization vs. decentralization in organizing the controller's department.* Houston: Scholars Book. (Original work published 1954)

Simon, H.A., & Levy, F.K. (1963). A note on the Cobb-Douglas function. *Review of Economic Studies, 30,* 93–94.

Stigler, G.J. (1961). The economics of information. *Journal of Political Economy, 69,* 213–225.

Theil, H. (1957). A note on certainty equivalence in dynamic planning. *Econometrica, 25,* 346–349.

von Neumann, J., & Morgenstern, O. (1944). *Theory of games and economic behavior.* Princeton, NJ: Princeton University Press.

Walters, A.A. (1963). Production and cost functions: An econometric survey. *Econometrica, 31,* 1–66.

Williamson, O. (1975). *Markets and hierarchies: Analysis and antitrust implications.* New York: Free Press.

Winter, S. (1971). Satisficing, selection, and the innovating remnant. *Quarterly Journal of Economics, 85,* 237–261.

Chapter 3

Animal Choice and Human Choice*

Howard Rachlin

Department of Psychology
State University of New York, Stony Brook

Except for differences in parameters and what would now be called differences in "interface" between organisms and environment, the laws of human and nonhuman choice, as Brunswik (1943) and Tolman (1938) saw them, are the same and can be studied in the same (or at least parallel) ways. Brunswik (1943), in an article entitled "Organismic Achievement and Environmental Probability" (from an address at a conference at which Hull and Lewin also spoke), cited his experiments with rats choosing between uncertain rewards in a T-maze in the same context as his experiments with humans making judgments of pictures of faces. Tolman (1938) felt that a rat's behavior at a choice point in a maze would lead to laws of choice, generalizable to all human behavior.

Yet, in the last 20 years or so, studies of animal choice (where "animal" includes "human"), and studies of choice exclusively limited to humans, have diverged. The theoretical stances and experimental techniques of the two areas now seem far apart. Although both approaches currently make use of economic models, the animal research is resolutely behavioral while the human research is resolutely cognitive.

While exemplifying the previous unity of theory of animal and human choice, Brunswik (1952) also prefigured the current division. He saw what he called "objective functional psychology," a synthesis of behaviorism and gestalt psychology, as taking two forms, both relying, ultimately, on "objective" relationships. The first form, which he himself preferred, he called "the empty organism approach." He said, "By applying this approach to distal-to-distal functional arcs bridging over the entire organism without descending into it, one may further gain scope and at the same time get around the hazardous construction of intervening variables. Such an approach may be characterized as 'without, yet about, the organism'" (p. 72).

* This article was written with the help of a grant from the National Science Foundation. I thank Leonard Green, John Kagel, and Alexandra Logue for valuable comments on earlier versions of the manuscript.

He cited Skinner's (1938) proposal that psychologists had better give up the nervous system and confine their attention to the "end terms" as an example of this approach. He compared the organism's bridging-over of temporal and spatial gaps to the effects of a lens that transforms an object on one side to a focused image on the other side. If one wants to understand the relationship between object and image, it would be a mistake to study the light inside or even at the surface of the lens. At those points there is no image. According to Brunswik (1952, p. 25), "A great variety of . . . relationships must be studied, including some that arch out very far in space or time." And "All we can hope for with respect to molar behavior is what Reichenbach and others have called 'probability laws.' Among these are correlation coefficients and other statistical measures of concomitant variation" (p. 28). Correspondingly, if one wants to understand functional behavior, Brunswik felt, it would be a mistake to study neurophysiology. The perceptual constancies, for instance, can be understood best in terms of relationships between objects on the one hand and overt behavior on the other. Currently, those psychologists studying choice using this approach have emerged out of the Skinnerian tradition, and often (although far from exclusively) have done experiments with nonhuman animal subjects exposed to concurrent schedules of food reward.

The second form of objective functional psychology, according to Brunswik (1952), is the one that Tolman took. Tolman went beyond simple probability laws to discuss "intervening variables" such as expectancies and cognitive maps. These variables, in Tolman's hands, were not dependent on introspection except in their formative stages. In theory, at least, they were "operationally anchored." This approach, that of modern cognitive psychology, has been adopted by modern decision theory and applied generally to human choice. According to Wallsten (1980, p. ix), "Recent years have seen important changes in research on behavioral decision theory in terms of a shift from a reliance on economic and statistical models to an emphasis on concepts drawn from cognitive psychology." Thus a unified approach to choice has split into behavioral and cognitive directions, the former studying animals and the latter studying only humans.

Aside from the subjects of their experiments, perhaps the most critical difference between animal and human studies of choice is their differing treatment, both in theory and in practice, of the concept of probability. Behavior, for the behavioral theorist, is (most directly) a function of "objective" relative frequencies of events. Behavior, for the cognitive theorist, is (most directly) a function of "subjective" probabilities of events. But there is not as much difference as there might seem to be between an objective and a subjective probability. *Both objective and subjective probabilities are representations of events as determined by theory.* The dependence on theory of what is said to be a subjective probability of an event is perhaps obvious. But, as the next section will show, objective probabilities are no less dependent on theory.

Behavioral and cognitive theories of choice will be compared using two examples of behavioral theories, Herrnstein's (1970) theory that animals *match* their choices (relative rates of response) to relative rates of reinforcement, and Rachlin, Battalio, Kagel, and Green's (1981) theory that animals behave so as to *maximize* value, and one example of a cognitive theory, Kahneman and Tversky's (1979) *prospect* theory, in which people are said to choose, from among gambles, the one of highest subjective value. It will be seen that the difference between current behavioral and cognitive theories lies more in their tone than in their substance.

Objective probability. In Brunswik's (1939) original animal studies with a T-maze, a probability was represented as the number of trials with food present in the goal box divided by the total number of trials (with food plus without food). In such an experiment, a particular sequence of trials, for instance *FNNNFNFF* (where *F* is a food trial and N is a nonfood trial) may have been drawn from a random number table with a probability of *F* and *N* of 0.5 but any finite sequence, no matter how long, is a specific sequence, not a random one. The initial or the final *F* in the example above may affect behavior more or less strongly than the *N*s nested in the middle of the series. Furthermore, an animal's behavior may be a function only of the two most recent trials. The probability of reward in the series above is *really* 0.5 only for a set of limited purposes, for instance, selecting at random from a bag containing balls labeled *F* and *N*. But the rat does not select trials at random. They are ordered in a *specific sequence,* and the sequence may affect behavior. It is not clear that each trial should be considered to be a unitary event, nor that the set of trials, as a whole, that comprises an experimental session should be marked off and isolated (for purposes of calculation of probability) from other trials during other sessions. Adding in other sequences can, of course, change the value one gets when calculating probability. Yet a probability based on the trials of one session and a probability based on the trials of two sessions are both *objective* probabilities. And it is also true that calculation of objective probabilities in *some* way is useful in predicting the rat's behavior. What holds for probability of events (with respect to trials) holds also for rate of events (with respect to time). It is up to theory as guided by the results of experiments to decide how to best represent the objective probability or rate of events. Without a theory, probability and rate are indeterminate.

It is important to emphasize that this indeterminancy of objective probability is not just behavioral variability, and it is not just a problem of choosing a convenient scale by which to measure rate. The indeterminacy holds equally for probability and rate of behavioral events as for probability and rate of environmental events.

This flexible view of probability and rate is a common feature of many post-Skinnerian approaches to behavior (Baum, 1973; Catania, 1971; Gibbon, Berryman, & Thompson, 1974; Herrnstein, 1970; Maier, Seligman, & Solomon, 1969; Rachlin, 1976; Rescorla, 1967; Staddon, 1980; Teitelbaum, 1977). In Figure 1, lines *A* and *B* are hypothetical records of two discrete events. Line *A* may represent pecks by a pigeon on key *A,* and line *B* may represent pecks on key *B*. Rate of pecking on key *A* and key *B* both depend on the time base used in calculating them. Time bases *V–W* and *X–Y* yield different rates from each other and from the wider time frame, *U–Z*.

Although records such as line *A* represent behavior of the whole organism, Figure 1 shows that two such behaviors can occur at the same time. It is an essential part of all post-Skinnerian behavioral theories that rates of two events may occur over the same time span, because correlations of events over time rather than individual events are the variables. It would be meaningless to ask what was a pigeon's rate of pecking at a given instant unless that instant were part of a larger time span and that larger time span were specified. This is a critical point. Consider instant *Y* in Figure 1. At the instant of *Y,* response *A* is not occurring, but it is not true that the rate of response *A* at that instant is zero. Rate of response needs an interval to have meaning; let us take interval *X–Z*. Once we have specified that interval we may then say that during the interval (which encompasses instant *Y*) the

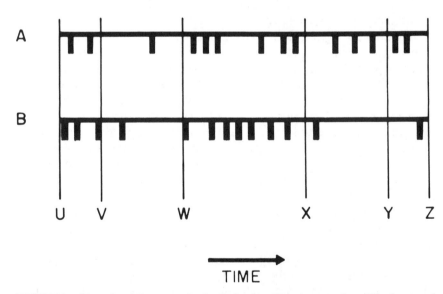

FIGURE 1. Lines *A* and *B* are records of a single pigeon's pecks at two keys. The downward pips represent pecks at keys *A* and *B*. The letters *U, V, W, X, Y,* and *Z* represent specific instants of time.

rate of response is *R1*. But if we take a different interval, say *V–Z,* the rate of response at instant *Y* would be different, say *R2.* It would be pointless (outside of a particular theory) to argue whether the rate of response at instant *Y* was really *R1* or *R2.*

The mathematics of calculus, is, of course, the way to obtain rates at a point. But differential calculus cannot be applied to the discrete events of Figure 1. As $\triangle t$ approaches zero, the rate at point-*Y* would approach zero. The proper calculus for such data as those of Figure 1 is *difference,* rather than differential calculus. Difference calculus uses a finite $\triangle t,$ and, for any given $\triangle t,$ yields an umbiguous instantaneous rate at each point. But different $\triangle t$s yield different rates. Therefore one needs a theory, before one begins to apply calculus, to decide on an appropriate interval.

Molar behavioral theories such as *matching* and *maximizing* can provide a $\triangle t.$ Each theory defines an appropriate range of $\triangle t$s as the range over which that theory holds (describes the data). As indicated above, matching and maximizing may hold at values of $\triangle t$ that do not completely overlap (although, in fact, they overlap considerably). Neither matching nor maximizing holds at an extreme molecular level. Both theories say that the organism integrates events over brief temporal intervals and that behavior is a function of that integral. All psychological theories do this to some extent (a tone, for instance, is often supposed to occur at an instant although it takes time for tones to occur), but molar behavioral theories such as matching and maximizing extend this integration over relatively long temporal intervals.

Avoidance behavior (Herrnstein & Hineline, 1966), choice among temporally extended events, as in concurrent chain schedules of reinforcement (Herrnstein, 1964), and self-control (Rachlin & Green, 1972) are all areas in which an animal's behavior is said to be a function of events at a temporal distance. Self-control, for instance, is defined by maximization theory in terms of a temporal interval (the $\triangle t$) over which maximization occurs. An animal that maximizes value over a brief interval may thereby fail to maximize value over a long interval. Such an animal is, by definition of the theory, behaving impulsively, while an animal that maximizes value over long intervals is (also by definition) showing self-control (Rachlin, 1974). Thus, a crucial development and comparative variable in maximization theory is the span of time over which value is maximized.

The interval $\triangle t$ is a *dependent* variable in maximization theory—it is a measure of self-control. Yet it is necessary to determine what $\triangle t$ is before deciding on how to describe the *independent* variable—the rate of reinforcement. The way this problem is handled in practice is by an iterative process where a $\triangle t$ is first arbitrarily chosen (or chosen by intuition) and then adjusted if necessary so as to provide the simplest or clearest or most esthetically pleasing explanation of the data (what Skinner calls "smooth curves").

Matching and maximizing may be viewed just as two ways in which this process is accomplished.[1]

The extension of both matching and maximizing theory to complex human behavior requires that $\triangle t$ be large. Human self-control, expectancy, belief and cognition can be explained by molar behavioral theory (as Brunswik pointed out) only in terms of widely extended temporal events.

Behavior is not raw data, simply observed. "Reinforcement rate," "response rate," and other behavioral terms are theoretical terms—ways in which theory represents data. Because behavior itself is bound up in theory, objections to the use of mental terms in a science of psychology on the grounds that those terms are imprecise or cannot be directly observed can be turned against the very notion of behavior itself.

Subjective probability. One might conceivably argue that subjective probabilities are more determinate than objective probabilities because they may be directly accessible to a human subject and reported verbally. But a human subject's verbal report of a probability may or may not coincide with the experimenter's calculation of probability, on the one hand, or with the subject's own choices or gambles on the other. The assumption that verbal report is a veridical indication of subjective probability is that of classical introspectionism, a method that was rejected by both Brunswik and Tolman and also by most modern cognitive psychologists. A review of the validity of verbal reports of cognitive processes by Nisbett and Wilson (1977) revealed that such reports were inconsistent with other measures of behavior, and that, while the other measures were often supportive of one or another cognitive theory, verbal reports seemed unrelated to theory when they were not actually disconfirmatory. Like other cognitive psychologists, decision theorists generally reject introspection as a direct indication of subjective probability (although they do not reject introspection as an object of study).

---

[1] Examples of misunderstanding on the arbitrariness of $\triangle t$ by behavioral theorists are common. For instance, Herrnstein and Vaughan (1980) devised a complex schedule in which contingencies were readjusted every 4 minutes. The pigeon subjects of these experiments behaved so that, if $\triangle t = 4$ min, matching explained their performance. Since the session consisted of concatenations of these 4-min intervals, matching also explained the pigeons' performance over the session. But, for $\triangle t << 4$ min, the pigeons' behavior is well described by maximization theory. However, by maximizing over the short interval, the pigeons failed to maximize over the session as a whole. Since there is evidence that the relevant $\triangle t$ for pigeons (choosing between reinforcers of various delays and amounts) may be only a few seconds, even after many months of training to extend it (Mazur & Logue, 1978), the result of Herrnstein and Vaughan's experiments are not inconsistent with maximization theory. The results show that pigeons lack self-control (maximize over short intervals at the expense of reinforcement in the long run). Herrnstein and Vaughan claim, erroneously, that these results are evidence against maximization theory.

The standard method used by decision theorists to present probabilities to human subjects attempts to bypass relative frequencies and expose the subject to probabilities "directly." Thus, the subject is presented with a gamble such as (from Kahneman & Tversky, 1979, p. 264):

Which of the following would you prefer?
(a) 50% chance to win 1000   (b) 450 for sure
    50% chance to win nothing

Often, these gambles are couched in the form of practical everyday problems. For instance (from Tversky & Kahneman, 1981, p. 453):

Imagine that the U.S. is preparing for the outbreak of an unusual Asian disease, which is expected to kill 600 people. Two alternative programs to combat the disease have been proposed. Assume that the exact scientific estimate of the consequences of the program are as follows:

If Program A is adopted, 200 people will be saved.

If Program B is adopted, there is ⅓ probability that 600 people will be saved, and ⅔ probability that no people will be saved.

Which of the two programs would you favor?

Occasionally, in decision experiments with humans, the hypothetical gambles are supplemented with coin tosses or drawing of balls from a bag and occasionally subjects are actually exposed to gambles in which money is won or lost. But the major theoretical work in this area is based on results with hypothetical gambles as illustrated above. A prospect represents both the probabilities and the amounts in verbal form. A possible advantage of verbal presentation of probabilities and amounts is that they are already encoded—they are already representations of events. If it is not possible to discover a subject's subjective representation of an event by simply asking, it may yet be possible to instill a representation directly into a subject's cognitive system by telling the subject what the representation should be. Behavior could then be studied as a function of such representations. If behavior were a function of expected value (probability times amount) based on the stated probabilities and amounts, the subjective probabilities and amounts could be said to equal the stated probabilities and amounts. But, as Kahneman and Tversky (1979) have conclusively shown, behavior is not a function of expected value based on the stated probabilities and amounts. In their prospect theory, both stated probability and stated amount must be *transformed* before they are combined. The theory provides transformation functions for both probability and amount by which stated values of each of these variables may be converted into subjective values. The subjective values are then multiplied so that behavior emerges as a function of *subjective* expected value.[2]

The cognitive study of choice thus differs from the behavioral study of choice with respect to how it modifies independent variables when behavior is not a simple function of those variables. The first recourse of a behavioral theory in the face of this problem is to reflect on the measurement of the variables themselves. As shown previously, by judicious choice of a timebase, objective probability may vary considerably. Thus, if behavioral maximization theory, for instance, finds that a subject does not maximize utility over a period of an hour, perhaps it may find that the subject maximizes utility over a period of a minute or a second.

Despite the wide lattitude for adjustment of objective probabilities by behavioral theories and of subjective probabilities by cognitive theories, subjects in both behavioral and cognitive experiments are still found to behave inconsistently. Both behavioral and cognitive theories of choice attempt to cope with this further inconsistency in their treatments of *context*.

Objective context. For the behaviorist, the variables that comprise the context of behavior are of the same sort as those that determine behavior directly. In Herrnstein's (1970) matching theory, the rate of a response is said to vary directly with the rate at which it is reinforced and indirectly with the overall rate of reinforcement for *all* responses. Overall rate of reinforcement is the behavioral context of the reinforcement of the individual response. Where behavior may appear inconsistent, the supposed overall rate of reinforcement is adjusted until behavior appears consistent (de Villiers, 1977). In behavioral maximization theory (Rachlin et al., 1981), the context of any behavior is the other behavior available to the subject. Context acts on a given behavior by means of the substitutability of those other behaviors for the one in question. The generality of the theory rests on its ability to describe the behavior of an animal over a series of constraints (schedules, contingencies, time periods, availabilities) with a single set of substitutabilities.

Subjective context. Consider the following two problems from Tversky and Kahneman (1981, p. 457):

---

[2] This is the normal case. Where the two possible outcomes of a gamble are both positive or both negative and the objective probabilities add to unity, however, prospect theory calculates the subjective value of a gamble by first extracting the subjectively certain portion of the outcomes and then adding the subjective expected value of the amount by which it might be augmented. For instance, if an alternative involves .8 probability to win $2 and .2 probability to win $6, the subject who chooses that alternative is sure to win at least $2. Thus the subjective equivalent of $2 is subtracted out and the alternative is evaluated as a chance of augmenting that (subjective) amount by nothing or augmenting it by (the subjective equivalent of) $4.

Problem 8 (N = 183): Imagine that you have decided to see a play where admission is $10 per ticket. As you enter the theater you discover that you have lost a $10 bill.

Would you still pay $10 for a ticket for the play?

    Yes (88 percent)   No (12 percent)

Problem 9 (N = 200): Imagine that you have decided to see a play and paid the admission price of $10 per ticket. As you enter the theater you discover that you have lost the ticket. The seat was not marked and the ticket cannot be recovered.

Would you pay $10 for another ticket?

    Yes (46 percent)   No (54 percent)

Here is Tversky and Kahneman's explanation of the results:

> The marked difference between the responses to problems 8 and 9 is an effect of psychological accounting. We propose that the purchase of a new ticket in problem 9 is entered in the account that was set up by the purchase of the original ticket. In terms of this account, the expense required to see the show is $20, a cost which many of our respondents apparently found excessive. In problem 8, on the other hand, the loss of $10 is not linked specifically to the ticket purchase and its effect on the decision is accordingly slight.

This explanation is based on their concept of "framing," in which stated amounts of money are transformed into subjective amounts by the subject, who represents them as *changes* in amount relative to some subjective set point or reference level. That reference level is partly brought into the experimental situation by the subject and partly caused by the way the problem is stated. The frame, in the case of problems 8 and 9, is the cognitive equivalent of Herrnstein's concept of overall rate of reinforcement. Both cognitive and behavioral theories can explain behavioral variation (and would explain the difference in subjects' responses to problems 8 and 9) in terms of variation of frame or context. The difference between cognitive and behavioral explanations, again, is just in their subjective or objective tone.

Cognitive decision theory says that the difference between problems 8 and 9 lies in the subject's subjective reference level for money. The subject's representation would differ in the two problems on the dimension of subjective *amount*. Behavioral matching and maximizing theories might also see the dimension of difference between problems 8 and 9 in terms of amount. They would say that the experimenter should calculate amount differently in the two problems, not that the subject calculates amount differently. Matching theory would perhaps say that the time base for calculating overall rate of reinforcement should be different in the two situations represented by the problems. In problem 8, the time base should be wider, encompassing all effective money transactions. In problem 9, the time base should be narrower, encompassing only transactions within the theater. Operationally, the difference between the cognitive and behavioral explanations seems virtually nil.

Behavioral maximization theory differs from behavioral matching theory and cognitive theory in its greater reluctance to alter measures of *value* and its emphasis on explaining differences in behavior in terms of differences in constraints (see Stigler & Becker, 1977). Maximization theory might see the difference between the situations represented by problems 8 and 9 in terms of a difference in constraints. Consider, for instance, the following hypothetical problem:

> Problem 9′: Imagine that you have decided to see a play, paid the admission price of $10 per ticket, and are now seated in your seat waiting for the curtain to rise. You decide to go to the rest room (being alone, you take your coat with you). By accident you walk out of the theater. The exit door locks behind you, you have no stub and the seat was not marked. Would you pay $10 for another ticket?

My own answer to the question is, "no way." A small sample of subjects ($N=4$) agrees with me and, I venture to guess, nearly 100% of subjects in a larger sample would agree with me too. But, it would seem, according to an analysis based on *value,* that problem 9′ is the same as problem 9. I respond "yes" in problem 8, "no" in problem 9, and "no way" in problem 9′ because the constraints in the situations represented by the three problems are different. In the situation represented by problem 8, I would not argue with the manager. In that represented by problem 9, I would put up a small fight to get into the theater. In that represented by problem 9′, I would put up quite a big fight to get into the theater again. My willingness to fight to get into the theater would be determined by the constraints on my behavior imposed by the situation. Tversky and Kahneman may complain that I misunderstood the problem, but that is the chance one takes when the independent variables of an experiment are already representations of events; a subject's representation of those events may differ in unanticipated ways from that of the experimenter.

The point here is that the theoretical adjustment, when it is made by the behaviorist, is made in the independent variable itself—in the behaviorist's representation of that variable—not in the subject's representation. Faced with a similar problem (failure to find choice to be a simple function of independent variables), the cognitivist cannot look to the same solution. The typical independent variables in a cognitive experiment, the verbally encoded probabilities and amounts, are fixed before the experiment begins. When they are found to be inadequate, the experimenter cannot change his own representation of events. Instead, he changes what is conceived to be the subject's representation of events, and it is said that the subject's representation is not "true." Thus, subjects in cognitive experiments are sometimes said to behave irrationally or less than rationally (March, 1978).

Rationality. The concept of rationality has a confusing history in economics and psychology. It has never had a place in modern animal choice theory, perhaps because animals were not considered rational creatures. But it has been used extensively in economics and human decision theory. As regards the behavior of a subject in a psychology experiment, the only way to test for rationality is through consistency. According to Tversky and Kahneman's (1981, p. 45) characterization of the lay notion of rational behavior, "a man could be judged irrational either because his preferences are contradictory or because his desires and aversions do not reflect his pleasures and pains." The latter instance is a version of the former. Pleasures and pains are exhibited by one set of choices, and desires and aversions by an overlapping set. If two sets of choices are consistent, then the man's behavior is rational; if the two sets are contradictory, then the man's behavior is irrational. Thus, in everyday language, rationality is often identified with consistency of behavior and irrationality with inconsistency of behavior. *But one behavior cannot contradict another behavior. It can only contradict a theory of behavior.* It is not irrational or inconsistent for the context or frame of a problem to affect behavior. As Tversky and Kahneman imply, if behavior is seen to be inconsistent, then the fault must lie with the theory, not the subject. A theory, cognitive or behavioral, that could adequately predict behavior as a function of a prospect (or event) and its frame (or context) would find no more inconsistency than a perceptual theory that viewed the subjective brightness of a spot of light as a joint function of the intensity of the spot and its surrounding frame. The tendency of some cognitive theorists to view behavior as irrational or inconsistent is thus a disguised fault of their theories.[3]

---

[3] Recently, Cohen (1981) argued that much of the "irrationality" found in human decision experiments could be considered rational if one judges it, not against *normative* concepts of rationality (that one might get from a book on logic), but by judging the behavior against the subject's own *intuitive* rationality. As Cohen admits, however, this argument depends on a distinction between a person's competence and performance. Cohen simply assumes everyone is logically competent. But behavioral theories go one step further and assume that there is no difference between competence and performance. Cohen assumes that it is possible to separate a person's reasoning, on one hand, from the (contextual) influences on reasoning of such factors as learning and motivation, on the other. Thus, according to Cohen, a person, by means of a faulty connection between (infallible) competence and (fallible) performance, may be seen as obtaining a state of affairs he or she does not actually want. For both maximization and matching theory, what people want is determined by what they do (see Rachlin et al., 1981, for a formulization of this principle), so their reasoning can never be faulty.

Human and animal subjects. The relation between objective and subjective events is such that a given objective event, depending on various features of the subjective context, can give rise to any of a number of subjective events. (For instance, the series *ABBBABAA* could be represented by a subjective probability of *B* anywhere from 0 to 1, depending on how the subject perceives the series.)

Suppose (a) that cognitive theories are correct that choice is a function of subjective events. Then behavioral theories, in looking for a relation between objective events and behavior, would be seriously mistaking the true independent variable. As the behaviorist varied the objective events, the subject might be holding the subjective events (hence, choice) constant. As the behaviorist held the objective events constant, the subject might be allowing the subjective events (hence, choice) to vary.

Suppose (b) that there was a way to directly vary the subjective events (by telling the subject what they should be), or to directly measure the subjective events (by asking the subject what they were). If both (a) and (b) were true, then choice experiments should use humans as subjects; only with humans could there be a meaningful independent variable in choice experiments. If supposition (b) were true, experiments presenting hypothetical gambles would be better than experiments presenting actual gambles, because hypothetical gambles would directly instill the subjective representations which in turn determine choice. Since nonhuman animals cannot understand hypothetical gambles, they could not then be subjects in choice experiments. But, whatever one concludes about supposition (a), supposition (b) is not true; subjective probabilities are not directly determinable. An exactly parallel argument may be made regarding objective probabilities, as follows:

The relation between subjective and objective events is such that a given subjective event, depending on various features of the objective context, can arise from any of a number of objective events. For instance, the subjective probability of *B* of 1/2 could represent any series of events, *A*s and *B*s, depending on how the theorist constructs subjective probability from objective events.

Suppose (a') that behavioral theories are correct that choice is a function of objective events (the "lens" model). Then cognitive theories in looking for a relation between subjective events and behavior would be seriously mistaking the true independent variable. As the cognitivist supposed the subjective events to vary, the objective events (or the critical relationships among them) might be constant (hence choice would be constant). As the cognitivist supposed the subjective events to remain constant, the objective events (or the critical relationships among them) might vary (hence, choice would vary).

Suppose (b') that there was a unique, agreed upon interpretation of each objective event. If both (a') and (b') were true, then choice experiments should use animals as subjects. If supposition (b') were true, experiments presenting actual gambles would be better than experiments presenting hypothetical gambles, because actual gambles contain objective probabilities which directly determine choice. If (as Kahneman & Tversky, 1979, say) actual gambles cannot practically and meaningfully be presented in laboratory situations to humans, they should not be subjects in choice experiments.

But whatever one concludes about supposition (a'), supposition (b') is not true. There is no unique, agreed upon interpretation of each objective event. The behaviorist's argument against using humans as subjects in choice experiments is no better than the cognitivist's arguments against using animals. It would seem desirable to test all theories, behavioral and cognitive, with both animal and human subjects. The fundamental observational datum that interacts with theory is, in both cases, the same. Both objective and subjective probabilities are theoretical constructions from that datum.

Let us now compare these constructions by considering how behavioral and cognitive theories handle a common problem—the relationship of symmetric to nonsymmetric choice.

Symmetric and nonsymmetric choice. Choice behavior, when it is studied as such in behavioral and cognitive experiments, is usually symmetric. In both types of choice experiments, subjects choose between alternatives with specific consequences for each alternative. In cognitive choice problems, the alternative responses are often, "A" or "B," "left" or "right," "Yes" or "No." In behavioral experiments with pigeons, rats, or humans, the choices often consist of responding to one of two symmetrically arranged keys, levers, or buttons. But when Tolman (1938) claimed that a rat's behavior at a choice point could stand, in some sense, for all behavior, he meant that a theory that explained symmetrical choice should be generalizable to explain asymmetrical choice. A theory that explains choice between a blue coat and a brown coat should, according to Tolman, also explain choice between buying a coat in the first place and not buying it. In behavioral practice, symmetric choice is literally symmetric. Alleys of a maze, keys, levers, or buttons may be presented symmetrically. The critical test of the generalizability of a behavioral theory of choice, then, is whether choice with multiple, symmetrical, available responses can be predicted from behavior with only one explicit response available. Is it possible, for example, to predict a rat's behavior in a symmetric T-maze from the rat's behavior in a straight alley? More abstractly, is it possible to predict the *relative* rate of response in a symmetric choice situation from the absolute rate of response in an asymmetric situation? This question has always been recognized as critical in behavioral theory (Logan, 1960), but was not adequately answered until recently. Herrnstein (1970) and de Villiers (1977) show how choice in a great variety of symmetrical and asymmetrical situations may be explained by a common formulation. Their tactic is to postulate a hypothetical reward for all responses available in the experimental situation other than those explicitly rewarded. This hypothetical reward is considered to be part of the behavioral context. Its value, estimated from an animal's behavior in one choice situation (symmetric or asymmetric), is then used to predict the animal's behavior in other situations. Rachlin et al. (1981) show how the degree of substitutability among various responses interacts with their symmetry. It is possible to predict a rat's choice between food and water (its relative rate of response on two levers) from the amount of work it will do to get food (its absolute rate of response on a single lever when only food is available) and the amount of work it will do to get water (its absolute rate of response on a single lever when only water is available).

The corresponding symmetry–asymmetry problem in cognitive decision theory has not been solved. Theories such as Kahneman and Tversky's prospect theory, that describe symmetrical choice between gamble-x and gamble-y, have not been able to describe asymmetrical choices: how much money a subject would pay for gamble-x and how much money a subject would pay for gamble-y (Einhorn & Hogarth, 1981; Payne, 1982). According to Payne (p. 382), "the lack of invariance across tasks that are seemingly similar (e.g., choice vs. bidding for the same gambles) is of concern to decision analysts and others whose job is to improve decision performance. . . . The lack of invariance also complicates the search for a small set of underlying principles that can describe observed behavior."

The problem, however, does not seem to lie in current cognitive theory, which is at least as sophisticated (and flexible) as any behavioral theory. Kahneman and Tversky's (1979) prospect theory, for instance, distinguishes clearly between amount and probability of reward, whereas behavioral theory often confounds them in rate of reward (but see Gibbon, 1977, for behavioral distinctions between rate and amount). If cognitive theory is at least as flexible as behavioral theory, why then can it not encompass symmetric and asymmetric choice? An obvious answer is that there is something wrong with the behavioral situations studied by cognitive psychologists. The concluding section briefly speculates on what that problem may be and how to correct it.

Precept and practice in choice experiments. The behaviorist may insist that contingencies or reinforcement determine behavior, but cannot insist that subjects in choice experiments must always come into contact with those very contingencies. In practice, people often make decisions without much contact with the critical contingencies. For instance, the contingency between sex and pregnancy certainly has a powerful effect on the decisions humans make, but at least half of our number have had no direct experience with the contingency. How contingencies come to have an indirect effect on behavior is a subject, it would seem, that might be investigated by experiments with hypothetical as well as actual events. Kahneman and Tversky (1979, p. 265) say, "The use of the method [of hypothetical problems] relies on the assumption that people often know how they would behave in actual situations of choice, and on the further assumption that the subjects have no special reason to disguise their true preferences." In the few cases where these assumptions have been put to the test, however, the results have not been encouraging. For instance, Ebbesen and Konecni (1975) could not predict the bail set by judges in a courtroom from their choices when faced with hypothetical bail-setting problems in the laboratory. Perhaps, as with hypothetical problems 8, 9, and 9 ', the difference lies between the constraints posed by the hypothetical problems and the actual constraints of the courtroom.

The fact that there is no simple relation between objective situations and the sorts of hypothetical problems posed by decision theorists is not a critical objection to the use of hypothetical problems. Although it is not possible to make straightforward generalizations from behavior with hypothetical problems, it may be possible to make some kinds of generalizations and it may be possible to develop better hypothetical problems—where straightforward generalizations can be made. Thus, the relationship between verbal and nonverbal choice problems would need to be studied. That relationship can only be studied with human subjects. Although the real life situations observed by Ebbeson and Konecni are instructive, variables cannot be easily manipulated outside of the laboratory. Thus, the development of ways to study human choice in the laboratory with meaningful nonverbal problems is of critical importance. Here the cognitive theorist may find that the techniques of the animal behaviorist will come nicely to hand. (See Catania, Matthews, & Shimoff, 1982, for a discussion of operant experiments with human subjects.) If adequate techniques could be developed and put to common use by cognitive and behavioral theorists, there is nothing in the theories per se that could prevent the unification of the study of choice that Brunswik and Tolman envisioned.

SUMMARY

Animal and human choice are currently studied in different ways. Animal choice is studied mostly with hungry pigeons or rats pecking keys or pressing levers in Skinner boxes. Behavioral theory attempts to describe and predict behavior in terms of rates of response and rates of food reinforcement. These rates appear to be objective, but their determination is no less dependent on theory than are so-called subjective variables.

Behavioral theory and cognitive theory seem to differ vastly, but cognitive theory, with its rejection of the validity of introspective report and its de-emphasis on the concept of rationality, has recently become more behavioral, while behavioral theory, with its molarity and flexibility in interpretation of rates of response and reinforcement, has become more like cognitive theory. It is argued here that the difference between molar behavioral theory and current cognitive decision theory is a difference more of tone than substance. If this argument is valid, the way stands clear for a unified theory of animal and human choice.

REFERENCES

Baum, W.M. (1973). The correlation based law of effect. *Journal of the Experimental Analysis of Behavior, 20,* 137–153.

Brunswik, E. (1939). Probability as a determiner of rat behavior. *Journal of Experimental Psychology, 25,* 175–197.

Brunswik, E. (1943). Organismic achievement and environmental probability. *Psychological Review, 50,* 255–272.

Brunswik, E. (1952). The conceptual framework of psychology. In *International Encyclopedia of Unified Science,* (Vol. 1), No. 10. Chicago: University of Chicago Press.

Catania, A.C. (1971). Elicitation, reinforcement and stimulus control. In R. Glazer (Ed.), *The nature of reinforcement.* New York: Academic Press, pp. 196–211.

Catania, A.C., Matthews, B.A., & Shimoff, E. (1982). Instructed versus shaped human verbal behavior: Interactions with nonverbal responding. *Journal of Experimental Analysis of Behavior, 38,* 233–248.

Cohen, L.J. (1981). Can human irrationality be experimentally demonstrated? *Behavioral and Brain Sciences, 4,* 317–371.

de Villiers, P. (1977). Choice in concurrent schedules and a quantitative formulation of the law of effect. In W.K. Honig & J.E.R. Staddon (Eds.), *Handbook of operant behavior.* Englewood Cliffs, NJ: Prentice-Hall.

Ebbesen, E.B., & Konecni, J.J. (1975). Decision making and information integration in the courts: The setting of bail: *Journal of Personality and Social Psychology, 32,* 805–821.

Einhorn, H.J., & Hogarth, R.M. (1981). Behavioral decision theory: Processes of judgment and choice. *Annual Review of Psychology, 32,* 52–88.

Gibbon, J., Berryman, R., & Thompson, R.L. (1974). Contingency spaces and measures in classical and instrumental conditioning. *Journal of the Experimental Analysis of Behavior, 21,* 585–605.

Gibbon, J. (1977). Scaler expectancy and Weber's law in animal timing. *Psychological Review, 84,* 279–325.

Herrnstein, R.J. (1964). Secondary reinforcement and rate of primary reinforcement. *Journal of the Experimental Analysis of Behavior, 7,* 27–35.

Herrnstein, R.J. (1970). On the law of effect. *Journal of the Experimental Analysis of Behavior, 13,* 243–266.

Herrnstein, R.J., & Hineline, P.N. (1966). Negative reinforcement as shock-frequency reduction. *Journal of the Experimental Analysis of Behavior, 9,* 421–431.

Herrnstein, R.J., & Vaughan, W., Jr. (1980). Melioration and behavioral allocation. In J.E.R. Staddon (Ed.), *Limits to action: the allocation of individual behavior.* New York: Academic Press.

Kahneman, D., & Tversky, A. (1979). Prospect theory: An analysis of decisions under risk. *Econometrica, 47,* 263–291.

Logan, F.A. (1960). *Incentive.* New Haven: Yale University Press.

Maier, S.F., Seligman, M.E.P., & Solomon, R.L. (1969). Pavlovian fear conditioning and learned helplessness. In B.A. Campbell & R.M. Church (Eds.), *Punishment and adversive behavior.* New York: Appleton-Century-Croft, pp. 299–343.

March, J.G. (1978). Bounded rationality ambiguity, and the engineering of choice. *Bell Journal of Economics, 5,* 587–608.

Mazur, J.E., & Logue, A.W. (1978). Choice in a "self-control" paradigm: Effects of a fading procedure. *Journal of the Experimental Analysis of Behavior, 30,* 11–17.

Nisbett, R.E., & Wilson, T.D. (1977). Telling more than we can know: Verbal reports on mental processes. *Psychological Review, 84,* 231–259.

Payne, N.J. (1982). Contingent decision behavior. *Psychological Bulletin, 92,* 382–402.

Rachlin, H. (1974). Self-control. *Behaviorism, 2,* 94–107.

Rachlin, H. (1976). *Behavior and learning.* San Francisco: W.H. Freeman.

Rachlin, H., Battalio, R., Kagel, J., & Green, L. (1981). Maximization theory in behavioral psychology. *The Behavioral & Brain Sciences, 4,* 371–388.

Rachlin, H., & Green, L. (1972). Commitment, choice and self-control. *Journal of the Experimental Analysis of Behavior, 17,* 15–22.

Rescorla, R.A. (1967). Pavlovian conditioning and its proper control procedures. *Psychological Review, 74,* 71–80.

Skinner, B.F. (1938). *The behavior of organisms.* New York: Appleton-Century.

Staddon, J.E.R. (Ed.). (1980). *Adaptation to constraint: The biology, economics and psychology of individual behavior.* New York: Academic Press.

Stigler, G.J., & Becker, G.S. (1977). De gustibus non est disputandum. *The American Economic Review, 67,* 76–90.

Teitelbaum, P. (1977). Levels of integration of the operant. In W.K. Honig and J.E.R. Staddon (Eds.), *Handbook of operant behavior.* Englewood Cliffs, NJ: Prentice-Hall.

Tolman, E.C. (1938). The determiners of behavior at a choice point. *Psychological Review, 45,* 1–41.

Tversky, A., & Kahneman, D. (1981). The framing of decisions and the psychology of choice. *Science, 211,* 453–458.

Wallsten, T.S. (1980). *Cognitive processes in choice and decision behavior.* Hillsdale, NJ: Erlbaum.

PART II
A CALL FOR DATA

One might be impressed with the sophisticated models and mathematical analyses proferred by economists in accounting for economic behavior. Yet, as experimental economists and psychologists, we are suspicious about such accounts when carefully constructed and controlled experimental research, necessary to assess the ability of these models to accurately predict behavior, are so conspicuously lacking. Leontief (1982) has noted that, in the *American Economic Review,* "the flagship of academic economic periodicals," the percentage of articles published in which no empirically-derived data are presented was about 67% over the years 1972 through 1981. The models developed by economists are based upon untested assumptions; yet "it is precisely the empirical validity of these *assumptions* on which the usefulness of these models depends" (Leontief, 1971). Leontief (1971) has further remarked on the "undue reliance on indirect statistical inference" and the need for empirical research.

When data are actually amassed, they are often aggregate data, based upon the behavior of large groups of subjects under imprecise and varying conditions. They are commonly collected as a byproduct of administrative processes and as such are often only indirectly related to the economic variables of interest. Limited sample sizes with limited variation in the relevant independent variables often make the predictive utility of such data suspect. There is a need, and a growing realization of this need, for alternative data sets, some to be derived from experimentally-controlled situations.

In his contribution, "The Role of Microdata in the Production of Economic Knowledge," F. Thomas Juster criticizes much in the standard approach to data collection as practiced by economists. He states, also, that "research economists have played virtually no role in the generation of economic microdata" and goes on to suggest reasons for "the lack of high-quality microdata in economics." Convinced of the value scientifically-generated data have for the production and growth of economic knowledge, Juster points out that "while the results of building economic models with good microdata are unknown and uncertain, the results of building models with existing data have been thoroughly explored in a number of areas. The results can fairly be described as unsatisfactory, and there is no compelling reason to suppose that the application of more refined estimation techniques and more fully developed theory to the same set of basic data will result in much improvement.''

While we are in agreement with Juster's analysis, we would more strongly argue for much greater emphasis upon the laboratory as a valuable, indeed necessary, source from which to generate data to conduct precise and demanding tests of theory.

REFERENCES

Leontief, W. (1971). Theoretical assumptions and nonobserved facts. *American Economic Review, 61,* 1–7.
Leontief, W. (1982). Academic economics. *Science, 217,* 104, 107.

Chapter 4

The Role of Microdata in the Production of Economic Knowledge*

F. Thomas Juster

Institute for Social Research
University of Michigan

INTRODUCTION

An assessment of the role of microdata in the production of economic knowledge—and speculation about its appropriate role in the future—leads to examination of a much broader range of problems. The right question to start with seems to be: What is the function of data in the production of economic knowledge? Putting the question this way suggests other questions: What is the current state of economic knowledge, and how has the character of the data inputs influenced its development? What is the relation between data and knowledge in other scientific disciplines, and, if the relation is different than in economics, why? What accounts for the present modes of generating and using data in economic research, and are these modes an efficient way to produce knowledge? And, finally, regardless of how the past is evaluated, are there reasons to suppose that the present modes of conducting economic research will be increasingly inefficient in the future, and that only a really drastic shift of emphasis—away from a concentration on analysis of existing data and towards the generation of sets of microdata driven by scientific priorities—will permit a rapid rate of growth in the stock of socially useful knowledge about economic behavior?

THE PRODUCTION OF ECONOMIC KNOWLEDGE

Questions about how to optimize the use of scarce resources to achieve specified objectives have always been of central concern to economists. Analysis

---

* This paper is a modified and updated version of Juster, F.T. (1970). Microdata, economic research, and the production of economic knowledge. *American Economic Review, 60,* 138–148. Permission granted.

of the costs and benefits of alternatives A and B comes as a matter of instinct to all of us, almost irrespective of the subject matter involved. But we have rarely, if ever, looked carefully at the economics of what economists do.

In analyzing the production of economic "knowledge," I prefer to define the term narrowly as the stock of qualitative and quantitative generalizations about economic relationships that are demonstrably "true."[1] Thus knowledge comprises a collection of analytical statements (other things equal, rent control will reduce the supply of new housing) and empirical statements (the proportion of income saved in the United States is usually between 4 and 8%).[2]

Economic knowledge is produced by professional economists using inputs of theoretical insights, statistical estimation techniques, and data. The data inputs are of several sorts.

Basic data can be defined as an empirical observation of a specific phenomenon—perhaps a transaction, perhaps a perception (whether objectively correct or incorrect), perhaps an activity. All basic data are thus microdata, since they must be observations relating to a single economic unit. Observations are defined as basic data that have been generated out of a specific research problem.[3] Processed data are basic data that have been adjusted in some way to make them more convenient or conceptually more appropriate for exploration of a specific problem; for the most part, processed data are also aggregates fashioned from microdata.

The production of knowledge will ordinarily require some use of all those inputs, although only the first, theoretical insights about relationships, seems indispensable. Knowledge can evidently be produced by theorizing about the necessary consequences of a set of relationships, given certain assumptions about objectives. Prior to the 1930s, most of the stock of economic knowledge was produced in exactly this way.[4] Where data inputs are part of the process, however, even the selection of one rather than another data input necessarily implies some organizing principle and hence some input of analytical skill.

---

[1] An extensive discussion of different attempts to classify concepts like knowledge and information can be found in Machlup (1962).

[2] It is important to distinguish between knowledge and what might be termed "interesting and intuitively plausible relationships," partly because one person's view of what is plausible may be different from another's, and partly because the social usefulness of these two kinds of knowledge is probably quite different. For example, demonstrably correct knowledge is likely to have a much greater impact on the formulation of public policy than interesting and intuitively plausible relationships. Moreover, where the latter are used as the basis for policy, the social returns are almost as apt to be negative as positive and hence may not average much above zero.

[3] The distinction between data and observations is discussed extensively in Morgenstern (1963).

[4] As a practical matter, even the purest of pure theorists probably always make some use of empirical information in the research process, even though it may be of a casual and highly impressionistic sort.

As a loose generalization, economists produce knowledge increments in one of two ways: (a) theorizing about the logical implications of some type of optimizing behavior; (b) applying a heavy dose of analytical skills to some set of existing data. Knowledge of the first sort is always qualitative and conditional; e.g., higher subway fares will reduce the quantity of subway rides demanded, other things equal.[5] Knowledge of the second sort is always quantitative and generally associated with specified conditions; e.g., a 5% increase in subway fares will eventually reduce the number of riders by 3%, provided that bus and taxicab fares remain unchanged. In research that is heavily empirical, a good part of the input of analytical skills may go into adjustment, manipulation, and transformation of either basic or processed data into processed data that have not previously existed.

THE STOCK OF ECONOMIC KNOWLEDGE

Serious quantitative economic research is a relatively young discipline—a half-century, more or less—compared to several centuries for qualitative economic analysis and very much longer for most of the physical sciences. What is a reasonable generalization about the results? If knowledge is defined as pertaining to relationships about behavior, with its implication that behavior can be predicted if its determinants are either known or can themselves be predicted, I suggest that economists possess a very large and often quite useful stock of qualitative knowledge but a remarkably skimpy, although rapidly growing, stock of quantitative knowledge.

If the focus is placed on knowledge useful in the formulation of public policy decisions, as distinct from private decisions of firms and households, the situation is probably even worse. For example, economists "know" that an increase in the minimum wage will tend to reduce the employment of marginally productive members of the labor force, and will tend to result in skilled labor and capital being substituted for unskilled labor in the production process. Similarly, it is known that an increase in personal income taxes will reduce the demand for consumption. But neither of these bits of knowledge is particularly helpful in the formulation of public policy, except insofar as they increase the odds that gross errors will be avoided. Changes in the minimum wage rate will have other consequences, both immediately and in the long run, than a tendency to reduce employment among the marginally productive, and some of these effects will or may be viewed as desirable by some welfare criteria. Similarly, changes in income taxation rates ordinarily comprise one part of a package of policies designed to achieve certain stabilization or equity objectives. Knowing the direction of the effect on, in the one case, unemployment, and in the other, consumption demand, is simply

---

[5] A qualitative statement is technically identical to a quantitative one that contains very wide limits—if subway rides "decline," they must fall by an amount between one and the present number of rides.

not good enough. What we have to know is the quantitative dynamics of these effects, and we need to know them with a good deal of precision.[6]

Some of these difficulties are probably traceable to the fact that economics has had little success in measuring the influence of social or economic forces which are slow to respond to changes and which represent side effects of policies designed for other purposes.

Environmental pollution, for example, can be viewed as an undesired consequence of growing wealth. Similarly, the attempt to put a floor under the living standards of the urban poor has apparently intensified the social and financial problems of urban areas because of its unintended effect on migration. And some of the evidence from income maintenance experiments suggests that providing a stable floor under family income increases the probability of divorce and separation. In short, effective public policies need to be based on general rather than partial equilibrium analysis and on long- rather than short- or intermediate-run dynamics. And even in the simpler world of partial equilibrium analysis and short-run dynamics, the quantitative economic relationships that constitute our best approximations to knowledge are notoriously unreliable and show little evidence of becoming less so. For example, the behavior of money GNP, the money stock and velocity during the early 1980s casts serious doubt on the wisdom of using monetary growth targets to guide the macro economy.

A KNOWLEDGE PRODUCTION FUNCTION

To recognize shortcomings in the stock of economic knowledge is neither novel nor especially useful. The existence of serious deficiencies is not inconsistent with optimality in resource allocation; economists know better than most that all types of output are subject to benefit-cost constraints, and knowledge is no exception. But perhaps matters are worse than they would have been had research resources within economics been allocated differently.

We can start by examining allocation parameters which describe how research economists spend their time. The alternatives are (a) theoretical analysis and empirical analysis of existing data; (b) generation of experimental microdata (observations) growing out of a specific research problem; (c) generation of microdata that is nonexperimental but is motivated by

---

[6] It obviously matters whether a 10% change in the minimum wage will cause a 1% or 100% change in unemployment, and we have to specify the time path of the employment effect. And the same is clearly true for changing income tax rates: every undergraduate with half a year of economics knows that increasing tax rates will reduce the demand for consumption, but recent experience suggests that we lack firm knowledge about the quantitative dynamics of that relationship. In short, for most purposes policy-makers need reliable estimates of empirical parameters, and economists have generally been unable to supply this need.

scientific priorities; and (d) generation of processed data, usually but not necessarily aggregates, from microdata. The relevant questions are: first, what are the values of these parameters in the knowledge production function for economics and for other scientific disciplines? Second, to the extent that differences exist among disciplines, is the nature and extent of the difference consistent with a priori and other evidence on efficiency in the research process?

On the first of these questions, hard data are not needed to make reasonable estimates. The proportion of professional skills devoted to the generation of either observations or microdata is very small in economics, while the proportion devoted to generating processed data is much larger than the first two but much smaller than the proportion concerned with analysis.[7] The great majority of professional economists devote virtually all of their efforts either to the training of future professionals, the study of purely theoretical problems, or the specification and analysis of quantative problems that use existing, and generally highly processed, data as the sole empirical input.

COSTS OF BASIC AND PROCESSED DATA IN ECONOMICS

Some of the forces that influence these choices are clear enough. The generation of economic data is a classic example of an activity characterized by economics of scale; the economies come in dissemination, not in production, and dissemination costs have been declining in real terms as a result of advances in data handling technology. Thus, the only reasons for the existence of competitive sets of data would be either quality differences or cost differences based on technological lags. Both should cause only temporary interruptions in the attainment of a long-run equilibrium solution where the costs of acquiring existing data are forced close to zero and where a single firm—often the government—produces the product.

The production of new microdata sets is extremely costly. Data from households or business firms are ordinarily obtained by personal contact that always involves the time of the unit being observed and often requires

---

[7] Although most of the professional skill inputs in the basic data function consist of economists employed by the federal government, the great majority of government professionals are concerned with the generation of processed data, not basic data. A few private organizations, for example, the NBER, devote some professional resources to the generation or improvement of processed data, and a much more modest fraction to generating observations or basic data. Other organizations, for example the Institute for Social Research at the University of Michigan or the National Opinion Research Center at the University of Chicago, use a large fraction of resources to generate observations and basic data. And some individuals make similar allocations, mainly on the generation of better processed data. But these are surely atypical allocations of effort for the profession as a whole, although that is probably less true now than it used to be.

the time of an observer. Both are labor intensive activities, and there has been limited success in increasing efficiency by substituting capital for labor.[8] Moreover, economic relationships at the micro level are subject to a good deal of nonsystematic variability that is of little intrinsic interest but which is able to obscure the relationship unless relatively large samples of observations are obtained. In effect, disturbances in economic relationships are large relative to the regularities that are of analytical interest, and, to insure that regularities can be measured, the sample must be big enough so that disturbances are well behaved.[9] The enormous cost of generating new microdata sets thus means that economists tend to use the best existing sets of data, even though they may be seriously deficient for research needs, a tendency that can be offset only if the high costs are balanced by equally high returns.

For the most part, the data inputs into economic research consist of processed rather than basic data, and economics is probably unique among the sciences in the proportion of professional resources that go into the processing and manipulation of basic data. The apparent reason is that much economic data can be fitted into a comprehensive "information system" characterized by a set of logical constraints. In economics, what is bought must be sold, what is produced must be either consumed or added to inventory, what is saved must be invested, and so on.[10]

The information systems character of much processed economic data is by no means an unmixed blessing. Since an information system is general purpose by definition, the data are unlikely to be optimal for any specific analytical use and will generally have to be modified or adjusted to fit requirements. For example, consumption as measured in the National Income Accounts is not conceptually appropriate for most studies of consumption behavior. It lumps together what basically represent investment decisions like the acquisition of automobiles and college educations with consumption decisions like the acquisition of food, gasoline, and theater tickets; it blends together real data reflecting observable decisions with imputations reflecting past decisions and estimates reflecting trend extrapolation, and in the process imports a smoothness to consumer behavior that may not exist; and so on.

---

[8] In some parts of the process—for example, editing the microrecords—mechanical methods have been able to replace labor intensive methods.

[9] The contrast with the physical sciences, where empirical regularities can often be observed with a sample of one, is quite marked. The noise level in physical experiments is reduced by incurring costs for equipment that essentially serves the function of eliminating disturbances.

[10] The existence of definitional constraints among variables has historically enabled economists to increase socially useful knowledge without making any use of data inputs at all: it is not essential to measure the money holdings of any economic unit to know that an increase in the supply of money must be held by someone, and that some of the variables which influence the demand for money will therefore be affected.

Second, information systems almost always contain aggregated data, and the system is designed to produce reasonably correct aggregates at the lowest possible cost. The microdata requirements of the system will thus be met, whenever possible, by using existing data generated by some record-keeping requirements.[11] Moreover, adjustment of the available microdata has a higher priority than improvements in the quality of the underlying microdata, since accuracy at the aggregate level is not necessarily dependent on accuracy at the micro level because of consistency checks within the system.

An extreme illustration is provided by our savings data. Despite the fact that there are no reasonably accurate microdata, aggregate savings can be estimated with fair accuracy as the difference between income and consumption.[12] And one of our most famous empirical generalizations about savings—that the saving/income ratio is secularly independent of the level of income—is based solely on the measurement of net investment in capital assets, which conveniently enough happens to be equal to observed saving.

In sum, cost considerations propel professional economists toward analysis of a relatively small collection of processed numbers that are readily accessible. That this generalization has many exceptions and that it is a better description of the past than the present does not vitiate its essential accuracy. It is broadly correct to describe empirical research in economics as a process that starts with an analytical model, specifies the data necessary to estimate the model, respecifies the model in terms of the best currently available set of processed data, then estimates parameters whose precise quantitative dimensions are heavily dependent on the skill and judgment of the investigator and whose interpretation is thus inevitably ambiguous. It is hardly ever true that economists choose to invest resources in measuring precisely what their analytical models specify.

DATA INPUTS IN THE PHYSICAL SCIENCES

An examination of the research process in other disciplines is instructive. In the physical sciences there is virtually no counterpart to the economists' collection of processed data. Empirical research in the physical sciences is based almost entirely on observations generated as an essential part of the research process itself, and a large proportion (probably more than half) of

---

[11] Both the conceptual clarity and the mechanical accuracy of record-keeping data are likely to be obscure unless the data have been generated by trained professionals as part of a specific research design. This is in general unlikely where the data come from a private industry source. See Morgenstern (1963).

[12] This may be an overly optimistic assessment of the accuracy of aggregate savings estimates. Still, it would probably be agreed that estimates of aggregate saving obtained by residual methods are more reliable than estimates obtained from aggregating microdata.

professional skills is devoted to the questions of what observable phenomena are to be measured and how can the measurement be made. A substantial fraction of the research budgets for sciences like biology, chemistry, physics, and astronomy goes for the procurement of equipment designed to permit extremely precise measurements of observed microphenomena, and another substantial fraction is spent on equipment whose function is to generate observations. Further, the ability of physical scientists to furnish laboratories with equipment like particle accelerators and cyclotrons designed to produce observable phenomena that can be studied, as well as with devices like electron microscopes, spectroscopes, and spectrometers whose function is to permit observation and measurement, is in considerable measure an outgrowth of the research process itself. The power and sophistication of accelerators or spectroscopes are determined largely by what needs to be observed and how accurately the observation needs to be measured, and both are the result of strong interaction between research scientists and equipment builders.

These differences in research methods are well known and hardly require documentation. It seems plausible that they are also one of the basic causes of differential rates of growth in scientific knowledge. Here, the contrast between developments in space, medicine, and weaponry and the contribution of economic knowledge to the formulation of public policy is rather marked. We can land men on the moon, reduce the incidence of diseases like polio and smallpox to virtually zero, and intercept a potential enemy missile within minutes of its appearance in the atmosphere because we can predict a great many physical consequences with extraordinary precision; but we could not predict the effects of the 1968 tax increase or the 1981–83 tax decrease, we have stong professional disagreements about the effects of changes in the money stock on economic activity, we were unable to foresee the debilitating effects of our present welfare system (and those who did probably also argued that the Social Security system would reduce private saving and thus economic growth), we invest very large sums in a program designed to enrich the educational environment for ghetto youngsters without knowing whether or not the beneficial effects are wholly transitory, and we spend over $100 billion a year on education without knowing whether half or twice that amount is optimal or whether what we do spend is efficiently allocated.

DIFFERENCES IN RESEARCH METHODOLOGY

While it thus seems reasonably clear that there are marked differences in the growth of socially useful knowledge among scientific disciplines, it is far from clear why these differences exist. The relatively unsatisfactory state of quantitative economic knowledge may be a consequence of the simple fact that economists are concerned with relationships of enormous complexity and have little or no possibility of being able to exercise experimental control. Alternatively, it may result from the relative youth of quantitative economics as a scientific discipline. It might, however, be the result of a sort of methodological hangover that causes a gap between private and social returns to different research strategies.

EXPERIMENTAL CONTROLS IN ECONOMIC RESEARCH

It is undeniably true that the social sciences face limitations in the control of experiments that physical sciences do not generally have to contend with. A controlled experiment requires that a change be imposed on the environment of whatever is being studied, and that the consequences of the change be observable and measurable. But economists cannot create a new "Great Depression" just to see how different the result would have been if monetary or fiscal policy had developed differently than was the case in 1929. Nor can we select students at random to go to 4-year colleges while constraining a control sample not to attend 4-year colleges, in order to measure the net contribution of education to earnings.

The limitation, however, is more apparent than real. Some problems can be explored by analyzing choices under a simulated and synthetic environment—a research design widely used in analysis of managerial decision making and marketing strategy. While it is true that a simulated environment may introduce a bias of important and unknown dimensions, the bias may be the same for alternative simulated changes. If so, and if the real influence of one of two simulated changes is known, the real influence of the other can be estimated from its simulated influence. This design has been used to examine the influence of interest rates on the demand for consumer credit, and a variation has been used to analyze the relation between alternative types of anticipations surveys and actual behavior.[13] And, during recent years, there has been a substantial growth in experimental simulations of decision-making, both for market decisions and nonmarket choices.[14] Much of this literature has simulated an environment in which real gains and losses accrue to participants, rather than hypothetical ones—a line of research that is very costly because participants have to be compensated.

Next, while social scientists cannot make adverse changes in the environment of micro-units in order to observe consequences, it is hard to see the objection to experimental controls involving a favorable change for some units and no change for others. Precisely this kind of experiment has been

---

[13] The first illustration is discussed in Juster and Shay (1964); the second in Juster (1966).

[14] The experimental literature dealing with markets is summarized by Plott (1982). Important references include Fouraker and Siegel (1963), Hoggatt (1959), Plott and Smith (1978), Smith (1962, 1982).

conducted to measure the work-leisure responses of welfare families faced with controlled marginal tax rates; to measure the effect of housing allowances on housing choices, on the quality of the housing stock, and on housing maintenance practices; and to measure the effectiveness of alternative ways to reintroduce the "hard core" unemployed into the job market.[15]

But even the "favorable change or no change" experimental design is not a real limitation. Suppose we do not know if a change will be favorable or not, for example, whether more heavily subsidized charges on urban mass transit systems will expand urban job opportunities, or whether group health insurance plans based on prepayment will provide equivalent health care at lower cost than plans based on fee-for-service. It is not unreasonable to suppose that a more active searching out of opportunities to use experimental designs could result in the generation of experimental data designed to analyze the consequences of alternative policies. In short, the limited vision of economists may have made a rigid constraint out of what ought to be no worse than a serious inconvenience.[16]

Finally, insistence on absolute experimental control as a prerequisite for scientific investigation is both unrealistic and unnecessary; it is a condition that is not always met, even in the "experimental" sciences.[17] In the behavioral sciences, the situation is generally much worse because certain "treatments" cannot be administered at all and because the relation between treatment and "effect" is obscured by uncontrollable "disturbances." But the function of experimental controls is to impound in ceteris paribus everything that disturbs the relation between treatment and effect. The best way to achieve this result is to create an environment without disturbances, where the treatment can be administered in varying doses. An alternative is to accept whatever differences in treatment happen to exist in the universe, measure the effects that have been produced by some combination of treat-

---

[15] See Lowry (1983); Manpower Demonstration Research Corporation (1980); Watts and Rees (1977).

[16] This general type of experimental design is widely used in private industry research, often for the purpose of determining optimum marketing strategy. For example, the impact of alternative advertising strategies has been studied by varying the advertising dosage for residents of selected geographic areas, then measuring the sales response to get estimates of incremental sales (and profits) per incremental dollar of advertising outlay. Some of these experiments cost enormous sums of money relative to expenditures on basic data generation, and one must assume that they are worth the cost because they continue to be undertaken.

[17] One cannot measure the flow of air in a wind tunnel without changing the flow that is being measured, since the measuring instrument itself represents an intrusion. Similarly, one cannot investigate the effects of genetic composition on cellular growth, which requires identification of the gene responsible for the appearance of mutant strains, without first isolating and then implanting a specific gene in a known complex of other genes—a procedure which in and of itself will necessarily produce changes in the cellular growth process under study.

ment and disturbances, and then remove the influence of disturbances via statistical procedures.

To do this successfully, however, a number of requirements have to be met. The treatment (say, change in income) should have a good deal of variation in the observable universe, as should the effect (say, consumption spending). All the disturbances (everything else besides income change that affects consumption) have to be completely specified, and it is essential that disturbances not be too highly correlated with the treatment. And everything has to be measurable and actually measured. The role of theory is critical—to specify the structure of all relevant disturbances as well as the relation between treatment and effect. And, as Morgenstern pointed out many years ago, the measurements have to be accurate.

The above set of requirements describes the objectives of quantitative studies in economics. But the objectives are not often met. They cannot be met in any study that uses processed and aggregated data to examine the time series relationships, for reasons that have been well known to economists for many years. Nothing is independent of anything else in economic time series, and no one has yet found a way to get around this problem. Additionally, if one believes that there are lots of important disturbances and not just a few, and if one further believes that the relation between treatment and effect is often influenced by the level of the treatment (nonlinearity) and that the influence of one disturbance will often depend on the level of other disturbances and on the level of the treatment (interactions), analysis of time series data is an unlikely prospect for discovering valid empirical relationships.

The shortcomings of existing microdata sets in meeting these objectives, while not so serious as those of time series, are serious enough. Many disturbances are of the sort that cannot be measured directly with existing microdata, and some cannot be measured directly at all because they are unobservable in principle (expected income, permanent income, desired stocks of durables, etc.). Sometimes, the influence of treatments or disturbances that are measured will depend on previous disturbances or treatments that were not measured. For example, the influence of high-quality teaching inputs on academic output cannot be detected unless we know the student's ability level to start with. Quality teaching, high test scores, and bright youngsters are quite apt to be found together, and we need to estimate the "value added" by teaching inputs of different qualities, not gross value as reflected by the strong positive association between test scores and teacher quality.

Although some of the problems with using microdata to test scientific hypotheses are not easily avoided because they involve difficult problems of measurement error that lack good solutions, others can be avoided by the use of longitudinal data designs. Having observations on the same units over time obviously helps to disentangle causality, and permits researchers to examine processes (e.g., the intergenerational transmission of economic status) that take a long time to become visible. Finally, longitudinal data enable researchers to control for a class of important but typically unmeasured disturbances—characteristics of individuals, such as ability, motivation, energy, and drive, that tend to be importantly related to outcomes and to be stable over time. In cross-section analyses, these characteristics will often have a strong influence on observed behavior, and they will usually be correlated with variables that are of major interest: thus their presence will contaminate the analysis. But in longitudinal data, the influence of such unobserved (and often unobservable) variables can largely be eliminated by a differencing procedure.[18]

DIFFERENCES IN SCIENTIFIC "AGE"

As regards the relative youth of quantitative economics as a scientific discipline, it is worth noting that all of the physical sciences with which economics can be adversely compared are, in fact, many centuries older, and their record during comparable stages of development is not especially noteworthy. To illustrate from a scientific discipline which faces precisely the same limitations as economics and other social sciences—inability to control the environment—it took over a thousand years for Copernicus, Kepler, and Galileo to overturn the solar and planetary motion theory of Ptolemy and Hipparchus, and another century or so before Newton was able to put all the pieces together.

Some analogies are worth noting. Development of the elaborate and ingenious Ptolemaic theory bears an uncomfortably close resemblance to quantitative analysis of time series relationships in economics. For example, if a Ptolemaic theorist were faced with an observation that could not be explained by the existing complex set of eccentric circles and epicycles, a new and of necessity perfectly circular epicycle would be invented to explain it. Moderns would of course say that the trouble with Ptolemaic theory was that it could not be tested empirically, since an observation that failed to fit received theory would be duly incorporated into a new and more complex theory. Hence a Ptolemaist never had any "degree of freedom" in the data. Given the amount of analytical ingenuity and computational power focused on the limited number of time series observations available in economics,

---

[18] There is a large and growing literature in the treatment of measurement errors in the analysis of microdata, and on the analytical advantages of longitudinal microdata sets. See Corcoran (1980); Jöreskog and Goldberger (1975); Jöreskog and Sorbom (1978); Lillard (1979a,b).

and the strong preference of model builders for linear systems, it is tempting to suggest that the empirical parameters in most time series models bear a much closer resemblance to Ptolemy's eccentric circles and epicycles than to the less esthetically pleasing but simpler (and ultimately more correct) theories of Copernicus and Newton.[19]

RESOURCE MISALLOCATION IN ECONOMIC RESEARCH

The above analysis suggests that resources used in economic research have been systematically misallocated; more specifically, that the relatively slow growth of socially useful knowledge in economics is a consequence of the fact that research economists have played virtually no role in the generation of economic microdata, because of a gap between social and private returns. In essence, the argument is: (a) that the private returns to economic research are not strongly correlated with the discovery of scientifically valid relationships, (b) that many such relationships cannot be isolated without very precise micro-observations specifically designed for the purpose, (c) that the requisite microdata sets are enormously costly relative to existing but inferior alternatives, and (d) that, because the costs are much higher and the private returns uncertain and not necessarily higher, economists have strong incentives to use existing and inferior data inputs in research even if the social returns are zero.

The evidence to support this set of propositions can hardly be called persuasive: very little of it is quantitative and much of it can be explained by quite different hypotheses.

RESEARCH DESIGN AND PRIVATE RETURNS

In research, choices are influenced by the stream of expected income as well as by abilities, aptitudes, and tastes. In economics, as in other scientific disciplines, expected income is related to the quantity and quality of research output. Some of the criteria by which research quality is judged seem to be common to all the sciences, and can be summed up by noting that research with a large amount of good theoretical content tends to be associated both with prestige and above average compensation. One can think of numerous reasons for this: correct theoretical specification is the cornerstone of in-

---

[19] It might also be noted that the Copernican and Newtonian view of planetary motion was not really accepted by astronomers until it proved capable of successfully predicting events that had not yet taken place. If the adequacy of our econometric models is judged by the same standard, all of us are Ptolemaists—and Newton, to say nothing of Einstein, has yet to make an appearance.

creases in knowledge, and empirical research that lacks this underpinning is unlikely to produce useful results.[20] Once we leave this common ground, however, marked differences appear. Research output in the physical sciences seems to be evaluated on the basis of the skill and ingenuity with which experiments are designed, as well as the theoretical importance and generality of relationships uncovered by the experiment. Any experiment can and will be replicated, often in order to refine or extend empirical results; hence, experimental errors are apt to be discovered fairly quickly.[21] Thus, the criterion for determining the quality of research output is that it must contribute to a solid base of tested empirical findings within a well-developed theoretical framework.

In economics, however, while analytical skill and empirical ingenuity also tend to be highly regarded characteristics of research output, there is no yardstick for differentiating output that will eventually come to be regarded as part of the fund of accumulated knowledge from output that, while interesting and ingenious, will eventually come to be viewed as wrong. And the private returns to the researcher are apt to be realized long before it is possible to evaluate the ultimate validity of the research output that determines returns.

Let me put the argument more concretely. Assume that you had a dissertation student writing on the question: "Other things equal, are retail prices higher in ghetto areas than suburban areas?" Further assume that data already available could be used to examine the problem, but that the data were, as usual, seriously deficient because they had, as usual, been obtained originally for quite different purposes—for example, say they consisted of total sales and average prices for classes of product and types of stores. The relevant set of observations are a large sample of specific transactions and dates—one jar of X-brand pickles at 35 cents per jar, sold on July 3 at store A, plus other supplementary data. Further assume that an extra 2 years would be required to collect and analyze the relevant data, and that additional costs would be incurred to raise the required funds. Given these facts, do you recommend that your dissertation student obtain the relevant observations or use existing data? I suggest that your student's professional reputation and expected income would be unaffected by the choice of research

---

[20] An interesting class of exceptions should be noted. It is possible to relate treatment to effect without knowing anything about the causal relation between the two. A good deal of useful medical knowledge apparently fits this description; e.g., doctors do not necessarily have to know why penicillin reduces the incidence of pneumonia deaths to know that penicillin is a useful treatment for pneumonia.

[21] The text presents too favorable a view of the precision and clarity of experimental findings in the physical sciences. As Fienberg (1981) notes, the empirical results on which the famous "oil drop" experiments of Milliken were based bear an uncomfortable resemblance to a procedure where the investigator highlights the experimental results that support the theory, and discards others that fit less well.

strategy, and hence that you could not in fairness recommend the investment of an extra couple of years in generating observations. Yet the social value of the two research designs is markedly different: one has the potential for providing a solid basis for policy decisions; the other does not.

This general line of analysis suggests that the basic reason for the lack of high-quality microdata in economics is the absence of any strong demand for it on the part of professional economists.[22] While the application of increasingly sophisticated analysis to a limited set of data may have been a reasonable strategy several decades ago, it seems quite unreasonable now— if for no other reason than the fact that the laws of variable proportions and diminishing returns are as applicable to the production of knowledge as to the production of more mundane types of output.

MICRODATA AND GROWTH IN ECONOMIC KNOWLEDGE

Is there any evidence to suggest that scientifically motivated microdata inputs will make a big enough contribution to the growth of economic knowledge to justify the costs of obtaining them?

First, all scientific disciplines in which rapid expansion of knowledge has taken place are characterized by the ability to make extremely precise measurements of microphenomena generated in an experimentally controlled environment. Moreover, the experience of the other sciences is that experimentally generated measurements have a strong feedback on theoretical development.[23]

Second, while the results of building economic models with good microdata are unknown and uncertain, the results of building models with existing data have been thoroughly explored in a number of areas. The results can fairly be described as unsatisfactory, and there is no compelling reason

---

[22] It is often argued that relevant but costly microdata sets have not been obtained in economics mainly because of limitations on resources imposed by the unwillingness of foundations and other grant organizations to fund costly projects of this sort. While there is doubtless some substance to the argument, its importance may be exaggerated. The evidence from the physical sciences can be interpreted as suggesting that research resources expand to meet the specifications of research designs, and that costly but essential research designs are not necessarily more difficult to fund than other designs. In short, research resources are responsive to the specification of professionals conducting the research, and the traditional view of an appropriate budget for research in economics is mainly a consequence of what economists themselves have said is necessary.

[23] Cases in point are Tycho Brahe's astronomical observations, from which Kepler was able to infer that the earth's orbit could be described as elliptical, and current explorations in physics designed to determine whether the shape of the electrical charge in elementary particles like electrons and neutrons is absolutely spherical or only approximately so, which, if true, would have "profound implication for elementary particles and nuclear structure theory." (See National Science Foundation, 1968.)

to suppose that the application of more refined estimation techniques and more fully developed theory to the same set of basic data will result in much improvement.

A few examples will illustrate the point. Large-scale models of aggregate economic activity in the U.S. have been constructed and tested over a period of years. The current models, while more sophisticated in both theoretical content and methods of statistical estimation than those developed a decade or so ago, still do not appear to provide appreciably better short-term predictions than purely autoregressive models with no economic content. The substantive models would not be superior at all if model builders were precluded from making subjective ad hoc adjustments to the forecasts produced by the model itself.[24]

Next, despite an immensely large investment of some of our most skilled professional resources, our understanding of the consumption–income relation is not very satisfactory if ability to predict is the test. Quantitative models of aggregate consumption expenditures do not provide appreciably better forecasts than those of a decade ago, and there are still serious disagreements at the theoretical level which cannot be resolved with existing data.

Third, and perhaps most directly relevant to the issue, we can contrast the development of scientific knowledge in two areas of economic inquiry (labor supply and saving behavior) where the distribution of inputs into the knowledge production function has been quite different during recent decades.[25] More specifically, the quantity of scientific observations entering into the production of knowledge has been vastly greater in the case of labor supply than in the case of saving behavior.

As a historical generalization, the supply of measurements available for analysis in these two areas was roughly equivalent until recent decades. Much analysis of labor supply was based on measures obtained in decennial censuses—employment, hours, occupation, and household income. For saving behavior, we have had access to household budget studies—of farmers, urban dwellers, and, occasionally, nationally representative samples—for a good many decades stretching back into the nineteenth century. Hence the supply of basic observations that could be used to formulate and test theories was roughly comparable in the two areas until the 1970s.

Starting in the late 1960s and continuing through the 1970s, however, there has been an enormous disproportion in the supply of relevant measurements with which labor supply or saving problems could be analyzed. This is partly happenstance—labor supply problems are closely linked to prob-

---

[24] This conclusion may be unfair to the model builders, since the subjective adjustments might themselves be dependent on the insight provided by the model.

[25] This part of the paper is taken from Juster and Miller (1983).

lems of income distribution and poverty, and political pressures in the society during the 1960s and early 1970s produced an explosion of high-quality measurements with which labor supply and poverty problems could be examined. These included the Survey of Economic Opportunity done at Census; the National Longitudinal Surveys, done partly by Census and partly by the National Opinion Research Center at Chicago; the Panel Study of Income Dynamics, begun in the late 1960s at the University of Michigan; the New Jersey/Scranton and Seattle/Denver Income Maintenance Experimental Data Bases collected by Mathematica and SRI; and the Time-Use Studies started in the mid-1960s at the University of Michigan. None of these data bases, with the exceptiion of the Income Maintenance Experiments, was explicitly designed to facilitate analysis of labor supply, but all are well-suited to that purpose and all have been extensively used for such analyses. Among them, these scientifically designed data bases have probably cost a cumulative sum in the area of several hundred million dollars—most of which is associated with the Income Maintenance Experiments where respondents had to be given cash grant opportunities as part of the experimental program. A number of these data bases are longitudinal, as their descriptions imply.

In contrast, data on saving behaviors have been obtained only infrequently and never longitudinally. Aside from the very early budget studies, of which the largest was conducted in the mid-1930s, saving studies have been conducted in 1950–51, 1962–63, and 1972–73 by the Bureau of Labor Statistics, and in 1961–62 by the Federal Reserve Board. As discussed later, empirical studies of saving behavior are particularly difficult to do well because the estimates are subject to large measurement errors. Although labor supply data have measurement error as well, there is no comparison in the magnitude of the measurement error problem between the two content areas.

There are, of course, extensive time-series data available on both problems. These data have been used extensively for analysis, depite the pervasive lack of independent variability that is always a characteristic of such data. But the measurement-error problem noted above for the microdata applies as well to the time-series data. There is no particular problem with the labor-supply information, which is widely regarded as having a high degree of accuracy at both the micro- and the macro-level. Not only are estimates of saving bedeviled by measurement error at the micro-level, but the two aggregate sources of saving data at the macro-level are impossible to reconcile. The National Income and Product Accounts (NIPA) data, the series most often used by analysts, have shown virtually no trend in the saving–income ratio throughout the post-war period, and earlier measurements going back into the nineteenth century also find no long-term trend in the ratio of either personal or national saving to income. But the saving data estimated from Flow of Funds sources indicate a very strong uptrend throughout the entire post-war period.

What have been the consequences of this uneven development of scientific measurements in two areas over the past decade or so? For labor supply problems, we have now arrived at well-defined estimates of the labor supply response to wage rates for the principal household earner and for family members other than the principal earner, as well as the labor supply response to changes in family income. We have a good deal of confidence that the labor supply response to a wage rate change for the principal earner is small, and is likely to be positively related to the wage change; we know that the labor supply response of marginal household earners is substantially greater than the response of the principal earner; and we know that the labor supply response to changes in non-wage income is modest for the principal earner but somewhat stronger for others.[26] We are beginning to understand that analysis of labor supply looks somewhat different if we take account of people's actual hours in productive activity at the work place rather than their "nominal" hours—the hours reported on conventional labor-market surveys like the Current Population Surveys.[27] And so on. In general we have wide agreement on theory, on parameter estimates, and on areas where further refinement is needed.

In contrast, the state of knowledge about saving behavior can only be described as in virtual chaos. There are still at least five theories of saving behavior with some professional standing, despite several decades of intensive analytical work by a large number of the profession's ablest practitioners. Even the old absolute income theory of Keynes still has some standing, and if more people analyzed Flow of Funds rather than NIPA data, it would have even more standing; the sociologically oriented Duesenberry hypothesis about relative income position continues to have adherents; the permanent income hypothesis originated by Friedman, although largely discredited in its extreme form, continues to live as an important element in the life-cycle hypothesis; and the life-cycle hypothesis of Modigliani, Ando, and Brumberg is probably the current favorite, especially if one includes the extended life-cycle version attributable to writers like Barro and Feldstein.[28]

---

[26] The current assessment of labor supply responses is somewhat different than would have been the case a decade ago. For example, the weight of the evidence would have suggested a small but negative response of the principal earner to a wage rate change, while now the evidence favors a small but positive response. See Borjas and Heckman (1978), Burtless and Hausman (1978).

[27] "Nominal hours" are the hours of work reported on conventional surveys like the CPS. "Actual hours" are nominal hours less hours not at the workplace (arriving late or leaving early), less hours spent on leisure activities ("visiting" with co-workers, scheduled or unscheduled breaks for coffee, etc.), less hours spent in formal or informal training. See Stafford and Duncan (1985).

But the simple fact is that none of these theories can be definitively proved or disproved with the available set of measurements related to saving behavior. We have yet to formulate a theory of saving behavior which has much prospect of fitting all the available facts—long-term constancy in the ratio of saving to income, a ratio of saving to income that varies positively with income in cross sections and varies monitonically with age instead of declining as people get older, a rising ratio of contractual commitments to total savings as a consequence of the growth of private pension arrangements, and the continual uncertainties associated with income trajectory, date of death, health status in old age, and the need to provide for one's surviving family members.

What we need is clearly a relatively error-free set of saving measurements that are longitudinal in nature, and which will enable us to examine the process of saving through time for the same households. As in all such cases, creation of that kind of measurement instrument will not guarantee that the profession will come as close to agreement about saving behavior as it has on labor-supply issues, but without such an instrument one can surely forecast a continuation of chaos.

It is possible to specify sets of microdata that are probably capable of being obtained and of resolving issues that have not been (and possibly cannot be) resolved in any other way. This seems to be true, for example, with regard to specification of the consumption–income relation, the effects of minimum wage legislation on unemployment, the monetary returns to education, the efficiency of schooling inputs, and the long-range consequences of income maintenance programs.[29]

Finally, even if high-quality experimentally designed microdata prove to be less useful than one would hope in the resolution of analytical problems, significant gains would almost certainly accrue in terms of sharpening our knowledge of both economic aggregates and of microdistributions. For ex-

---

[28] The literature here is enormous. The key ideas can be found in Ando and Modigliani (1963); Barro (1978); Duesenberry (1949); Feldstein (1976); and Friedman (1957). Much of the literature is summarized in Mayer (1972).

[29] One of the distinctive characteristics of the microdata sets with the capacity to resolve these issues is that the observations must cover an extended period of time. If consumption behavior is influenced by expected income, and if the latter is in turn influenced by the level and structure of actual income during past periods, precise measurements of both income and consumption covering the relevant past are essential inputs into a properly specified model. Since precise measurement of the past may be impossible, the only solution may be to accumulate data on a current basis until enough time has elapsed. And some of these problems, e.g., measuring the efficiency of schooling inputs, may require even more elapsed calendar time. Here, the output that one wants to relate to school inputs is really post-school performance, and it is likely to be a decade or so after the completion of schooling before an adequate measure of performance can be obtained.

ample, even if it still proved impossible to predict consumption behavior on the basis of experimental microdata specifically designed for that purpose, we would at least have as a by-product a rich collection of consumption, income, and savings estimates that would be available as inputs into information systems.

THE TECHNOLOGY OF MICRODATA GENERATION

One of the most striking differences between the social and physical sciences lies in the technology of measuring empirical phenomena. Extraordinary advances in the power and sophistication of measuring instruments have been made in the physical sciences.[30] In economics, with the exception of sampling procedures, our measurement technology is very little different today than it was two or three decades ago. A few studies have been made of the errors involved in responses to simple factual questions asked by interviewers—our standard measurement technique.[31] But there has been no serious attempt to explore the cost and effectiveness of alternative technologies.

Moreover, existing methods typically assume that the objective is to obtain information from each of a preselected random sample, with little regard to the trade-off between sample design and data quality. In the design of household surveys, for example, use is rarely made of the extensive system of tautological relationships that form the basis of our aggregate information systems data. These surveys are not designed to exploit the fact that changes in assets must equal the difference between income and consumption expenditures provided the consumption categories are comprehensive and asset changes are defined to exclude capital gains, presumably because the survey sponsors do not like to ask respondents to resolve apparent inconsistencies. Yet it is hard to think of a framework better designed to reduce measurement errors than the application of a consistency check.[32]

In a similar vein, sponsors of microdata collections are seldom prepared to compensate behavioral units for the time and annoyance involved in the

---

[30] In large part, these advances are a direct consequence of the demands by research scientists for instruments capable of increasingly finer resolution, as noted earlier. Since the point of many physical experiments would be lost in the absence of sufficiently precise measurements, there is strong incentive for physical scientists to involve themselves directly in the process of designing instrumentation. Much of this emphasis doubtlessly results from the fact that physical scientists are accustomed to specify both the process by which experimental phenomena are to be generated and the procedures by which the phenomena are to be observed and measured.

[31] For example, see Maynes (1968). Morgenstern (1963) is concerned mainly with errors of aggregated data.

[32] The statement in the text is oversimplified, since some use is made of consistency checks. A common procedure is to use consistency tests to eliminate cases of doubtful reliability. But the acceptable range is very wide, since ± 10% is often viewed as satisfactory when comparing direct consumption estimates with estimated income less savings. But a 10% error in consumption means a possible error of many times that percentage in savings estimates.

observation. In the behavioral sciences, after all, it is not possible to measure relevant behavior without the cooperation and assistance of the unit being observed. But the measurement process inevitably involves at least the cost of time and, for some units, annoyance as well. A straightforward agreement with sample respondents to trade accuracy and consistency in the set of variables being measured against compensation for the time and inconvenience involved, might well be a more efficient procedure than the current practice of appealing to the social conscience of respondents.[33]

Finally, experience strongly suggests that a greater allocation of professional skills toward the problems of generating relevant microdata sets should eventually produce completely new measurement techniques that are vastly superior to the modified versions of existing techniques suggested above. It is probably useless even to speculate about potential developments, but they might possibly be tied to generating observations via preprogrammed computerized methods. If Nielsen can observe television preferences without the need for a physical observer, why cannot economists obtain transactions data in the same way? The point is that the learning process is apt to pay handsome and totally unexpected dividends in the form of much better methods than can now be specified.

CONCLUDING REMARKS

Let me close by listing a collection of points ranging from omissions to implications. First, some omissions:

1) The particular research areas discussed above are mainly a reflection of my own interests and do not necessarily constitute the most crucial or the most manageable problem areas. For example, less attention has been given to research on the behavior of firms than to research on the behavior of households: the reason is my greater familiarity with the latter.

2) Although my concern has been with the generation of scientifically motivated observations, there is abundant evidence that our general purpose information systems are badly in need of greater resources. To cite two recent cases in point: at a critical juncture in the economy, when the consequences of policy errors are likely to be more serious than usual, our basic measure of money supply has behaved so erratically that it is hard to place much credence in it, and our basic measure of consumption has a well-deserved reputation for looking very different after the annual revision than it did while being reported currently. It is difficult enough to formulate economic policy when the key variables are known within tolerable limits; it is next to impossible when the actual course of events over the past several months will be known only sometime next year.

---

[33] The methodological literature on improving the reliability and validity of survey responses is summarized in Cannell, Miller and Oksenberg (1981).

Finally, some implications:

1. The main thrust of this paper has been that the generation of precise sets of micro-observations growing out of the analytical requirements of a specific research problem is likely to provide a much more promising method of expanding economic knowledge in the future than the application of more sophisticated, analytical, and statistical techniques to existing data. A strong case can be made for this argument if it is true that accurate micro-observations are in fact obtainable at "reasonable" cost. Evidently, this task may prove to be impossible at any cost, or to be possible but so costly as not to be worthwhile.[34] There seems no way to tell except to try, and the right way to try is clearly with a pilot study designed to explore feasibility.

2. If the research process needs to be refocused on generating micro-observations, it is probably true that organizational restructuring will be needed also. Large-scale "research firms" may have to replace the individual "research entrepreneur" to some extent.

3. If the argument in this paper is correct and there is a gap between private and social returns to alternative research strategies, it follows that normal market forces cannot by themselves bring about the necessary reallocation of research resources. The point at which effective pressure can be exerted is probably at the level of organizations that finance research—foundations and government. If projects designed to generate the data required to test hypotheses are treated in a kindly way and other projects are not, one would expect to see more research of the first sort and less of the second.

4. The budgetary implications of the research strategy outlined here are formidable. Looking only at research on households, for example, one can make rough guesses about orders of magnitude. Assume we are really talking about a sample more like 100,000 units than 10,000, about an observation period more like 10 years than 2, and about a cost per annual observation

---

[34] Two points should be noted. First, to the extent that the experimental microdata required for particular research problems need to be obtained from either of our basic types of micro-units, firms and households, considerable economies of scale in research uses ought to be possible. Using households to illustrate the possibilities, there are few important problems in economic research that do not require precise measurement of a common set of variables over an extended period of time. Investigation of the demand for consumption, the demand for money, the response to price changes, the returns to education, the allocation of time in non-market activities, the formation of expectations, the demand for household capital goods, and the determinants of marriage and birth rates—all require collection of a large common set of variables plus a smaller collection of variables specifically oriented to each problem. Thus a single sample could be used to examine a wide range of additional information. Such a research-oriented sample would have to be large enough so that the observational intrusion on any one unit could be kept within manageable proportions. Second, it may be possible to recoup some of the financial costs by charging fees in excess of marginal costs. For example, the enormously costly Project Talent data appear to be available on this basis. There are thorny problems of research structure and organization involved in this area, however, and they cannot be resolved in this paper.

more like $200 than $20. That comes out to a nicely rounded total of $200 million over 10 years, or $20 million per year—about half the total NSF appropriation for research in the social sciences, but still probably less than NSF now appropriates for the generation of experimental data in physics, in biology, in chemistry, and in astronomy. Just to get some additional perspective, the total is about a fifth of the probable cost of the 1980 decennial census.

5. The most significant returns from the research strategy outlined here may not begin to appear until a good many years after the investment has begun, primarily because long-run and general equilibrium effects cannot be observed until a good bit of calendar time has elapsed. And significant social returns are unlikely to appear at all unless professional economists involve themselves, as well as their junior associates and graduate assistants, directly in the data-generating process.

REFERENCES

Ando, A., & Modigliani, F. (1963). The "life cycle" hypothesis of savings: Aggregate implications and tests. *American Economic Review, 53,* 53–84.

Barro, R. (1978). *The impact of social security on private saving.* Washington, DC: American Enterprise Institute.

Borjas, G., & Heckman, J. (1978). Labor supply estimates for public policy evaluation. *Proceedings of the 31st annual meeting* (pp. 320–331). Chicago: Industrial Relations Research Association.

Burtless, G., & Hausman, J.A. (1978). The effect of taxation on labor supply: Evaluating the Gary negative income tax experiment. *Journal of Political Economy, 86,* 1103–1130.

Cannell, C., Miller, P.V., & Oksenberg, L. (1981). Research on interviewing techniques. In S. Leinhardt (Ed.), *Sociological methodology.* San Francisco: Jossey-Bass.

Corcoran, M. (1980). Sex differences in measurement error in status attainment models. *Sociological Methods and Research, 9,* 199–217.

Duesenberry, J.S. (1949). *Income, savings, and the theory of consumer behavior.* Cambridge, MA: Harvard University Press.

Feldstein, M. (1976). Social security and saving: The extended life cycle theory. *American Economic Review, 66,* 77–86.

Fienberg, S. (1981). *Statistics and the scientific method: Comments on and reactions to Friedman* (Tech. Rep. No. 196). Pittsburgh: Carnegie-Mellon University, Department of Statistics.

Fouraker, L.E., & Siegel, S. (1963). *Bargaining behavior.* McGraw-Hill.

Friedman, M. (1957). *A theory of the consumption function.* Princeton, NJ: Princeton University Press.

Hoggatt, A.C. (1959). An experimental business game. *Behavioral Science, 4,* 192–203.

Jöreskog, K.G., & Goldberger, A.S. (1975). Estimation of a model with multiple indicators and multiple causes of a single latent variable. *Journal of the American Statistical Association, 70,* 631–639.

Jöreskog, K.G., & Sorbom, D. (1978). *LISREL: Analysis of linear structural relationships by the method of maximum likelihood* (User's guide, version IV). Uppsala, Sweden: Uppsala University.

Juster, F.T. (1966). *Consumer buying intentions and purchase probability: An experiment in survey design* (Occasional paper 99). New York: National Bureau of Economic Research.

Juster, F.T., & Miller, R.B. (1983, May). *Impacts of changes in methods and technology on social science research.* Paper presented at meetings of the American Association for the Advancement of Science, Detroit.

Juster, F.T., & Shay, R.P. (1964). *Consumer sensitivity to finance rates: An empirical and analytical investigation* (Occasional paper 88). New York: National Bureau of Economic Research.

Lillard, L.A. (1979a). *Wages and hours in earnings dynamics* (Paper series P-6165). Santa Monica, CA: Rand Corporation.

Lillard, L.A. (1979b). *Estimation of permanent and transitory response functions in panel data: A dynamic labor supply* (Paper series P-6292). Santa Monica, CA: Rand Corporation.

Lowry, I.S. (Ed.). (1983). *Experimenting with housing allowances.* Cambridge, MA: Oelgeschlager, Gunn & Hain.

Machlup, F. (1962). *The production and distribution of knowledge in the United States.* Princeton, NJ: Princeton University Press.

Manpower Demonstration Research Corporation. (1980). *Summary and findings of the national supported work demonstration.* Cambridge, MA: Ballinger.

Mayer, T. (1972). *Permanent income, wealth, and consumption.* Berkeley: University of California Press.

Maynes, E.S. (1968). Minimizing response errors in financial data: The possibilities. *Journal of the American Statistical Association, 63,* 214–227.

Morgenstern, O. (1963). *On the accuracy of economic observations* (2nd ed.). Princeton, NJ: Princeton University Press.

National Science Foundation. (1969). *Annual Report.* Washington, DC: Author.

Plott, C.R. (1982). Industrial organization theory and experimental economics. *Journal of Economic Literature, 20,* 1485–1527.

Plott, C.R., & Smith, V.L. (1978). An experimental study of two exchange institutions. *Review of Economic Studies, 45,* 133–153.

Smith, V.L. (1962). An experimental study of competitive market behavior. *Journal of Political Economy, 70,* 111–137.

Smith, V.L. (1982). Microeconomic systems as an experimental science. *American Economic Review, 72,* 923–955.

Stafford, F.P., & Duncan, G.J. (1985). The use of time and technology by households in the United States. In F.T. Juster & E.P. Stafford (Eds.), *Time, goods and well-being.*

Watts, H.W., & Rees, A. (Eds.). (1977). *The New Jersey income maintenance experiment* (Vols. II & III). New York: Academic Press.

PART III

ANIMAL MODELS IN BEHAVIORAL ECONOMICS

While the study of nonhuman animals has been a mainstay of psychological and biological theory and research, such study has been, until recently, unheard of, even dismissed, within economics. Indeed, it has even been stated that "in economics, of course, experiments are not possible" and "in economics, we cannot perform controlled experiments in a laboratory" (Samuelson, 1973, p. 362 and 66, respectively). This position is now changing. The extensive work conducted by psychologists and biologists, which demonstrates behavioral as well as physiological continuity across species, suggests that the laws of economic behavior would be virtually unique among behavioral principles if they did not apply (with some variation, obviously) to the behavior of nonhuman organisms. Furthermore, if economics is defined as "the study of the allocation of scarce resources among unlimited and competing resources" (Rees, 1968, p. 472), then psychologists, biologists, and ecologists have been involved in the study of economic behavior for quite some time. The use of nonhuman animal experimentation to study economic behavior is an emerging research area.

As Hursh and Bauman note in their chapter, "Economics and psychology can succeed as behavioral sciences as long as theory is grounded in precise experimentation..." The many advantages of the laboratory and animal-based research—precise control, cost-effectiveness, the ability to greatly reduce observational errors from those generally obtained in studies with large groups of humans, and the chance to test more precisely and formally the assumptions and predictive consequences of theories that for ethical or practical reasons might not be possible with other subject populations—all greatly extend the scope and precision of psychological and economic theory.

Of course, we are not suggesting that the results of such animal experimentation be blindly applied to human behavior. But, as we have noted elsewhere: "once we get an idea of the general relation of the preference structures of animals (as revealed by their indifference contours) to the indifference contours of humans, we may test the manipulation of constraints with animals other than humans before applying such manipulations to humans. The alternative is the current practice of trial and (sometimes costly) error with humans themselves" (Rachlin, Battalio, Kagel, & Green, 1981, p. 381). Furthermore, the issue of the generalizability of the results obtained with nonhuman animals to humans is an empirical one, and not to be dismissed a priori. Finally, we remind the reader of Rachlin's suggestion (see Part I) that, in the study of choice, for example, a unification of cognitive and behavioral theory and research may only be possible when they "put to common use" the techniques offered from both human and non-human research approaches. In this section of the book, then, we present contributions by psychologists and economists who study the behavior of nonhuman organisms under controlled, laboratory conditions in an attempt to integrate the two fields of study.

In previous papers, Lea (1978) and Allison (1979) have noted the empirical similarities between reinforcement theory in psychology and demand theory in economics. In his present contribution, "Animal Experiments in Economic Psychology," S.E.G. Lea discusses reasons for animal learning theorists' interest in economic psychology. He considers the potential problems of the generalizability of animal work, the question of rationality, and the role of animal experiments in the study of economic behavior. After reviewing research already conducted, Lea argues for the continued use of nonhuman animal experimentation in the study of "economic psychology." The continuities between nonhuman and human economic behavior are convincingly demonstrated.

Stating that "laboratory experimentation based on behavioral analysis is the most powerful method for defining, testing, and refining economic theory," Steven R. Hursh and Richard A. Bauman show how the concepts of supply and demand can be operationally defined and studied with nonhuman animals. Their review of animal experimentation on such economic concepts as substitution, elasticity of demand, and open versus closed economies points up the importance of this research both for psychology and economics. As they argue at the beginning of their chapter, "The Behavioral Analysis of Demand":

> Experimental psychology has only recently been applied to economic problems. Laboratory methods for studying animal behavior are highly refined but, in many cases, the language of behavioral psychology and traditional laboratory practices require modification before they can be applied to problems of economics. This enterprise permits economists to benefit from controlled laboratory testing and to capitalize on the psychologist's precise language for the analysis of the behavior of the individual organism. At the same time, the psy-

chologist gains access to a rich body of descriptive relations formulated by economists to explain the behavior of consumer populations, a kind of ethology of human behavior, which a complete theory of behavior must eventually explain.

The study of intertemporal choice has played a prominent role in economic theory and has received considerable attention in the psychological literature. Generally, when offered a choice between a smaller, but more immediate, outcome (reward) and a larger, but delayed, outcome, subjects choose the smaller reward. However, this preference reverses when the delay between the availability of this choice and the availability of the smaller reward is increased. Furthermore, Rachlin and Green (1972) showed that experimental subjects will make a commitment far in advance of the rewards in order to insure receipt of the larger, but delayed reward. Recent models of choice developed by psychologists predict this reversal in preference from the smaller to the larger, more delayed reward (see Green, 1982, for a review). As John H. Kagel and Leonard Green show in their chapter, "Intertemporal Choice Behavior: Evaluation of Economic and Psychological Models," such preference reversals as time between choice and availability of the rewards is varied are incompatible with standard economic models. The authors also discuss the implications of such behavior obtained with nonhuman subjects, for understanding comparable human behavior. The interrelations between psychology and economics, the value of studying animals in laboratory situations, and the potential significance of such work to human behavior are thus made evident.

In "Stability, Melioration, and Natural Selection," William Vaughan, Jr. and R.J. Herrnstein criticize the use of optimality principles in behavioral analyses. The first, and shorter, part of their paper deals with the use of optimality principles in situations where individuals are faced with a set of constraints that they cannot alter, a game against nature, so to speak. The discussion here extends an ongoing debate in the recent psychology literature (Herrnstein & Vaughan, 1980; Kagel, Battalio, & Green, 1983; Prelec, 1982; Rachlin, 1983; Rachlin, Battalio, Kagel, & Green, 1981, with commentary). The second and longer part of their paper criticizes the relevance of optimality concepts in a group, or multiple-person setting, in which agents must take into account the reactions to their decisions by the other agents in the group. Their criticisms of game theory here reflect, in part, Simon's criticism that "...it is virtually impossible to define an unambiguous criteria of rationality for this class of situations (or, what amounts to the same thing, a definitive definition of the 'solution' of a game)." (However, see Johansen, 1982, for an interesting defense of the traditional Nash equilibrium solution to noncooperative games and its relationship to individual "rationality.") More importantly, Vaughan and Herrnstein point out that in prisoner dilemma-type games, the mutual defection solution (which is a dominant strategy under appropriately defined conditions) is not optimal for the group as a whole in the sense that all players can be made better off, and that evolutionary processes are likely to exhibit sub-optimality in this respect. The recent book by Axelrod (1984) dealing with the evolution of cooperation in prisoner dilemma games is particularly relevant supplemental reading here.

REFERENCES

Allison, J. (1979). Demand economics and experimental psychology. *Behavioral Science, 24,* 403–415.

Axelrod, R. (1984). *The evolution of cooperation.* New York: Basic books.

Green, L. (1982). Self-control behavior in animals. In V.L. Smith (Ed.), *Research in experimental economics* (Vol. 2), (pp. 129–150). Greenwich, CN: JAI Press.

Herrnstein, R.J., & Vaughan, W., Jr. (1980). Melioration and behavioral allocation. In J.E.R. Staddon (Ed.), *Limits to action: The allocation of individual behavior* (pp. 143–176). New York: Academic Press.

Johansen, L. (1982). On the status of the Nash type of noncooperative equilibria in economic theory. *Scandinavian Journal of Economics, 84,* 421–441.

Kagel, J.H., Battalio, R.C., & Green, L. (1983). Matching versus maximizing: Comments on Prelec's paper. *Psychological Review, 80,* 380–384.

Lea, S.E.G. (1978). The psychology and economics of demand. *Psychological Bulletin, 85,* 441–466.

Prelec, D. (1982). Matching, maximizing, and the hyperbolic reinforcement feedback function. *Psychological Review, 89,* 189–230.

Rachlin, H. (1983). How to decide between matching and maximizing: A reply to Prelec. *Psychological Review, 90,* 376–379.

Rachlin, H., Battalio, R., Kagel, J., & Green, L. (1981). Maximization theory in behavioral psychology. *The Behavioral and Brain Sciences, 4,* 371–417.

Rachlin, H., & Green, L. (1972). Commitment, choice and self-control. *Journal of the Experimental Analysis of Behavior, 17,* 15–22.

Rees, A. (1968). Economics. In D.L. Sills (Ed.), *International encyclopedia of the social sciences* (Vol. 4). New York: Macmillan.

Samuelson, P. (1973). *Economics* (9th ed.). New York: McGraw-Hill.

Chapter 5

Animal Experiments in Economic Psychology*

S.E.G. Lea

Department of Psychology
University of Exeter, UK

Economic psychology is now growing rapidly in influence and importance, and it should be no surprise that more and more fields of psychology are now being seen to have an economic aspect. But to some readers, at least, it must seem very odd that one of the areas where a rapproachement between economics and psychology is now eagerly pursued is that of animal learning. Who would expect to find energetic discussion of microeconomic theory going on among the Skinner boxes and rat cages of the operant laboratory?

My intentions in this paper are threefold. First, I want to try to explain this interest in economic psychology among those studying animal learning and behavior. Secondly, I shall discuss some of the limitations and advantages of animal experimentation as a research technique in economic psychology. I shall argue that, though the limitations are real enough, the compensating advantages are sufficient to make at least a small-scale use of animal research well worth-while. Finally, I shall review experiments that have already been carried out.

OPERANT PSYCHOLOGY AND ECONOMICS

The first thing we have to understand is just how little contact there has been in the century between economics and psychology as they are studied in the English-speaking world. The dominant American and British schools in both disciplines have their philosophical roots in British empiricism, but long before either psychology or economics became truly empirical, the two subjects had lost contact. Psychologists might occasionally poke fun at the

* This chapter is based on a paper delivered to the Annual Colloquium of the European Group for Research in Economic Psychology, held at Leuven in August 1980. This chapter was previously published in the *Journal of Economic Psychology,* vol. 1 (1981), pp. 245–271, and is reprinted here by permission of North-Holland Publishing Company.

absurd nature of "economic man" (e.g., McDougall, 1920, p. 11), and occasionally economists have found time to reply explicitly (e.g., Friedman,
1935, Ch. 1; Florence, 1927; Ch. 4). But in general terms, what has happened,
as Reynaud (1954) documents, is that economic theory has been steadily
purged of psychological content, to the point where even the minimal interdisciplinary contact afforded by mutual mockery has largely ceased.

Of course there are areas where economists and psychologists have
always worked alongside one another, even in the anglo-saxon world. Industrial and occupational psychology is one; so is advertising, and, in general,
the empirical study of consumer behavior. It is probably significant that
these are "applied" areas, and of low prestige within mainstream psychology: similarly, consumer science, which is one branch of economics that
does draw on psychology, is of low prestige in economics. An important
turning point for economic psychology occurred with the publication of a
review of decision theory in the *Psychological Bulletin* (Edwards, 1954).
This paper made explicit a convergence that had occurred between economics and psychology in the study of choice, and led many psychologists to at
least a limited study of the literature of economics. Edwards' paper has
been influential. But why should it have any effect within operant psychology? Decision theory is essentially cognitive: it presumes that behavior is
determined by rational choices. Operant psychology, on the other hand, is
normally thought of as radically behavioristic, and it presumes that behavior is determined by habits, conditioned by histories of reinforcement.

Perhaps, however, it is not really so odd that operant psychologists
should be interested in economics. What really unites operant psychologists
is not a blind faith in the ideas of B.F. Skinner, or even the use of the methodology he introduced, but a conviction that an important determinant of
behavior is the environmental consequences it produces. Operant behavior
is instrumental behavior. And the two most fundamental kinds of economic
behavior, working and buying, are also essentially instrumental. Skinner
long ago (1953, Ch. 25) speculated that economic behavior might be understood in terms derived from instrumental conditioning; and the profoundly
behavioristic trend of modern microeconomic theory, especially of the "revealed preference" approach (Samuelson, 1938), is also clearly congenial to
the radical behaviorist. Thus, paradoxically, the long march of economics
away from psychological content has actually brought it closer to operant
psychology. Of course there are still differences between economists and
operant psychologists: for example, to an economist, contingency between
behavior and its outcome should be enough to make the outcome affect
behavior, while most psychologists would also regard contiguity as necessary. Even this, however, has been disputed (e.g., Baum, 1973).

Two other factors have been important in drawing the attention of
operant psychologists towards economics. First, one of the liveliest areas of

current research in operant psychology is the study of choice (or, to use the approved behavioristic term, concurrent schedules of reinforcement). It has been given a powerful impetus by the existence of a number of quantitative formulations: the best known is the "matching law" first proposed by Herrnstein (1961), which fits a considerable range of data with fair accuracy (see, for example, de Villiers, 1977). The matching law attempts to state, in quantitative terms, the consequences of the assumption that choice behavior is the result of competing habitual tendencies ("Choice is behavior in the context of other behavior," Herrnstein, 1970, p. 255). It has long seemed that the most radical alternative assumption would be that choice behavior is optimal, which, in the case of an animal in a Skinner box, would imply that the subject would act so as to maximize the overall rate at which rewards are delivered. A number of optimizing theories have been proposed (e.g., Shimp, 1969); but once it became necessary to think in terms of optimal choice, it was natural that attention would turn, first to the psychological literature on optimal decision (e.g., Edwards, 1954, 1961) and then to the field where optimizing theory has been developed in most detail, economics.

But "operant psychology" does not just consist of those still carrying out fundamental research with rats and pigeons in Skinner boxes. Another important influence comes from those who seek to put operant principles into effect, for example in educational or clinical psychology—the behavior modifiers. And recent developments in behavior modification have also constrained operant psychologists to think about economics. In an ambitious and original clinical research project, Ayllon and Azrin (1968) sought to apply reinforcement principles to raise the level of behavior in an entire ward of severely regressed schizophrenic patients. A considerable merit of their study was the care they took to identify possible rewards. They produced a list of some 30 items or classes, ranging from the obvious (e.g., preferred foods) to the far less obvious (e.g., an extra religious service). Clearly many of these could not be delivered as immediate consequences of, say, a patient brushing her own teeth in the morning, and Ayllon and Azrin therefore introduced "tokens," which were given to the patients as rewards whenever they performed any desired response, and could be exchanged for any of the range of "backup reinforcers."

Ayllon and Azrin's rationale for the token system lay in the well established principle of conditioned reinforcement, which had been studied in detail in animals (reviewed by Kelleher & Gollub, 1962, for example), and shown to extend to the use of tokens at least in rats (Malagodi, 1967) and apes (Cowles, 1937; Wolfe, 1936). But obviously they had also set up a kind of miniature economic system, as they recognized in the name they gave their project—the Token Economy. Token economics had considerable success, and soon spread widely; and it was not long before those managing them began to run into essentially economic problems such as inflation and excess saving, not to mention fraud and theft. It was clear that a science of "token economics" (Atthowe, 1973) would be needed. The first serious attempt to apply economic principles to understand behavior in a token economy was made by Winkler (1971), and a series of papers has followed (e.g., Battalio, Kagel, & Reynolds, 1977b; Battalio et al., 1973; Schroeder & Barrera, 1976a, b; for a review, see Winkler, 1980). Clearly, token economies (and related systems, some of which are now being developed purely for experimental purposes; see Miles, 1975, for a summary) can be expected to play a considerable part in the development of economic psychology as an experimental discipline. And it is hard to imagine a better setting for a simultaneous consideration of conditioning principles and economic theory.

ADVANTAGES AND LIMITATIONS OF EXPERIMENTS WITH ANIMALS

Most economic psychologists would, I think, readily concede that token economies offer interesting new research possibilities. It is much less obvious that more traditional operant psychology has anything to offer to economic psychology.

The Species Extrapolation Problem

All psychological research with animals is bedevilled by the difficulty of deciding how far, if at all, we can expect results obtained with other species to be applicable to man; and the situation is made worse by a history, at least in American psychology, of extrapolating too eagerly. Thus Osgood's (1953) textbook could seriously refer to the albino rats as "our furry white test-tube" (1953, p. 393), while Skinner (1938) saw the rat as a "representative" organism and its lever-pressing as a "typical" response. But rats are not simplified people; they show rat behavior, not simplified human behavior; and rat behavior has its own laws and complexities, constrained presumably by the rat's ecological niche, and they are not typical of any other species' behavior. Extrapolations can never be made without explicit justification. (For more discussion of the species extrapolation problem in psychology generally, see, for example, Heim, 1979; Lea, 1979b.) This is the fundamental limitation on using animal experiments, and it can only be compensated by other advantages, never directly negated.

The Need for Experiments

Just as the species extrapolation problem is an irreducible disadvantage to experimental work with animals, so too there is one irreducible advantage. Using animals, we can carry out experiments that cannot be done any other way. It is a common complaint among economists that theirs is not an experimental discipline. (Some would argue that this is, and should be, true of economic psychology too, e.g., Morgan, 1972.) Others have argued that experimentation in economics is now seriously possible; Naylor (1972), for example, points to the New Jersey income maintenance experiments, as well as to the experimental literature on choice, flowing from Edwards's (1954) work. New fields of experimental study, for example of bargaining behavior (Smith, 1976), are being opened up. And in consumer science, the possibility of experimental study of demand curves has long been recognized (e.g., Whitman, 1942; Bennett & Wilkinson, 1974), though as Doyle and Gidengil (1977) point out, remarkably little real progress has been made in nearly three decades of research in this area, and it is perhaps no accident that a very modest attempt to bring psychology to bear on the problem (Lea, 1978) rapidly found a niche in at least one economics textbook (Hirshleifer, 1980). Nonetheless, there are some experiments that economists just cannot do. We cannot find the form of the demand curve for bread by repeated doubling, or halving, its price throughout the economy. Even if the experiment were practicable (as it might be in a token economy), it would not be ethically acceptable. But if we could construct a model economy inhabited by rats, the experiment would be easy. And there are many other textbook economic phenomena, that have similarly never been observed outside the covers of a textbook, which could easily be examined in such an experiental economy. This is the most basic argument for animal experiments in economic psychology.

The Question of "Rationality"
A second, apparently fundamental problem in using animal experiments lies in the different ways in which we normally explain the behavior of humans and animals. Economists assume that behavior is rational: operant psychologists assume that it is the product of habit determined by particular schedules of reinforcement. Surely these assumptions must be contradictory (Cross, 1980)?

Put like this, the question about rationality in fact confuses two distinct issues. The first is a question about the description of behavior: can we, by assuming rational choice, generate adequate quantitative descriptions of how people behave in the economy, or the economy as a whole behaves? The second is a question about the mechanism by which behavior is produced. Habit is, presumably, "blind"; rational choice involves previewing in imagination the consequences of different courses of action, and choosing the one with the best outcome. Whichever one of these questions we consider, however, it turns out not to pose an insuperable objection to the use of animals.

Rationality as Mechanism
Consider the question of mechanism first. Previewing in imagination might plausibly be held to be a uniquely human capacity, because it seems to depend on the possession of language. However, it may well turn out that the

difference in cognitive capacity between human beings and other animals
has been grossly overestimated. Psychologists are now looking at animal
cognition much more seriously than they have for several decades (see
Hulse, Fowler, & Honig, 1978), and we can no longer rule out the possibility
that animals could be "rational" in the sense of being capable of forethought
(Midgley, 1979). Equally, almost every psychologist interested in economics
has pointed out that people are certainly not rational, in this sense, all the
time, or even much of the time (e.g., McDougall, 1920; Simon, 1955). The
real issue for the relevance of animal experiments is, therefore, whether people, when they behave according to habit, are governed by the same laws as
animals are when *they* are behaving according to habit. So distracted have
we been by the issue of *total* rationality versus *total* irrationality, that there
are no readily available data to answer this question. However, recent developments in the study of human operant behavior under schedules of reinforcement (reviewed by Lowe, 1979) suggest an answer: at least in the laboratory,
people behave very differently from animals in instrumental response tasks
—if, but only if, they are old enough to have language, and they construe
the situation as one in which a problem has to be solved. If they approach it
uninquisitively, or do not see the instrumental performance as being under
study, behavior approximates what is classically produced by animals, as
documented by Ferster and Skinner (1957). If Lowe's conclusions turn out
to be truly general, it will be clear that animal studies have considerable
potential for understanding some parts of economic behavior, provided
they are coupled with a theory as to when, and to what extent, habit rather
than reason will govern human behavior. It is significant here that the most
successful approaches to economic psychology have been those which have
elaborated just such a theory (see Katona, 1975, esp. pp. 219–222; Reynaud,
1974, esp pp. 104–133).

Rationality as Descriptive
Given the behavioristic slant of modern economics, however, the more important question about rationality is the descriptive one. It may be applied
either at the level of individual behavior, or of the economy as a whole, but
in either case its form is similar. Robustly monodisciplinary economists may
admit that individuals sometimes behave irrationally, but still (e.g., Friedman, 1935) argue that the assumption of rationality works: it makes correct
predictions. Therefore, it should be retained.

The argument is incorrect, because it ignores the possibility that assumptions other than rationality might make the same, successful, predictions. In
fact, some of the animal experiments that have been done in economic psychology even run the risk of being called trivial (e.g., Cross, 1980), just
because they only demonstrate phenomena which were well known before,
like the downward slope of the demand curve. Such experiments are in no
sense trivial. If rats produce "orthodox" demand curves, then either rats

are rational, and so experiments with rats must be admitted as relevant, or else important economic phenomena can be founded on assumptions other than rationality, and so there is no reason why the assumption of rationality should dominate theoretical economics as it now does.

Even if the pragmatic defence of the rationality assumption were logically sound, it would not be an argument against taking animal experiments as evidence: for optimization models, as functional descriptions of behavior, are now almost as common in animal psychology as they are in economics (e.g., Rachlin, Battalio, Kagel, & Green, 1981; Staddon & Motheral, 1978). In the past few years, there has been a convergence of interests between subgroups within economics, psychology, and behavioral ecology, in which the use of such models represent a common point of reference (see Houston, 1980; Staddon, 1980). This illustrates a further advantage of using animal experiments: it furthers that interdisciplinary spirit which is an essential part of economic psychology (see Reynaud, 1974), and extends it not only into experimental psychology, but also into biological science proper.

Corresponding to each of the arguments I have just advanced in favor of animal experiments, there are clear dangers. Too much time spent demonstrating that well known economic phenomena also occur in rats would be wasted time. There is no need to demonstrate experimentally that some phenomenon can be predicted by reinforcement theory as well as economic theory, if a mathematician can demonstrate it analytically. Similarly, too much time spent testing the consequences of innumerable slightly different optimizing models would also be wasted. Reynaud (1974, p. 22) has justly criticised laboratory studies of choice for being exclusively concerned with testing formal models. The real use of animal experiments is surely not for testing old hypotheses.

Related to these two dangers is a third. Laboratory experiments are, or should be, abstracted from any historical context. But economic psychology has made most progress when it has abandoned this abstract plane and concentrated on specific economic behavior, recognizing that it is partly determined by a particular history. For example, "discretionary income" is one of Katona's most successful concepts. But, as Katona himself makes clear (1975, p. 21 ff.), it only makes sense within a bourgeois state at a particular stage of its development. And it is neither accident nor disgrace that Katona's entire economic psychology has had to be revised to accommodate the new economic era of the 1970s (Katona & Strumpel, 1978). Animal experiments must not be allowed to distract our attention from the historical determination of economic behavior.

Optimization and Mechanism

I have attempted to resolve the vexed rationality or optimality problem by splitting it into two, a problem about the mechanism of behavior and a problem about its description. It should be obvious that I have borrowed this argument from ecology. Ecology and economics have much in common, as the similarity of their names suggests. One important commonality is a concern with adaptation to scarcity of resources, and in both disciplines an important method of investigation is to find the optimal solution to a given resource allocation problem. But the diciplines differ in their reason for accepting optimization as relevant. In economics, the argument is mechanistic: rational forethought should lead at least some agents to the optimal solution. In ecology, the argument depends on natural selection: individuals showing optimal behavior will leave a disproportionate number of descendants, so that optimal behavior will eventually predominate. Natural selection has been claimed to occur at the economic level, of course: even if we ignore the early "Social Darwinists," there are modern examples, such as Hirshleifer's (1977) treatment of the effects of competition between firms. But with these exceptions, the different ideas about the origins of optimality lead to different approaches to psychological knowledge. Ecologists readily recognize that the evolutionary imperative for optimization provides only an ultimate cause for behavior: within the lifespan of the individual organism, we must look for some proximate mechanism that will explain how the organism manages to produce what will be, at best, only roughly optimal behavior, or optimal behavior within a narrowly defined range of circumstances. Economists, on the other hand, tend to see optimality as a sufficient explanation in itself, and as likely to be universal rather than situationally restricted.

Now, it is arguable that economics is precisely the science of human ecology, and that rationality is the mechanism that humans, uniquely, have evolved to ensure optimal behavior in the face of scarce resources. In that case, my division of the rationality problem into mechanism and description would be false. But it seems to me much more likely that the mechanisms that ensure near-optimal behavior in our species will have something in common with the mechanisms that do the same job in other species. A clear understanding of the relation between optimal behavior and learning processes in other species should provide a model for an improved understanding of the same relation in man. The recent experiments on, for example, the relations between the ecological theory of optimal foraging and animal learning (Kaufman—see Collier & Rovee-Collier, 1981; Lea, 1979a) are therefore of particular relevance to economic psychology.

The Medium of Exchange

The kind of "model economy" experiment I have advocated above is open to at least one serious objection. Modern economic behavior is powerfully influenced by a factor which seems to be unique to human life, namely the use of a medium of exchange. Smith (1908, Book I, Ch. II) indeed argued that exchanging was one of the defining marks of humanity. This is an exaggeration: as I have argued elsewhere (Lea, 1980), division of labor is a kind of exchange and is ubiquitous in the animal kingdom. But the use of a medium of exchange, namely money, does seem to be uniquely human.

In fact, however, this is one of the more promising areas for future animal experimentation in economic psychology, because it has been shown that animals of many species can be trained to perform instrumental responses that are rewarded only by tokens such as poker chips or ball bearings, the tokens being exchanged later for, say, food (e.g., Cowles, 1937; Malagodi, 1967; Wolfe, 1936). Skinner (1953, p. 79) has suggested that token reinforcement provides an explanation for humans' use of money, and Castro and Weingarten (1970) argue that research into token reinforcement is an essential part of an experimental approach to economics.

Of course, token reinforcement experiments have their limitations, as Lea and Webley (1981) discuss in greater detail. In most of them, as in conditioned reinforcement experiments generally, the conditioned reinforcer is associated with just one kind of primary reward (Bolles, 1967, p. 392). While some primitive moneys function like this (Einzig, 1966, p. 424 ff.; Grierson, 1978), modern money certainly does not. But the behavior produced by tokens is very interesting. Chimpanzees in the prewar token experiments were seen to beg tokens from each other (Nissen & Crawford, 1936); it is even said that one of them, in a "delayed redemption" experiment, wrapped her tokens in a lettuce leaf and went to sleep with this as a pillow. Less obviously related to known human behaviors, and perhaps the more interesting for that, is "misbehavior" towards tokens, as when pigs root them (Breland & Breland, 1961) or rats chew them (Boakes, Poli, Lockwood, & Goodall, 1978). Perhaps we have here a link to some of the strange human behaviors toward money discussed by the psychoanalysts (e.g., Ferenczi, 1952).

The Unpredictable Rat

The token studies lead on to my final argument in favour of animal experiments. It is one that may seem odd, even perverse, but I believe it is quite important. Excessive formalism is, as I have said, a danger to the laboratory experimentalist. It is compounded by the fact that, given the power of modern techniques for controlling behavior, it would be quite easy to construct a simulated economy within which rats would be almost certain to behave like Marshallian, or Marxian, consumers, or in which the whole economy would almost certainly obey perfectly the dictates of Keynes or even Friedman. We could thus lend these over-simplified schemata an undeserved psychological plausibility. But the key word here is "almost." A live animal retains the capacity to surprise us in a way that a mathematical model never can, as when the ape puts her poker chips under her pillow. There may therefore be some value in simulating economic processes with animals just for the sake of seeing familiar problems in a new light—in fact, through the animal's eyes. It is possible that the experimental subjects will behave in ways that would never, otherwise, have occurred to us, and which can throw light on quite different phenomena in human economic behavior.

There is another important kind of unpredictability. To make an experiment work, contingencies and assumptions must be translated into hardware (and maybe software). Deutsch (1956, p. 15) has commented on the salutary effect this can have, in making loose thinking and hidden assumptions painfully obvious.

The Role of Animal Experiments

To summarize, therefore, animal experiments seem likely to have two major uses in economic psychology. The first is to support existing economic knowledge: to confirm what we strongly suspect but cannot rigorously prove from available human data. The second is to challenge existing knowledge, by offering new interpretations of economic phenomena, and new and perhaps surprising phenomena within attempts to simulate the economy.

As an example of these two roles, consider a paper by Rachlin, Kagel, and Battalio (1980), concerning choice between nonsubstitutable rewards. This paper draws on data from pigeons working in operant experiments: on a psychological theory (the "matching law" of Herrnstein, 1961, 1970); and on economic methodology (equilibrium analysis). What is produced is, in effect, a sophisticated alternative to the usual accounts of cross-price elasticities of demand. Thus, existing economic knowledge is supported (the effect of the price of one commodity on purchase of another is demonstrated in a novel way), while accepted economic theory is challenged by the provision of an explicit alternative account of both psychological and economic phenomena.

CURRENT ANIMAL EXPERIMENTS IN ECONOMIC PSYCHOLOGY

To some readers, who have perhaps never seen a Skinner box, still less handled a rat, all my talk of what operant psychology has done or can offer must seem like so many vague promises. The time has now come to redeem them by reviewing more systematically the work that has already been done in animal economic psychology.

Literature Surveys

So far, animal experimentation in economic psychology is in its infancy. However, there is a considerable body of data in the psychological literature which is of economic relevance even though it was gathered with no thought of economics in mind, and a number of authors have brought this relevance out in different ways.

For example, Skinner (1938) devised what he called the "fixed ratio schedule of reinforcement," in which the subject has to perform an instrumental response (for a rat, this might be pressing a lever) a fixed number of times before getting a reward (perhaps a pellet of food). It is quite possible to arrange that the subject lives in the experimental apparatus, and has continual access to the schedule but no other source of the reward (the free behavior situation: Logan, 1964). The animal's situation is then clearly analogous to that of a consumer who has free access to some commodity, but only on paying a fixed price per unit. And it turns out that analogous data are produced.

Figure 1 shows some data I gathered together from a variety of studies by different authors where animals had free access to fixed-ratio schedules of various kinds of reinforcement (Lea, 1978, Fig. 1). The results are plotted as the number of rewards taken, as a function of the fixed ratio schedule, with log scales on both axes. Now, in this form, these data are in effect demand functions—they show how the amount of a commodity (reward) consumed per unit time varies as a function of its price (the fixed ratio schedule). To compare with them, Figure 2 shows some "real" economic demand curves

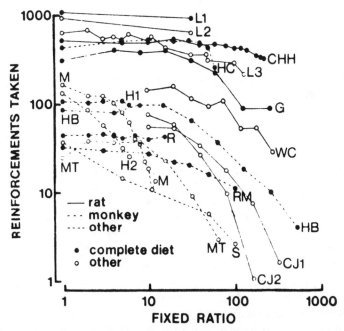

FIGURE 1.   Demand curves of animal consumers as plotted by Lea (1978). "Fixed ratio" is the price each unit of the reward ("commodity"), to be paid in leverpresses or similar responses. Copyright © 1978 by the American Psychological Association. Reprinted by permission of the publisher and author.

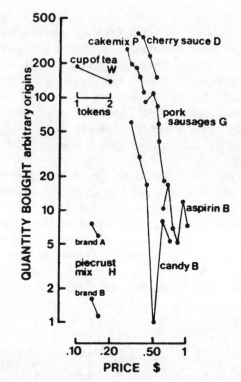

FIGURE 2. Demand curves found by direct experiments on consumer behavior, collected by Lea (1978). Copyright © 1978 by the American Psychological Association. Reprinted by permission of the publisher and author.

which I extracted from a number of experimental studies in the consumer behavior literature (Lea, 1978, Fig. 2). And finally, Figure 3 shows demand data from Stone's (1954) monumental econometric studies of the U.K. economy in the inter-war period (Lea, 1978; Fig. 4).

Of course there are differences between these three sets of data, and in the review paper where I originally collected them, I went on to discuss the origin and significance of those differences. But there are also important similarities. Most obviously and simply, whether our subjects are rats or human consumers, an increase in price leads to a decrease in demand, and when our subjects are rats (Fig. 1) we have the opportunity to study that effect over three log units of price variation, instead of the tiny range typically encountered in econometric studies.

The data shown in Figure 1, or very similar collections, have been considered by other authors for other purposes. Allison (1979) reviews some of them, and some econometric data, with the aim of showing how they both fit into a "conservation" model of fixed ratio performance (Allison, 1976).

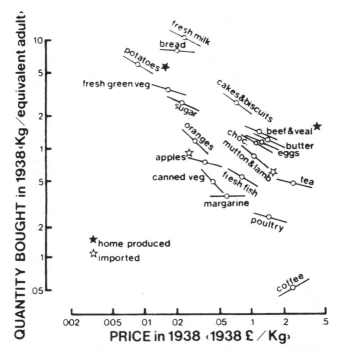

FIGURE 3. **Demand data from the econometric studies of Stone (1954). The points show observed mean price-quantity combinations; the lines through them indicate observed elasticities. Copyright © 1978 by the American Psychological Association. Reprinted by permission of the publisher and author.**

This approach of Allison's is important: although there are problems with the conservation model, it is capable of being extended and modified (e.g., Allison, Miller, & Wozny, 1979; Lea, 1981), and it bears important affinities to Lancaster's (1966) "new theory" of consumer demand. And Allison's approach represents a first attempt to use a specific, quantitative theory developed within operant psychology to make sense of economic data. It has not been tested very rigorously yet, but so far results are interesting and promising.

Battalio, Kagel, and Green (1977a) have also made use of some of the data shown in Figure 1, for a different kind of economic analysis. They consider an animal under a fixed-ratio schedule of reinforcement to be like, not a consumer purchasing a commodity, but an employee working under a piece rate. They therefore consider the data shown in Figure 1 as an opportunity to study labor supply, and the labor-leisure choice, in animal workers. In point of fact, it makes very little difference whether we view these data as referring to work, or purchase: unless we provide a medium of exchange, there is no logical difference between the two (Castro & Weingarten, 1970).

Other bodies of psychological data have also been reviewed from an economic point of view. Hursh (1980) and Lea (1980) have both been concerned with the supply side of supply–demand equilibrium, and with the predictions made by the notion of equilibrium itself. In both these cases, it once again turns out that existing data from animals like rats make quite good economic sense.

Explicitly Economic Experiments

I turn now to experiments that have been done, using animals, with the direct intention of investigating economic principles. Logically, I ought to include here at least the early studies of token reinforcement already mentioned (e.g., Cowles, 1937; Nissen & Crawford, 1936; Wolfe, 1936), but that would open too wide a field; it would also distract attention from the modern developments in operant psychology which are my particular concern in this paper.

The first explicitly interdisciplinary animal studies to appear were those of Kagel et al. (1975) (also described by Rachlin, Green, Kagel, and Battalio, 1976). These were straightforward experiments on the revealed-preference approach to demand theory. Individual rats were kept in two-lever Skinner boxes, and allowed to make a fixed number of lever presses (a "budget") per day. Different rewards were available, on different fixed ratio schedules of reinforcement, for pressing the two levers. After performance had stabilized under one set of conditions, one of the fixed ratios ("prices") was increased, while the lever press "budget" was adjusted so that the combination of rewards previously taken was still, in principle, obtainable. (In economic terms, these were "compensated" price changes.) The question asked was whether the rats would reduce intake of the now more "expensive" reward, and increase intake of the other. It was duly observed that the rats did behave like this. Furthermore, the extent of the substitution depended on the nature of the rewards offered. Where they were food (standard laboratory rat diet) and water, rather little substitution occurred. Where they were two different American sweet drinks (root beer and Tom Collins mix), there was much more substitution. These results are consistent with economic demand theory and they are, of course, not at all surprising. Less predictable was the fact that, at one point, when the "price" of food was sharply increased, one rat ceased to "spend" all its budget of lever presses; as a result, its intake of food reduced sharply, and it lost weight. This is the kind of observation that I had in mind earlier, when I suggested that the unpredictability introduced by a live subject might aid serendipity: and it led Rachlin et al. (1976) to some interesting speculative comparisons with Hamermesh and Soss's (1974) theory of the economic origins of suicide.

In a further series of similar experiments reported by Kagel, Battalio, Green, and Rachlin (1980), uncompensated price changes were used. It was found that changes in consumption were again mainly consistent with economic theory. Downward curves were generally more elastic than under compensated price changes, as would be expected from economic considerations. These two series of experiments have been summarized and compared by Kagel, Battalio, Rachlin, and Green (1981). Another experiment on the substitutability of reinforcers, by Lea and Roper (1977), was inspired by Lancaster's (1966) theory that consumers demand goods, not for their own sake, but for the sake of characteristics they incorporate; and that, if we know what the characteristics are, we can predict what substitutions will occur as prices change. Rats in a two-lever Skinner box were exposed to a range of fixed-ratio schedules on one lever with reinforcement consisting of pellets of a complete diet, so that a demand curve for food could be plotted. The consequences of pressing the other lever varied. Under one condition, it was ineffective. Under another, presses were rewarded with pellets of sugar, according to a fixed-ratio 8 schedule. Under a third condition, the reward (again on FR 8) was not sugar, but pellets of the same mixed diet as was used to reinforce presses on the main lever. As predicted, we found that the elasticity of demand for food from the main lever changed sharply as a function of the alternative schedule. The demand curves are shown in Figure 4: with no alternative reward, demand was very inelastic; with a moderately

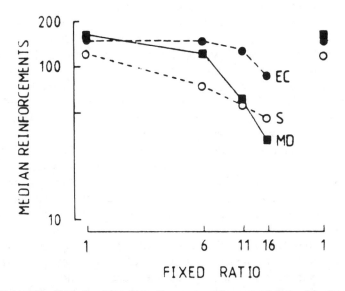

FIGURE 4.   The effect of making alternative commodities on rats' demand for food pellets. "Fixed ratio" is the number of leverpresses to be "paid" for each food pellet. Curve EC shows demand with no alternative commodity: S and MD, with sucrose pellets or identical food pellets, respectively, available at a price of 8 leverpresses per pellet. The detached points at the right represent a return to fixed ratio 1 conditions at the end of the experiment. From Lea and Roper (1977). Copyright © 1977 by the Society for the Experimental Analysis of Behavior, Inc. Reprinted by permission.

substitutable alternative, it was moderately inelastic; and with the maximally substitutable alternative, another source of the identical reward, it was elastic.[1]

Yet another experiment on substitution under price changes has been reported by Battalio, Kagel, Rachlin, and Green (1981). This used pigeons as subjects, and manipulated the relative prices of food and water. Again the results were generally consistent with economic theory, but with two interesting additions. First, the results of price changes in opposite directions were not always symmetrical: it appeared that, having been forced to take food and water in some new proportion by a new price combination, the birds suffered a "change in tastes." Secondly, as well as carrying out a "comparative static" analysis of asymptotic behavior under different prices, as in previous work, Battalio et al. studied the process of adjustment to new prices. They found it to be very rapid (it was complete in under 24 hours). It did not, as they had hoped, explain the asymmetries mentioned above.

The next experiment I want to mention is an unpublished one of my own. I introduce it not because it has very much merit, but because it illustrates a slightly different approach to economic experimentation with animals. It is concerned with the supply side of the supply–demand problem; we wanted to know whether rats would "speculate," in the sense of increasing the price they would pay for a commodity that was, or was going to be, in short supply (unpublished data of Lea and Nicholas, described by Lea, 1980).

The apparatus used is illustrated in Figure 5. It consisted of a large complex maze, containing a number of small chambers which were, in effect, single-lever Skinner boxes. Five rats lived in this apparatus, and got all their food and water as rewards on different schedules of reinforcement in the various chambers. This was an attempt to provide a more complex situation than the simple one- or two-lever Skinner boxes used in the experiments I have described so far, and so lend the experiment greater face validity as a simulation of an economic system. I have used this equipment in a number of other experiments (e.g., Graft, Lea, & Whitworth, 1977). In the one that concerns us here, two of the chambers offered mixed diet food reward, two offered water, and a fifth offered sucrose pellets—sometimes. The number of sucrose pellets available each day, to all the rats together, was varied. Instead of using fixed-ratio schedules of reinforcement in this experiment, we used variable-interval schedules, which allow the actual "price" paid for each reward to be determined by the vigor of the subject's responding. And we duly found that, as the available supply of sugar pellets decreased, the number of lever presses made per pellet increased. In other words, the rats were influenced by shortage in just the same way as human consumers sometimes are.

Reaction to shortage may be thought of as a *social* effect on demand (though it remains to be seen whether the effect shown by Lea and Nicholas's

[1] See Hursh and Bauman (this volume) for a reexamination of these results (ed.).

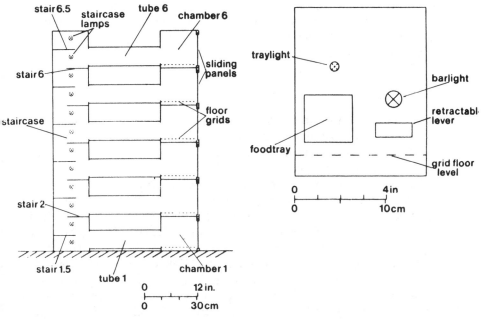

FIGURE 5. Apparatus used by Graft, Lea, and Whitworth (1977) to provide a "miniature economy" for rats. The left panel shows a cross-section through the entire apparatus; the right panel shows the operant equipment, located on the right walls of the top five chambers. Copyright © 1977 by the Society for the Experimental Analysis of Behavior, Inc. Reprinted by permission.

rats had a social origin). Another social effect has been studied by Kennedy (unpublished data reported by Lea, 1980). Kennedy was pursuing Scitovsky's argument (1976) that luxuries are a source of "pleasure," which comes chiefly from stimulation and differs from the "comfort" provided by more basic goods. He therefore argued that rats living socially should show more elastic demand for sucrose pellets—a "luxury"—than isolated rats, who had no alternative, social, source of stimulation. Demand for ordinary food pellets, however, should not be affected. His experiment, though limited in scope, strikingly confirmed this prediction.

Comparison of elasticities also appear in a recent experiment by Hursh and Natelson (1981), in which rats lived in a chamber where they could obtain food by pressing one lever or electrical stimulation of their brains (ESB) by pressing another. Instead of using fixed-ratio schedules of reinforcement, Hursh and Natelson used variable intervals, which control the mean time between rewards rather than the number of responses made; however, indirectly, schedule changes do produce indirect changes in the responses made per reward (Hursh & Natelson's Figure 5). They found that demand for ESB was very much more elastic than demand for food, indicating that they are distinctly different commodities, a point that has been much disputed in the literature of physiological psychology. This experiment is notable in that it uses economic concepts to illuminate a point *within* psychology: the benefits of animal experiments in economic psychology accrue in both the constituent disciplines.

CONCLUSION

Although much of the experimental work I have cited has been exploratory, it is beginning to form quite a substantial corpus. Of the various possible benefits of animal experimentation, one at least has been realized: interdisciplinary continuity has been convincingly demonstrated.

There have been a few glimpses of more solid benefits. Allison's (1979) work on the form of demand curves provides one; another comes from the unexpected effects of price changes reported by Rachlin et al. (1976) and Battalio et al. (1981). The irreversibilities after price changes are the more interesting because similar effects have been reported in token economies (Battalio et al., 1973, 1974; Hayden, Osborne, Hall, & Hall, 1974). They are also of practical importance: irreversible change of tastes following a reversible price change is precisely what a marketer is trying to achieve when he or she makes us a "free" or reduced price offer (cf. Engel, Kollat, & Blackwell, 1973, p. 535). Similarly, Kagel et al. (1981) note that, although in strict economic theory uncompensated demand curves need not always be downward sloping, in practice in animal experiments they always are. This is a useful generalization, which is supported by the wider data base considered by Lea (1978); see Figure 2.

Although one or two nontrivial empirical generalizations are beginning to emerge, the comment, made by both Cross (1980) and Stafford (1980) (a propos of a paper by Kagel & Battalio, 1980), seem fair: experiments to date demonstrate what economists aleady knew rather than providing new hypothesis or new ways of thinking. Thus their main thrust is to establish the credibility of the experimental method rather than to shake the foundations of economic doctrine. Those of us who work with animals in economic psychology would see this as an essential preliminary phase, but we have to admit that we have yet to prove we can advance beyond it.

I should be far from wanting to see large-scale graduate programs in comparative-consumer psychology, as Jacoby (1975) once mischievously proposed. But I am convinced that there is a future for animal experimentation in economics, at least on a small scale. The convergence of interests of operant psychologists and behavioral ecologists, focusing on optimization models, makes it certain that both these groups of behavioral scientists will be quarrying economics for ideas for some years to come. What remains to be seen is whether this will become a two-way traffic: whether economists, and indeed economic psychologists, will know how to make use of data from animal experiments.

REFERENCES

Allison, J. (1976). Contrast, induction, facilitation, suppression and conservation. *Journal of Experimental Analysis of Behavior, 25,* 185-198.

Allison, J. (1979). Demand economics and experimental psychology. *Behavioral Science, 24,* 403-415.

Allison, J., Miller, M., & Wozny, M. (1979). Conservation and behavior. *Journal of Experimental Psychology: General, 108,* 4-34.

Atthowe, J.M. (1973). Token economics come of age. *Behaviour Therapy, 4,* 646-654.

Ayllon, T., & Azrin, N. (1968). *The token economy.* New York: Appleton-Century-Crofts.

Battalio, R.C., Kagel, J.H., & Green, L. (1977a). Labor supply behavior of animal workers: towards an experimental analysis. In V.L. Smith (Ed.), *Research in experimental economics,* (Vol. 1). Greenwich, CT: JAI.

Battalio, R.C., Kagel, J.H., & Reynolds, M. (1977b). Income distributions in two experimental economies. *Journal of Political Economy, 85,* 1259-1272.

Battalio, R.C., Kagel, J.H., Rachlin, H., & Green, L. (1981). Commodity choice behavior with pigeons as subjects. *Journal of Political Economy, 89,* 67-91.

Battalio, R.C., Kagel, J.H., Winkler, R.C., Fisher, E.B., Jr., Basmann, R.L., & Krasner, L. (1973). A test of consumer demand theory using observations of individual consumer purchases. *Western Economic Journal, 11,* 411-428.

Battalio, R.C., Kagel, J.H., Winkler, R.C., Fisher, E.B., Jr., Basmann, R.L., & Krasner, L. (1974). An experimental investigation of consumer behavior in a controlled environment. *Journal of Consumer Research, 1,* 52-60.

Baum, W.M. (1973). The correlation-based law of effect. *Journal of the Experimental Analysis of Behavior, 20,* 137-153.

Bennett, S., & Wilkinson, J.B. (1974). Price-quantity relationships and price elasticity under in-store experimentation. *Journal of Business Research, 2,* 27-33.

Boakes, R.A., Poli, M., Lockwood, M.J., & Goodall, G. (1978). A study of misbehavior: token reinforcement in the rat. *Journal of the Experimental Analysis of Behavior, 29,* 115-134.

Bolles, R.C. (1967). *Theory of motivation.* New York: Harper and Row.

Breland, K., & Breland, M. (1961). The misbehavior of organisms. *American Psychologist, 61,* 681-684.

Castro, B., & Weingarten, K. (1970). Towards experimental economics. *Journal of Political Economy, 78,* 598-607.

Collier, G.H., & Rovee-Collier, C.K. (1981). A comparative analysis of optimal foraging behavior: laboratory simulations. In A.C. Kamil & T.D. Sargent (Eds.), *Foraging behavior.* New York: Garland. pp. 39-76.

Cowles, J.T. (1937). Food-tokens as incentives for learning by chimpanzees. *Comparative Psychology Monographs, 14,* 1-96.

Cross, J.G. (1980). Some comments on the papers by Kagel and Battalio and by Smith. In J. Kmenta & J.B. Ramsey (Eds.), *Evaluation of econometric models* (pp. 403-406). New York: Academic Press.

Deutsch, J.A. (1956). *The structural basis of behaviour.* Cambridge, England: Cambridge University Press.

de Villiers, P. (1977). Choice in concurrent schedules and a quantitative formulation of the law of effect. In W.K. Honig & J.E.R. Staddon (Eds.), *Handbook of operant behavior.* Englewood Cliffs, NJ: Prentice-Hall. pp. 233-287.

Doyle, P., & Gidengil, B.Z. (1977). A review of in-store experiments. *Journal of Retailing, 53*(2), 47-62.

Edwards, W. (1954). The theory of decision making. *Psychological Bulletin, 51,* 380-417.

Edwards, W. (1961). Behavioral decision theory. *Annual Review of Psychology, 12,* 473-498.

Einzig, P. (1966). *Primitive money* (2nd ed.) Oxford: Pergamon.

Engel, J.F., Kollat, D.T., & Blackwell, R.D. (1973). *Consumer behavior* (2nd ed.). New York: Holt, Rinehart and Winston.

Ferenczi, S. (1952). The ontogenesis of the interest in money. In S. Ferenczi (Ed.), *First contributions to psychoanalysis* (pp. 319–331). London: Hogarth. (Originally published 1914.)

Ferster, C.B., & Skinner, B.F. (1957). *Schedules of reinforcement*. New York: Appleton-Century-Crofts.

Florence, P.S. (1927). *Economics and human behaviour*. London: Kegan Paul, Trench and Trubner.

Friedman, M. (1935). *Essays in positive economics*. Chicago, IL: University of Chicago Press.

Graft, D.A., Lea, S.E.G., & Whitworth, T.I. (1977). The matching law in and within groups of rats. *Journal of the Experimental Analysis of Behavior, 27*, 183–194.

Grierson, P. (1978). The origins of money. In G. Dalton (Ed.), *Research in economic anthropology, vol. 1.* (pp. 1–35). Greenwood, CT: JAI Press.

Hamermesh, D.S., & Soss, N.M. (1974). An economic theory of suicide. *Journal of Political Economy, 82*, 83–98.

Hayden, T., Osborne, A.E., Hall, S.M., & Hall, R.G. (1974). Behavioral effects of price changes in a token economy. *Journal of Abnormal Psychology, 83*, 432–439.

Heim, A.W. (1979). The proper study of psychology. *New Universities Quarterly, 33*, 135–154.

Herrnstein, R.J. (1961). Relative and absolute strength of response as a function of frequency of reinforcement. *Journal of the Experimental Analysis of Behavior, 4*, 267–272.

Herrnstein, R.J. (1970). On the law of effect. *Journal of the Experimental Analysis of Behavior, 13*, 243–266.

Hirschleifer, J. (1977). Economics from a biological viewpoint. *Journal of Law and Economics, 20*, 1–52.

Hirschleifer, J. (1980). *Price theory and applications (2nd ed.)*. Englewood Cliffs, NJ: Prentice-Hall.

Houston, A.I. (1980). Godzilla v. the creature from the black lagoon: ethology v. psychology. In F.M. Toates & T.R. Halliday (Eds.), *Analysis of motivational processes* (pp. 297–318). London: Academic Press.

Hulse, S.H., Fowler, H., & Honig, W.K. (1978). *Cognitive processes in animal behavior*. Hillsdale, NJ: Erlbaum.

Hursh, S.R. (1980). Economic concepts for the analysis of behavior. *Journal of the Experimental Analysis of Behavior, 34*, 219–238.

Hursh, S.R., & Natelson, B.H. (1981). Electrical brain stimulation and food reinforcement dissociated by demand elasticity. *Physiology and Behavior, 26*, 509–515.

Jacoby, J. (1975). Consumer psychology as a social psychological field of action. *American Psychologist, 30*, 977–987.

Kagel, J.H., & Battalio, R.C. (1980). Token economy and animal models for the experimental analysis of economic behavior. In J. Kmenta & J.B. Ramsay (Eds.), *Evaluation of econometric models.* (pp. 379–399). New York: Academic Press.

Kagel, J.H., Battalio, R.C., Green, L., & Rachlin, H. (1980). Consumer demand theory applied to choice behavior of rats. In J.E.R. Staddon (Ed.), *Limits to action.* (pp. 237–267). New York: Academic Press.

Kagel, J.H., Battalio, R.C., Rachlin, H., & Green, L. (1981). Demand curves for animal consumers. *Quarterly Journal of Economics, 96*, 1–15.

Kagel, J.H., Battalio, R.C., Rachlin, H., Green, L., Basmann, R.L., & Klemm, W.R. (1975). Experimental studies of consumer demand using laboratory animals. *Economic Enquiry, 13*, 22–38.

Katona, G. (1975). *Psychological economics*. New York: Elsevier.

Katona, G., & Strumpel, B. (1978). *A new economic era*. New York: Elsevier.

Kelleher, R.T., & Gollub, L.R. (1962). A review of positive conditioned reinforcement. *Journal of the Experimental Analysis of Behavior, 5*, 543–597.

Lancaster, K.J. (1966). A new approach to consumer theory. *Journal of Political Economy, 74,* 132–157.

Lea, S.E.G. (1978). The psychology and economics of demand. *Psychological Bulletin, 85,* 441–466.

Lea, S.E.G. (1979a). Foraging and reinforcement schedules in the pigeon: optimal and non-optimal aspects of choice. *Animal Behaviour, 27,* 875–886.

Lea, S.E.G. (1979b). The art of being an experimental psychologist. *New Universities Quarterly, 33,* 166–176.

Lea, S.E.G. (1980). Supply as a factor in motivation. In F.M. Toates & T.R. Halliday (Eds.), *Analysis of motivational processes.* (pp. 153–177). London: Academic Press.

Lea, S.E.G. (1981). Concurrent fixed-ratio schedules for different reinforcers: a general theory. In C.M. Bradshaw, E. Szabadi, & C.F. Lowe (Eds.), *Quantification of steady-state operant behavior.* (pp. 101–112). Amsterdam: Elsevier.

Lea, S.E.G., & Roper, T.J. (1977). Demand for food on fixed-ratio schedules as a function of the quality of concurrently available reinforcement. *Journal of the Experimental Analysis of Behavior, 27,* 371–380.

Lea, S.E.G., & Webley, P. (1981). *Théorie psychologique de la monnaie.* Paper read at the August meeting of the European Group for Research in Economic Psychology, Paris.

Logan, F.A. (1964). The free behavior situation. In D. Levine (Ed.), *Nebraska symposium on motivation* (Vol. 12). (pp. 99–131). Lincoln, NE: University of Nebraska Press.

Lowe, C.F. (1979). Determinants of human operant behaviour. In M.D. Zeiler & P. Harzem (Eds.), *Advances in analysis of behaviour.* (Vol. 1: Reinforcement and the organization of behaviour). (pp. 159–192). Chichester, England: Wiley.

Malagodi, E.F. (1967). Acquisition of the token reward habit in the rat. *Psychological Reports, 20,* 1335–1342.

McDougall, W. (1920). *An introduction to social psychology* (15th ed.). London: Methuen.

Midgley, M. (1979). *Beast and man.* London: Methuen.

Miles, C.G. (Ed.). (1975). *Experimentation in controlled environment.* Toronto: Addiction Research Foundation.

Morgan, J.N. (1972). A quarter century of behavioural research in economics, persistent problems and diversions. In B. Strumpel, J.N. Morgan, & E. Zahn (Eds.), *Human behavior in economic affairs.* (pp. 15–34). Amsterdam: Elsevier.

Naylor, T.H. (1972). Experimental economics revisited. *Journal of Political Economy, 80,* 347–352.

Nissen, H.W., & Crawford, M.P. (1936). A preliminary study of food-sharing behaviour in young chimpanzees. *Journal of Comparative Psychology, 22,* 383–419.

Osgood, C.E. (1953). *Method and theory in experimental psychology.* New York: Oxford University Press.

Rachlin, H., Kagel, J.H., & Battalio, R.C. (1980). Substitutability in time allocation. *Psychological Review, 87,* 355–374.

Rachlin, H., Battalio, R.C., Kagel, J.H., & Green, L. (1981). Maximization theory in behavioral psychology. *Behavioral and Brain Sciences, 4,* 371–388.

Rachlin, H., Green, L., Kagel, J.H., & Battalio, R.C. (1976). Economic demand theory and psychological studies of choice. In G.H. Bower (Ed.), *The psychology of learning and motivation* (vol. 10). (pp. 129–154). New York: Academic Press.

Reynaud, P.L. (1954). *La psychologie économique.* Paris: Riviere.

Reynaud, P.L. (1974). Précis de psychologie economique. Paris: Presses Universitaires de France (English translation: *Economic psychology,* New York: Praeger, 1981.)

Samuelson, P.A. (1938). A note on the pure theory of consumer behavior. *Economica N.S., 5,* 61–71; 353–354.

Schroeder, S.R., & Barrera, F.J. (1976a). Effects of price manipulation on consumer behavior in a sheltered workshop token economy. *American Journal of Mental Deficiency, 81,* 172–180.

Schroeder, S.R., & Barrera, F.J. (1976b). How token economy earnings are spent. *Mental Retardation, 14*(2), 20–24.

Scitovsky, T. (1976). *The joyless economy*. New York: Oxford University Press.

Shimp, C.P. (1969). Optimal behavior in free-operant experiments. *Psychological Review, 76,* 97–112.

Simon, H.A. (1955). A behavioral model of rational choice. *Quarterly Journal of Economics, 69,* 99–118.

Skinner, B.F. (1938). *The behavior of organisms*. New York: Appleton-Century-Crofts.

Skinner, B.F. (1953). *Science and human behavior*. New York: Macmillan.

Smith, A. (1908). *An inquiry into the nature and causes of the wealth of nations*. London: Bell. (Originally published 1776).

Smith, V.L. (1976). Experimental economics: induced value theory. *American Economic Review* (Papers and Proceedings), *66*(2), 274–279.

Staddon, J.E.R. (1980). *The limits to action*. New York: Academic Press.

Staddon, J.E.R., & Motheral, S. (1978). On matching and maximising in operant choice experiments. *Psychological Review, 85,* 436–444.

Stafford, F.P. (1980). Some comments on the papers by Kagel and Battalio and by Smith. In J. Kmenta & J.B. Ramsey (Eds.), *Evaluation of econometric models*. (pp. 407–410). New York: Academic Press.

Stoner, R. (1954). *The measurement of consumers' expenditure and behavioiur in the United Kingdom 1920–1938* (Vol. 1). Cambridge, England: Cambridge University Press.

Whitman, R.H. (1942). Demand functions for merchandise at retail. In O. Lange, F. McIntyre, T.O. Yntema (Eds.), *Studies in mathematical economics and econometrics* (pp. 208–221). Chicago, IL: University of Chicago Press.

Winkler, R.C. (1971). The relevance of economic theory and technology to token reinforcement systems. *Behaviour Research and Therapy, 9,* 81–88.

Winkler, R.C. (1980). Behavioural economics, token economies, and applied behavior analysis. In J.E.R. Staddon (Ed.), *Limits to action*. (pp. 269–297). New York: Academic Press.

Wolfe, J.B. (1936). Effectiveness of token rewards for chimpanzees. *Comparative Psychology Monographs, 12,* no. 5 (whole no. 60).

Chapter 6

The Behavioral Analysis of Demand*

Steven R. Hursh
Richard A. Bauman

Walter Reed Army Institute of Research
Washington, DC

Economists and psychologists have more in common than an interest in predicting human behavior. Each has been held to the test of predicting behavior in the natural environment, either the future inclinations of the consumer or the future dispositions of an unruly child. The common failure of both disciplines under such tests has often been taken as a confirmation of man's inherent freedom and, consequently, an indictment of the scientific status of economics and psychology.

Without minimizing the difficulties of predicting human behavior, such "naturalistic" tests are a problem for any science. For example, precise descriptions of gravitational force and aerodynamics are available, but the test of these "laws" is not their ability to predict the trajectory of a falling leaf but their ability to predict lift and flow patterns of idealized objects under highly controlled wind conditions. The success of a new aircraft design, in turn, validates this scientific process and the engineering based on physical theory. The failure of a new design points to a flaw in either the physical theory or the engineer's translation to practice, and is not evidence for the inherent "freedom" of physical objects.

By analogy, failures of psychology and economics to predict behavior in the natural environment are not grounds for rejecting their status as a science. Economics and psychology can succeed as behavioral sciences as long as theory is grounded in precise experimentation and tested in the design of social practices. In this chapter, we will describe how the precision of labora-

---

* The views of the author(s) do not purport to reflect the position of the Department of the Army or the Department of Defense (para 4-3, AR 360-5).

In conducting the research described in this report, the investigator(s) adhere to the "Guide for the Care and Use of Laboratory Animals," as promulgated by the Committee on Care and Use of Laboratory Animals of the Institute of Laboratory Animal Resources, National Research Council.

37

tory behavioral science can be applied to the definition of economic and psychological theory. Testing theory in the design of social institutions and practices is more a problem for clinicians and applied economists, and will not be discussed here (but see Volume 2 in this series).

Experimental psychology has only recently been applied to economic problems. Laboratory methods for studying animal behavior (our "models" and "wind tunnels") are highly refined, but, in many cases, the language of behavioral psychology and traditional laboratory practices require modification before they can be applied to problems of economics. This enterprise permits economists to benefit from controlled laboratory testing and to capitalize on the psychologist's precise language for the analysis of the behavior of the individual organism. At the same time, the psychologist gains access to a rich body of descriptive relations formulated by economists to explain the behavior of consumer populations, a kind of ethology of human behavior, which a complete theory of behavior must eventually explain. In the first several sections, we will discuss some simple concepts and definitions that are fundamental to "economic experimentation."

Supply and Demand

For the economist, the behavior of the individual consumer considered in the ideal case reflects an equilibrium between the supply of a commodity and the consumer's demand; on the one hand, how much gasoline will be produced at current prices, on the other hand, how much consumers will buy at those prices. This equilibrium process is diagrammed in Figure 1. Price, on the x-axis, is translated as responses-emitted-per-reinforcer; in most animal experiments, there is no medium of exchange. Quantity consumed, on the y-axis, represents the rate at which reinforcers, such as food, are earned and consumed. We have adopted here the scientific convention of displaying the usual independent variable, price, on the x-axis, in contrast to many economic textbooks.

The first determiner of equilibrium is the *supply curve* (*s* in Figure 1) or schedule, which can be translated as the environmental constraints on obtaining the commodity, expressed as quantity per unit time provided at a given price. As the price paid per unit goes up, the rate of production increases. In behavioral experiments supply is controlled by a *schedule of reinforcement,* a procedural rule that determines what quantity and/or pattern of responding is required for each unit of reinforcement. The second determiner of equilibrium is the *demand curve* (*d* in Figure 1), which describes the amount that the subject will consume at a given price or the price that will be paid for a given rate of consumption. As price increases, consumption generally decreases. Demand is a joint product of the nature of the commodity under study, the context of alternatives, and the reinforcement schedule/constraint.

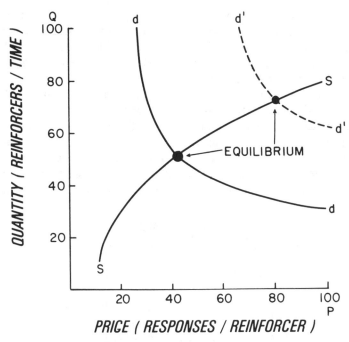

FIGURE 1.   The theoretical basis for behavioral equilibrium based on the intersection of the subject's demand (d) and the environment's supply (s). An increase in demand is shown as d' with the consequent change in equilibrium point.

Equilibrium is the stable outcome of these two curves, shown in Figure 1. Where they intersect is the only point of agreement between the subject's demand and the environment's constraint on supply. Given a stable pair of demand and supply curves, a single behavioral outcome is observed—a certain price is paid and a certain quantity is consumed. If demand increases, for example, when colder temperatures increase the requirement for food calories, the demand curve moves to the right, shown as d' in Figure 1. The new equilibrium moves upward and to the right, implying a higher price and a greater rate of consumption, all else being constant.

To map a demand curve you must observe its intersection with a set of supply curves; demand is the outcome of a simple experiment, not a hypothetical construct. One such experiment is illustrated in Figure 2, top panel. Here, the various supply curves were determined by a simple fixed-ratio (FR) constraint between responding and reinforcement; a certain number of responses is required for each unit of reinforcement. In essence, each test schedule (S_1, S_2, S_3, S_4, S_5) sets a fixed price for food represented by a vertical supply curve. Each intersection is an equilibrium point, and a demand curve is formed by connecting the equilibrium points. Since supply is precisely controlled by pre-arranged schedules and all other conditions are held constant, we are assured that the shifts in consumption reflect changes along a single demand curve. This eliminates the problems encountered when observing shifts in equilibrium in a natural economy where changes in both supply and demand can occur together.

Constraints on supply may be more complicated, as indicated in the bottom panel of Figure 2. Here reinforcement was constrained by a minimum average elapsed time since the last reinforcer, with only one response required after that time. This variable-interval (VI) constraint sets no rigid price for each reinforcer, but rather the relationship between price and rate of consumption is a negatively accelerated function. The maximum rate of consumption is the mean interreinforcement interval set by the schedule.

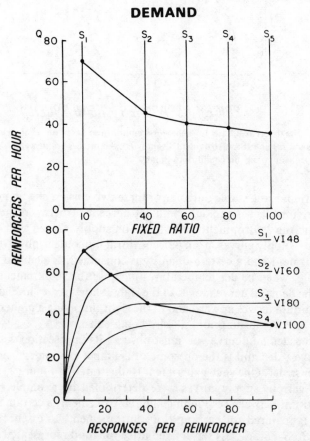

FIGURE 2. Two examples of demand curves as might be determined by using either FR schedules (top panel) or VI schedules (bottom panel) to control supply (S_1, S_2, S_3, etc.); i.e., rate of reinforcers obtainable as a function of changes in responses "paid" per reinforcer.

Approximated supply curves (S_1, S_2, S_3, S_4) are shown for variable intervals ranging from 48 sec to 100 sec. Again, the demand curve is the function described by connecting the equilibrium points under each schedule.

The demand curve mathematically determines the overall rate of responding, or for economists, total expenditure (unit price times the quantity consumed under each equilibrium condition). Figure 3 depicts the rates of responding associated with the equilibrium points of the gently sloping demand curves of Figure 2. Response rate must increase with price (or FR value) in the top panel to minimize the changes in consumption shown in Figure 2. Likewise, in the bottom panel, response rates will increase with increasing VI schedules if the demand curve shows minimal changes in consumption across increases in price. These concepts are illustrated by data

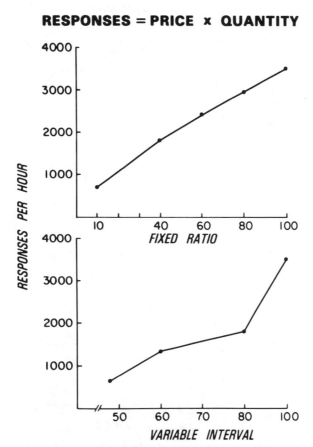

FIGURE 3. The two response rate functions derived from the demand curves in Figure 2. Price at each equilibrium point was multiplied by the quantity consumed and plotted as a function of the schedule of reinforcement, FR (top panel) or VI (bottom panel).

from an experiment reported by Collier, Hirsch, and Hamlin (1972) (see Figure 4). Two rats lived in chambers 24 hours a day and pressed levers for their food. The number of responses required for each 45-mg bite of food was increased across conditions using FR schedules. The observed changes in consumption resulting from these progressive increases in price map a demand curve for food in the top panel of Figure 4. In this closed environment, with no other supply of food, the quantity consumed decreased slowly relative to the increase in price. This resistance of consumption to decrease with increases in price is referred to as *inelastic* demand. The bottom panel of Figure 4 shows that, in order for consumption to resist reduction by increases in price, response rate or total expenditure of behavior to obtain the

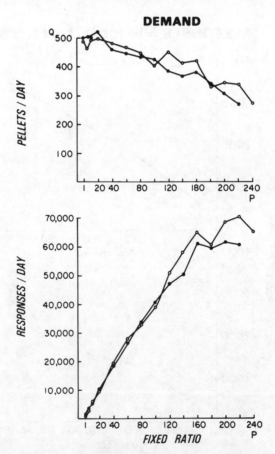

FIGURE 4.   Top panel: The demand curve for food pellets by two rats working 24 hrs per day. Bottom Panel: The response rate functions associated with these demand curves. Data reported by Collier, Hirsch, and Hamlin (1972).

commodity must increase. Inelastic demand implies a positive relationship between price and response rate. In the next section, we will discuss more extensively the relations between demand elasticity and response rate, and illustrate those relationships with data drawn from the behavioral laboratory.

Demand Elasticity

During the past 25 years, a principal concern of behavioral psychology has been the study of variables that control response rate or performance output (Ferster & Skinner, 1957; Catania & Reynolds, 1968; Schoenfeld, 1970; Zeiler, 1977). Research has implicated a number of important variables, including: (a) the rate (Catania & Reynolds, 1968), probability (Felton & Lyon, 1966; Powell, 1968), and immediacy of reinforcement (Chung, 1965; Chung & Herrnstein, 1967; Hursh & Fantino, 1973; Shull, Spear, & Bryson, 1981); (b) the amount and quality of reinforcement (Catania, 1963b; Hawkins & Pliskoff, 1964; Iglauer & Woods, 1974; Miller, 1976; Hursh, 1978; Hursh & Natelson, 1981); and (c) the availability of alternative sources of reinforcement (Herrnstein, 1970; Lea & Roper, 1977). These variables parallel the economic factors of (a) price and supply, (b) the nature of the commodity, and (c) the context of substitutes, all of which relate to the demand curve and elasticity. The shape of the demand curve relates directly to total expenditure, the economic equivalent of response rate. A fuller appreciation of these economic variables which alter demand can extend psychology's understanding of response rate. At the same time, the methods of experimental psychology can be applied to economics to directly test the theory of demand with individual laboratory subjects. In this section, we will begin this analysis by comparing the relation between elasticity of demand curves and the shapes of response rate functions.

Figure 5 is a distillation of the mathematical relationships between different demand curves and the corresponding response rate functions. The top three rows of the figure illustrate three simple demand curves that imply monotonic response rate functions. The first is the gently sloping curve that shows a relatively small change in consumption (Q) with large changes in price (P). This inelastic demand curve produces a monotonically *increasing* response rate function. The pure case would have a negative slope with absolute value less than one when plotted in double logarithmic coordinates (elasticity coefficient, E.C., less than 1, see third column). The third case is a steeply sloping *elastic* demand curve that corresponds to a monotonically *decreasing* response rate function. In its pure form, this demand curve would have a negative slope with absolute value greater than one in log-log coordinates (E.C. greater than 1). The second case defines the boundary condition between *inelastic* and *elastic* demand, a demand curve with a negative slope equal to one, unit elasticity. Here, consumption decreases in equal proportion to increases in price, and the corresponding response rate function is constant.

These pure cases can be used to describe demand elasticity within the bounds of some practical situation. More often than not, the demand curve will not be linear in logarithmic space, and elasticity will vary along the extent of the demand curve, labelled here "mixed elasticity" (Figure 5, fourth row). In this case, the slope of the curve at each point determines its *point elasticity*. The case illustrated in the fourth row is a demand curve that is linear in arithmetic coordinates and nonlinear in logarithmic coordinates. The implied response rate function is bitonic, increasing along the inelastic portion of the demand curve and decreasing along the elastic portion. In the following sections, we will illustrate specific environmental conditions that influence elasticity including a case of mixed elasticity.

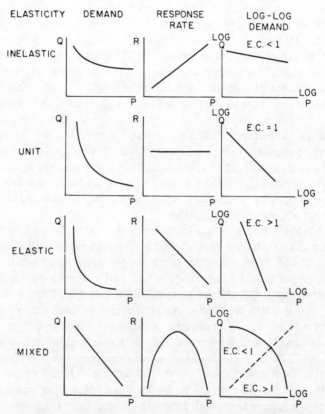

FIGURE 5. Definitions of inelastic, unit elastic, elastic, and mixed demand in terms of the demand curves, the response rate curves, and the elasticity coefficients of the log-log demand curves (see text for explanation).

VARIABLES INFLUENCING DEMAND

Different Commodities
Economists have long stipulated that all commodities are not equally important to the consumer. Some are more essential than others. Findley (1959) compared the work output per day by a monkey for food, water, and general illumination (light). Across conditions of the experiment, Findley increased the number of responses required for each reinforcer, using FR schedules of reinforcement in a manner analogous to the top panel of Figure 2. In the top panel of Figure 6, we see that consumption of food and water was much less sensitive to changes in price than was "consumption" of light. In the bottom panel, work output went up for food across all prices,

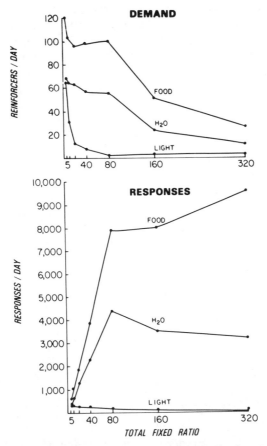

FIGURE 6. Demand curves and response output functions for food, water, and light by one monkey writing 24 hrs per day reported by Findley (1959).

indicating inelastic demand; work output for water increased to a point then decreased, indicating that demand shifted from being inelastic to elastic; and work output for light decreased across all prices, indicating consistently elastic demand. Notice that, when water and light were both cheap (FR 5), consumption of each was about equal, and their "values," measured as response output in this nearly free choice situation, were equivalent (see Premack, 1965). Nevertheless consumptions were not equally resistant to increases in price; as price increased, the slope of the light demand curve decreased much more rapidly than the slope of the water demand curve. This means that elasticity, a measure of performance change, is distinct from reinforcer "value," a measure of performance output in a single defining situation.

Findley (1959) measured demand by directly varying the price (FR schedule). Hursh and Natelson (1981) used interval schedules of reinforcement to compare demand by rats for food and reinforcing electrical brain stimulation (EBS). Figure 2, bottom panel, illustrates the use of interval schedules to determine a demand curve. Two rats lived individually in chambers containing two levers. One provided half-second trains of EBS; the other provided 45-mg food pellets. The schedules of reinforcement for each were

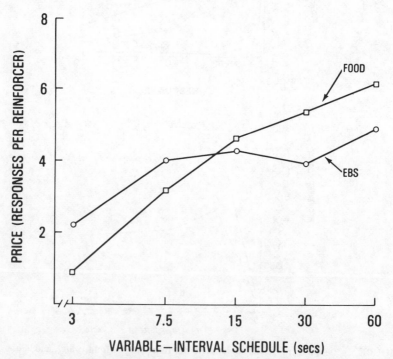

FIGURE 7.   Mean price (responses per reinforcer) emitted by three rats for electrical brain stimulation (EBS) and food as a function of the variable-interval schedules arranged concurrently for both reinforcers. Data reported by Hursh and Natelson (1981).

always equal VI schedules. The mean durations between available reinforcers was increased across conditions from 3 sec to 60 sec, with intermediate steps at 7.5, 15, and 30 seconds and a replication at 3 sec. This schedule does not set a specific price for each reinforcer but rather sets the maximum rate of consumption by limiting the average time between available reinforcers. Figure 7 shows, however, that, typically, as this time parameter increases it has the effect of increasing the measured price (responses per reinforcer). Figure 8 (top panel) shows the demand curves for each commodity based on these measured increases in price. Consumption of food decreased only slightly with increases in price (inelastic demand) while consumption of EBS decreased steeply across the same prices (elastic demand). As expected, response output for food increased across VI schedules while responding for EBS decreased (Figure 8, bottom panel).

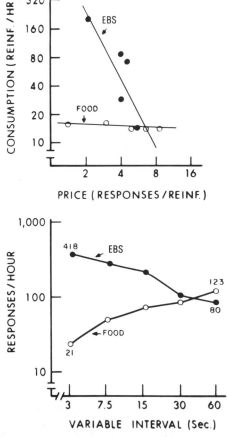

FIGURE 8.   Top panel: Mean demand curves from three rats for electrical brain stimulation (EBS) and food. Bottom panel: Mean response rates for the same subjects across VI schedules. Data reported by Hursh and Natelson (1981).

This experiment even more dramatically demonstrates the independence of demand elasticity and reinforcer value. Under the conditions of stimulation intensity and duration of this experiment, the subjects produced more EBS than food in nearly all conditions and emitted more responses for it; in that sense, the value of EBS was greater than food. Yet food consumption was defended at all costs, while consumption of EBS was readily surrendered under increasing prices; food demand was more inelastic than EBS demand.

Income

Income is a variable that can be used to reveal differences between the demand elasticity of "luxuries" and "necessities." When income is reduced, one's consumption of "luxuries" is reduced so that consumption of "necessities" can be preserved. Economists have explained this by noting that, when income goes down, all prices increase in terms of percent of income. If all prices go up (as in the previous example with food versus EBS), then consumption of elastic commodities ("luxuries") will decline more rapidly than consumption of inelastic commodities ("necessities").

To change income involves a change in some common variable required to obtain all commodities. For the human consumer, this is usually a reduc-

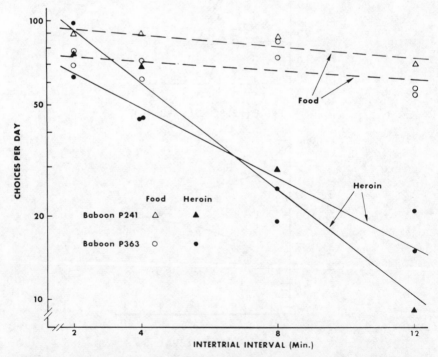

FIGURE 9.   Choices per day for food and heroin infusions as a functional intertrial interval (trials per day) by two baboons working 24 hrs per day. Data reported by Elsmore et al. (1980).

tion in available money income. A change in income for nonhuman subjects can be modelled by *limiting the opportunities to respond,* in the absence of a medium of exchange. Rachlin, Green, Kagel, and Battalio (1976) controlled income by limiting the total number of responses the subjects could emit during the test session. They explored the trade-off relationship between income and unit price. Their subjects did not maintain a constant intake under increasing unit price, even when the price increases were compensated for by increases in income. Price-induced decreases in consumption were greater for "luxuries" such as tom collins mix than for "necessities" such as food and water. They did not systematically study the effects of decreasing income independent of changes in price. Elsmore, Fletcher, Conrad, and Sodetz (1980) manipulated income by limiting the opportunities to make a choice between two commodities, food and heroin. Their results confirm the relations among income, elasticity, and demand. Two baboons living in test chambers had two pushbuttons, one that delivered food pellets and one that produced an infusion of heroin through a catheter. Intermittently throughout the day, lights came on behind the pushbuttons to indicate that a choice could be made. This was a "trial." Only one item, either food or heroin, was permitted during each trial. Income was reduced by reducing the number of trials per day (i.e., increasing the amount of time between trials). The price of each commodity in terms of responses per trial was equal for food and heroin, and was held constant across changes in income. Nevertheless, as trials per day were reduced, the baboons gave up more heroin choices than food choices, as shown in Figure 9. The dashed lines, indicating food choices, sloped downward much less steeply than the solid lines, indicating heroin choices. This would suggest that heroin was more of a "luxury" than was food and that demand for heroin was more elastic, even though the subjects were heroin-dependent and not food-deprived. Elsmore et al did not directly measure demand in this experiment, but, in another experiment with monkeys, he did vary FR schedules for heroin and food. As expected, consumption of heroin declined more steeply with price than did consumption of food, indicating greater demand elasticity (see Hursh, 1980, Figure 13).

Substitution

A major focus of behavior analysis has been the study of the relationship between response rate for one reinforcer and the availability of alternative reinforcers (e.g., Findley, 1958; Herrnstein, 1961; Catania, 1963, Chung & Herrnstein, 1967; de Villiers, 1977). Since these studies involve two or more responses and associated reinforcers, these experiments have been considered studies of "choice." These experiments have uncovered a variety of procedural variables that control choice, such as delay of reinforcement, rate of reinforcement, number of reinforcers, and cost of reinforcers. Unfortunately, almost all the experiments have used identical and perfectly substitutable reinforcers for all alternatives, a bit like studying consumer behavior in a store with only one product on the shelves. Economists have had a corresponding interest in consumer choice. Their focus has been an analysis of how the demand curve for one commodity is altered by the availability and price of alternative commodities. The economic analysis has stressed interactions among different commodities which may not be perfectly substitutable for each other. However, much of the economic analysis has been conducted in the absence of direct experimental manipulation of these interactions with individual consumers. In this section, we will discuss the experimental analysis of substitution effects on elasticity of demand.

Very few experiments have systematically varied levels of substitution and then mapped changes in demand or demand elasticity. Lea and Roper (1977) have reported changes in demand for food pellets as the price of the food was increased under three different situations: with no alternative food available, with sucrose available, or with identical food pellets available. Figure 10 shows the three demand curves for the test food across the three situations: empty compartment alternative; FR 8, sucrose alternative; and FR 8, identical mixed diet alternative. Considering the slope of the three demand curves between the two end points, FR 1 and FR 16, the elasticity of demand (slope of the function) was least for no alternative, greater with sucrose available, and greatest with identical food available. Elasticity of demand, then, is in part a function of the context, the availability of substitutes.

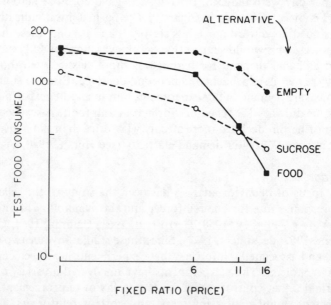

FIGURE 10.   The effect of the availability of alternatives to food on the demand for food. Two alternatives are a second food (squares) and sucrose (open circles). No alternative (solid circles) was a third condition. (Lea & Roper, 1979)

The change in elasticity in this experiment was not uniform, however. At low prices, i.e., between FR 1 and FR 6, the slope of the demand curve with the poor substitute, sucrose, was actually slightly greater than the slope of the demand curve with the perfect substitute, food pellets. This seemingly inconsistent result can actually be understood within the context of utility theory, which will be discussed later.

Another way to vary the degree of substitution is suggested by optimal foraging (Krebs, 1978; Krebs, Houston, & Charnov, 1980). One important factor determining the likelihood of leaving one patch of food and foraging in another is the travel cost—time and effort—involved in moving between the patches (Baum, 1982). In other words, identical food in another patch is not perfectly substitutable for food in the current patch if any significant amount of time must be spent in moving to the other patch. While travel might have other effects as well, one effect could be to change the substitutability relation between the two foods by imposing a temporal separation. Substitutability in this case might be inversely proportional to travel time. In behavioral experiments, this factor has been varied across a broad range, from simultaneously available alternatives requiring a travel time less than several seconds (concurrent schedules), to consecutively available alternatives requiring a "travel" time of a few minutes (multiple schedule), to a single alternative varied every few weeks (successive conditions of an experiment). Illustrations of data from each of these categories are displayed in Figure 11. In each experiment, the supply of food was controlled by ratio schedules. Shown in these examples is consumption (reinforcers per hour) from one schedule as its price relative to the available alternatives (if any) was increased. The slope of these demand curves indicates the general elasticity of demand. The dashed line indicates a slope of unit elasticity. A slope more negative than the dashed line indicates elastic demand; a slope less negative than that line indicates inelastic demand. The first case (Figure 11, panel A) is a representative function based on data from several experiments in which two sources of identical food were simultaneously available (concurrent schedules) and differed only in price (Green, Rachlin, & Hanson, 1983; Herrnstein & Loveland, 1975; Shrimp, 1973). Consumption of food from one alternative is plotted as a function of its price relative to the price of the other alternative. At a value of 0.5 on the x-axis, the two prices were equal. Above and below this point, consumption was exclusively from the source with lower price. As the price of one alternative was made greater than the price of the other, there was a rapid shift in consumption almost exclusively to the other, cheaper alternative. This steep transition is characteristic of a highly elastic demand curve.

In the second case (Figure 11, panel B), rats in our laboratory were provided identical food from two different schedules available at separate times (multiple schedule). Representative data from one subject are shown. The left and right levers of a two-lever test chamber were associated with two

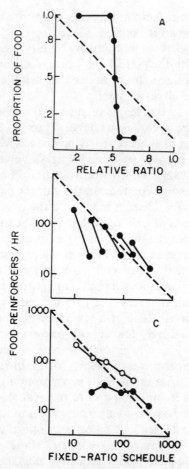

FIGURE 11. The effect on the elasticity of demand for food of increasing temporal separation between the opportunity to earn one food and the opportunity to earn food from a second source. Demand curves less steep than the dotted line are inelastic, and those more steep are elastic. *Panel A.* Demand curve representing shift in food consumption from one variable-ratio schedule to a second, concurrently-available variable-ratio schedule. *Panel B.* Each pair of connected points shows changes in consumption within a multiple FR,FR schedule in which the smaller ratio was always half the larger ratio. Absolute ratio size of both schedule components increases from left to right as conditions change. *Panel C.* Demand for food delivered at the lower ratios (open circles, upper points in B) and at higher ratios (closed circles, lower points in B). The points along a single function show consumptions *across* conditions.

different FR schedules with the value on the left always one-half the value on the right. Lights above the levers signalled when each was activated; periods of access to the left and right levers were 2 and 4 minutes, respectively, and alternated in irregular sequence. In each condition, a demand curve was constructed based on the two prices on the left and right levers and the two associated rates of food consumption. In successive conditions of the experiment, the value of both FR schedules were doubled from the previous condition. Five conditions were studied, giving five separate demand curves. Unlike the previous example in panel A with simultaneous presentation of food alternatives, consumption was not exclusively to the alternative with the lower price. Nevertheless, with sequential presentation of alternatives and a temporal separation of just several minutes, consumption was much greater from the lever with the lower price, and the demand curves were all elastic, with slopes greater than minus one. The elastic demand in Panel B implies that the response rate under the lower FR component exceeded that of the higher FR component, so that the subjects not only consumed more per hour under the lower FR but also made more responses per hour as well.

In the third case (Figure 11, panel C), these same values were replotted to show the demand curve for a particular lever *across conditions of the experiment*. In this case, consumption from one lever one week was a poor substitute for the consumption from that same lever the next week. The demand curves for the lower ratio lever (open circles) and the higher ratio lever (closed circles) both have slopes less than one, indicative of inelastic demand. In contrast to Panel B, the inelastic demands in Panel C imply that, at higher FRs, subjects consumed less per hour but responded at a higher rate.

These examples indicate that temporal separation modulates substitutability. These three cases parallel, in the first case, a comparison of prices for two identical items side-by-side in one store; in the second case, a comparison of prices for identical items in two different stores; and, in the third case, a comparison of prices for identical items across months of shopping, as might be produced by inflation. The shapes of the demand curves are consistent with the changes in substitutability caused by differences in temporal separation, ranging from a step-like vertical demand curve in the first case, to a steeply sloping elastic demand curve in the second, to a less steeply sloping inelastic demand curve in the third. Furthermore, the degree to which temporal separation effects substitutability may depend, in part, on the nature of the commodity itself. Heat, for example, is poorly stored, and even a small temporal separation might eliminate any substitution of one source for another. This would imply an inelastic demand curve under all conditions except those providing a simultaneous choice. Food, on the other hand, can be stored physiologically as fat or externally. Temporal separation does not prevent a large degree of substitution of one food source for another.

Open and Closed Economies
Substitution effects have been a factor in most previous behavioral studies with animals. Until recently, these experiments were conducted with the subjects made artificially hungry through a program of controlled food deprivation. This insured that the animals would emit high and steady levels

of responding during the test sessions, and eliminated weight and hunger as variables in the experiment. The usual procedure involved reducing the animals to about 80% of their free-feed weight (a safe procedure with the subjects used) and having them work for a small portion of their daily food in the experiment. However, this procedure usually required a supplemental ration of food after the test in the home cage to hold body weights constant, a substitutable source of reinforcement. None of these studies evaluated the economic impact of providing supplemental food to hold motivation constant.

This kind of procedure, in which the level of total daily consumption is independent of the level of responding and consumption during the session, has been labelled an *open economy* (Hursh, 1980). In more recent experiments, subjects have been studied under conditions that leave total daily

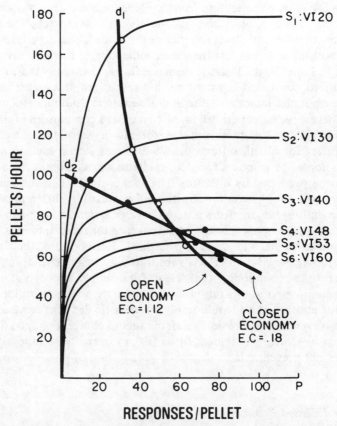

FIGURE 12.   Demand curves for food pellets determined with varying schedules in a closed economy (closed circles) and an open economy (open circles). Data are from Hursh (1978); computations are explained in legend of Figure 13.

consumption under the control of the subject's own adjustment to the schedule of reinforcement, either in limited test sessions (e.g., Hursh, 1978) or in live-in test environments (e.g., Collier, Hirsch & Hamlin, 1972; Collier, Hirsch, & Kanarek, 1977; Hursh & Natelson, 1981). This kind of arrangement has been labelled a *closed economy* (Hursh, 1980). As might be expected, changes in performance and consumption under variations in supply —schedule of reinforcement—are very different in the two types of economic context (Hursh, 1978, 1980). In general, elasticity of demand is high in an open economy, so that response rate decreases with increases in price (FR) or decreases in reinforcer density (VI). In contrast, elasticity of demand is low in a closed economy for an essential commodity like food, and response rate increases under similar increases in price or decreases in reinforcer density. A direct comparison of these two situations is shown in Figure 12. These demand curves were obtained by varying the variable-interval schedules for food across conditions with no other food available in the session (Hursh, 1978). In the closed economy, the demand curve has a negative slope of only 0.18, (inelastic) while in the open economy the demand curve has a negative slope of 1.12 (slightly elastic).[1] Figure 13 shows that the inelastic demand of the closed economy was associated with a dramatic increase in response rate across increases in VI schedule. The slightly elastic demand of the open economy was associated with a slight decline in response rate across the same range of VI schedules. (See, also, Catania, 1963b, and Catania & Reynolds, 1968, for similar results in an open economy.)

The difference between an open and closed economy may be understood as different cases of temporal separation modulating substitutability. An open economy is a kind of multiple schedule in which food is available from both the test session and, later, from the hand of the experimenter in the home cage. By contrast, the closed economy arranges a test session as a single schedule varied across conditions. As depicted for these two schedule arrangements in Figure 11, the temporal separation effect predicts generally more elastic demand in the multiple schedule, open economy, than in the single schedule, closed economy.

Mixed Elasticity
In the previous examples of elastic and inelastic demand (figure 12), we referred to the slope of the demand curve, its elasticity, as if it were a constant. Referring to Figure 5, recall that a demand curve that is linear when plotted in log-log coordinates has constant elasticity. For many demand curves, a linear approximation is accurate within a limited range of prices, as in the previous examples. Such is not the case when a broad range of

---

[1] In both cases, the slopes of the demand curves were estimated using a best-fit linear regression analysis applied to the log-transformed data, as is typical for the analysis of elasticity.

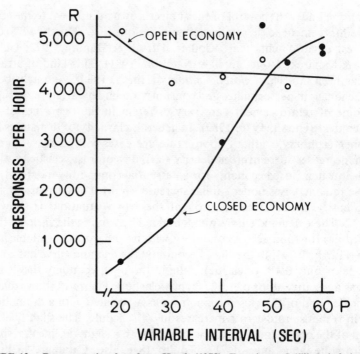

FIGURE 13. Representative data from Hursh (1978), Experiment I (filled circles) and Experiment II (open circles), showing response rate as a function of variable-interval schedules. Data were computed from the sum of responses to two concurrent VI schedules for food as a function of the average variable-interval between food pellets from both schedules.

prices is sampled, as in the two cases shown in Figure 14. Here, two monkeys earned their daily ration of food and water under FR schedules (closed economy). A wide range of FR schedules was used to study the relation between food and water consumption and the price of food. The FR schedule for water was constant at 10 presses. The baseline schedule for a concurrently available source of food was FR 10. When performance stabilized, the ratio for food was increased by 10% on successive days, up to a final value of 308. Because food consumption declined to between 1/5 and 1/8 of baseline levels, the FR was immediately returned to 10 following FR 308. The top two panels show the demand curves for food and the "cross-price" change in water consumption for the two monkeys. Approximate curves have been drawn through the points for clarity. It is evident that, even in these log-log coordinates, the demand curves for food were not linear throughout their extent and elasticity was "mixed." At low prices up to about FR 30, almost no change in consumption occurred and elasticity of demand was zero. At medium prices up to about FR 212, consumption declined but with a slope less than minus 1, inelastic demand. For high prices between FR 212 and FR

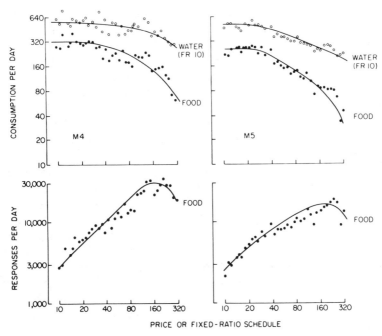

FIGURE 14. Demand curves with mixed elasticity (top panels) and the corresponding bitonic response rate functions (bottom panels) for each of two monkeys (left and right panels, respectively).

308, consumption declined more steeply and demand was elastic. These nonlinear demand curves yielded, in the bottom two panels, response rate functions that had an inverted U shape. Responding increased rapidly at first, leveled off, then took a sharp dip at very high prices. There is only a suggestion of the slope of the descending limb of the inverted U; further increases in price would have restricted food consumption to the point of posing a health hazard to the monkeys. Nevertheless, these demand curves illustrate the general case of nonlinear demand and mixed elasticities.

Figure 14 also shows the decreases in consumption of water that accompanied the increases in the price of food. This was a "cross-price" change in demand typical of a complementary relation between two commodities, the topic of the next section.

Cross Demand Relations
The previous sections have shown that substitution seems to be a major determiner of demand elasticity. The slope of a demand curve, its elasticity, was a function of the availability of substitutes as price was changed. We now consider how consumption of a constant price alternative varies with changes in the price of another commodity. It is precisely these changes

which indicate which alternatives in the context of all alternatives are substitutes, and which are not. Specifically, if the consumption of a constant alternative increases as the price of another increases, then we can say that the constant alternative substitutes for the one with increasing price. On the other hand, if the consumption of the constant alternative decreases, then we can say that it complements the one with increasing price. Together, these changes are referred to as "cross-price" shifts in demand.

Similar changes in demand can be observed by changing the rate of consumption or supply of one commodity and observing changes in the price that the subject is willing to pay for alternatives. Economists seldom consider this kind of cross demand relation separately, since changes in supply usually produce changes in price. We treat it separately here because interval schedules of reinforcement most directly alter the rate of consumption, and only secondarily alter price. Figure 7 illustrates how changes in an interval schedule can have the effect of changing price. An increase in supply is equivalent to a reduction in interval length and the associated price. If the supply of one commodity increases and the price paid for a constant alternative decreases, we can say that the constant alternative is a substitute. If, when the supply of one commodity increases, the price paid for a constant alternative also increases, then we can say that the constant alternative is a complement.

Hursh (1978) studied precisely these kinds of cross demand relations with two monkeys in a closed economy. The supply of one food was varied, and the prices paid for two constant alternatives were measured. One alternative was an identical food, and the other alternative was water. The experiment illustrated both a substitution effect for the identical food and a complementary effect for the water. Each monkey had available three levers, two of which provided access to food and a third which provided access to water. The supplies of food and water were controlled by VI schedules of reinforcement: one food and the water were constant at VI 60 sec access, while the second food alternative was a VI with mean value varied across conditions to allow relatively frequent access (VI 15 sec) at one extreme, relatively scarce access (VI 480 sec) at the other extreme, and four intermediate levels. Thus, the supply of one commodity was varied ("variable food") and expenditures for two alternatives was measured ("constant food" and "constant water"). Figure 15 shows the changes in price paid (responses per reinforcer) for the two constant alternatives (food, top panel; water, bottom panel) as the number of food pellets per hour from the variable food source was increased. In the top panel, we have depicted the changes in price paid for the constant food as the variable food supply was increased from zero pellets per hour to 58 per hour. The prices paid decreased and the equilibrium points moved from right to left. We have drawn in hypothetical demand curves to relate this figure to the diagram in Figure 1. Demand for one food decreased as the supply of a substitutable food was increased.

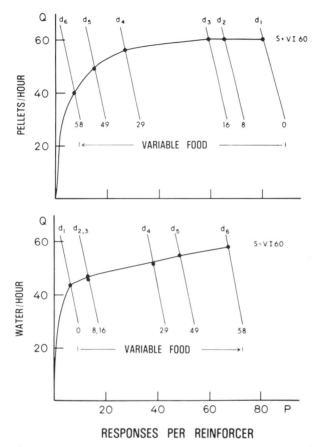

FIGURE 15.   Top panel: *Substitution*—reductions in demand for one food source (d_1, d_2, d_3, etc.) as a function of increases in the supply (and reductions in price) of a substitutable food source (8,16,29, etc. pellets per hr). Bottom panel: *Complementation*—increases in demand for water (d_1, d_2, d_3, d_4, etc.) as a function of increases in the supply (and reductions in price) of a complementary commodity—food. Data from Hursh (1978).

A quite opposite relation was found for the alternative water schedule, shown in the bottom panel of Figure 15. As the supply of the variable food schedule was increased, prices paid for water increased from left to right. Demand for this complement increased as the supply from the variable food source was increased.

In this experiment, the complete demand curves could not be drawn, since only one equilibrium point (supply schedule) was studied for each level of restriction of the variable commodity. Meisch and Thompson (1973) have reported more complete results of changes in food supply in relation to demand for ethanol. Figure 16 is a reanalysis of their data plotted in log-log coordinates. For each of two levels of food intake, seven prices (FR schedules) were arranged for sips of ethanol solution by rats. Food-satiated subjects had free access to food in their home cages. Food-deprived subjects were given just enough food in their home cages to maintain them at 80% of their free feeding weights. Two complete demand curves were observed and, as would be expected of substitutes, demand for ethanol was uniformly increased with restriction of food intake. Consumption of ethanol appeared to substitute for lost consumption of food.

Bernstein and Ebbesen (1978) reported substitution effects which did not occur along a physiological dimension. In this multiple baseline study (Dunham, 1971), a variety of activities such as reading, sewing, artwork, and candlemaking were available to human volunteers who were confined to a laboratory apartment 24 hours per day. During a baseline period of unrestricted access, time spent engaging in each of the activities was recorded. One activity was then artificially restricted so that the baseline amount of this activity was no longer available. It was found that the newly available

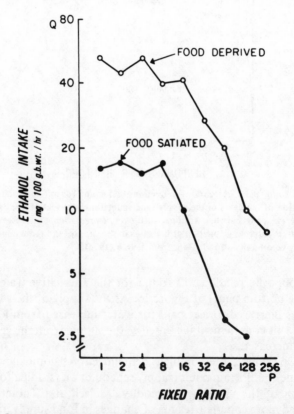

FIGURE 16.   Increase in demand for ethanol when shifted from a food satiated baseline to a food deprived baseline. Data from Meisch and Thompson (1973) replotted in log-log coordinates.

time was not redistributed uniformly to all the remaining activities, but was selectively distributed to certain specific alternatives depending on which activity was restricted. For example, when reading was restricted, artwork increased but candelmaking did not. These selective increases in time engaged in one activity as the availability of another was restricted was taken as evidence for a relatively greater substitution relation between the activities.

In this example with humans, the substitution observed did not seem to be based on any biological "need" but was based on some property of the individual's experience, what might be described by economists as a "psychological" effect. The one example of complementarity between food and water described earlier (Figure 15, bottom panel; see Hursh, 1978) clearly could have been based on some biological process, since the levels of consumption of food and water did vary conjointly as a function of supply and price. The subjects may have been responding to defend some preferred ratio of food and water, or "water balance" (Bolles, 1961; Collier & Knarr, 1966; Kutscher, 1969). More recently, that experiment was repeated with a procedural change that held the consumption ratios constant across a wide range of changes in responding. The purpose was to see if complementary changes in food and water responding would occur if the overall consumption of food and water were constant. Food could be obtained by pressing either of two levers, and water could be obtained by pressing a third lever. The supply of both food and water was regulated by three equal VI schedules. Because some responding was maintained by each schedule, the overall consumption of food and water remained roughly constant as the cost of one food was increased. Cost was manipulated by requiring an additional fixed ratio of leverpresses, a "tax," once food was made available by one of the food VI schedules. The untaxed food supply and water were unavailable during the time that the fixed ratio was being completed. This time, however, was excluded from the total session time, and so did not reduce the time available for the consumption of food or water. The size of this tax, the FR value, was increased across conditions, and the changes in price paid during the VI schedules for the constant water alternative was measured. In Figure 17, we have plotted this change in demand in terms analogous to Figure 15. The lines d_1 through d_6 are hypothetical demand curves for water which show that, as the tax on the target food schedule increased from FR 1 (beneath d_1) to FR 240 (beneath d_6), the price paid for water decreased and demand decreased (moved to the left). This decrease occurred despite the fact that overall consumption of food and water remained invariant except at the highest tax of FR 240. In this study, the complementary relation between food and water was therefore not physiologically forced by the dependence of water consumption on food consumption (cf. Rachlin & Krasnoff, 1983). Complementarity is, as economists have long taken for granted, a fundamental form of interaction among different reinforcers (Rachlin, Kagel, & Battalio, 1980; cf. Herrnstein, 1974).

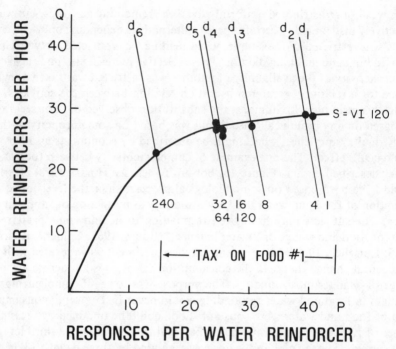

FIGURE 17.   Decreased responses per water reinforcer, and decreased water consumption $(d_1 \rightarrow d_2 \rightarrow d_3 \rightarrow d_4 \rightarrow d_5 \rightarrow d_6 \rightarrow)$ as the fixed ratio of leverpresses (tax) required for the delivery of a concurrently available source of food, was increased. Each fixed ratio was required after food was made available by a VI 120-sec schedule.

THE ORIGIN OF DEMAND

Constraint, Choice, and Utility

So far, the concept of substitution has been applied intuitively to explain general variations in demand elasticity and response rate based on the economic context. Elasticity of demand is said to increase as the economic context provides closer substitutes to the commodity under study. Substitutes may be concurrently available approximations to the test commodity, or they may be time-delayed opportunities to obtain the same commodity. In either case, the theoretical mechanism for the action of substitutes on demand and response rate remains to be specified. In this section, the basics of the theory of consumer demand will be used to explain the origin of the demand curve and the effect of substitution on elasticity of demand and response rate.

The classical theory of consumer behavior conceives of demand in a context of choice. In the limit, the geometry of this context is a consumption space partitioned by a very large number of axes along which are scales for

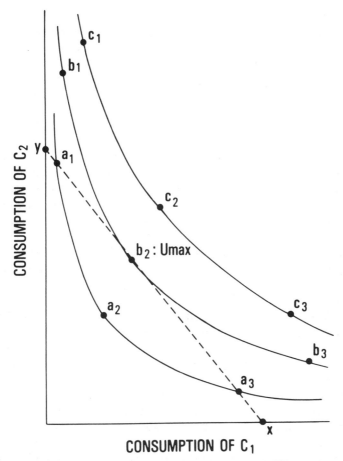

FIGURE 18.   In the space between the C_1 and C_2 axes are three indifference curves, and a constraint line which intersects with the C_1 and C_2 axes at x and y. x amount of C_1 will be consumed if no income is spent on C_2, and conversely, y amount of C_2 will be consumed if no income is spent on C_1. Where the contraint line and the highest indifference curve are tangent, utility is maximized, U_{max}.

individual commodities. Certain axioms of demand theory allow individual commodities to be aggregated so that the degenerate form of the consumption space is two axes. Along one is plotted the consumption of the target commodity, and along the other is plotted the consumption of all other commodities. In Figure 18, the vertical axis scales the consumption of the target commodity, C_2, and the horizontal axis scales an aggregate of consumption of all other commodities. In laboratory studies of the consumption space, C_1 is commonly defined as activities other than work for commodity C_2, or, in other words, "leisure" with respect to C_2. The units of the commodity space are, then, along the x-axis, time spent not working for C_2

(total time minus time spent working), and, along the y-axis, time spent consuming C_2. Each point in the consumption space represents some combination of time spent consuming C_2 and time spent in other activities, C_1.

In any real situation, constraints exist that make certain combinations inaccessible. One constraint is the tradeoff relation between C_1 and C_2, how much leisure must be given up to obtain a certain level of consumption of C_2. The fixed-ratio schedule is one such tradeoff (see Green, Kagel, & Battalio, 1982). It specifies that, for any level of C_2 consumption, a certain amount of responding must be expended. That responding required for C_2 precludes consumption of other commodities within the context, C_1. This ratio constraint is represented by the line x–y. To obtain increasing amounts of C_2, a certain proportional amount of leisure, C_1, must be forfeited. A ratio constraint is a line with negative slope equal to the inverse of the ratio itself. When total time is spent responding for C_2 and no C_1 is consumed, level y of C_2 is earned. When total time is spent responding for commodities in the context and no C_2 is earned, level x of C_1 is earned.[2] To predict which combination of C_1 and C_2 a subject will choose from among the set of available combinations, x–y, requires a decision criterion. Utility theory provides one such criterion. Let's suppose that the combination of C_1 and C_2 consumptions represented by a_2 has some total value or utility. There are other points within this space that represent other combinations which have that same total utility. Points a_1 and a_3 represent other such combinations and the curve drawn through them connects all points in this space having that same level of utility. This curve is called an indifference contour. Other indifference contours may be drawn at different distances from the origin, representing different levels of utility. Points b_1, b_2, and b_3 lie on another indifference contour with total utility equal along its extent and higher in utility than the curve connecting a_1, a_2, and a_3. It is assumed that, given a choice between any combination of consumptions on the a curve and any combination on the b curve, a subject will choose one on the b curve. Given a choice between any two points on one curve, the subject would be, of course, indifferent, the defining property of the curve.

Given a set of choices between accessible combinations of C_1 and C_2 along line x–y, for example, a_1, b_2, and a_3, the subject will choose that combination on the higher utility contour, b_2. That point is also the point of maxi-

---

[2] In the current example, the constraint line is referred to as the "budget line" by economists. A more general mathematical form of the constraint line is what researchers in behavioral psychology refer to as the "feedback function," i.e., the rate of reinforcement provided by a schedule of reinforcement as a function of response rate (Baum, 1973; Rachlin & Burkhard, 1978; Staddon & Motheral, 1978; Heyman & Luce, 1979; Prelec & Herrnstein, 1978; Prelec, 1982; Nevin & Baum, 1980). In addition, the feedback function is methematically related to the supply schedule shown in Figures 1 and 2. In that case, the x-axis is price paid rather than response rate or leisure expended, but a simple transformation would make them equivalent (Hursh, 1980, pg. 222).

mum utility, U_{max}, since it is the one combination that just touches the higher indifference contour and thus yields the highest possible utility. Points on the c contour have higher utility but are inaccessible given the constraint represented by line. x–y. The U_{max} point (b_2) is equivalent to the equilibrium point shown in Figure 1, the level of consumption observed under the constraint of one supply schedule, line x–y.

Substitution and Elasticity

The shape of the indifference contour determines the exact point of tangency and maximum utility. As one moves along an indifference contour, say from b_1 to b_3, some amount of C_2 is given up and some amount of C_1 is substituted to hold total utility constant. Since total utility remains constant, we can say that the utility gained from C_1 equals the utility lost from C_2. To that degree, the two are substitutes. Notice that, in the region of the curve from b_1 to b_2, it takes a small amount of C_1 to make up for a large loss of C_2. Just the opposite is true moving from b_2 to b_3. These curves, then, represent by their shape the nature of substitution between C_1 and C_2. As we will see later, the straighter the contours, the more similar (substitutable) are the two commodities.

Suppose that we vary the slope of the constraint line across conditions of the experiment by varying the FR value. These variations in FR constraint specify how much of all other commodities, C_1, must be traded for any given level of consumption of C_2. Since a loss of C_1 is measured as an increase in work for C_2, then each FR constraint is equivalent to the *price* of C_2, responses per reinforcer. Variations in the price of C_2 are represented in the top panel of Figure 19. Price increases as one moves from line P_1 to line P_6 (price is inversely proportional to slope). For each constraint a different U_{max} (filled points) and a certain level of consumption, Q_1 to Q_6, is observed. As expected, as price increases, consumption of C_2 decreases. Connecting the U_{max} points gives us a *price-consumption* curve, levels of consumption of both C_2 and C_1 associated with each price constraint. The price–consumption curve relates the price of a commodity to the levels of consumption that have maximum utility. The price–consumption curve conveys the same information described by the demand curve for that one commodity. The bottom panel of Figure 19 is a demand curve generated by plotting the consumption levels, Q_1 to Q_6, as a function of the prices, P_1 to P_6, connected by the price–consumption curve in the top panel. (See Appendix 1 for a mathematical derivation of the demand curve from the constraint line and the point of maximum utility.)

To understand how *elasticity* of demand is controlled by substitution, we need to consider more closely the factors that determine the shape of the price–consumption curve. It is that shape which determines the slope of the demand curve. Referring again to the top panel of Figure 19, notice that the price–consumption curve is based on the tangent points between the con-

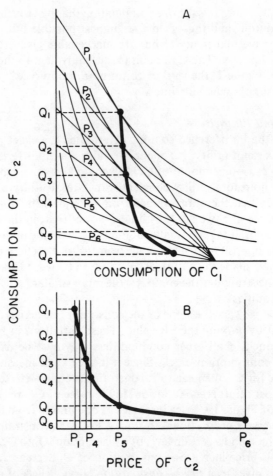

FIGURE 19. In Panel A, the points of tangency between individual FR constraint lines (budget lines) radiating from the C_1 axis and one of the six indifference curves are connected to form a curve of optimal consumption (dark line). At each unit price of C_2, the optimal consumption of C_2 in indicated, i.e., Q_1, Q_2, Q_3, etc. In panel B, the optimal consumptions (Q_1, Q_2, Q_3, etc.) are plotted above each price, and the connected points form the optimal demand curve for C_2 (see Appendix I).

straint lines and the indifference contours. The location of those points depends entirely on the shape of the contours, since the constraint lines are determined by the procedure of the experiment. The indifference contours are usually thought of as a family of curves based on a general utility function. The specifications of that function are debatable; we do not as yet have enough data to single out one function as more useful or representative than another (see Rachlin, Kagel, & Battalio, 1980; Staddon, 1979). For the purposes of this chapter, we have chosen a simple form suggested by Rachlin, Kagel, and Battalio (1980):

$$U = x_1 Q_1{}^y + x_2 Q_2{}^y \qquad (1)$$

This function states that the Value, U, of any contour is the sum of the consumption levels of the two commodities, Q_1 and Q_2, each raised to a power, y, and each weighted by a factor, x_1 and x_2, respectively. The exponent, y, determines the shape of the contours; x_1 and x_2 are scaling factors which determine the location of the contours in utility space based on the relative size of each unit of C_1 and C_2.

Since y determines the shape of the contours, it also may be thought of as representing the substitution relation between C_1 and C_2. For example, when y is equal to 1.0, then the contours are straight lines running diagonally, with negative slope equal to the ratio of the reinforcer sizes, x_1/x_2. If x_1 equals x_2 (as with identical food pellets of constant size), then, no matter where one starts on the contour, one can precisely compensate for a loss of C_1 with an equal gain of C_2. Each contour would represent a simple sum of the reinforcers from sources C_1 and C_2, and points along each contour would represent different combinations of C_1 and C_2 that sum to the total represented by that contour.

Less than perfect substitutability between C_1 and C_2 is represented by exponents, y, less than 1.0. The easiest way to appreciate the relationship between substitutability, y, and demand elasticity is to graph examples similar to Figure 19 based on different values of y. Figure 20 depicts five examples, ranging from perfect substitution, $y = 1.0$, to independence, $y = 0.0$, to complementarity, $y = -\infty$. In the four columns of this figure, we have summarized the major functions considered so far and their interrelationships based on utility theory. The four functions are the price–consumption curve, the demand curve, the cross demand relation, and response rate. The axes for these four functions are labelled in the legend at the bottom of the figure.

Consider first the price–consumption curves and the corresponding demand curves for commodity C_2, the first two columns. It is clear that, for this utility function, as y approaches zero, the slope of the demand curve decreases from nearly vertical (highly elastic) to a slope of -1.0, unit elasticity. When y is negative, elasticity of demand decreases further to a curve that is highly inelastic at $y = -\infty$. In other words, as commodity C_2 becomes less and less like anything else available in the context, demand becomes more and more inelastic. (See Appendix II for the mathematical definition of elasticity in terms of the utility function.)

The derivation of the demand curve from a more general framework of choice within a context of many commodities is very similar in logic to Herrnstein's (1970, 1974) derivation of the law of simple action from the

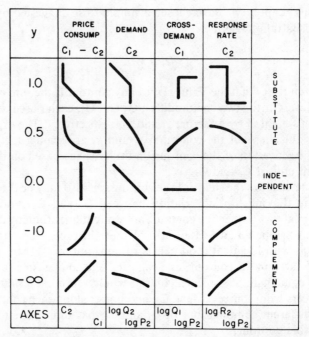

y	PRICE CONSUMP $C_1 - C_2$	DEMAND C_2	CROSS-DEMAND C_1	RESPONSE RATE C_2	
1.0					S U B S T I T U T E
0.5					
0.0					INDE-PENDENT
-10					C O M P L E M E N T
-∞					
AXES	C_2 C_1	$\log Q_2$ $\log P_2$	$\log Q_1$ $\log P_2$	$\log R_2$ $\log P_2$	

FIGURE 20. Five values for *y* appear in column one. Along each row, the price consumption curve, demand curve for C_2, cross demand curve, and response rate function for C_2 are drawn for each value of *y*. The axes labels for each column are shown along the last row. Down the last column are the regions of substitution, independence, and complementarity associated with the y values in column one.

matching law of choice within a context of many reinforcers. The economic approach is more general in the sense that it can accommodate demand for commodities that have varying substitutability relationships with the commodities in the context, whereas the original statement of the law of simple action rested on an assumption of perfect substitutability among all commodities. More recent extensions of that matching law have added parameters which could accommodate varying degrees of substitutability (Baum, 1974; Davison & Tustin, 1978) but, as Rachlin, Kagel, and Battalio (1980; see also Appendix I) point out, such an extension is easily derived from the principles of constraint and utility and, in fact, may make most sense within a broader economic framework.

Theoretical demand curves based on changes in the substitution parameter, *y*, square well with the actual data presented in Figures 10 and 11. In Figure 11, elasticity of demand decreased with increases in temporal separation between the substitutable alternatives. In Figure 10, based on the Lea and Roper (1977) experiment, elasticity of demand increased with increasingly similar alternatives parallel to the top three panels of the second column of

THEORETICAL DEMAND

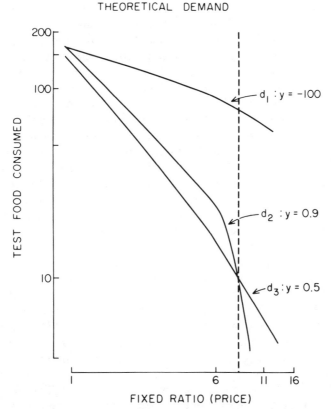

FIGURE 21.   Three values of y (-100, 0.90, 0.50) and Eq 3b (from Appendix I) were used to plot three hypothetical demand curves which appeared similar in shape to those reported by Lea and Roper (1977), shown here as Figure 10.

Figure 20. Those demand curves were troublesome for Lea and Roper because elasticity of demand was not *always* greatest for the case involving nearly perfect substitutes, particularly at low prices of food. That result is actually consistent with the predicted demand curves based on the utility function used here. Figure 21 shows three demand curves plotted on the same axes as Figure 10, but based, instead, on three hypothetical price–consumption curves associated with substitution constants, y, of 0.9, 0.5, and -100. When substitution is low, the demand curve is nearly horizontal (d_1). When substitution is high, as between the identical foods in the Lea and Roper experiment, the demand curve becomes nonlinear (d_2). This sharply bent demand curve makes intuitive sense. At prices less than the alternative food (FR 8, to the left of the dashed line), consumption will be little affected by the availability of the identical but more costly alternative. Changes in consumption in this range of prices are dictated strictly by the increasing price within a context of limited income. As soon as price exceeds that of the alternative (to the right of the dashed line), consumption shifts entirely to the other source of food, and the demand curve plummets to zero.[3] This step-like effect does not occur with intermediate substitutes (d_3), such as food and sucrose. At prices of food below that of the alternative (to the left of the dashed line), elasticity will actually be greater in comparison to sucrose than in comparison to another identical food. Although the food is cheaper than sucrose, it does not totally substitute for it; for example, it doesn't taste sweet. Increases in the price of food will shift some consumption to sucrose, increasing elasticity in that range of prices. For prices of food above that of sucrose (to the right of the dashed line), consumption does not go to zero, because sucrose does not totally substitute for food; for example, it doesn't contain many needed nutrients. These theoretical curves closely approximate the actual curves in Figure 10, and provide one explanation for the "inconsistencies" described by Lea and Roper.

Derivation of Cross Demand Relations

The price–consumption curve contains information about consumption of C_1 as well as C_2, and, in that sense, conveys more information than a demand curve. In particular, it is possible to draw cross demand changes in consumption of C_1 as a function of price changes for C_2. Those curves are shown in the third column of Figure 20. Comparing the changes in consumption of C_2 to the comparable changes in consumption of C_1, we see that, for positive values of y (e.g., 1.0 and 0.5), consumption of C_1 goes up as consumption of C_2 is driven down by its price. This is indicative of a substitutable relation between C_1 and C_2. When y is negative (e.g., -10 and $-\infty$), consumption of C_1 varies in the same direction as consumption of C_2, indicative of a complementary relation. In fact, in the hypothetical case of $y = -\infty$, the two consumptions parallel each other perfectly and the ratio of consumptions of C_1 and C_2 is constant. Finally, when y is zero, consumption of C_1 is unaffected by changes in consumption of C_2 and, in this sense, C_1 is independent of C_2. These cross demand effects have been discussed earlier and are shown in Figure 15 and 17. Again, the extrapolations from utility theory agree with the empirical results.

Demand and Response Rate

As indicated in Figure 5, response rate or expenditure functions are strictly related to the demand curves. In Figure 20, the right-most column of curves shows response rate for C_2 as a function of its price. When y is positive,

---

[3] Perfect substitutability would imply $y = 1.0$ and would produce a demand curve that makes a discrete transition to zero precisely at FR 8. We have used a $y = 0.9$ since the two foods were spatially and temporally separated and, therefore, not perfectly substitutable. This yields a steep but continuous transition to zero in the vicinity of FR 8.

indicating a substitutable relation to the context, response rate for C_2 decreases with increases in price. When y is negative, indicating a complementary relation to the context, response rate for C_2 increases with increases in price. Finally, when y is zero, indicating independence from the context, response rate is constant across changes in price.

These relationships have been confirmed in a number of laboratory experiments. Herrnstein and Loveland (1975) have shown that, when relative price of one food source is varied in comparison to an identical food alternative, the responding for one tends to be a step function of its price relative to the alternative. When its price is less than the alternative, responding is exclusively for it; when its price is greater than the alternative, there is little or no responding for it. This corresponds closely to the response rate function in Figure 20 with y equal to 1.0 (see Figure 11, Panel A; see also Green, Rachlin, & Hanson, 1983).

In a number of other experiments in which the price of food was varied in a context that contained complements such as water (e.g., Hursh, 1978; Collier, Hirsch, & Hamlin, 1972), response rate increased uniformly with increases in price. These results correspond to negative values of y.

Few experiments have explored reinforcers that are truly independent of the context where y equals zero. One possible exception is Hursh and Natelson (1981), described earlier. Recall that rats worked for both electrical brain stimulation and food on two simultaneously available levers. At one point in the study, the intensity of brain stimulation was increased by a factor of 2.5 for the remainder of the study. This change had a dramatic effect on the level of demand and response rate for brain stimulation. Yet it had virtually no effect on the level or elasticity of demand for food or responding to obtain food. While this study demonstrated a high degree of independence of food responding from the level of demand for brain stimulation, it was not entirely consistent with the theoretical demand curves shown in Figure 20. The elasticity of demand for brain stimulation was much greater than unit elasticity corresponding to a y value of zero (see Figure 8, top panel).

FUTURE DIRECTIONS

The observation that the same event can have different effects at different times has led psychologists and economists alike to look to the environmental context for the explanation. Substitution and complementarity are context effects modulating motivation which are extraordinarily important for a complete theory of behavior. Under one set of circumstances, such as an open economy where substitution is allowed to occur and demand is elastic, response output declines with decreases in the size or rate of reinforcement and increases in price. Under another set of circumstances, such as a closed economy where substitutes are not available, the very same change in reinforcement or price will produce an increase in response output (see Figure 5; Hursh, 1980).

The practical significance of this effect is clear. One could not predict that a fourfold increase in the price of gasoline would produce only a 10% reduction in consumption without considering that there are few, if any, acceptable substitutes for gasoline. Imagine the effect on movie attendance of a fourfold increase in the price of a theatre ticket. Given the broad array of comparable substitutes, such a change would be disastrous for the movie industry. Yet movie producers have attempted to preserve an audience in the face of rising prices by reducing the substitutability of other forms of entertainment. Large screen special effects, stereo and Dolby sound, and explicit sex all serve to distinguish movies from the closest competition, the television. Not surprisingly, the television industry has responded to close the gap with large screen television projectors, subscription television with "adult" subject matter, and, soon, stereo sound.

These are the obvious effects of substitution, the ones economists have long discussed. A behavioral analysis suggests that these "economic" variables may operate with all choices and for each individual and, furthermore, provides a methodology for studying the effects of these variables on individuals. This leads to a consideration of substitution effects at a more subtle level. Could substitution explain differences in impact of the same therapy for inpatients and outpatients? For the inpatient, few substitutes for the social approval from the therapist are available; for the outpatient, an array of family and community substitutes may be available. Could complementarity explain the covariance of certain social rituals and alcoholism, or the increase in smoking among women as more women move into the business world? An understanding of these "economic" factors may aid our understanding of significant patterns of behavior, and could even point the way to amelioration of their important health effects. (See Volume 2 in this series for some of this.)

Much of this remains speculative until the full spectrum of substitution effects are explored in the laboratory. In Appendix I, we extrapolate one theoretical road map for this exploration. Figure 22 is a three-dimensional portrayal of the relationship between the substitution parameter, y, and the level and elasticity of demand. The downward sloping curves between the consumption and price axes are demand curves. This figure shows that the downward curvature (elasticity) of the demand curves is modulated by the y dimension, substitutability. With negative values of y, the curves slope gradually and are inelastic (the left-hand portion of the surface). With positive values of y, the curves slope more steeply and are elastic (the right-hand portion of the surface). At present, we have only scant data about this theoretical surface, primarily at the extremes of substitution and complemen-

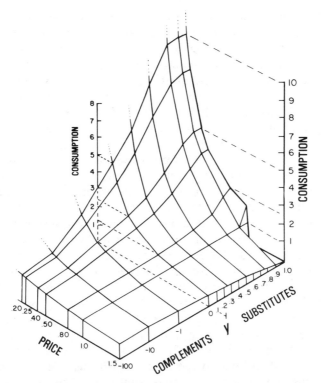

FIGURE 22.   Consumption of commodity two is plotted as a function of price at each of nine *y* values. The resulting demand curves were connected to form a consumption surface which is divided at *y* = 0 (independence) into regions of substitution and complementarity. The dotted lines project from the demand curve at 0 onto the left consumption axis and from the demand curve at 1.0 onto the right consumption axis.

tarity. One direction for future research will be to explore the intermediate cross sections of this space by manipulating the number and kind of commodities available within the context. The result of such an endeavor would be, on the one hand, to verify the usefulness of the theory itself and, on the other hand, to describe specific cross demand relations and test their trans-situational generality.

A corollary of this theme is the relationship between temporal separation and substitutability. Choices are not usually made in the abstract, disconnected from time and space. Whether to purchase a car from one dealer or another has as much to do with timing and opportunity as it has with such "rational" factors as cost, function, and reliability. One may readily choose a more expensive car because it is available now and is close by. In this sense, temporal separation and substitutability are related to issues of "self-control" (see Rachlin & Green, 1972; Green, 1982). Choices often involve a trade-off between the quality or amount of reinforcement and delays to obtain them (Green & Snyderman, 1980; Navarick & Fantino, 1976). These factors are no more "psychological" than the concept of substitution is "economic." Factors such as temporal separation, what ethologists call "search" and "travel" costs (Kaufman & Collier, 1981; Kaufman, 1979), and what psychologists have called "changeover" costs (Baum, 1982) are all related to variations in substitutability and may be understood in the context of variations in the demand curve. Together they are an important concept for a theory of behavior.

Earlier, we speculated that the difference between open and closed econmies may be understood as an example of differences in temporal separation, with the open economy arranging a relatively brief separation between the test commodity and substitutes outside the experiment. This analysis suggests, then, that the open–closed distinction is not categorical but, rather, defines extremes of a continuum of openness and closedness. An understanding of open and closed economies will be achieved when we isolate the variable that moves a test environment between the two extremes.

Finally, we will have to consider the nature of the commodities themselves. It is likely, for example, that not all commodities support the open-closed distinction. Electrical brain stimulation displays a highly elastic demand curve even when studied in a closed economy. It is unlikely that arranging an "open" economy of brain stimulation would make demand any more elastic. Other reinforcers that support inelastic demand curves may not be susceptible to modulation by substitutes. One example is heat. Subjects will work to maintain a comfortable ambient temperature (Weiss & Laties, 1960), and this process may support an inelastic demand curve if a very cold environment would prevail otherwise. Subjects might show substitution between simultaneously available sources of heat, but it is likely that even a small temporal separation will eliminate any substitution effect. Heat as a reinforcer is poorly stored; substitution across a temporal separation presumes some capacity to maintain an adequate supply of the commodity during the period of transition.

SUMMARY

Laboratory experimentation based on behavioral analysis is the most powerful method for defining, testing, and refining economic theory. In this chapter, we have reviewed behavioral methods as applied to nonhuman laboratory animals and have shown how economic theory can accommodate those results. This enterprise benefits economists by providing controlled laboratory methodology and a precise language for analysis of the behavior of individual subjects; psychologists benefit by gaining access to a broad theoretical framework formulated by economists.

The most basic concept is the equilibrium of supply and demand. Supply is experimentally controlled by a schedule of reinforcement. Demand is determined by the level of consumption observed across a range of prices. Response rate is determined by the equilibrium point at each price. If the demand curve decreases slowly with increases in price (inelastic demand), then response rate will increase with increasing price; if the demand curve decreases rapidly with increases in price (elastic demand), then response rate will decrease with increasing price.

The slope of the demand curve, its elasticity, is controlled by the nature of the target commodity itself, by the context of available substitutes and complements, by the temporal separation between the target commodity and alternatives, and by the nature of the economic system, open or closed.

Cross demand relations are manifest as changes in the consumption of alternatives as a result of changes in the price or supply of the target commodity. If consumption of an alternative increases as the price (FR schedule) of the target commodity increases, then we say that the alternative is a substitute. On the other hand, if consumption of an alternative decreases with increasing price of the target commodity, then we say that it is a complement. Similar distinctions may be made by altering the supply (VI schedule) of the target commodity and observing changes in the price paid for alternatives. These interactions may be physiologically based, as with changes in food consumption altering demand for water (see Figure 15), or they may be based on less obvious mechanisms, as when artwork increases with a decrease in time allowed for reading (Bernstein & Ebbesen, 1978).

Differences in demand elasticity and cross demand relations may be theoretically derived from an analysis of the environmental constraints limiting the available combinations of activities and a choice criterion based on maximization of utility within the set of available alternatives. The central premises of this theory are a consumption space (Figure 18) showing the universe of potential activities, the constraint line showing the set of available combinations of activities, and the indifference contours which show those combinations of activities with equal value or utility. The tangent of the constraint line to the highest indifference contour specifies the point of theoretically maximum utility, and predicts the observed equilibrium point. The curvature of the indifference contours represents the degree of mutual substitutability between the two commodities, or the target commodity and the context of alternatives. This shape is determined by the utility function and the value of its parameters.

By varying the constraint line to reflect changes in a typical FR schedule, one can construct a theoretical price–consumption curve. This, in turn, leads to a presentation of the demand curve based on the utility function chosen and the value of its parameters. The exponent of the utility function (y) alters the curvature of the contours and denotes differences in substitutability between the two commodities or the target commodity and the context. This substitutability parameter directly controls the elasticity of the predicted demand curve, with positive exponents less than or equal to one indicative of elastic demand, negative exponents indicative of inelastic demand, and a zero exponent indicative of unit elasticity. These predicted demand curves are surprisingly consistent with the small set of available data.

Cross demand relations are also predicted by utility theory, with positive values of y indicative of substitutes, negative values indicative of complements, and a value of zero indicative of independent commodities. Again, the available data appear consistent with these predictions.

Utility theory provides a basis for describing the relations between performance (or demand) for one commodity, and the type and amount of available alternatives, the context. This theory embraces many of the same factors that have led psychologists to propose choice theories such as the generalized matching law. The economic framework provides a unique interpretation of the functional significance of matching in terms of substitution and complementarity (see Rachlin, Kagel, & Battalio, 1980). Furthermore, it provides a connection between a general choice theory (utility maximization) and elasticity of demand, a predictor of the absolute response rate function. Few behavioral theories of choice have been extended to account for changes in absolute response rate (cf. Herrnstein, 1970; Rachlin, 1973), and none have the same breadth of applicability. None of the accounts based on matching can accommodate an inelastic demand curve, i.e., an inverse relation between the quantity of reward and absolute rate of response (Timberlake, 1977; Hursh, 1980; Hursh & Natelson, 1981) or complementarity, i.e., a direct relation between the quantity of one reward and absolute rate of response for an alternative reward (Hursh, 1978, 1980).

While economic theory has made a substantial contribution to the theoretical framework for describing choice, demand, and absolute response rate, behavioral analysis and laboratory methods provide an unparalleled empirical basis for these concepts at the level of individual subjects. While much remains to be done, we have enough data now to be assured that economic concepts originally conceived by observation of whole markets can have relevance for understanding changes in the behavior of individuals.

REFERENCES

Baum, W. (1973). The correlation based law of effect. *Journal of the Experimental Analysis of Behavior, 20,* 137–153.

Baum, W. (1974). On two types of deviation from the matching law: Bias and undermatching. *Journal of the Experimental Analysis of Behavior, 22,* 231–242.

Baum, W. (1982). Choice, changeover, and travel. *Journal of the Experimental Analysis of Behavior, 38,* 35–50.

Bernstein, D., & Ebbesen, E. (1978). Reinforcement and substitution in humans: A multiple-response analysis. *Journal of the Experimental Analysis of Behavior, 30,* 243–253.

Bolles, R.C. (1961). The interaction of hunger and thirst in the rat. *Journal of Comparative and Physiological Psychology, 54,* 580–584.

Catania, A.C. (1963a). Concurrent performances: Reinforcement interactions and response independence. *Journal of the Experimental Analysis of Behavior, 6,* 253–263.

Catania, A.C. (1963b). Concurrent performances: A baseline for the study of reinforcement magnitude. *Journal of the Experimental Analysis of Behavior, 6,* 299–300.

Catania, A.C., & Reynolds, G.S. (1968). A quantitative analysis of the behavior maintained by interval schedules of reinforcement. *Journal of the Experimental Analysis of Behavior, 11,* 327–383.

Chung, S.-H. (1965). Effects of delayed reinforcement in a concurrent situation. *Journal of the Experimental Analysis of Behavior, 8,* 439–444.

Chung, S.-H, & Herrnstein, R.J. (1967). Choice and delay of reinforcement. *Journal of the Experimental Analysis of Behavior, 10,* 67–74.

Collier, G., & Knarr, F. (1966). Defense of water balance in the rat. *Journal of Comparative and Physiological Psychology, 61,* 5–10.

Collier, G., Hirsch, E., & Hamlin, P.H. (1972). The ecological determinants of reinforcement in the rat. *Physiology and Behavior, 9,* 705–716.

Collier, G., Hirsch, E., & Kanarek, R. (1977). The operant revisited. In W.K. Honig & J.E.R. Staddon (Eds.), *Handbook of operant behavior.* New York: Prentice-Hall.

Davison, M., & Tustin, R. (1978). The relation between the generalized matching law and signal-detection theory. *Journal of the Experimental Analysis of Behavior, 29,* 331–336.

de Villiers, P. (1977). Choice in concurrent schedules and a quantitative formulation of the law of effect. In W.K. Honig & J.E.R. Staddon (Eds.), *Handbook of operant behavior.* New Jersey: Prentice-Hall.

Dunham, P.J. (1971). Punishment: Method and Theory. *Psychological Review, 78,* 58–70.

Elsmore, T.F., Fletcher, G.V., Conrad, D.G., & Sodetz, F.J. (1980). Reduction of heroin intake in baboons by an economic constraint. *Pharmacology, Biochemistry and Behavior, 13,* 729–731.

Felton, M., & Lyon, D.O. (1966). The post-reinforcement pause. *Journal of the Experimental Analysis of Behavior, 9,* 131–134.

Ferster, C.B., & Skinner, B.F. (1957). *Schedules of reinforcement.* Englewood Cliffs, NJ: Prentice-Hall.

Findley, J.D. (1958). Preference and switching under concurrent scheduling. *Journal of the Experimental Analysis of Behavior, 1,* 123–144.

Findley, J.D. (1959). Behavior output under chained fixed-ratio requirements in a 24-hour experimental space. *Journal of the Experimental Analysis of Behavior, 2,* 258.

Green, L. (1982). Self-control behavior in animals. In V.L. Smith (Ed.), *Research in experimental economics* (Vol. 2). Greenwich, CT: JAI Press.

Green, L., & Snyderman, M. (1980). Choice between rewards differing in amount and delay: Toward a choice model of self control. *Journal of the Experimental Analysis of Behavior, 34,* 135–147.

Green, L., Kagel, J.H., & Battalio, R.C. (1982). Ratio schedules and their relationship to economic theories of labor supply. In M.L. Commons, R.J. Herrnstein, & H. Rachlin (Eds.), *Quantitative analysis of behavior (Vol 2): Matching and maximizing accounts.* Cambridge, MA: Ballinger.

Green, L., Rachlin, H., & Hanson, J. (1983). Matching and maximizing with concurrent ratio-interval schedules. *Journal of the Experimental Analysis of Behavior, 40,* 217–224.

Hawkins, T.D., & Pliskoff, S.S. (1964). Brain stimulation intensity, rate of self-stimulation, and reinforcing strength: an analysis through chaining. *Journal of the Experimental Analysis of Behavior, 7,* 285–288.

Herrnstein, R.J. (1961). Relative and absolute strength of response as a function of frequency of reinforcement. *Journal of the Experimental Analysis of Behavior, 4,* 267–272.

Herrnstein, R.J. (1970). On the law of effect. *Journal of the Experimental Analysis of Behavior, 13,* 243–266.

Herrnstein, R.J. (1974). Formal properties of the matching law. *Journal of the Experimental Analysis of Behavior, 21,* 159–164.

Herrnstein, R.J., & Loveland, D.H. (1975). Maximizing, and matching on concurrent ratio schedules. *Journal of the Experimental Analysis of Behavior, 24,* 107–116.

Heyman, G.M., & Luce, R.D. (1979). Operant matching is not a logical consequence of maximizing reinforcement rate. *Animal Learning and Behavior, 7,* 133–140.

Hursh, S.R. (1978). The economics of daily consumption controlling food- and water-reinforced responding. *Journal of the Experimental Analysis of Behavior, 29,* 475–491.

Hursh, S. (1980). Economic concepts for the analysis of behavior. *Journal of the Experimental Analysis of Behavior, 34,* 219–238.

Hursh, S., & Fantino, E. (1973). Relative delay of reinforcement and choice. *Journal of the Experimental Analysis of Behavior, 19,* 437–450.

Hursh, S., & Natelson, B.H. (1981). Electrical brain stimulation and food reinforcement dissociated by demand elasticity. *Physiology and Behavior, 26,* 509–515.

Iglauer, C., & Woods, J.H. (1974). Concurrent performances: Reinforcement by different doses of intravenous cocaine in rhesus monkeys. *Journal of the Experimental Analysis of Behavior, 22,* 179–196.

Kaufman, L.W. (1979). *Foraging strategies: Laboratory simulations.* Unpublished doctoral dissertation, Rutgers University.

Kaufman, L.W., & Collier, G. (1981). The economics of seed handling. *The American Naturalist, 118,* 46–60.

Krebs, J.R. (1978). Optimal foraging: Decision rules for predators. In J.R. Krebs & N.B. Davies (Eds.), *Behavioral ecology.* Sunderland, MA: Sinauer Associates.

Krebs, J.R., Houston, A.I., & Charnov, E.L. (1980). Some recent developments in optimal foraging. In A.C. Kamil & T. Sargent (Eds.), *Foraging behavior: Ecological, ethological and psychological approaches.* New York: Garland STPM Press.

Kutscher, C.L. (1969). Species differences in the interaction of feeding and drinking. *Annals of the New York Academy of Sciences, 157,* 539–552.

Lea, S.E.G., & Roper, T.J. (1977). Demand for food on fixed-ratio schedules as a function of the quality of concurrently available reinforcement. *Journal of the Experimental Analysis of Behavior, 27,* 371–380.

Mansfield, E. (1970). *Microeconomics.* New York: W.W. Norton & Company.

Meisch, R.A., & Thompson, T. (1973). Ethanol as a reinforcer: Effects of fixed-ratio size and food deprivation. *Psychopharmacologia, 28,* 171–183.

Miller, H.L. (1976). Matching-based hedonic scaling in the pigeon. *Journal of the Experimental Analysis of Behavior, 26,* 335–345.

Naverick, D.J., & Fantino, E. (1976). Self-control and general models of choice. *Journal of the Experimental Psychology: Animal Behavior Processes, 2,* 75–87.

Nevin, J.A., & Baum, W. (1980). Feedback functions for variable-interval reinforcement. *Journal of the Experimental Analysis of Behavior, 34,* 207–217.

Powell, R.W. (1968). The effect of small sequential changes in fixed-ratio size upon the post-reinforcement pause. *Journal of the Experimental Analysis of Behavior, 11,* 589–593.

Prelec, D. (1982). Matching, maximizing, and the hyperbolic reinforcement feedback function. *Psychological Review, 89,* 189–230.

Prelec, D., & Herrnstein, R.J. (1978). Feedback functions for reinforcement: A paradigmatic experiment. *Animal Learning and Behavior, 1,* 181–186.

Premack, D. (1965). Reinforcement theory. In D. Levine (Ed.), *Nebraska symposium on motivation* (Vol. 13). Lincoln: University of Nebraska Press.

Rachlin, H. (1973). Contrast and matching. *Psychological Review, 80,* 217–234.

Rachlin, H., & Burkhard, B. (1978). The temporal triangle: response substitution in instrumental conditioning. *Psychological Review, 85,* 22–48.

Rachlin, H., & Green, L. (1972). Commitment, choice, and self-control. *Journal of the Experimental Analysis of Behavior, 17,* 15–22.

Rachlin, H., Green, L., Kagel, J.H., & Battalio, R.C. (1976). Economic demand theory and psychological studies of choice. In G.H. Bower (Ed.), *The psychology of learning and motivation* (Vol. 10). New York: Academic Press.

Rachlin, H., Kagel, J.H., & Battalio, R.C. (1980). Substitutibility in time allocation. *Psychological Review, 87,* 355–374.

Rachlin, H., & Krasnoff, J. (1983). Eating and drinking: An economic analysis. *Journal of the Experimental Analysis of Behavior, 39,* 385–403.

Schoenfeld, W.N. (1970). *The theory of reinforcement schedules.* Englewood, NJ: Prentice Hall.

Shimp, C.P. (1973). Probabilistic discrimination learning in the pigeon. *Journal of Experimental Psychology, 97,* 292–304.

Shull, R., Spear, D., & Bryson, A. (1981). Delay or rate of food delivery as determiners of response rate. *Journal of the Experimental Analysis of Behavior, 35,* 129–143.

Staddon, J.E.R. (1979). Operant behavior as adaptation to constraint. *Journal of Experimental Psychology: General, 108,* 48–67.

Staddon, J.E.R., & Motheral, S. (1978). On matching and maximizing in operant choice experiments. *Psychological Review, 85,* 436–444.

Timberlake, W. (1977). The application of the matching law to simple ratio schedules. *Journal of the Experimental Analysis of Behavior, 27,* 215–217.

Weiss, B., & Laties, V. (1960). Magnitude of reinforcement as a variable in thermoregulatory behavior. *Journal of the Experimental Analysis of Behavior, 53,* 603–608.

Zeiler, M. (1977). Schedules of reinforcement: the controlling variables. In W.K. Honig & J.E.R. Staddon (Eds.), *Handbook of operant behavior.* Englewood Cliffs, NJ: Prentice-Hall.

APPENDIX I

Figure 18 is a commodity space in which each point can be represented by a quantity Q_1 of commodity C_1 and a quantity Q_2 of commodity C_2. Income, I, and the unit price of each commodity, P_1 and P_2, restrict Q_1 and Q_2 to those locations on or below the line:

$$Q_2 = \frac{I}{P_2} - \frac{P_1}{P_2}Q_1 \qquad (1)$$

Figure 18 shows that utility is maximized at the point where the budget line and the utility function are tangent (point U_{max} in Figure 18). At the point of tangency, the demand for C_1 and C_2 is optimal.

Now imagine that similar budget lines are added, radiating from a fixed location along the C_1 axis and that each line is tangent to a single indifference curve as in Figure 19, panel A. Because the C_1-intercept is the same for each budget line, the slopes of these lines depend exclusively on P_2, the price of commodity C_2. Therefore, the various points of tangency represent optimal quantities of C_1 and C_2 as the price of C_2 varies. More specifically, as P_2

varies the points of tangency trace a trajectory in (Q_1, Q_2) coordinates which economists refer to as the "price consumption curve" (Mansfield, 1970). This function shows the optimal consumption for C_1 and C_2 at different prices of C_2. When this optimal level of C_2 is replotted as a function of its price, P_2 (Figure 19, panel B), the resulting function is the demand curve for the consumer who maximizes values.[4] This analysis implies that the form of utility function that determines the shapes of the indifference curves also determines the form of the optimal demand function.

A first step toward deriving the function of optimal demand is to solve for the maximum of a utility function. The following simplified form of utility function was proposed by Rachlin et al. (1980):

$$U = x_1 Q_1^y + x_2 Q_2^y$$

Q_1 and Q_2 are physical quantities of commodities C_1 and C_2. The degree to which C_1 and C_2 are substitutable is captured by y. The parameter y is a number less-than-or-equal-to 1.0 which transforms the physical quantities into their psychological equivalents. The actual density of the completely substitutable substance in a unit of C_1 and C_2 is represented by x_1 and x_2. The amount transformations therefore use these unit values to locate the total value of a commodity along the scale of utility.

The classical theory of consumer demand invariably uses the Lagrangian multiplier λ to solve for maximum utility. λ and the income restriction: $I = P_1 Q_1 + P_2 Q_2$ are used to form the function:

$$L = U - \lambda [P_1 Q_1 + P_2 Q_2 - I]$$

L is identical to U because what appears in parenthesis equals zero. Therefore, by differentiating L with respect to Q_1, Q_2 and λ, and evaluating each derivative at zero, U is maximized. Thus,

$$\frac{\partial L}{\partial Q_1} = \frac{\partial U}{\partial Q_1} - \lambda P_1 = 0$$

$$\frac{\partial L}{\partial Q_2} = \frac{\partial U}{\partial Q_2} - \lambda P_2 = 0$$

$$\frac{\partial L}{\partial \lambda} = I - P_1 Q_1 - P_2 Q_2 = 0$$

---

[4] A price consumption curve can be constructed by drawing a group of budget lines from virtually any fixed location along either the C_1 or C_2 axis. By varying this location along a single axis, income is affected because the common intercept of a family of budget lines is the point at which the price and quantity of one commodity equals total income. By switching a single location from one axis to the other, e.g., from the C_1 axis to the C_2 axis, the optimal consumptions switch from being a function of P_2 to being a function of P_1. The C_2 axis is used for most economic representations of the price consumption curve.

By solving for λ and evaluating both derivatives of U, we find:

$$\frac{x_1yQ_1^{y-1}}{P_1} = \frac{x_2yQ_2^{y-1}}{P_2}$$

which, when rearranged, reveals that:

$$\frac{x_1}{x_2} \frac{Q_1^{y-1}}{Q_2^{y-1}} = \frac{P_1}{P_2}. \tag{2}^5$$

This expression shows that utility is maximized at the point along the indifference curve where the slope of this curve equals the slope of the budget line. By using the budget line (Equation 1) to solve for Q_1 and substituting this solution into Equation 2, we find:

$$\frac{x_1}{x_2} \left[\frac{I - Q_2P_2}{P_1Q_2} \right]^{y-1} = \frac{P_1}{P_2}$$

Taking logarithms, rearranging terms, and solving for Q_2 reveals the following demand function for $y < 1.0$ and $0 < P_2 < I$.

$$Q_2 = I \left[\frac{P_1^s}{(KP_2^s + P_1^s)P_2} \right] \tag{3a}$$

where s equals $y/(1 - y)$ and K equals x_1/x_2.

This general function can be simplified by assuming a common x-intercept for a family of budget lines and by assuming that the density of the substitutable substance in a unit of C_1 and C_2 is equal. Given these assumptions, P_1 will equal 1.0 and x_1 will equal x_2. Equation 3a will therefore reduce to:

$$Q_2 = \frac{I}{P_2 (1.0 + P_2^s)} \tag{3b}$$

Equation 3b was used to illustrate the effects of price and substitution on consumption of C_2. Consumption was calculated at each of seven prices

---

[5] The price of food for a hungry animal is typically defined as the ratio of responses (R) to reinforcements (Q). Substituting each price, R_i/Q_i, into the equation for maximum utility reveals a form of the generalized matching relation (Baum, 1974). The resulting equation, $R_1/R_2 = (x_1/x_2)[(Q_1/Q_2)]^y$, is identical to Eq 9 in Rachlin et al. (1980), and implies that perfect matching will occur if an animal maximizes the utility of reinforcement, and the commodities C_1 and C_2 are perfect substitutes ($y = 1.0$). The response ratio will undermatch the reinforcement ratio if C_1 and C_2 are imperfect substitutes ($y < 1.0$), and antimatching, an inverse relation between the response ratio and the reinforcement ratio, will occur if C_1 and C_2 are complements ($y < 0$).

(0.20, 0.25, 0.40, 0.50, 0.80, 1.00, and 1.50), while income remained constant at 2.0. This was done at each of eight values of y (1.00, 0.75, 0.50, 0.25, 0.0, -1.00, -10.00, and -100.00), and is shown in Figure 22. Here, the individual demand curves are plotted between the P_2 and y axes and are joined to form a consumption surface.

The Consumption Surface

First, notice that each demand curve slopes downward to the right. This means that consumption for C_2 decreases as its price increases. When C_1 and C_2 are imperfect substitutes $(0 < y < 1.0)$ consumption declines steeply as price increases. As C_1 and C_2 become increasingly complementary $(y < 0)$ the effect of price on consumption decreases until at $y = -100$, the demand curve approaches a horizontal line, a form never quite reached even for perfect complements.

At values of the parameter y equal to 1.0, 0.0, and $-\infty$, the expressions for the demand curve are simplified versions of Equation 3b. In each case the substitution parameter, s, vanishes and consumption of C_2 depends entirely on the price of C_2 (P_2) and total income, I. Table 1 gives the specific expressions for the demand curve at these values of y.

The demand curves at y equals 1.0 and y equals 0.0 illustrate the effect of income on consumption (see Table 1). Consider prices of C_2 less than 1.0, the point at which the price of C_2 equals the price of C_1. When y equals 1.0, the consumption of C_2 is twice what it is when y equals 0.0 (see Figure 22, dashed lines). This occurs because, when C_1 and C_2 are perfect substitutes,

TABLE 1.   Effect of y on the Form of the Demand Function

y	s	Q_2
1.0	∞	$I(\frac{1}{P_2})$, $P_2 \leq 1.0$
		0, $P_2 > 1.0$
.50	1	$\dfrac{I}{P_2(1 + P_2)}$
.25	.33	$\dfrac{I}{P_2(1 + P_2{}^{.33})}$
0	0	$\dfrac{I}{2}(\dfrac{1}{P_2})$
-10	$-.91$	$\dfrac{I}{P_2(1 + P_2{}^{-.91})}$
-100	$-.99$	$\dfrac{I}{P_2(1 + P_2{}^{-.99})}$
$-\infty$	-1.0	$\dfrac{I}{(1 + P_2)}$

total income is spent on C_2; when C_1 and C_2 are totally independent, only half the income can be spent on C_2. Beyond a price of 1.0, the price of C_2 exceeds the price of C_1. No amount of C_2 will be consumed if C_1 is a perfect substitute. As C_2 and C_1 become less substitutable, increasing fractions of income must be spent on C_2 to maximize total utility. When C_2 and C_1 are totally independent, i.e., y equals 0.0, half the income is spent on C_2 even when its price exceeds that of C_1.

Substitution

The effect of substitution on consumption can be seen in Figure 22 by tracing the connected points at each of the seven prices. At prices less than 1.0, these points decrease as y decreases. This means that consumption of C_2 declines as C_1 and C_2 become increasingly less substitutable.

The effect of substitution on consumption is reversed beyond 1.0, at which point consumption is independent of y. When P_2 is greater than P_1, consumption increases monotonically as C_2 and C_1 become increasingly less substitutable. For example, at P_2 equal to 1.5 and y equal to 1.0, no amount of C_2 will be consumed, because its price exceeds the price of C_1, a perfect substitute. As C_1 and C_2 become increasingly less substitutable, the suppressive effect of higher P_2 on the consumption of C_2 is offset by the fact that value can no longer be maximized by exclusively choosing the commodity of lowest price. Consequently, the consumption of C_2 increases.

Own-Price and Cross-Price Effects.

Figure 22 showed that the consumption of C_2 declined at all values of s as price of C_2 increased. The substitution relation affected the general curvature of the demand curve but did not affect its basic form. A more complicated effect on demand for C_2 emerges when we consider not the effect of its own price on the demand for C_2, but the effect of the cross-price P_1, on the demand for C_2. Rewriting Equation 3a by dividing the numerator and denominator by $P_1{}^s$, we find that:

$$Q_2 = \frac{I}{[K(\frac{P_2}{P_1})^s + 1]\,P_2}$$

Notice that the effect of P_1 is in the denominator of the price ratio, P_1/P_2, and its position in this ratio depends on the sign of s, the substitution parameter. When C_1 and C_2 are substitutes, s will be positive and P_1 will remain in the denominator. Therefore, increases in P_1 will *increase* Q_2 at a given I and P_2. At the same time, increases in P_1 *decrease* Q, in terms of its own demand equation. Thus when C_1 and C_2 are substitutes, cross-price and own-price changes in consumption are opposite in direction. At some extreme value of P_1, consumption, Q_1, vanishes and the ratio of P_2 to P_1 in the denominator approaches zero. At this point, Q_2 will equal I/P_2 or $I = Q_2 P_2$.

When C_1 and C_2 are complements, s will be negative and the positions of P_1 and P_2 will be reversed. Therefore, increases in P_1 will not only have the own-price effect of decreasing Q_1, but will have the cross-price effect of decreasing Q_2. As P_1 continues to increase, both Q_1 and Q_2 decrease together. This correlated decrease in Q_1 and Q_2 is consistent with the empirical definition of complementarity.

APPENDIX II

The change in the shape of the demand curve as price changes is captured by a normalized measure of its slope known as the elasticity of demand. One representation of demand elasticity is:

$$e = \frac{-dQ}{dP}\left(\frac{P}{Q}\right)$$

The ratio dQ/dP is the derivative of the demand curve and P/Q is the ratio of the price that was changed to the quantity that was changed. Because dQ and dP are inversely related, the minus sign ensures that e will be positive.

An explicit expression for e can be derived by substituting the derivative of Equation 3b into the general equation for e. The derivative of Equation 3b is:

$$\frac{dQ_2}{dP_2} = -Q_2 \frac{1 + \frac{s}{y}P_2^s}{P_2(1 + P_2^s)}$$

By substituting this derivative into the equation for e and cancelling, the following expression is obtained for the elasticity of demand:

$$e = \frac{1 + \frac{s}{y}P_2^s}{1 + P_2^s}$$

This equation shows that like the demand function (Equation 3b) e is affected by price and substitutibility, but unlike the demand function e is not affected by income. The effects of price and substitutibility on e are shown in Table 2, where in each cell e appears as a unique combination of y and P_2. The rows of this table show that e increases continuously as price increases at all magnitudes of y except zero and 1.0. This unit elasticity of demand is a special case of constant elasticity which occurs if demand is a power function of price.[6] Since demand is a power function of price when y equals either zero or 1.0, two sufficient conditions for constant elasticity of demand are perfect substitutability and independence of value.

TABLE 2. *e* Values for Combinations of P_2 and y

y	Price			
	.25	.50	1.0	1.5
1.0	1.0	1.0	∞	∞
.50	1.20	1.33	1.50	1.60
0	1.0	1.0	1.0	1.0
−10	.20	.41	.54	.63
−∞	.20	.33	.50	.60

A final point to be made is that e decreases as y decreases at each price. This means that the shape of the demand curve is increasingly less affected by price as C_1 and C_2 become less substitutable (see the demand curve for $y = -100$ in Appendix I). But, again, it should be mentioned that, even at the hypothetical limit of perfect complementarity, demand continues to be affected by price.

---

[6] A second representation of demand elasticity is, $-[(dQ/Q)(dP/P)]$. This ratio of ratios reveals that e will be constant only if a uniform price increase causes the same relative reduction of demand at all prices. Consequently, only when this special tradeoff between q and p is true will demand be a power function of price.

Chapter 7

Intertemporal Choice Behavior: Evaluation of Economic and Psychological Models*

John H. Kagel

Economics Department
University of Houston

Leonard Green

Department of Psychology
Washington University

I. INTRODUCTION

In choosing between contemporaneously-available alternatives such as food and water, consumption and leisure, root beer and Tom Collins mix, pigeons and rats reliably respond to changes in prices and income along the lines of standard textbook theories in economics. Real income constant (Slutsky compensated) price changes reliably result in increased (decreased) consumption of the good whose price decreased (increased). Similarly, nominal income constant price changes reliably result in satisfaction of the law of demand (Battalio, Kagel, Green, & Rachlin, 1981; Kagel, Battalio, Green, & Rachlin, 1980; Kagel, Battalio, Rachlin, & Green, 1981; Lea, 1978). Responses to these changes are typically quite rapid and do not require extensive "training"; substituting out of higher priced goods into cheaper ones appears to be a natural part of an animal's repertoire.

The fact that pigeons and rats behave quite efficiently in contemporaneous choice situations, quite rationally as economists define it, suggests

* This paper was written while the first author was a National Fellow at the Hoover Institution, whose research support is gratefuly acknowledged, as is that of the National Science Foundation. The experiment underlying the analysis was supported by NIH Grant 1 RO3 MH32655-01 to Leonard Green. Valuable comments were received from participants at the Interdisciplinary Seminar on Decision Analysis at Stanford University. An earlier version of this paper was presented at the Western Economic Association Meetings, 1982.

that laboratory animals may serve as a model for providing insight into human economic behavior. In this context, the question naturally arises of whether there are important situations where standard textbook theory and the animals' behavior part company, and if so what kind of insights animals can provide us into these situations. The present paper deals with one such area, dynamic choice behavior. In this paper, we present experimental results demonstrating that, while animals act as if present value calculations of alternative outcomes guide choices, they display dynamic inconsistencies: With short delays between choice and outcomes, smaller, more immediate payoffs are preferred to larger, more delayed ones; but with longer delays between choice and outcomes, the larger, more delayed outcome is chosen. In presenting these results, we analyze them in terms of economic models of intertemporal choice, and contrast predictions from these models with competing psychological models of choice.

Preference reversals of the sort identified here are contrary to predictions of the most common intertemporal choice models employed in the economics literature. The potential for such reversals has been recognized for some time, most notably by R.H. Strotz (1956), who noted that there was no reason to presume that individuals were endowed at birth with the special sorts of preference structures resulting in temporally consistent choices. This in turn has spawned a literature aimed at modeling the basis for such inconsistencies, characterizing mechanisms capable of achieving consistency, such as precommitting choices, parental training, etc., and examining the general economic implications of this behavior, as in decisions to save and invest. The experiments reported on here provide clear evidence for taking this literature seriously as they provide unambiguous evidence for the reversal phenomenon.

The latter part of the paper attempts to provide a better understanding of intertemporal choice behavior in animals, and its implications for understanding comparable human behavior. Do the persistent "self-control" problems observed in laboratory animals have adaptive value in nature, and would we expect similar adaptive consequences to shape human behavior? What sorts of environmental factors lead to greater or lesser "self-control" in animals, and what are the implications for understanding comparable behavior in humans? While we recognize the hazards inherent in drawing parallels between the behavior of laboratory animals and that of humans operating in advanced industrialized economies, there are clear advantages to the controlled investigation of behavior which the use of laboratory animals permit (see also Hursh & Bauman, this volume). This second factor, in conjunction with the clear parallels between animal and human behavior already established in consumer demand and labor supply behavior, are what we offer in support of the analysis in this section of the paper.

Section II specifies the "standard" intertemporal choice model employed in the economics literature and, for comparative purposes, predictions drawn from reinforcement theory in psychology with respect to the outcomes of primary interest. Section III specifies the procedures and results of our particular experiment which investigated the theory. The implications for rejecting the standard economic model in terms of insuring temporal consistency in choices are dealt with in Section IV. We conclude with a discussion of the potential adaptive value of the extreme "self-control" problems observed in pigeons and rats, the environmental forces resulting in more or less "self-control," and the implications for understanding human intertemporal choices.

II. THE STANDARD ECONOMIC MODEL AND ITS RELATIONSHIP TO PSYCHOLOGICAL THEORIES OF CHOICE

In the conventional model for analyzing intertemporal choice problems where the concern is with aggregate consumption levels, C_t, in different time periods, t, the consumer is viewed as maximizing a quasi-concave utility function of the sort

$$V = U[C_0, C_1, \ldots, C_t, C_{t+1}] \tag{1}$$

subject to a wealth constraint. To derive testable hypotheses about behavior, special assumptions about the nature of the utility function, Equation 1, are commonly employed. The conventional assumptions are that the utility function is strongly separable over time (see Deaton & Muellbauer, 1980, for the implications of separability assumptions) and that the value of consumption differs between dates by a constant time bias parameter, ρ. Thus, the utility function, Equation 1, is conventionally replaced by

$$V = \sum_{t=\tau}^{T} \frac{U(C_t)}{(1+\rho)^{t-\tau}} \tag{2}$$

where $(T - \tau)$ is the decision maker's time horizon and τ is the point at which decisions are made. (See MaCurdy, 1981; and Olson & Bailey, 1981, for recent examples of formulations along these lines.)

As expressed in Equation 2, the intertemporal utility model makes a number of predictions which are readily testable. Interestingly, one of the weakest predictions concerns the time bias parameter, ρ, with the only requirement for negatively sloped, convex indifference surfaces being that $\rho > -1$. However, with a few notable exceptions such as Stigler and Becker (1977), most economists take a positive time bias for granted, based on either intuitive judgments about how individuals behave or on indirect arguments in terms of positive market interest rates and uncertainty.[1] Reinforcement theory in psychology actually predicts a positive time bias, since the principle of immediacy of reinforcement holds that, between any two reinforcers, C_t and C_{t+n}, the more immediate one is more effective, all other things being equal.

Assuming a positive time bias, both reinforcement theory and the standard economic model predict that one can find a sufficiently large payoff, $C_{t+n} > C_t$, such that the decision maker is willing to "wait it out," choosing the larger more delayed payoff. Both formulations also assume some degree of forward-looking behavior in the sense that in choosing between alternative consumption streams with the same initial outcome, subsequent events affect choice, albeit with reduced effectiveness. Although lifetime allocation models are quite popular these days in economics, the length of the time horizon appears to be, in practice, considerably less than this. For example, estimates of the time horizon within the context of the permanent income hypothesis range between 1 and 10 years (Mohabbat & Simos, 1977), while Friedman (1957) suggests that a 3-year time horizon is a good approximation. Reinforcement theory takes the time horizon to be an empirically determinable parameter, subject to considerable interspecies differences, as well as individual differences due to previous histories (i.e., reinforcement contingencies; see, e.g., Logue, Rodriguez, Peña-Correal, & Mauro, 1984).

The standard economic model implies that choices between alternatives are temporally consistent in the sense that preferences between C_t and C_{t+n} are independent of the time, τ, at which choices are made. In other words, if C_t is preferred to C_{t+n} at time τ, then it should also be preferred at time $\tau + s$. It is this last implication of the model, that of consistent intemporal choices, that has aroused more skepticism in the literature, beginning with Böhm-Bawerk (1923) and, most notably, with Strotz (1956).[2]

Reinforcement theory as such makes no predictions concerning temporal consistency. However, the matching law, the leading quantitative choice model within the context of reinforcement theory, predicts preference reversals as a function of the time interval $(t - \tau)$. In choosing between alternatives C_t and C_{t+n}, the simple matching law holds that choice is based on the ratio of consumption values times the inverse of the delay ratio:

$$\frac{V_t}{V_{t+n}} = \left(\frac{C_t}{C_{t+n}}\right) \cdot \left(\frac{(t+n-\tau)}{(t-\tau)}\right) \qquad (3)$$

---

[1] Olson and Baily (1981) recently reexamined these arguments and found most of them unconvincing. Yet they still concluded, on the basis of indirect evidence, that there must be either a positive time bias or sharply diminishing marginal utility of consumption. Their arguments assume that equation 2 of the text is valid. As we will see shortly, it is not.

[2] The assumptions embodied in equation 2 are sufficient to insure consistent intertemporal choice. See Hadar (1971, pp. 233–242) for a good discussion of necessary and sufficient conditions.

so that when $V_t/V_{t+n} > 1$, C_t is chosen in favor of C_{t+n}. As the value of τ is increased, there will come a point when $V_t/V_{t+n} < 1$; C_{t+n} would then be chosen in favor of C_t (Baum & Rachlin, 1969; Rachlin & Green, 1972). In other words, consumption is discounted by the time delay between choices and reinforcement, so that preference reversals are bound to occur with variation in the time delay.[3]

The matching law formulation can be derived as a special case of discounting with a variable time bias

$$V = \sum_{t=\tau}^{T} \phi(t-\tau)U(C_t) \qquad (4)$$

The discounted value formulation in Equation 4 differs from Equation 2 in that we have replaced the exponential rate of time discounting in the standard model with a general time bias factor $\phi(t-\tau)$. When $\phi(t-\tau) = (t-\tau)^{-1}$, $U(C_t) = C_t$, and subjects are choosing between alternatives with a single outcome in the relevant time horizon, then $V_t = C_t/(t-\tau)$ so that the predictions of the matching law follow directly from Equation 4. We refer to Equation 4 as the variable time bias specification since it permits the time bias to vary systematically with $t - \tau$.

III. MYOPIA AND INCONSISTENCY IN CHOICE

Psychologists have extensively studied the relationship between time delay and choice with laboratory animals. Preference reversals as a function of time have been suggested in several studies using rats and pigeons (Ainslie, 1974; Deluty, 1978; Rachlin & Green, 1972). While suggestive, the evidence for such reversals has not been conclusive. For example, in Ainslie's (1974) experiment only three out of ten subjects showed preference reversals in terms of coming to choose the larger, more delayed outcome on more than 50% of the trials, when the time between choice and receipt of outcomes was increased. In the Rachlin and Green (1972) study, all five birds increased their preference for the larger, more delayed reward as the delay to the outcomes increased; however, only three of these subjects actually reversed their preference.

The present experiment provides a clear demonstration of preference reversals as predicted in Equation 3. It also serves to characterize the pro-

---

[3] The matching law formulation is related to Weber's law, which suggests that discrimination between different values of any physical continuum depends more on the ratio of the values than on the absolute difference between them. Accordingly, increasing the time delay between choice and outcomes, holding the time difference between the two reward alternatives constant, reduces the time delay ratio and hence the perceived difference between alternatives. However, recent research shows that the absolute differences in delay also affect choice. As the absolute delay values are varied while the ratio is held constant, preference for the smaller more immediate alternative also varies (Green & Snyderman, 1980; Navarick & Fantino, 1976).

cedures and results of intertemporal choice experiments as commonly conducted by psychologists.

A. Experimental Procedures

The experiment consisted of a series of discrete choice trials, one of which is illustrated in Figure 1. (For complete details of the procedure used in this experiment, see Green, Fisher, Perlow, & Sherman, 1981). Each trial consisted of a choice period, a constant (30 second) time period during which choices became available, and an outcome period of constant duration (10 seconds), irrespective of the outcome chosen. Subjects (pigeons) could choose between a small reward, C_t (2 seconds access to a grain hopper), available at the start of the outcome period, or a larger payoff, C_{t+n} (6 seconds access to grain), available at the end of the outcome period. To determine consistency of intertemporal choices, the time within the 30-second choice period when the choice keys became available, τ, was varied from 2 to 28 seconds.

Each day, the birds faced 66 independent trials of the sort shown in Figure 1. There were 16-forced-choice trials at the beginning of the session, during which only one of the choices was available on each trial to insure familiarity with the alternatives. These were followed by 50 free-choice trials. Experimental conditions were maintained for a minimum of 15 days,

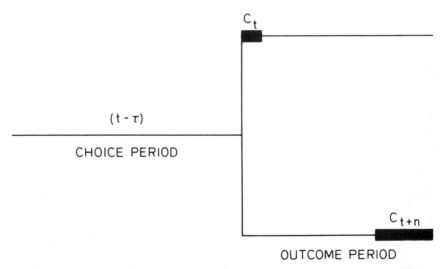

FIGURE 1. Structure of a single trial for studying choice between time-dependent outcomes (Green et al., 1981). Subjects chose between different size payoffs, C_t and C_{t+n}, occurring at different points in the outcome period. Total trial time and length of outcome periods remained constant across experimental conditions and outcomes chosen. The point within the trial period, τ, at which choices between the two payoffs were permitted was varied across experimental conditions.

and were only changed when the distribution of free choices had stabilized. Sequencing of experimental conditions varied, with two pigeons starting with short delay intervals $(t - \tau)$ and progressing to longer ones, with the other two birds starting with the longest delay interval and progressing to shorter delays. Pigeons were maintained at 80% of normal body weight throughout and subjected to constant pre-trial deprivation conditions in order to insure constancy of background conditions.

B. Experimental Results and Discussion

Closed circles in Figure 2 show the percent of larger, more delayed outcomes chosen as a function of $t - \tau$, the time between choice and availability of C_t, for each of the four birds studied. Values reported are means over the last 5 days of each condition, with the bars indicating ± one standard error of the mean for observations over this period. Each bird's initial condition was replicated with mean choices over the last 5 days of these periods indicated by Xs.

When choices became available close to the outcome period $(t - \tau < 5)$, every bird strongly favored C_t, the smaller more immediate outcome. The

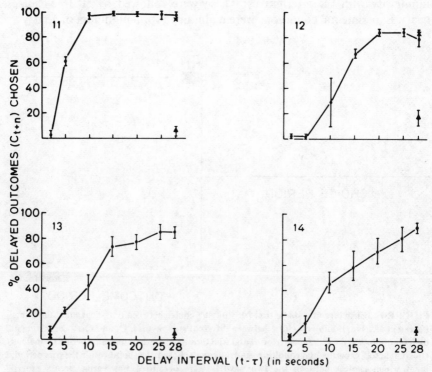

FIGURE 2.   Effects of varying time delay, $t - \tau$, on percentage of delayed outcomes chosen (from Green et al., 1981). See text for explanation.

nearly exclusive preference for alternative C_t here means that the pigeons failed to maximize total food intake. What is particularly important to note about this behavior is that the blackout period following C_t equalized the total time between choice trials, irrespective of the alternative chosen. Some psychologists have (mistakenly) taken this as evidence against maximization theory as currently employed in economics (Mazur, 1981).[4] Many psychologists (for example, Ainslie, 1975) have characterized this behavior as a "self-control problem," with the implication that the animals simply do not have the ability to act in their own best interest. While we might be surprised at the relatively large positive time bias the pigeons have, or be appalled at their short time horizons, the failure to maximize food intake is perfectly consistent with the standard representation, equation 2, given a sufficiently large positive time bias.

As the time interval, $t - \tau$, between choice and outcomes increased, however, preferences reversed and every bird came to choose C_{t+n}, the larger, more delayed outcome. The pigeons are now maximizing total food intake. However, these preference reversals are incompatible with the standard representation, equation 2, which does not allow for such reversals.

The triangles in Figure 2 show the results from a control condition in which subjects chose between $\overline{C}_t$ and C_{t+n}, but where $\overline{C}_t = C_{t+n}$ (the amount of consumption obtained from both alternatives was now equal), with no other changes in the choice procedures. Pigeons overwhelmingly preferred $\overline{C}_t$, the more immediate outcome. Since this comparison was made at a point $t - \tau$ where subjects previously preferred C_{t+n} to C_t, it rules out explanations of the preference reversals in terms of subjects' inability to distinguish delay differences between the alternatives from such a distance.

The reversals in preference as $t - \tau$ increased are inconsistent with the assumption of a log linear time bias factor in the standard representation. Pigeons tend to "over-value" more proximate satisfactions relative to more distant ones, as Strotz and others suggested is the "natural" state of affairs for humans. This is more in keeping with predictions of the matching law and the variable time bias specification, equation 4.

The matching law and the variable time bias specification are only two of several possible ways to characterize choice in Figure 2. An additive commodity characteristics formulation, along the lines suggested by Lancaster (1966), can be employed to explain both the "self-control" problem with short delay intervals and the preference reversals with increases in the delay interval. In terms of this formulation, preference for the smaller more immediate alternative involves a willingness to forego increased consumption in favor of earlier delivery, with very little weight attached to differences in

---

[4] Failure to maximize food intake has also been reported in labor supply experiments where pigeons give up consumption in favor of increased leisure (Battalio, Green, & Kagel, 1981; Green, Kagel, & Battalio, 1982). Of course, such data do refute simple "wealth" maximizing models.

post-reinforcement delays.[5] The addition of a constant delay increment to both alternatives narrows differences with respect to the delay characteristic, while holding differences with respect to consumption characteristics constant. As long as preferences are normal with respect to both of these characteristics, this change in relative prices with respect to the delay characteristic is bound to result in increased choice of the larger, more delayed alternatives, resulting in the preference reversals observed.

One advantage of an additive characteristic formulation is that it would naturally account for both nonexclusive choice and systematic variations in choice frequencies between the two alternatives as a consequence of subjects' optimally mixing characteristics. Both the matching law (Equation 3), and the variable time bias specification (Equation 4) fail to account for nonexclusive preference; to do so would require a generalization of these models in terms of probabilistic choice concepts (see Luce & Suppes, 1965, for a review of such models). Interpretation of the experimental results in terms of a commodity characteristics approach is supported by a sequential analysis of choices within experimental sessions which showed a nearly uniform distribution of choice for the C_{t+n} outcome. This rules out income effects or changes in deprivation levels during the experimental session as factors responsible for the nonexclusive choice often observed. This interpretation leaves unanswered the question of *why* delays between choice and reinforcement carry so much weight relative to either post-reinforcement delays or consumption. Some ecologists have argued that such a weighting scheme might have important survival characteristics in natural habitats. We return to this question in the next section.

The results of Figure 2 can also be explained in terms of a model in which choice is determined on the basis of additive *differences* in commodity characteristics. This model implies intransitivities in choice as well as preference reversals (Tversky, 1969). None of the other choice models considered up to this point permit intransitivities. For example, in terms of Equation 1, choices at short delay intervals were over alternatives of the sort $A = (0, C_s, 0, 0, \ldots)$ vs. $B = (0, 0, C_L, 0, \ldots)$ where $C_L > C_s$. At longer delay intervals, choices were over alternatives of the sort $C = (0, 0, \ldots, C_s, 0, \ldots)$ vs. $D = (0, 0, \ldots, 0, 0, C_L, 0, \ldots)$. Preference reversals as a function of the delay interval imply that A.P.B. (*A* is preferred to *B*) and D.P.C., which is consistent with equation 1 as well as with an additive characteristic formula-

---

[5] A constant elasticity of substitution utility function of the sort

$$U = \frac{\alpha_1}{V} (C)^V + \frac{\alpha_2}{V} (\frac{1}{t-\tau})^V + \frac{\alpha_3}{V} (\frac{1}{t_B})^V \; ; V < 1, \; \sum_i \alpha_i = 1$$

where C, $t - \tau$, and t_B represent consumption, the time delay between choice and consumption, and the post-reinforcement blackout period, respectively, is sufficient to generate the results characterized in the text.

tion. An intransitivity, on the other hand, would imply A.P.B., B.P.C., but C.P.A., or A.P.B., B.P.D., but D.P.A. Although we are virtually certain that preference would be transitive over the alternatives employed here, we might be able to induce intransitivities using alternatives of the sort C and D and an alternative of the sort $E = (0, 0, \ldots, 0, \ldots, 0, C_k, 0, \ldots)$, where $C_k > C_L > C_s$, and a delay even longer than that under alternative D. Experiments are currently underway to test for this possibility.

As already noted, the results of the experiment reported here do not stand in isolation (see Ainslie & Herrnstein, 1981, for similar results). For example, Deluty (1978) reports preference reversals with rats choosing between brief immediate shocks compared to longer delayed ones; with short delays $(t - \tau)$, rats preferred the longer but more delayed shock, only to switch their preference as $t - \tau$ increased. This is consistent with the results reported in Figure 2, since with shock, the outcomes C_t and C_{t+n}, in terms of Equations 3 and 4, presumably take on negative values. In addition, research by Fantino (1966) indicates that choices are responsive to changes in the magnitude of the payoffs, C_t and C_{t+n}, as Equations 3 and 4 predict. Fantino (1966) also showed that pigeons are somewhat sensitive to post-reinforcement delays associated with the more immediate alternative, C_t, when the delays were quite long. While pigeons heavily discount future outcomes and/or have a limited time horizon, preferences are affected by the temporal locus of events subsequent to the first reinforcement, as required by the variable time bias specification, Equation 4 (also see Shull, Spear, & Bryson, 1981).

IV. IMPLICATIONS OF REJECTING THE
STANDARD ECONOMIC MODEL

Rejection of the standard model, Equation 2, in favor of Equation 4 has several implications for intertemporal choice behavior. Primary among these is the problem of consistent planning. With an intertemporal value function like that of Equation 4, if the decision maker has complete flexibility of choice and the opportunity to revise decisions, then reconsideration of plans may lead previously chosen alternatives to now be rejected. In interactive settings involving other economic agents, revisions of prior commitments are typically constrained by legally binding contracts, positive transaction costs, and the possibility of a continuing series of interactions among agents. The only implication that rejection of the standard model has for these situations is that one need not rely *exclusively* on assumptions of prior malevolence on the part of the decision maker in order to generate motives for the rejecting of previous commitments. The simple reconsideration of plans at a later point in time, when preferences have reversed, also serves as sufficient motivation.

In cases where the cost of revising plans are internalized in the individual, auxiliary mechanisms must be relied upon for achieving temporal consistency in choices. When these mechanisms are successful in averting inconsistencies, the individual is commonly characterized as exhibiting "self-control." Further, actions may be taken which appear irrational in a world characterized by Equation 2, for example precommitting future choices, but which serve as mechanisms for achieving consistent planning.

Numerous mechanisms for achieving self control have been proposed in the literature (Ainslie, 1975; Elster, 1979; Strotz, 1956; Thaler & Shefrin, 1981). Two of the most commonly suggested ones are: (a) Precommitting behavior through choosing options which make a future activity unavailable or which dramatically increase the costs associated with particular actions. Examples consist of voluntary decisions by some professors to have their 9-month salary paid in 12 installments in order to regulate spending in the absence of summer income, and the repeated decisions by large numbers of people to overwithhold on their income taxes as a device for saving income; and (b) Learning self-control as a result of parental and social influences. Such learning might result either in direct modification of the discount function and/or in learning to employ both overt and covert commitment strategies when appropriate.

There is evidence that pigeons and rats can exhibit "self-control" with the aid of these two mechanisms also. For example, in choosing between small immediate (C_t) and larger delayed rewards (C_{t+n}), Rachlin and Green (1972) gave pigeons the choice to precommit in favor of C_{t+n} or to retain flexibility in choosing between the two. The structure of their experiment is characterized in the decision tree in Figure 3. Options C_t and C_{t+n} were selected so that at choice node n_1, C_t was preferred to C_{t+n}. Choices at n_0 gave access to either the flexible choice node, n_1, or the commitment alternative, $n_{1'}$, with its single outcome C_{t+n}. With long time delays between n_0 and n_1 and $n_{1'}$, when C_{t+n} would have been preferred to C_t, the pigeons chose the commitment alternative ($n_{1'}$) and thus received the delayed larger reward (C_{t+n}). Although the flexible choice alternative (n_1) *could* have led to the same reward outcome, the pigeons chose the commitment alternative.

The choice of the commitment alternative in Figure 3 involved a cost in terms of loss of flexibility in future choices. That the pigeons responded so as to limit their future choice is all the more striking given that they seem to prefer choice to no choice under other circumstances. For example, in choosing between two alternatives, m_1 and $m_{1'}$, with m_1 having several identical outcomes any one of which could be obtained, and $m_{1'}$ having a single positively valued alternative of equal expected value, pigeons prefer the multiple outcome alternative (Catania, 1980).

Other research shows that pigeons can be "taught" self-control. That is, with appropriate training they come to choose large delayed outcomes in

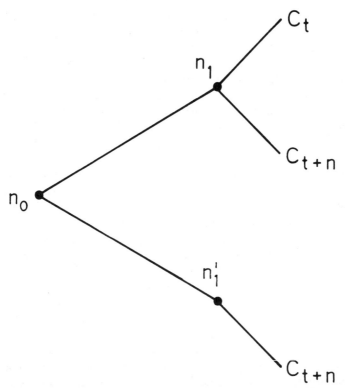

FIGURE 3. Structure of the Rachlin and Green (1972) precommitment experiment. Choice at node n_0 led to the flexible choice node, n_1, where subjects could choose between C_t and C_{t+n} or to the commitment node, $n_{1'}$, which only permitted choice of C_{t+n}. At n_1, the pigeons chose the smaller more immediate reward, C_t. As the time delay between n_0 and n_1 and $n_{1'}$ was increased, the pigeons now chose the commitment alternative, $n_{1'}$, thus ensuring receipt of the larger, more delayed reward, C_{t+n}.

favor of small immediate ones at short-delay intervals significantly more often than control groups which have not received such training. Mazur and Logue (1978) offered their pigeons a choice between 6 seconds of food delayed by 6 seconds or 2 seconds of food delivered immediately. The birds consistently chose the small, immediate reward. However, when first placed under a procedure in which both rewards were delayed 6 seconds, the birds, of course, almost always chose the larger reward. Then, over the course of 1 year, the delay to the smaller reward was gradually reduced to zero. These experimental subjects now chose the delayed reward significantly more often than did the control pigeons not exposed to this fading procedure. However, there was considerable variability in the effectiveness of identical training methods, with one subject choosing the larger delayed outcome 90% of the time and another choosing it only 15% of the time. Also, it is unclear exactly what changes have occurred in terms of Equation 4. One possibility is that the discount factor $\phi(t-\tau)$ has simply become relatively less extreme at small values of $t-\tau$, in which case inconsistencies would re-emerge with appropriate changes in the size of the payoffs and differential time delays associated with the alternatives. On the other hand, the original discount function might have been replaced by one that was log linear or perhaps even constant so that something more akin to Equation 2 would effectively characterize decisions. Alternatively, the birds might have learned some kind of covert commitment strategy to forestall their preference for the smaller, immediate reward, in which case the degree to which this strategy generalizes to other situations is of considerable interest. Answers to these questions require further investigation. Nevertheless, the research clearly shows that one can modify the effective rate of time discounting even in pigeons, albeit with considerable residual variability.

Although a precommitment strategy for achieving consistent intertemporal planning is inexplicable in terms of a utility function such as Equation 2, the use of such mechanisms appears to rest on underlying economic contingencies. Thus, in the Rachlin and Green (1972) experiment, the pigeons only started to use the precommitment alternative when the delay intervals were long enough such that they would have preferred the larger delayed alternative anyway, not before.

There is also data to suggest that implementation of "learning" mechanisms for inducing consistent choice of larger more delayed outcomes is functionally related to the underlying economic contingencies. For example, Mischel's (1974) work with children in the United States shows that preferences for larger delayed, as compared to smaller immediate, outcomes increases systematically with childrens' ages. In marked contrast, Bochner and David (1968), using procedures similar to Mischel's, found no significant differences in time bias in Aboriginal school children in Australia as a function of their ages. There can be little doubt that the United States economy emphasizes substantially greater reliance on human and physical capital than would the native Aboriginal economy.

Although we have argued that reliance on commitment strategies and learning mechanisms does not eliminate the role of standard economic contingencies in determining when to employ these mechanisms, rejection of the standard model (Equation 2) would certainly seem to imply a much slower response to changes in the underlying economic conditions than if agents were born into the world with preference structures which satisfied the model's restrictions. The standard model, in ignoring the need to rely on learned behavior mechanisms for achieving temporal consistency, ignores the residual impact of these mechanisms on behavior once conditions have changed. However, while we accept their contention that rejection of the standard model (equation 2) in favor of learned response rules implies a substantially slower adjustment to changes in economic conditions and greater efficiency losses than a world in which the standard model held, we are skeptical of Thaler and Shefrin's (1981) suggestion that there exist situations in which commitment strategies (or rules) completely thwart a response to changes in economic conditions, as in their example where saving becomes an imperative in its own right so that the introduction of a mandatory pension plan results in a zero offset in nonpension savings. In support of this position, we would note that animal learning studies indicate that it is not uncommon for prior training to retard the adjustment to a new set of experimental conditions, and that prior training can at times produce lasting residual effects on behavior. However, it is rarely the case that prior experience completely eliminates adjustments to changes in reinforcement contingencies, as long as the information feedback loop concerning changes in the choice set is preserved. Most of the economic research in applied consumer demand behavior reaches much the same conclusion.

V. CONCLUSIONS AND IMPLICATIONS

The results of recent experiments indicate that animals' choices between time-dependent outcomes can be characterized in terms of a present discounted value formulation. In this context, pigeons and rats show a high positive time bias, but they can be induced to wait longer with sufficient compensation. The "natural" structure of preferences is such that choices are dynamically inconsistent; preferences reverse as the time interval, $t - \tau$, between choice and outcome is varied. Such preference reversals are incompatible with the standard representation, Equation 2, with its assumption of an exponential rate of time discounting. Rather, the animals' time bias function, $\phi(t - \tau)$, is one which overvalues more proximate satisfactions relative to more distant ones.

The pigeons' preferences for the smaller more immediate reward with short delay intervals ($t - \tau < 5$) shown in Figure 2 has often been characterized as a self-control problem, with the implication that it is not in the animal's best interest. However, it is not clear to us that, from a broader perspective, this is indeed the case. The "natural" rate of time discount the animal is observed to have in the laboratory is the result of evolutionary pressures in its natural habitat. For species living in a competitive environment with no property rights, there is an inherent uncertainty associated with obtaining deferred outcomes. If the probability of loss increases with the passage of time, then, at short delay intervals, small differences in time to reinforcement could give rise to substantial uncertainty discounts, resulting in "impulsive," yet optimal, behavior. Further, if the probability of loss were a negatively accelerated function of the time delay, then the optimal behavior pattern would be to overvalue more proximate outcomes relative to more distant ones, giving rise to the sort of preference reversals observed here. Thus, the time discount patterns of subjects observed in the laboratory may well have evolved as optimal responses to the uncertainties associated with waiting in nature.

While it is purely conjectural, although not completely outlandish, to argue that similar evolutionary forces shaped the "natural" rate of time discount for humans, there do appear to be strong parallels between pigeons' choices over time-dependent outcomes and those of humans. To be sure, there are clear differences in order of magnitude between subjective rates of time discounting. But to judge by the frequent concerns of economists and psychologists, and common observations of children, there are clear parallels in the tendency to overvalue more proximate outcomes relative to more distant ones. These tendencies appear to be far from universally arrested in the growth process, to judge by responses to hypothetical choices (Thaler, 1981; A. Tversky, personal communication, 1982) as well as actual choices in unfamiliar situations where the impact of prior training is minimized (Solnick, Kannenberg, Eckerman, & Waller, 1980).

If we accept the parallelism between human and animal behavior, then one of the more interesting practical implications of the results reported here is the maleability of the time bias parameter in the longer run as a result of appropriate learning sequences. Mazur and Logue's (1978) results indicate that training can temper even the strong positive time bias of pigeons, albeit with considerable residual variability. As previously noted, Mischel's (1974) work with children suggests the importance of training in humans. In addition, Grosch and Neuringer (1981, experiment 6) found that successful preliminary experiences significantly enhanced pigeons' ability to choose and wait for more preferred, delayed outcomes than when they had unsuccessful or mixed successful and unsuccessful preliminary experiences. Mischel (1974) and others have found similar expectancy effects in studies with children. Differences in the time bias parameter translate directly into different decisions on whether to save or to invest in either physical or human capital when forced with identical market rates of return, which in turn have important effects on income. Consequently, to the extent that these learning effects are embedded in the family and in neighborhood influences, as they surely must be given the importance of observational learning in humans, they will contribute to "poverty cycles," an absence of intergenerational mobility in family members' and ethic groups' standing in the distribution of earnings (see Maital & Maital, 1977, for similar suggestions).[6]

---

[6] An early statement of the "cycle of poverty" issue is found in Irving Fisher (1907, quoted in Maital & Maital, 1977, p. 184):

The effect will be that...an inequality in the distribution of capital is gradually effected, and this inequality, once achieved, tends to perpetuate itself. The poorer a man grows, the keener his appreciation of present goods is likely to become.

or more succinctly, "The smaller the income, the higher is the preference for present, over future income" (p. 185).

This parallelism in behavioral processes also suggests the viability of using animals as models to better understand the structure of intertemporal preferences and to test hypotheses for which it is difficult, if not impossible, to obtain unambiguous data on humans (see chapters by Lea and by Hursh and Bauman, this volume). For example, it has often been suggested that time bias varies inversely with income and wealth (Fisher, 1960). That is, the time bias is greater at lower income levels. This proposition can be readily investigated using laboratory animals free from the confounds of cultural, learning, and expectancy factors likely to be encountered in similar research with humans. If Fisher's hypothesis is indeed correct, it would be an important contributing factor to poverty cycles and income dispersion, and would require entirely different sorts of government programs to correct for than if these poverty cycles were primarily caused by other factors, such as expectancy effects.[7]

Finally, problems of self-control have at times been attributed to a lack of will power or to conflicts between competing energy systems in the psyche (Thaler & Shefrin, 1981; see also Green, 1982, for a review). Some writers have even argued that the development of self control typically results from "a rearrangement of the inner space of the person, *without any causal mechanisms being set up in the external world*" (Elster, 1979, p. 37, emphasis added). The analysis presented here (see also Green, 1982, and Rachlin, 1974) suggests that self-control problems are likely to arise in situations having an important temporal component to them, and that "will power" rests in part on the behavioral history of the organism and the availability of commitment devices. Further, since pigeons are able to effectively display self control, we must either accept the notion that they have will power or psyches with multiple energy systems, or treat these concepts as heuristic expressions. In either case, we look for both time bias and its associated characteristic of self control to be determined on the basis of the contingencies with which organisms and their environments interact.

V. SUMMARY

Animals' choices between time-dependent outcomes can be characterized in terms of a present discounted value formulation. Subjects display positive time bias: They choose a more immediate outcome even when such an outcome provides a lesser payoff than does a delayed outcome. Subjects can be induced to choose the more delayed outcome when it provides sufficient reward. However, choices are dynamically inconsistent: Preferences over

---

[7] Research addressing this issue has produced somewhat mixed results. Snyderman (1983) and Eisenberger and Masterson (in press) find evidence in favor of Fisher's hypothesis, while Christensen-Szalanski, Goldberg, Anderson, and Mitchell (1980) find just the opposite result. Experiments are underway in our laboratory to try to reconcile these different results.

outcomes reverse themselves as the time interval between choice and outcome is varied. Specifically, a subject's preference for a lesser, more immediate outcome reverses for the larger, more delayed outcome as the time to the reward outcomes increases. Such behavior is incompatible with standard economic models, but is predicted by a psychological model of choice. Implications of rejecting the standard model were drawn along with evidence supporting alternative formulations. Conclusions were reached for understanding comparable human behavior.

REFERENCES

Ainslie, G.W. (1974). Impulse control in pigeons. *Journal of the Experimental Analysis of Behavior, 21,* 485–489.

Ainslie, G. (1975). Specious reward: A behavioral theory of impulsiveness and impulse control. *Psychological Bulletin, 82,* 463–496.

Ainslie, G., & Herrnstein, R.J. (1981). Preference reversal and delayed reinforcement. *Animal Learning & Behavior, 9,* 476–482.

Battalio, R.C., Green, L., & Kagel, J.H. (1981). Income-leisure tradeoffs of animal workers. *American Economic Review, 71,* 621–632.

Battalio, R.C., Kagel, J.H., Green, L., & Rachlin, H. (1981). Commodity choice behavior with pigeons as subjects. *Journal of Political Economy, 89,* 67–91.

Baum, W.M., & Rachlin, H. (1969). Choice as time allocation. *Journal of the Experimental Analysis of Behavior, 12,* 861–874.

Bochner, S., & David, K.H. (1968). Delay of gratification, age and intelligence in an aboriginal culture. *International Journal of Psychology, 3,* 167–174.

Böhm-Bawerk, E.V. (1923). *The positive theory of capital* (Tr. by W. Smart). New York: G.E. Stechert & Co., reprint.

Catania, A.C. (1980). Freedom of choice: A behavioral analysis. In G.H. Bower (Ed.), *The psychology of learning and motivation* (Vol. 14). New York: Academic Press.

Christensen-Szalanski, J.J., Goldberg, A.D., Anderson, M.E., & Mitchell, T.R. (1980). Deprivation, delay of reinforcement, and the selection of behavioral strategies. *Animal Behavior, 28,* 341–346.

Deaton, A., & Muellbauer, J. (1980). *Economics and consumer behavior.* Cambridge, England: Cambridge University Press.

Deluty, M.Z. (1978). Self-control and impulsiveness involving aversive events. *Journal of Experimental Psychology: Animal Behavior Processes, 4,* 250–266.

Eisenberger, R., & Masterson, F.A. (in press). Effects of prior learning and current motivation on self-control. In M.L. Commons, J.A. Nevin & H. Rachlin (Eds.), *Quanitative analyses of behavior* (Vol. 5): *Reinforcement value.* Cambridge, MA: Ballinger.

Elster, J. (1979). *Ulysses and the sirens: Studies in rationality and irrationality.* Cambridge, England: Cambridge University Press.

Fantino, E. (1966). Immediate reward followed by extinction vs. later reward without extinction. *Psychonomic Science, 6,* 233–234.

Fisher, I. (1960). *The theory of interest.* London: MacMillan.

Friedman, M. (1957). *A theory of the consumption function.* Princeton, NJ: Princeton University Press.

Green, L. (1982). Self-control behavior in animals. In V.L. Smith (Ed.), *Research in experimental economics* (Vol. 2). Greenwich, CT: JAI Press.

Green, L., Fisher, E.B., Jr., Perlow, S., & Sherman, L. (1981). Preference reversal and self-control: Choice as a function of reward amount and delay. *Behaviour Analysis Letters, 1,* 43-51.

Green, L., Kagel, J.H., & Battalio, R.C. (1982). Ratio schedules of reinforcement and their relation to economic theories of labor supply. In M.L. Commons, R.J. Herrnstein, & H. Rachlin (Eds.), *Quantitative analyses of behavior* (Vol. 2): *Matching and maximizing accounts.* Cambridge, MA: Ballinger.

Green, L., & Snyderman, M. (1980). Choice between rewards differing in amount and delay: Toward a choice model of self control. *Journal of the Experimental Analysis of Behavior, 34,* 135-147.

Grosch, J., & Neuringer, A. (1981). Self-control in pigeons under the Mischel paradigm. *Journal of the Experimental Analysis of Behavior, 35,* 3-21.

Hadar, J. (1971). *Mathematical theory of economic behavior.* Menlo Park, CA: Addison-Wesley.

Kagel, J.H., Battalio, R.C., Rachlin, H., & Green, L. (1981). Demand curves for animal consumers. *Quarterly Journal of Economics, 66,* 1-15.

Kagel, J.H., Battalio, R.C., Green, L., & Rachlin, H. (1980). Consumer demand theory applied to choice behavior of rats. In J.E.R. Staddon (Ed.), *Limits to action: The allocation of individual behavior.* New York: Academic Press.

Lancaster, K.J. (1966). A new approach to consumer theory. *Journal of Political Economy 74,* 132-157.

Lea, S.E.G. (1978). The psychology and economics of demand. *Psychological Bulletin, 85,* 441-466.

Logue, A.W., Rodriguez, M.L., Peña-Correal, T.E., & Mauro, B.C. (1984). Choice in a self-control paradigm: Quantification of experience-based differences. *Journal of the Experimental Analysis of Behavior, 41,* 53-67.

Luce, R.D., & Suppes, P. (1965). Preference utility and subjective probability. In R.D. Luce, R.R. Bush, & E. Galanter (Eds.), *Handbook of mathematical psychology* (Vol. 3). New York: Wiley.

MaCurdy, T. (1981). An empirical model of labor supply in a life-cycle setting. *Journal of Political Economy, 89,* 1059-1085.

Maital, S., & Maital, S. (1977). Time preference, delay of gratification and the intergenerational transmission of economic inequality: A behavioral theory of income distribution. In O.C. Ashenfelter & W.E. Oates (Eds.), *Essays in labor market analysis.* New York: Halstead Press.

Mazur, J. (1981). Optimization theory fails to predict performance of pigeons in a two-response situation. *Science, 214,* 823-825.

Mazur, J., & Logue, A.W. (1978). Choice in a self-control paradigm: Effects of a fading procedure. *Journal of the Experimental Analysis of Behavior, 30,* 11-17.

Mischel, W. (1974). Processes in delay of gratification. In L. Berkowitz (Ed.), *Advances in experimental social psychology* (Vol. 7). New York: Academic Press.

Mohabbat, K.A., & Simos, E.O. (1977). Consumer horizon: Further evidence. *Journal of Political Economy, 85,* 851-858.

Navarick, D.J., & Fantino, E. (1976). Self-control and general models of choice. *Journal of Experimental Psychology: Animal Behavior Processes, 2,* 75-87.

Olson, M., & Bailey, M.J. (1981). Positive time preference. *Journal of Political Economy, 89,* 1-25.

Rachlin, H. (1974). Self control. *Behaviorism, 2,* 94-107.

Rachlin, H., & Green, L. (1972). Commitment, choice and self-control. *Journal of the Experimental Analysis of Behavior, 17,* 15-22.

Shull, R.L., Spear, D.J., & Bryson, A.E. (1981). Delay or rate of food delivery as a determiner of response rate. *Journal of the Experimental Analysis of Behavior, 35,* 129-143.

Snyderman, M. (1983). Optimal prey selection: The effects of food deprivation. *Behaviour Analysis Letters, 3,* 359–369.

Solnick, J.V., Kannenberg, C.H., Eckerman, D.A., & Waller, M.B. (1980). An experimental analysis of impulsivity and impulse control in humans. *Learning and Motivation, 11,* 61–77.

Stigler, G.J., & Becker, G.S. (1977). De gustibus non est disputandum. *American Economic Review, 67,* 76–90.

Strotz, R.H. (1956). Myopia and inconsistency in dynamic utility maximization. *Review of Economic Studies, 23,* 165–180.

Thaler, R. (1981). Some empirical evidence on dynamic inconsistency. *Economics Letters, 8,* 201–207.

Thaler, R., & Shefrin, H.M. (1981). An economic theory of self-control. *Journal of Political Economy, 89,* 392–406.

Tversky, A. (1969). Intrasitivity of preferences. *Psychological Review, 76,* 31–48.

Chapter 8

Stability, Melioration, and Natural Selection*

William Vaughan, Jr.
R.J. Herrnstein

Department of Psychology
Harvard University

Optimality principles pervade the physical, biological, and social sciences (Rosen, 1967) to such a degree that it has been suggested that optimization as such is a central principle of science in general (Bordley, 1983). Within physical optics, for example, Fermat's principle of least time states, briefly, that a ray of light moving through a medium will minimize, mathematically if not dynamically, its travel time. More general is Maupertius's principle of least action: in any mechanical system in which energy is conserved, action is minimized. Still broader is the second law of thermodynamics: all closed systems achieve equilibrium by maximizing entropy. Within evolutionary biology, species are often said to be evolving toward maximization of fitness. In physiology, individual organisms are pictured as systems of adaptive homeostatic mechanisms (Cannon, 1939) shaped by natural selection to approach optimality.

Notions of optimality also have a long history in theorizing about human nature or human behavior. For Aristotle, mankind was unique for its rational soul, in addition to the vegetative and animal souls allotted to lesser forms of life. To be rational was to calculate the costs and benefits of alternative courses of action, and to behave accordingly. Jeremy Bentham, the great utilitarian, said: "Nature has placed mankind under the governance of two sovereign masters, *pain* and *pleasure*. It is for them alone to point out what we ought to do, as well as to determine what we shall do" (Bent-

* Preparation of this paper was supported by Grants No. 586-7801 and IST-8511606 from NSF to Harvard University. We are grateful for helpful criticism of an earlier draft by G.C. Homans, A. Houston, J.R. Krebs, R.D. Luce, and the Editors. It is unlikely that all their concerns are resolved here, but it was useful to try to do so within the framework we are suggesting.

ham, 1789, p. 1). A rational society, he believed, would employ a "felicific calculus" to maximize pleasures and minimize pain. With the formalization of economics in the nineteenth century, rationality was more precisely translated into maximization of utility. Consumers, according to standard microeconomic theory, tend to distribute their income so as to maximize total utility. In recent times, evolutionary biology has drawn on economic analysis to promote the idea that animal behavior, as well as human, is best described within an optimality framework.

Although optimality explanations are obviously both fruitful and attractive (see Shoemaker, 1982, for a general discussion of these issues), it is our view that they are special cases of a still more general class of explanations, and that the more general class is a more appropriate heuristic for science. Systems that are said to be tending toward optimality are necessarily also tending toward stability. (We are not considering systems exhibiting limit cycles or which are chaotic, although in principle our argument could be extended to them.) The distinction between optimality and stability may, as a practical matter, be irrelevant to the physical sciences; in physics or chemistry, equilibria are not said to be better than disequilibria, only more stable. A falling stone is no longer thought to be improving itself by coming to rest on the ground, as it was in Aristotelian physics. But in the life sciences, the idea of optimization has not been merely a synonym for stability, as we will show below. As long as optimality and stability are not synonymous, it should be possible to decide whether the stability achieved by a given system is also optimal in any nonvacuous sense. Since an optimal equilibrium implies stability, but not vice versa, the normative assumption of an explanation should be no more specific than stability, with the claim for optimization requiring some further evidence beyond stability itself.

Stability analysis is largely associated with the qualitative analysis of differential equations, initiated by Poincaré in the late nineteenth century (Kline, 1972). In many cases, it is not possible to obtain analytic solutions to a differential equation. Indeed, the exact form of an equation may not be known, due to possible errors of measurement. In cases such as these, the qualitative approach is an attempt to obtain a global picture of the dynamic system under study. (Introductory discussions include Ashby, 1963, and Smale, 1980. Arnold, 1973, and Hirsh & Smale, 1974, are more advanced.)

The basic sorts of question one seeks to answer involve what states of a system constitute points of stable equilibrium, points of unstable equilibrium, and transient states. In the latter case, in what direction is the system moving? If the system is changed slightly, does the global picture change radically or not? In the study of a complex dynamic system, the theoretical framework should not unduly constrain the conclusions reached regarding the nature of the system. The assumption of optimality as used in the life sciences (particularly those dealing with behavior) seems to us unnecessarily constraining. Its thrust is often not so much examination of real-world data, but interpretation: given the data, is it possible to hypothesize intuitively a plausible dimension that is being maximized? Stability analysis, on the other hand, is more closely tied to data, as is required by the qualitiative analysis of transient and stable states of a system. Rather than interpretation, the thrust of stability analysis should be experimentation (or, if that is impossible, the statistical approximation of quasi-experimentation).

The particular contrast between optimization and an alternative form of stabilization that will concern us first is in regard to the experimental analysis of behavior, where the alternatives can be illustrated by economic maximization (Rachlin, Battalio, Kagel, & Green, 1981; Rachlin, Green, Kagel, & Battalio, 1976; Staddon & Motheral, 1978), on the one hand, versus melioration (Herrnstein, 1982; Herrnstein & Vaughan, 1980; Vaughan, 1981, 1985, 1986; Vaughan, Kardish, & Wilson, 1982) on the other. The question is: do organisms distribute their time among options so as to optimize some plausible quantity, e.g., overall rate of reinforcement, or do they tend to distribute more time to better options, even if the overall reinforcement rate suffers? According to the first view, each form of behavior must somehow be sensitive to its impact on one overriding goal, such as maximization of reinforcement rate (or value or utility).[1] According to the second view, various response alternatives literally compete with each other for the organism's time and/ or energy, without regard to overall impact. The alternative theories have much in common—both of them picture a behaving organism as goal-directed or cybernetically moving toward an equilibrium state, which is to say, a stability point. Both theories belong in the tradition of reinforcement theory, with its usual implications for practical prediction and control, as well as its historical antecedents in utilitarianism and hedonism. However, since only one of them can reasonably be characterized as optimizing, the other alternative represents a sharp break with the past.

Inasmuch as maximization is a central assumption of economic theory, the confrontation with melioration must bear on economics as well as psychology. Moreover, to the extent that the formal structure of biological evolutionary selection resembles that of reinforcement, an elucidation of the abstract properties of either structure should illuminate both of them. The clash between maximization and melioration has, in fact, already been joined within biology, though not usually called by those names. (The exception is Dawkins, 1982, p. 46, who had independently proposed "meliorizing" as an alternative to biological maximization.) It should later be apparent how striking the parallel is between biology's dichotomy of group selection versus gene selection, and psychology's dichotomy of maximization versus melioration.

---

[1] No theoretical distinction will be drawn here between "reinforcement," "value" or "utility," only syntactic ones that should become apparent below. It would be easy to collapse the three terms into one, but doing so might result in unfamiliar usages for the various disciplines involved.

In contrast to the usual optimality analysis, the general analysis being suggested here does not prejudge the issue of whether or not animal behavior is optimal. The state of a dynamic system may be characterized as a point within a phase space. The geometry of that space serves to characterize both transient and stable states of the system. Presumably, some such geometry describes the transient and stable states for behavior. While various forms of stability (and instability) are possible, only certain stability points are nonvacuously optimal. The question, then, is whether the stable states are also the optimal states in any meaningful sense.

MAXIMIZATION AND MELIORATION OF INDIVIDUAL BEHAVIOR

The assumptions of present day economics regarding consumer behavior may be found in any microeconomic text (e.g., Mansfield, 1975). A consumer may be assumed to have a fixed income which is to be distributed among a number of alternatives, or commodities. Each commodity is such that more of that commodity, all other things being equal, increases total utility, although in a decreasing manner. In the ideal case, the consumer is assumed to have knowledge of all options and what they entail. We are ignoring questions of cardinal versus ordinal utility and risky versus certain prospects, since they are not germane to the present discussion.

The main assumption about consumer behavior is that resources are distributed so as to maximize utility. In *The Theory of Political Economy,* Jevons (1871, p. 24) stated, "I may have committed oversights in explaining its details; but I conceive that, in its main features, this theory, whether useful or useless, must be the true one." Jevons's position rested largely upon intuition and common-sense observations of human behavior (e.g., "every person will choose the greater apparent good"). More recently, intuition and common sense have been replaced by pragmatism. Samuelson (1947, p. 22), for example, says, "... it is possible to derive operationally meaningful restrictive hypotheses on consumers' demand functions from the assumption that consumers behave so as to maximize an ordinal preference scale of quantities of consumption goods and services." Maximization, in short, is a useful assumption, but note that Samuelson quite properly does not suggest that it alone allows the derivation of "meaningful" hypotheses.

The analysis of consumer behavior does not usually specify the process leading to maximization of utility, but it is not hard to supply one (for more efficient single-variable optimization techniques, see, for example, Adby & Dempster, 1974, or Walsh, 1975). To be concrete, suppose there are two commodities, a and b. C_a and C_b represent the total amount of income spent on a and b, while U_a and U_b represent the utility derived from each. Let $C_a +$

$C_b = 1$, (fixed income), and the graph of U_{a+b} (total utility) as a function of C_a be unimodal with no inflection points.

Suppose a certain proportion of income is being spent on a; call this C_a*. Then C_b* ($= 1 - C_a*$) is being spent on b. This distribution of income will give rise to some total utility, $U_{a+b}*$. Let C_a* now be alternately increased by an arbitrarily small amount, to C_a*^+, and decreased to C_a*^-. The increase produces total utility $U_{a+b}*^+$, and the decrease produces total utility $U_{a+b}*^-$. Now consider the following process:

$$d \frac{C_a}{C_a + C_b} \Big/ dt = f_x (U_{a+b}*^+ - U_{a+b}*^-) \tag{1}$$

Here, f_x is strictly monotonically increasing and passes through the origin. Then, if $U_{a+b}*^+$ is greater than $U_{a+b}*^-$, C_a will tend to increase over time. That is, if an increase in income distributed to a gives rise to a gain in total utility, Equation 1 specifies that more income will be distributed to a, and vice versa. The process is shown in Figure 1. In this figure, overall utility, U_{a+b}, is plotted as a function of proportion of income spent on a (C_a). For a particular value of C_a (labeled C_a*), it can be seen that $U_{a+b}*^+$ is greater than $U_{a+b}*^-$, and hence Equation 1 specifies that more income should be distributed to a. The point labeled $C_a$max is such that utility is maximized; the process specified by Equation 1 will come into equilibrium at this point.

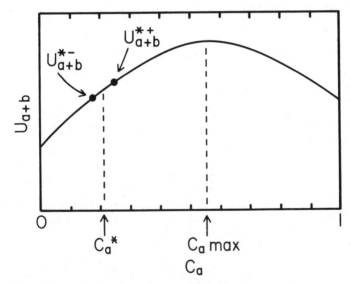

FIGURE 1. Starting at C_a*, behavior should shift to $C_a$max for a maximizer, for at $C_a$max, total utility, U_{a+b}, is maximized. See text for explanation.

At equilibrium (given that exclusive preference has not been reached) we have:

$$U_{a+b}*^+ = U_{a+b}*^-$$ (2)

Since the distance from C_a*^- to C_a*^+ is assumed to be arbitrarily small, Equation 2 is tantamount to the slope of the function for total utility being zero at $C_a$max. Given the assumptions made above regarding the shape of that function, satisfaction of Equation 2 is also equivalent to maximization of utility.[2]

Melioration may be characterized as follows. Again consider two alternatives, a and b, with V_a and V_b being a strictly increasing function of reinforcement per unit time obtained at each alternative. Let T_a and T_b represent times spent at a and b, with $T_a + T_b = 1$ (total time is constant). Melioration specifies:

$$d \frac{T_a}{T_a + T_b} / dt = f_x(V_a - V_b)$$ (3)

The function, f_x, is assumed to be differentiable, strictly monotonically increasing, and $f_x(0) = 0$ (see Vaughan, 1985, p. 387 for further discussion of this formulation). That is, if the value of a exceeds that of b, relatively more time will come to be distributed to a. The process specified by Equation 3 comes into equilibrium (given that exclusive preference has not been reached) when:

$$V_a = V_b.$$

That is, the value of a equals that of b.

---

[2] It is usually assumed that the utility gained from any commodity is a strictly monotonically increasing, negatively accelerated function of income spent on that commodity. Given this, maximization of utility is equivalent to:

$$\frac{dU_a}{dC_a} = \frac{dU_b}{dC_b}$$ (5)

That is, C_a and C_b must be such that the slopes of the respective utility functions are equal. Suppose the slope for a were greater than that for b. Moving a small amount of money from b to a would then cause a drop in U_b that is more than offset by the gain in U_a. Only at equality is no advantageous redistribution possible.

Equation 5 is suggestive of the following process:

$$d \frac{C_a}{C_a + C_b} / dt = f_x(\frac{dU_a}{dC_a} - \frac{dU_b}{dC_b})$$ (6)

where f_x has the properties specified for Equation 1. According to Equation 6, if the slope for commodity a exceeds that for commodity b, then, over time, relatively more resources will be distributed to a, and vice versa. At equilibrium, Equation 6 equals zero, and utility is maximized, as defined by Equation 5.

For animals working on a typical operant reinforcement schedule, the assumption is made that the value of a situation is a strictly monotonically increasing function of rate of reinforcement[3] in that situtation: $V_i = g(R_i/T_i)$, where R_i represents number of reinforcements in situation i; further, $g(0) = 0$. We then have the matching law (Herrnstein, 1970):

$$\frac{T_a}{T_b} = \frac{R_a}{R_b} \tag{4}$$

The operation of melioration (Eq. 3) is shown in Figure 2. Here, the value of a (V_a) and b (V_b) are shown as a function of time spent at a (T_a). For a particular value of T_a (labeled T_a*), the value of a exceeds that for b ($V_a* > V_b*$). Under these conditions, Equation 3 specifies that more time should be distributed to a. Equilibrium is reached at the point labeled $T_a$mel.

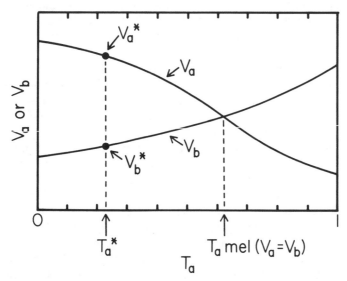

FIGURE 2.   Starting at T_a*, time allocation should shift to $T_a$mel for a meliorator, for at $T_a$mel, the reinforcing values of the competing alternatives are equalized. See text for explanation.

As a general rule, optimization analyses of behavior do not focus on the process (e.g., Eq. 1) but rather on the equilibrium state (e.g., Eq. 2). Equation 2 may be deduced from Equation 1, given suitable boundary conditions (such as unimodality). The converse, however, is not in general true: it is not necessarily the case that the process in Equation 1 can be uniquely in-

---

[3] The "reinforcement" of which behavior is a relatively simple and direct function may sometimes seem to be objectively specified, as by a certain number of food pellets or the like. In principle, however, it is subjective in approximately the same sense as the economic concept of "utility."

ferred from the outcome in Equation 2. Consider a concurrent variable-ratio, variable-ratio (*conc* VR VR) experiment (Herrnstein & Loveland, 1975), a procedure in which one alternative always pays off with a higher probability than the other, and the two pay-offs are otherwise identical. Although this experiment has been cited as evidence of optimization (e.g., Krebs, 1978; Rachlin et al., 1976), it is actually ambiguous with regard to discriminating between Equations 1 and 3. On *conc* VR VR, both an optimization process and melioration will drive an organism toward exclusive preference for the better alternative.

Figure 3 is a graphical representation of a *conc* VR VR experiment. Here R_a/T_a and R_b/T_b stand for the local rates of reinforcement in situations a and b, and $(R_a + R_b)/(T_a + T_b)$ represents overall rate of reinforcement. Here we assume that V_i is a strictly increasing function of R_i/T_i, that U_{i+j} is a strictly increasing function of $(R_i + R_j)/(T_i + T_j)$, and that T_a (proportion of time at alternative a) is equivalent to C_a (proportion of income spent on a). For any particular distribution of resources between 0 and 1, V_a is greater than V_b, so T_a should increase (by Eq. 3). Further, an increase in C_a will increase U_{a+b}, so C_a should increase (by Eq. 1). Under these conditions, then, both melioration and maximization predict exclusive preference for a.

Economics makes assumptions about consumer behavior not so much to study consumer behavior per se, but to facilitate deducing consequences of theories that include consumer behavior as one facet. In the large aggregations that economic theory addresses, we lose contact with individual behavior and its fine structure. Lakatos (1970) points out that scientific research programs may be characterized as consisting of a hard core, which it has been decided data cannot refute, and a protective belt of auxiliary hypotheses, which must bear the brunt of disconfirming instances. Within economics, maximization of utility by consumers is usually part of the hard core, not subject to empirical test. For behavioral analysis, on the other hand, assumptions which serve merely to protect the accepted view of consumer behavior should be dropped. The behavior of individual organisms is the ultimate subject matter for behavioral analysis, so at its hard core there should be no assumptions about the form of fundamental behavioral laws, including maximization of utility. Rather, it need merely be assumed that behavior obeys laws that can be stated at the behavioral level of analysis.

Within the study of animal behavior, data purporting to verify a maximization hypothesis have typically come from one of two areas: studies of animal behavior in the wild (in which the contingencies tend to be largely ratio-like), and studies in the laboratory employing the traditional interval and ratio schedules. The processes specified by Equations 1 and 3, however, are such that they should apply to any arbitrary schedule. (Indeed, one description of the aim of the experimental analysis of behavior is to be able, given any arbitrary schedule, to specify how the organism will behave.)

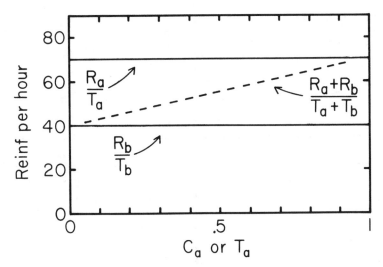

FIGURE 3. Showing a concurrent variable-ratio, variable ratio schedule on which alternative a is more valued than alternative b. Both maximization and melioration predict exclusive preference for a.

Some artificially contrived schedules of reinforcement provide decisive evidence in choosing between maximization and melioration.

Figure 4 dramatizes how different maximization can be from melioration, given appropriate reinforcement feedback functions. In Panel A, overall rate of reinforcement (the dashed line) is constant as more or less time is spent at either alternative, so by maximization all points are points of neutral equilibrium. However, alternative a pays off better than alternative b, so, by melioration, behavior should shift toward a.

In Panel B, overall rate of reinforcement increases as behavior shifts toward b, shown by the dashed line. In addition, the same contingencies as before hold for melioration: for any distribution of time, the local rate of reinforcement (and hence the value) of alternative a exceeds that for b. If the subject is sensitive to changes in overall rates of pay, it should always tend toward b; if sensitive only to local rates of pay, it should prefer a. Maximization thus predicts exclusive preference for b, while melioration predicts exclusive preference for a.

In Panel C, the rate of reinforcement on alternative a equals that on b, so by melioration all points are points of neutral equilibrium. In addition, overall rate of reinforcement increases as behavior shifts toward b, so by maximization it should do so.

Finally, in Panel D, the rate of reinforcement is the same for both alternatives, as well as for overall rate of reinforcement. By either melioration or maximization, all distributions of behavior are points of neutral equilibrium.

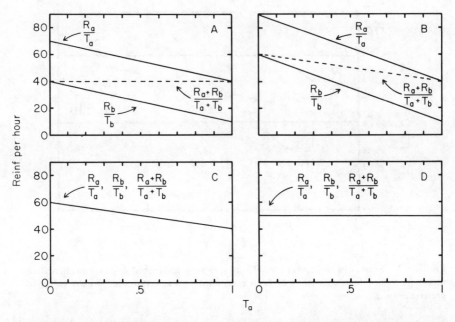

FIGURE 4.   A. Reinforcement rate for alternative a (R_a/T_a) always exceeds that for alternative b (R_b/T_b). Overall reinforcement (($R_a + R_b)/(T_a + T_b$)) (dashed line) is constant and independent of distribution of behavior (T_a). B. Reinforcement rate for a again always exceeds that for b, but overall reinforcement is maximized when b is preferred exclusively. C. Reinforcement rate is equal for a and b at all distributions of behavior, but overall reinforcement is again maximized when b is preferred exclusively. D. Reinforcement rate, for both alternatives and overall, remains constant for all distributions of behavior.

Within the domain of concurrent schedules with identical reinforcers, panels A, B, and C may well exhaust the ways in which maximization may be discriminated from melioration, in the sense of having the contingencies of reinforcement for the competing responses at odds with that for responding as a whole. Although these exact experiments have not been run, the abstract principles they exemplify have all been empirically tested. Panel A corresponds to the experiment shown in Figures 5.6 and 5.7 of Herrnstein and Vaughan (1980), using concurrent alternatives with flat local reinforcement functions. Panel B corresponds to Vaughan (1981), described below (see Figure 8), as well as Vaughan, Kardish, and Wilson (1982), also described below. And Panel C corresponds to Figure 5.9 of Herrnstein and Vaughan (1980), in which the two local rates of reinforcement were equal to each other, but varied as a function of the distribution of behavior. It is presumably of some significance that in all of these cases, the melioration process (Equation 3) describes the allocation of behavior across alternatives better than the maximization process (Equation 1). Only in those special cases in which the two processes converge do subjects maximize (see Herrnstein, 1982).

In summary, maximization constitutes a direct translation of rationality into behavioral language. All choices are viewed as depending on their relation to one central dimension, overall utility. Equilibrium is supposedly reached when no possible redistribution of activities can increase overall utility. In contrast, melioration portrays an organism as a set of competing response tendencies, a system that is "rational" only in certain special environments (Vaughan, 1984). If one response pays off more than another, the first will increase even if the overall payoff thereby suffers. At equilibrium, all surviving responses pay off at the same average rate. Response categories that do not achieve that high a rate of pay disappear. A meliorating organism is a maximizing organism if it has an infinite capacity to redefine response categories to suit prevailing contingencies of reinforcement, for then the optimal distribution of responses in any situation would be treated as a single response category in its own right, and it would be chosen exclusively as a result of melioration (Herrnstein, 1982). For a creature capable of learning new response configurations, melioration pushes toward maximization. However, no evidence has been provided for infinite response plasticity in any species. To the extent that the topography of response categories is not entirely determined by contingencies of reinforcement, a meliorating organism may fail to maximize.

The main virtue of stability analysis is that it focuses research on the qualitative, global properties of behavior, allowing questions regarding more precise refinements to be addressed at a later point. The major disagreement separating advocates of maximization and melioration concerns the nature of the variables governing behavior (cf. Equations 1 and 3). This is not a question requiring a precise mathematical answer. It requires a demonstration of functional relationships (or lack thereof) between environmental and behavioral variables.

For example, consider the experiment reported by Vaughan, Kardish, and Wilson (1982). Pigeons were exposed to a concurrent VI 3 min VI 3 min schedule, and distributed approximately half their time to each, an outcome consistent with both maximization and melioration. Next, a VI 1 min schedule was added, with the property that it only advanced while the pigeons worked on one of the original schedules, but delivered reinforcement (if one were available) when they were working on the other schedule. According to maximization, the pigeons should have increased their time on the side causing the third schedule to run (since this increased overall reinforcement); according to melioration, they should have spent more time on the other side (since the local rate of reinforcement on that side was now higher). The pigeons in fact shifted toward the side with the higher local rate of reinforcement, at a cost in overall reinforcement. For present purposes, the relevant feature of the experiment is that the variables purported to govern behavior by a maximization or a melioration process had opposite signs. It was not the precise outcome that mattered, but the qualitative one: more time came to be spent on one side than the other. The qualitative answer is an obvious, but essential, first step in the analysis of a dynamic system, for it precludes one of the two alternative processes.

Now consider the question of whether a slight change in a system results in an insignificant, or a significant, change in performance. On variable-interval schedules, responses are reinforced after varying and arbitrary intervals of time. Maximization holds that the moderately high response rates typically seen in pigeons derive from the positive, albeit shallow, slope of the function relating obtained reinforcement rate to response rate on the schedule, up to some rate of work at which the marginal response cost just balances the marginal gain in reinforcement. By means of a change in procedure (Vaughan, 1976), the slope of the function relating reinforcement to behavior can be made zero over a wide range of rates of work. According to maximization, the change in behavior should be dramatic; melioration would appear to predict no change in behavior (see also Prelec, 1983b). Changing the slope to zero has been shown to have little if any effect on behavior.

NATURAL SELECTION AND REINFORCEMENT

Parallels between evolution and operant conditioning have often been pointed out (e.g., Gilbert, 1972; Herrnstein, 1964; Skinner, 1981; Staddon & Simmelhag, 1971). Certain basic features of the parallel are not fortuitous, since the main question that one seeks to answer, concerning either evolution or individual behavior, is how adaptation comes about. For biological adaptation, prescientific accounts usually involved some sort of divine intervention or creation. The extraordinary adaptation of creatures to their environment has probably always been taken as evidence of God; in certain circles, it still is, as contemporary creationists exemplify. For individual behavior, prescientific accounts rely not so much on divine creation as on individual creativity or free will. Except to a small community of behavioral analysts, deterministic philosophers, and the like, adaptive behavior continues to be taken as evidence for individual autonomy.

Prescientific accounts of biological or behavioral adaptation postulate an agency outside of natural law, divine creation, or free will, beyond science and hence not subject to its causal analysis. Not surprisingly, a scientific analysis moves the agent back within the domain of natural law, back into biology or psychology. Darwin's theory of evolution noted that individuals vary along a number of dimensions. If given phenotypic values confer a greater ability to survive and reproduce than others, and are based on genetic differences, then selection will occur. Over time, this mechanistic process leads to adaptation. What God is said to do in an act of creation, evolution does, though presumably more slowly, by the sifting process of natural selection.

Variation and selection also provide a key to behavioral adaptation. A single organism's behavior varies, some of it leading to outcomes that influence the strength of those behaviors. The notions of reinforcement and punishment play the same roles in behavioral analysis as reproductive success and failure play in evolutionary biology. Selection thus again operates over time to produce adaptation by a mechanistic process; free will is said to achieve the same result instantaneously by insight.

The parallel between evolution and individual behavior goes beyond variation and selection. In each case, prescientific accounts serve both to seem to answer vexing questions and to give people an inflated sense of their worth (in the case of evolution) or their options (in the case of individual behavior). It is therefore not surprising that reactions to the scientific account tend to be virulent. John Herschel, a contemporary of Darwin, referred to natural selection as "the law of higgeldy-piggeldy" (see Hull, 1973). Koestler (1968) has referred to behaviorism as "a monumental triviality."

On the face of it, adaptation by means of variation and selection would appear to be a recipe for maximization—of fitness in the case of evolution, and of reinforcing value in the case of behavior. Nevertheless, a closer look at the process of evolution leads to a different conclusion, just as a closer look at behavior does.

NATURAL SELECTION AND STABILITY

In an introductory chapter, Davies and Krebs (1978, p. 2) discuss two approaches to theorizing within behavioral ecology. The first is optimality theory: "...natural selection should tend to produce animals which are maximally efficient at propagating their genes and therefore at doing all other activities...." They then point out a limitation of optimality theory: an individual's best solution to a problem may depend on what others in a population are doing. As a result, a different approach is warranted, which is to find what is termed an evolutionarily stable strategy (ESS). This consists of a strategy such that if most members of a population adopt it, it is not susceptible to invasion by some other strategy. That is, the system is stable. Whether, in addition to being stable, an ESS is also optimal for a species is a question we reserve for later, but note here that the constrast between optimality and an ESS has essentially the same dimensions as that between utility maximization and melioration, in each case pitting a rule for optimal stability against a rule for stability per se.

The use of optimality considerations in evolution is usually traced to Wright (1932) (although McCoy, 1979, points out that Janet, 1895, made similar proposals). Wright pictured a species as occupying an area in a

2-dimensional "landscape" onto which were projected contours of equal adaptive value. In general, evolution would consist in the species climbing the steepest slope in its vicinity. While picturesque, this conception of maximization has serious defects (see, for example, Maynard Smith, 1978). Given a number of adaptive peaks, where a "hill-climbing" species lands depends on initial conditions and may be a local, rather than global, maximum. The hill-climbing metaphor fails to provide a credible model of global maximization. It actually comes closer to being a model of an ESS, although, for an ESS, the genes, rather than the species as a whole, must do the "climbing."

If, in contrast, what one means by maximization is simply maximization (however achieved) of the mean reproductive fitness of individuals across a population, then one is driven to accept group selection, for a conspecific's offspring would be as potent in selection as one's own. From the standpoint of mean reproductive fitness, even one's own genes would have no special status in comparison with any conspecific's. Based on numerous observations which appeared to suggest that animals behave altruistically (for the good of the group), Wynne-Edwards (1962) argued at length for the pervasiveness of just the sort of group selection that would maximize mean reproductive fitness. But his argument ultimately failed for two reasons, as other optimalists soon pointed out. A more limited form of altruism was shown to be derivable from kin selection, which is, in turn, derivable from individual rather than group selection (Hamilton, 1964). To the extent that a kin's genes match one's own, this more limited altruism reduces to egocentricism, as far as natural selection is concerned. Moreover, a population of altruists is in any case unstable in principle, inasmuch as genes for selfishness, should they arise, will spread throughout the population (Dawkins, 1976).

Besides the problems with group selection based on mean fitness maximization, the very concept of maximizing adaptiveness is plagued with difficulty. Williams (1966), exemplifying the traditional optimalist view, says, "Natural selection would produce or maintain adaptation as a matter of definition. Whatever gene is favorably selected is better adapted than its unfavored alternatives" (p. 25). But what happens as a matter of definition tells us nothing about the world. Williams goes on to say that "the theoretically important kind of fitness is that which promotes ultimate reproductive survival" (p. 26). But can a mechanistic selective process conceivably promote "ultimate" survival? Consider, for example, Hardin's (1968) discussion of the tragedy of the commons, the risk of irreversibly overutilizing the environment. At some point during human evolution, man survived while closely related forms did not, presumably a reflection of man's greater fitness. Suppose that one component of that fitness was having sufficient intelligence to graze animals or build factories. But now, it turns out, mankind's intelligence or forbearance may be insufficient to prevent its own demise through overexploitation of the collective resources. In such a context, "ultimate reproductive survival" is a paradoxical concept at best, for a less bright species would not have grazed animals or built factories.

The above discussion has implicitly assumed that the fitness of a particular genotype is independent of the relative frequency of the genotype within a population. An analysis of the alternative, frequency-dependent fitness, was initiated by Fisher (1930), who sought an answer to why the ratio of the two sexes usually approaches one to one. A traditional optimalist might have answered that an equal number of males and females is good for the species, since it maximizes the probability of opposite sexes meeting, hence mating, or that females should greatly exceed males, if each male can fertilize many females. Fisher (making some assumptions about the transmission of gender that we may neglect here) reasoned that, if a population contained more males than females, females would then have greater fitness than males (inasmuch as the average female's genes would be more highly represented in the next generation than the average male's). The opposite argument applies if females outnumber males. Hence, any deviation from a one-to-one ratio (or, possibly some other stable ratio, if parental investments are taken into account) creates conditions which automatically tend to reestablish that ratio. An equilibrium sex ratio should be approximated whether or not it is good for the species.

Since Fisher's analysis of sex ratios, the notion of frequency-dependent selection has established itself firmly. A convenient example is Maynard Smith's (Maynard Smith, 1974, 1976, 1982; Maynard Smith & Price, 1973) game-theoretic analysis of animal conflict. Why, Maynard Smith wondered, are conflicts often settled without actual bloodshed? On the face of it, fighting one's opponent to the death would appear to confer greater fitness on an individual than allowing a vanquished opponent to escape. But from the group selectionist standpoint, ritualized combat may seem advantageous inasmuch as it allows the combatants to survive and reproduce. In fact, as Maynard Smith showed, neither the simple individualistic nor the group selection answer realistically captured the actual selective contingencies.

Maynard Smith's approach is exemplified by a hypothetical species (see fuller discussion in Maynard Smith, 1982, and Dawkins, 1976), individuals of which may use either one or the other, but not both, of two strategies when confronting another individual of the same species.[4] We assume the strategy used is under genetic control. The first strategy is termed "hawk" and is characterized by the individual always fighting until one of the combatants wins and the other loses; the loser is always injured. The second strategy is termed "dove." If a dove meets a hawk, it runs away; the hawk

---

[4] For our purposes, it is sufficient to consider only the case in which the strategies are mutually exclusive for any particular individual and reproduction is asexual; fuller treatments also attempt to deal with individuals that can employ either strategy and with sexual reproduction.

wins the contest, but neither is hurt. If a dove meets a dove, both posture for a while. Both doves lose time, and one wins the contest and the other loses, but neither is injured.

Next we must set values relating the outcomes of contests to fitness. Let us assume that winning a contest confers 50 fitness points on the winner and 0 on the loser; that an injury costs 100 points; and that time spent posturing costs 10 points. If a hawk meets a hawk, one will win and the other will lose and in the process be injured. The average payoff to a hawk meeting a hawk is therefore -25 ($= (+50$ for winner -100 for loser)/2). If a hawk meets a dove, the hawk wins the contest, hence gains 50 points, while the dove runs away and loses 0. If a dove meets a dove, both waste time posturing; in addition, one wins and one loses. The average payoff for a dove meeting another dove is therefore 15 ($= (+50$ $-20)/2$).

Now imagine a population consisting either of all doves or all hawks. In a population of doves, the average payoff to each individual is 15 points. But if a mutant hawk appears, it will win all contests. Hence, in a pure dove population, a hawk always receives 50 points, so hawk genes would tend to sweep the population. In contrast, in a population of hawks, the average payoff to each individual is -25. If a dove mutant appears, its average payoff is 0. Since this is greater than -25, dove genes will tend to sweep the population. Both pure dove and pure hawk populations are therefore unstable: a mutant with the opposite strategy will have greater fitness than the population average. Figure 5 shows the fitnesses for hawk and dove as a function of the proportion of the population playing dove. Given the particular parameters used here, a stable mix of hawks and doves would have 5/12 doves and 7/12 hawks.

From Figure 5 it can be seen that, at stability (evolutionarily stable strategy, or ESS), the average fitness for each individual is 6¼, independent of whether the individual is a hawk or a dove. The average fitness for each individual at all proportions of doves and hawks is plotted as the dashed curve. The equality of fitness for doves and hawks is a necessary (though not sufficient) condition for stability: if they were not equal, the strategy with greater fitness would subsequently constitute a higher proportion of the population, until equality was achieved. Note further that the average fitness at equality of 6¼ is suboptimal for the group; it is, for example, less than what could be achieved in an all dove population, which is 15. In this example, stability and optimality, in the sense of the maximum average fitness per individual, are mutually incompatible.

It could be countered, at this point, that, even though the species as a whole is not maximizing fitness, competing forms are in fact doing just that: given the context of individuals, the hawk or dove gene would each lose fitness by increasing its proportion above that at the ESS. But that, in fact, would be to grant that evolution is a melioration, rather than a maxi-

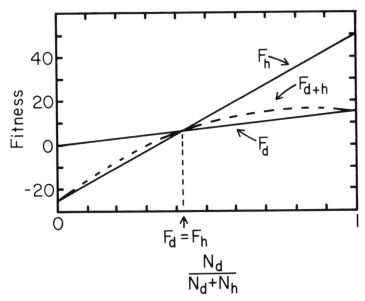

FIGURE 5. Fitness for "doves" (F_d) and for "hawks" (F_h) as a function of the proportion of doves in the population. N_d and N_h refer to the number of doves and hawks, respectively. At a fitness of 6¼, the two forms equalize in average fitness. The evolutionarily stable strategy (ESS) thus predicts 5/12 as the dove proportion. The total average fitness across doves and hawks (F_{d+h}) is given by the dashed curve.

mization, process. The parallel has been drawn between an individual with its various responses and a species with its various genes. Just as an individual's responses do not act in concert for the benefit of the individual, so the genes of a species do not act in concert to increase the species' fitness. In both cases, equilibrium is achieved, not necessarily at an optimum, but at a point where the meliorating elements are equally benefited, which is to say, at the point specified by the matching law.

In a discussion of the competitive exclusion principle, Ayala (1972) has discussed the necessary and sufficient conditions for two competing species to achieve a stable mix, as distinguished from one species excluding the other. For a stable mix, there must, first, exist a mix such that individuals of the two species have equal fitness, which means that over time their relative numbers remain constant. Second, given a deviation from that mix, the species whose relative representation has increased must simultaneously move to a lower individual fitness than the other: a deviation from equality drives the population back toward a mix that restores the equality point for fitnesses. If either or both of the two conditions are not met, in the long run one of the species will competitively exclude the other. Similar dynamics govern the competition between genetic polymorphisms within a species.

Frequency-dependent selection has been shown empirically to lead either to stable mixes or exclusions (for reviews, see, for example, Ayala & Campbell, 1974; Clarke, 1979), illustrated by Batesian mimicry and Mullerian mimicry, respectively (Fisher, 1930). In Batesian mimicry, a palatable species resembles a noxious one, thereby gaining in fitnesss by being less often taken as prey. Now consider a genetically polymorphic species with two phenotypes, one exhibiting mimicry of a noxious second species, and the other, of a noxious third species. The two forms are not themselves noxious, but they gain fitness by resembling noxious species. Whenever the proportion of one of the two forms rises, its ratio to the mimicked species also rises, other things being equal. Predators should then tend to favor it over the other phenotype, because its probability of noxiousness has fallen. As predators consume more of the first phenotype, its probability of noxiousness rises, reducing consumption, and so on. The two forms thus tend toward a stable mix, the specific value of which depends on the various parameters.

In Mullerian mimicry, two noxious species resemble each other, so that a predator that has encountered one will tend to avoid both. Here, the species is itself noxious and so is the species it resembles. Consider a noxious polymorphic species showing Mullerian mimicry for one or the other of two other noxious species. If one of these forms is more frequent than the other, it will tend to increase in frequency, since predators will have more often encountered it and discovered its noxiousness (disregarding effects of variations in degrees of noxiousness). At stability, only the more frequent form remains.

Harding, Allard, and Smeltzer (1966) discuss a case of frequency-dependent selection in lima beans. Over generations, plants that were heterozygotic at a particular locus tended to constitute about 7% of the otherwise homozygotic population. Experimental tests showed that heterozygotes had lower fitness in the presence of other heterozygotes than in the presence of homozygotes. The authors suggested that the frequency-dependence might have resulted from competition between the heterozygotes. At about 7% heterozygosity, fitness for heterozygotes approximately matched that for homozygotes.

Since frequency dependence is self-evidently an essential consideration in selection, it has attracted considerable theoretical, as well as, empirical attention (e.g., Slatkin, 1978; Ayala, 1972; Dawkins, 1976, 1980, 1982; Clarke, 1979). For our purposes, however, the detailed complications are beside the point. Instead, we shall represent Ayala's necessary and sufficient conditions for stable mixes graphically (see Figure 6), by plotting the fitness differences between individuals in two competing species (or two competing forms in one species) as a function of the relative sizes of the two populations, N_a and N_b. In order to achieve a stable mix, the interaction between the species or forms must conform to a function that intersects zero on the ordinate in Figure 6 with a negative slope (or a discontinuous approxima-

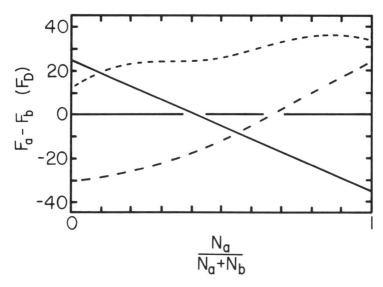

FIGURE 6. Difference between fitness of form a and form b (F_D) as a function of proportion of the population adopting form a. Only the solid line (sloping downward to the right) illustrates the condition for a stable mix of two populations. That line plots the fitness-difference function for hawks and doves (see Figure 5). Lower dashed line is unstable because any deviation from a fitness difference of zero is self-amplifying. Upper dashed line predicts exclusion of b by a.

tion to a negative slope) at the intersection. The actual function drawn by the solid line is, in fact, derived from the hypothetical hawks and doves (see Figure 5). It has already been shown that, in this example, stability is suboptimal.

As long as fitness a exceeds fitness b, the population will shift toward a, and vice versa. If the fitness-difference function intersects zero with positive slope, then fitness-equality will be unstable, since deviations on either side of equality are self-amplifying (see lower dashed function in Figure 6). Under these conditions, the population will become totally a or b, depending on initial conditions. Besides intersections with positive or negative slope, the fitness-difference function may simply not intersect zero, illustrated by the upper dashed function in Figure 6. Here, the a's would prevail, and it would look like a case of frequency-independent selection, although, strictly speaking, the function should at least have zero slope to justify that term (see discussion of Figure 7, below).

In a case of strict frequency-independent selection, the stable state is also necessarily optimal in the maximization-of-fitness sense. The more fit form simply excludes the less fit form. However, for the other kinds of stability, whether with an ESS mix of the two forms or competitive exclusion by one form, maximization of fitness depends on aspects of the fitness-difference

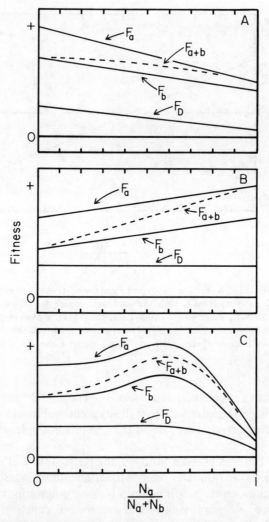

FIGURE 7. Fitness for form a (F_a), for b (F_b), average total fitness (F_{a+b}) and the differences between fitnesses of a and b (F_D), as a function of proportion of a's. In all three panels, b would be excluded by a, since the fitness-difference functions (F_D) are always positive. Exclusion by a minimizes over-all fitness (F_{a+b}) for panels A and C, and maximizes it for panel B.

functions that have no necessary bearing on the stability point. Figure 7, for example, contains three sets of contingencies that would yield populations of all a's given the principles of competitive exclusion. In each panel, form a has greater individual fitness (F_a) than form b (F_b) at all relative frequencies, so the population would shift to a's exclusively. However, only for panel B does an all a population maximize over-all fitness (F_{a+b}); for the other panels, an all a population minimizes over-all fitness. Frequency-independent selection, which is not illustrated here, would not only have a line of zero slope for the fitness-difference function (F_D; that is $F_a - F_b$), but lines of zero slope for the individual fitnesses of a and b.

In this discussion, we may seem to have neglected the possible influence of genetic changes that could modify the competing forms, hence the stability point. Ayala (1972), for example, has observed such changes in competing populations of fruit flies under laboratory conditions, when a new genetic form disrupts an established equilibrium and then establishes a new level. The emergence of fitter forms is, of course, crucial in natural selection and in speciation, but, given a mutation, the underlying process determining whether and to what extent it survives appears to be no different from the selection processes already described and diagrammed in Figures 6 and 7. Whether the modified form excludes its competition or establishes a new stable mix at a different frequency depends on whether the fitness-difference function passes through zero with negative slope. If the new form has a lower average fitness than that at the prevailing equilibrium point, it simply disappears, which is the case for most mutations.

Another way suboptimal ESS may be superseded has been described in detail by D.S. Wilson (1980). Instead of modeling natural selection as if it took place within a homogeneous medium in which the genetic composition (including the genetic variance) is uniform across all localities, Wilson argues for the relevance of what he calls "structured demes." Competition often occurs within localities with varying genetic compositions. The localities may differ in the equilibria they establish for gene frequencies, but they may also differ in how productive they are over-all. The localities may be mutually isolated to varying degrees. In such a model, genes compete locally, but localities themselves also compete as they send out colonizers in proportion to their own fecundities. It has been shown formally (if not empirically) that the notion of structured demes, under suitable circumstances, allows a population as a whole to move toward increasing reproductive fitness. The process appears to be the evolutionary analogue to learning new configurations of movements for an individual organism. The melioration process, in either case, operating at a more inclusive level of synthesis, drives the system toward genuine optimization. It remains to be shown how or where the concept of structured demes is relevant to natural selection.

We have been ignoring the rates at which equilibrium is approached by various systems, focusing instead only on the direction in which a system moves. Under some conditions, however, the rates of change can have strong effects. Consider a population of all doves, with an average fitness of 15, and assume it is competing with a second population of animals having an average (and stable) fitness of 10. Two processes will then occur simultaneously: the dove population will gain hawks (by mutation) and approach an average fitness of $6\frac{1}{4}$ (see Figure 5); and, of the two competing populations, the one with higher fitness will tend to competitively exclude the other. If the hawk-dove population approaches equilibrium quickly, but competitive exclusion occurs slowly, the hawk-dove population will go extinct (since it, with a fitness of $6\frac{1}{4}$, competes with a population with a fitness of 10). If the two processes are reversed in terms of speed, the other population will go extinct (since it, with a stable fitness of 10, faces a population with a fitness of nearly 15).

Our general conclusion with regard to ESS versus optimization is largely consistent with Dawkins's (1980). In the case of frequency-dependent selection, an ESS analysis or something similar is clearly required, both by existing data and by a logical analysis of the selective process. In the case of frequency-independent selection, an ESS and an optimality analysis lead to the same outcome. But just because of this ambiguity (recall the concurrent VR VR experiment mentioned earlier), cases involving frequency-independent selection cannot tell us whether the process of evolution acts to maximize average fitness, or whether fitter forms displace less fit forms, without regard to maximization. Frequency-dependent selection provides, in effect, an experimental test of the two hypotheses, and it favors ESS. Dawkins concludes that "it seems parsimonious to abandon the phrase 'optimal strategy' altogether, and replace it with ESS" (p. 357). In our view, an ESS analysis is preferable not so much because it is parsimonious, but because it is more nearly *correct*.

THE GENERALITY OF STABILITY ANALYSIS

Students of behavioral analysis may recognize that the foregoing analysis of evolutionary equilibrium directly parallels the melioration analysis of behavioral equilibrium. Figure 8 shows reinforcement-rate differences between alternative responses in two settings as a function of the time allocated to one of them (see also Prelec, 1983a, Ch. 2, Figure 3). Panel A plots the hypothetical schedule shown in Figure 4 (B), for which alternative a always reinforces at a higher rate than alternative b, but overall rate of reinforcement varies directly with time allocated to b. The rates or other qualities of reinforcement for a pair of alternatives would always differ by a constant amount ($R_a/T_a - R_b/T_b$ is positive and constant), but the overall level of reinforcement would be an increasing linear function of the time spent on the less reinforcing alternative (alternative b in Figure 8). As indicated, melioration ("M") here calls for exclusive choice of a, notwithstanding the optimality ("O") of choosing b exclusively. In evolutionary terms, this would be a case of suboptimal competitive exclusion.

Panels B and C illustrate what, in Ayala's terms, would be called a stable mix of competing (response) forms. Rates of reinforcement for each of a pair of alternatives depended on how much time the subjects (pigeons) were spending at the alternatives. For example, in Panel B it can be seen that from 0-.125 spent at alternative a, the reinforcement rate was higher at a (R_a/T_a) than b (R_b/T_b), but from .875-1.0 spent at alternative a, reinforce-

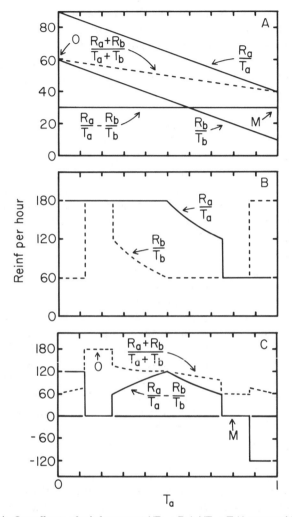

FIGURE 8. A. Overall rate of reinforcement $((R_a + R_b)/(T_a + T_b))$ grows with allocation to b, but a produces a higher rate of reinforcement than b at all allocations. Value is maximized (0) by exclusive preference for b, but melioration (M) predicts exclusive preference for a. This is the hypothetical experiment graphed in Figure 4, Panel B. B. Vaughan's procedure (1981) for distinguishing between maximization and melioration. Local rates of reinforcement for a (R_a/T_a) and b (R_b/T_b) are shown as a function of proportion of time spent at a (T_a). C. Overall rate of reinforcement $((R_a + R_b)/(T_a + T_b))$ and differences between local rates of reinforcement $(R_a/T_a - R_b/T_b)$. Rather than maximizing (flat region shown by 0) subjects meliorated (region shown by M).

ment rate was higher at b. The function $R_a/T_a - R_b/T_b$ in Panel C shows reinforcement rate differences at all allocations of time, while the function $(R_a + R_b)/(T_a + T_b)$ shows overall reinforcement rate. This complex function was examined by Vaughan (1981) because it simultaneously provided two tests of the melioration concept. First, it sharply separated the melioration (M) from the optimization (O) equilibrium (see Panel C). Secondly, it provided two points (actually, regions) of intersection with equality in reinforcement rate, only one of which had the negative slope required for stable mixed equilibria. As melioration predicts, pigeons exposed to this schedule all stabilized in the region labelled M, at a substantial cost in reinforcement. Their initial preference has been set at the optimal level, labeled 0, so the shift to M was all the more impressive confirmation of melioration. In this experiment, reinforcement could have been maximized simply by not changing behavior, yet the pigeons changed anyway, as melioration dictated.

The correspondence between maximization of fitness and maximization of utility (i.e., reinforcement) on the one hand, and ESS and melioration, on the other, should now be evident. Evolution and behavioral allocation are analogous processes, because both arise from selection among competing forms (Herrnstein & Vaughan, 1984). Within evolution, a given species does not survive because individual members work for the sake of a common good (e.g., maximization of reproductive fitness). Rather, forms with greater reproductive fitness displace those with lesser fitness, even at a cost in average fitness. Similarly, a given behavior does not survive because it serves a common goal (e.g., maximization of satisfaction). Rather, if one behavior earns more reinforcement than another, allocation shifts toward the first, even if overall reinforcement decreases. At stability, the remaining forms match in average fitness or in reinforcement. If a new form (of genotype or response) arises and survives, it is likely to find a new stability point at a higher fitness or higher reinforcement, because a new form is unlikely to survive unless it does. But, as the hypothetical examples have proved, higher stability points (either for behavior or genes) can in principle cause a reduction in overall reinforcement or fitness, depending on the underlying contingencies.

In evolutionary biology, the underlying contingencies of reproductive fitness are inherent in the interactions among species and their environments. Needless to say, the interactions can be so obscure that great scientific effort is necessary to uncover them. The all too common examples of disrupted ecology owing to the presumably innocuous introduction or removal of a species testify to the subtleties of determining in advance where a new ESS is to be established (e.g., May, 1983).

In contrast, in behavioral analysis, the contingencies of reinforcement are usually chosen in advance by the experimenter. What evolutionary biologists must discover painstakingly, experimental psychologists simply program into computers that run their experiments. This control over contingencies no doubt helps explain why behavioral analysts have (or think they have) discovered the invariance governing behavioral stability, and also why biologists often find psychological experiments too artificial to be applied to species in nature. Nevertheless, because the behavioral contingencies are transparent, it is relatively easy to see that stability is characterized by equal reinforcement rates for the competing responses (the matching law). Although it is not particularly easy to see that the same formal principle determines biological stability, replacing reinforcement with fitness, that has nevertheless been the conclusion of many theorists.

For a time, behavioral biologists believed that the optimizing assumption was ideal for them, because of a notion about evolution. Davies and Krebs (1978), for example, argued for behavior being optimal because it derived from evolution, and evolution tended toward optimal forms. But if natural selection among genotypes tends toward stability regardless of optimality, a different implication should be drawn. In light of the new evolutionary outlook, the argument by analogy at this point is that behavior, too, should tend toward stability, rather than optimality. Dawkins and Krebs (1979) discuss cases in which natural selection appears to lead species to extinction. Similarly, there are many examples of behavioral adaptations turning against the animals that use them.

Consider an experiment on fly larvae reported by Loeb in 1890 (described by Fraenkel & Gunn, 1940). In moving about a larva swings its head from side to side. If one side is darker than the other, it turns its body slightly in that direction as it moves, and continues the swinging motion. By means of this process, it tends to move away from the light in natural situations, presumably an adaptive behavior for a vulnerable and meaty larva.

Loeb placed a number of larvae in a test tube situated at a right angle to a window where, because of the placement of a screen, the part of the tube near the window received dim light. The part of the tube away from the window received bright light. The window was the source of the incident light throughout the tube. By sampling in various directions, the larvae oriented themselves away from the window. Most of them crossed over into the bright light, and continued to move away from the light. By moving away from the window they ended up in the bright end of the test tube. What is adaptive in most natural settings was maladaptive here, but the larvae behaved in their usual way.

Pigeons, presumably, are more advanced than lima beans or fly larvae. Vaughan (1981), in the experiment described above, subjected pigeons to a schedule in which one alternative reinforced more than another. However, distributing more time to the better alternative reduced the reinforcement from both alternatives. As we have suggested, the pigeons were apparently insensitive to the optimal strategy, and instead meliorated, choosing the locally better, but ultimately more costly, alternative.

Do people do any better? Hardin (1968) (discussed above) suggests that we should not assume that they do. Overexploitation of the environment is a case in which the more immediate reinforcers of indulgence outweigh the delayed reinforcers of forbearance and the long-term consequence is disastrous. On an abstract level, the response of fly larvae, pigeon, and man appear identical. We may conceptualize it as follows. Two situations are sampled (the fly larva samples two light intensities, the pigeon samples reinforcement rates on two keys, the man samples polluting versus not doing so). In all cases, there is a shift in the direction of the contingent payoff: the larva orients away from the window, the pigeon shifts toward the locally better alternative, the man pollutes. In all cases, the long-term effect is maladaptive: the larva ends up in the brighter light, the pigeon receives a lower rate of reinforcement, man degrades his environment.

If man differs at all, it is that knowledge of long term consequences favors setting up new contingencies of reinforcement (Ainslie, 1975; Herrnstein, 1982). For example, a tax or fine for polluting may be sufficient to reduce its reinforcement to the point where it ceases to have a net negative effect on the environment at large. The shift may be viewed as a case of optimization, but it is still an example of melioration, as Figure 9 shows. Without the fine or tax, polluting is more reinforcing than not polluting; with a penalty, which the figure depicts as graded beyond some level of indulgence, pollution is held to any arbitrarily low level. A public policy like this may be

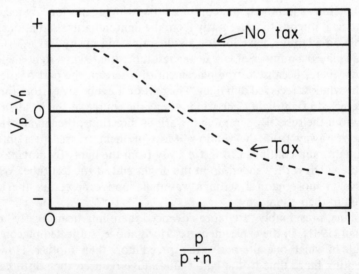

FIGURE 9. Difference between value of polluting (V_p) and value of nonpolluting (V_n), as a function of proportion of industrial residue that constitutes pollution. Without a tax for polluting, the potential polluter always earns more reinforcement for polluting than for not polluting, as illustrated by the solid line. A graduated tax for polluting (e.g., proportion of polluted versus nonpolluted acres of land or cubic yards of effluent) produces the dashed curve. Melioration predicts that pollution will shift from 1 to the abscissa proportion corresponding to the point of intersection with zero on the ordinate.

viewed as a change in reinforcement schedules that exploits melioration to drive behavior toward what is taken to be optimization. In fact, the difficulty people have in creating such presumably rational contingencies of reinforcement, for either their own behavior or for society as a whole, is further evidence for melioration as the controlling process for even human behavior.

Where does economics fit here? In fact, economists typically assume that, among competing behaviors (i.e., competing commodities), a stable mix *must* reflect some sort of diminishing marginal substitutability, allowing individual optimization to be preserved. The underlying contingencies of utility are neither discovered (as in biology), nor programmed (as in behavioral analysis), with only rare exceptions. Instead, having assumed that the consumer optimized, economists derive what the utility functions must have been.

Though assuming *individual* optimization, economists have often noted that groups may nevertheless fail to optimize collective (or average) outcomes. The field of welfare economics (e.g., Bohm, 1973) is concerned to delineate, to the extent logically possible, the concept of a social welfare function: How is aggregate welfare affected by changes in individual consumption? However, because interpersonal comparisons of utility are meaningless (a corollary of ordinal, rather than cardinal, utility functions), the question admits of no single answer. Under the usual assumptions of economics, there are, rather, an infinity of Pareto-optimal points, a state of market such that no person could do any better without someone else being made worse off. In spite of the plethora of points of optimization, a violation of Pareto-optimality may be easily constructed.

In the classical "prisoner's dilemma," both prisoners must choose an unpreferred alternative in order to maximize total gain, which is yet one more example of frequency-dependent outcomes. If either or both prisoners tried to maximize individually, the total outcome would suffer (and Pareto-optimality violated). Schelling's (1978) generalization of the dilemma to multiperson groups is, in fact, formally equivalent to our characterization of individual behavior or the ESS analysis of natural selection. If almost everybody carries a tow cable in his car, for example, then it is probably better not to carry one, since it costs something and the other car needed to tow you in any event probably has one. If almost nobody carries a tow cable, it is no doubt advantageous to buy one. The equilibrium state for tow cables versus no tow cables may or may not be optimal for drivers as a whole, depending on the contingencies (and disregarding the incommensurability of individual utilities). Schelling's analysis assumes that individual participants simply choose the better alternative at any given proportion of tow cables, as individual maximization would imply. In fact, individuals themselves do not generally maximize unless, under the contingencies of reinforcement, maximization and melioration converge. For the tow-cable example, at any given frequency of tow-cables, the choice confronting an individual is a binary choice between a larger and a smaller reinforcement, for which both melioration and maximization give the same answer. It is only when the competition among an individual's own responses have the kinds of frequency-dependent contingencies discussed earlier that maximization at the individual level breaks down, just as collective outcomes may be suboptimal if the individual contingencies are frequency dependent (as in the prisoner's dilemma or the tow-cable example).

Groups of individuals may form coalitions that circumvent suboptimal equilibria. They may, for example, form a tow-cable association which identifies its members by stickers on the cars' rear windows. The members promise to help only each other with towing. Similarly, members of labor unions forgo the possibility of improving their salaries by individual effort and negotiation, and rely on collective bargaining instead. In every facet of social life there may be risks in the unrestrained pursuit of advantage. The social contract itself replaces the Hobbesian confrontation of all against all. Like the structured demes of population biology, or the restructured resonse categories of individual behavior, people sort themselves into aggregations, which then interact. How and why these groups arise are questions that lie outside our concern here, except to note that they complete the parallel we have tried to draw at three levels of analysis.

At the genetic, behavioral, or collective levels, elements selected by individual consequences achieve equilibria that may or may not maximize the variable involved in selection. Individual genes selected for fitness may or may not maximize total fitness; responses strengthened by reinforcement may or may not maximize total reinforcement; participants recruited by outcomes may or may not maximize a group's collective outcome. A stable equilibrium involving mixtures rather than total exclusion—of genes, responses, or participants—must always obey a matching law, an equality (assuming commensurabilty) in the ratio of the frequency of each element to its selective principle: genes to their fitness, responses to their reinforcement, participants to their outcomes.

SUMMARY

The assumption that the behavior of organisms conforms to principles of optimization has derived strength from two distinct sources: the rationalistic perspective, absorbed by economic theory in the nineteenth century (people act to maximize satisfaction or utility), and the maximization of fitness assumption within evolution (a maximally fit organism will, as a corollary, act to maximize rate of reinforcement). Thus, a deduction from the evolutionary argument serves to complement an earlier argument for rational behavior.

Our position, first, is that behavior and evolution each exemplify a single principle of variation and selection, and, second, the principle can lead to equilibria that need not be optimal. Data that have previously been said to verify optimization are, we suggest, actually ambiguous with regard to distinguishing between optimization and a principle of melioration. And, given situations that allow one to discriminate between the two processes, the data unequivocally favor melioration.

REFERENCES

Adby, P.R., & Dempster, M.A.H. (1974). *Introduction to Optimization Methods*. London: Chapman and Hall.

Ainslie, G. (1975). Specious reward: A behavioral theory of impulsiveness and impulse control. *Psychological Bulletin, 82*, 463-496.

Arnold, V.I. (1973). *Ordinary differential equations*. Cambridge, MA: MIT Press.

Ashby, W.R. (1963). *An introduction to cybernetics*. New York: Wiley.

Ayala, F.J. (1972). Competition between species. *American Scientist, 60*, 348-357.

Ayala, F.J., & Campbell C.A. (1974). Frequency-dependent selection. *Annual Review of Ecology and Systematics, 5*, 115-138.

Bentham, J. (1789). *An introduction to the principles of morals and legislation*. London: D. Payne & Son.

Bohm, P. (1973). *Social efficiency: A concise introduction to welfare economics*. New York: Wiley.

Bordley, R.F. (1983). A central principle of science: Optimization. *Behavioral Science, 28*, 53-64.

Cannon, W.B. (1939). *The Wisdom of the Body* (Rev. Ed.). New York: Norton.

Clarke, B.C. (1979). The evolution of genetic diversity. *Proceedings of the Royal Society*, London, B, *205*, 453-474.

Davies, N.B., & Krebs, J.R. (1978). Introduction: Ecology, natural selection and social behavior. In J.R. Krebs & N.B. Davies (Eds.), *Behavioural ecology: An evolutionary approach*. Sunderland, MA: Sinauer.

Dawkins, R. (1976). *The selfish gene*. Oxford: Oxford University Press.

Dawkins, R. (1980). Good strategy or evolutionarily stable strategy? In G.W. Barlow & J. Silverberg (Eds.), *Sociobiology—beyond nature/nurture*. Boulder, CO: Westview Press.

Dawkins, R. (1982). *The extended phenotype*. San Francisco: Freeman.

Dawkins, R., & Krebs, J.R. (1979). Arms races between and within species. *Proceedings of the Royal Society*. London: B, *205*, 489-511.

Fisher, R.A. (1930). *The genetical theory of natural selection*. Oxford: Oxford University Press.

Fraenkel, G.S., & Gunn, D.L. (1940). *The orientation of animals*. Oxford: Oxford University Press.

Gilbert, R.M. (1972). Variation and selection of behavior. In R.M. Gilbert & J.R. Millenson (Eds.), *Reinforcement: Behavioral analyses*. New York: Academic Press.

Hamilton, W.D. (1964). The genetical theory of social behavior, I & II. *Journal of Theoretical Biology, 7*, 1-16, 17-32.

Hardin, G. (1968). The tragedy of the commons. *Science, 162*, 1243-1248.

Harding, J., Allard, R.W., & Smeltzer D.G. (1966). Population studies in predominately self-pollinated species, IX. Frequency-dependent selection in Phaseolus lunatus. *Proceedings of the National Academy of Sciences, 56*, 99-104.

Herrnstein, R.J. (1964). Will. *Proceedings of the American Philosophical Society, 108,* 455–458.

Herrnstein, R.J. (1970). On the law of effect. *Journal of the Experimental Analysis of Behavior, 13,* 243–266.

Herrnstein, R.J. (1982). Melioration as behavioral dynamism. In M.L. Commons, R.J. Herrnstein, & H. Rachlin (Eds.), *Quantitative analyses of behavior, Vol. II: Matching and maximizing accounts.* Cambridge, MA: Ballinger.

Herrnstein, R.J., & Loveland, D.H. (1975). Maximizing and matching on concurrent ratio schedules. *Journal of the Experimental Analysis of Behavior, 24,* 107–116.

Herrnstein, R.J., & Vaughan, W., Jr. (1980). Melioration and behavioral allocation. In J.E.R. Staddon (Ed.), *Limits to action: The allocation of individual behavior.* New York: Academic Press.

Herrnstein, R.J., & Vaughan, W., Jr. (1984). Evolutionary and behavioral stability. *Behavioral and Brain Sciences, 7,* 10.

Hirsh, M.W., & Smale, S. (1974). *Differential equations, dynamical systems, and linear algebra.* New York: Academic Press.

Hull, D.L. (1973). *Darwin and his critics.* Cambridge, MA: Harvard University Press.

Janet, A. (1895). Considerations mechaniques sur l'evolution et le problem des especes. *C.R. 3me Congr. Int. Zool.,* Leyde, 136–145.

Jevons, W.S. (1871). *The theory of political economy.* London: Macmillan.

Kline, M. (1972). *Mathematical thought from ancient to modern times.* New York: Oxford University Press.

Koestler, A. (1968). *The ghost in the machine.* New York: Macmillan.

Krebs, J.R. (1978). Optimal foraging: Decision rules for predators. In J.R. Krebs & N.B. Davies (Eds.), *Behavioural ecology: An evolutionary approach.* Sunderland, MA: Sinauer.

Lakatos, I. (1970). Falsification and the methodology of scientific research programmes. In I. Lakatos & A. Musgrave (Eds.), *Criticism and the growth of knowledge.* Cambridge, England: Cambridge University Press.

McCoy, J.W. (1979). The origin of the "adaptive landscape" concept. *American Naturalist, 113,* 610–613.

Mansfield, E. (1975). *Microeconomics* (2nd ed.). New York: Norton.

May, R.M. (1983). Review of *Food Webs* by S.L. Pimms. *Science, 220,* 295–296.

Maynard Smith, J. (1974). The theory of games and the evolution of animal conflicts. *Journal of Theoretical Biology, 47,* 209–221.

Maynard Smith, J. (1976). Evolution and the theory of games. *American Scientist, 64,* 41–45.

Maynard Smith, J. (1978). Optimization theory in evolution. *Annual Review of Ecological Systems, 9,* 31–56.

Maynard Smith, J. (1982). *Evolution and the Theory of Games.* Cambridge, England: Cambridge University Press.

Maynard Smith, J., & Price, G.R. (1973). The logic of animal conflict. *Nature, 246,* 15–18.

Prelec, D. (1983a). *Choice and behavior allocation.* Unpublished doctoral thesis, Harvard University Press.

Prelec, D. (1983b). The empirical claims of maximization theory: A reply to Rachlin, and Kagel, Battalio, and Green. *Psychological Review, 90,* 385–389.

Rachlin, H., Battalio, R., Kagel, J., & Green, L. (1981). Maximization theory in behavioral psychology. *The Behavioral and Brain Sciences, 4,* 371–417.

Rachlin, H., Green, L., Kagel, J.H., & Battalio, R.C. (1976). Economic demand theory and psychological studies of choice. In G.H. Bower (Ed.), *The psychology of learning and motivation* (Vol. 10). New York: Academic Press.

Rosen, R. (1967). *Optimality principles in biology.* New York: Plenum.

Samuelson, P.A. (1947). *Foundations of economic analysis.* Cambridge, MA: Harvard University Press.

Schelling, T.C. (1978). *Micromotives and macrobehavior.* New York: Norton.

Schoemaker, P.J.H. (1982). The expected utility model: Its variants, purposes, evidence and limitations. *Journal of Economic Literature, 20,* 529–563.

Skinner, B.F. (1981). Selection by consequences. *Science, 213,* 501–504.

Slatkin, M. (1978). On the equilibrium of fitnesses by natural selection. *American Naturalist, 112,* 845–859.

Smale S. (1980). *The mathematics of time.* New York: Springer-Verlag.

Staddon, J.E.R., & Motheral, S. (1978). On matching and maximizing in operant choice experiments. *Psychological Review, 85,* 436–444.

Staddon, J.E.R., & Simmelhag, V.L. (1971). The "superstition" experiment: A reexamination of its implications for the principles of adaptive behavior. *Psychological Review, 78,* 3–43.

Vaughan, W., Jr. (1976). *Optimization and reinforcement.* Unpublished doctoral thesis, Harvard University.

Vaughan, W., Jr. (1981). Melioration, matching, and maximization. *Journal of the Experimental Analysis of Behavior, 36,* 141–149.

Vaughan, W., Jr. (1984). Giving up the ghost. *Behavioral and Brain Sciences, 7,* 501.

Vaughan, W., Jr. (1985). Choice: A local analysis. *Journal of the Experimental Analysis of Behavior, 43,* 383–405.

Vaughan, W., Jr. (1986). Choice and punishment: A local analysis. In M.L. Commons, J.E. Mazur, J.A. Nevin, & H. Rachlin (Eds.), *Quantitative analyses of behavior. Vol. 5: Effects of delay and intervening events on reinforcement value.* Hillsdale, NJ: Erlbaum.

Vaughan, W., Jr., Kardish, T.A., & Wilson, M. (1982). Correlation versus contiguity in choice. *Behavioral Analysis Letters, 2,* 153–160.

Walsh, G.R. (1975). *Methods of optimization.* London: John Wiley.

Williams, G.C. (1966). *Adaptation and natural selection.* Princeton, NJ: Princeton University Press.

Wilson, D.S. (1980). *The natural selection of populations and communities.* Menlo Park, CA: Benjamin/Cummings.

Wright, S. (1932). The roles of mutation, inbreeding, crossbreeding and selection in evolution. In D.F. Jones (Ed.), *Proceedings of the Sixth International Congress of Genetics,* (Vol. 1). Menasha, WI: Brooklyn (NY) Botanic Garden.

Wynne-Edwards, V.C. (1962). *Animal dispersion in relation to social behaviour.* Edinburgh: Oliver and Boyd.

PART IV

RESEARCH REVIEWS

Within neoclassical economic theory, both individual and market behavior have been traditionally analyzed under the assumption of perfect information on the agent's part. For example, in choosing between commodities the consumer is assumed to face a single set of prices that are known prior to his or her choice. It took George Stigler's seminal papers in the early 1960s for economists to face up to the fact that, indeed, this was rarely the case, and that recognition of this fact had important implications for understanding economic behavior.

Since that time, there has been considerable research, both theoretical and empirical, on the effects of imperfect information on the existence, uniqueness, and efficiency of market equilibria, both in labor and consumer product markets. Louis L. Wilde's review article ("Consumer Behavior Under Imperfect Information: A Review of Psychological and Marketing Research as it Relates to Economic Theory") deals with research in consumer product markets. The paper concentrates on the process of information acquisition, reviewing experimental and empirical evidence related to individual consumer behavior under imperfect information, and the resulting implications for economic theories of market performance. Economic behavior under imperfect information is an important area of mainstream economic research, with important implications for a number of issues in both micro- and macroeconomics. Wilde's paper represents a fertile area of interaction between economics and psychology, since much of the empirical work in the area has been conducted by psychologists and marketing experts, while Wilde and a number of other economists are engaged in developing the implications of this work for economic theories of market behavior and public policy.

The interrelations among behavioral biology, economics, and psychology are increasingly apparent in the study of animal foraging. While biologists and ethologists have historically approached the study of foraging using a naturalistic or seminaturalistic setting, this research gains greater rigor and control when pursued in the laboratory of the experimental psychologist. However, given the potential artificiality of the laboratory, greater value can be derived if both approaches converge on the study of foraging, providing complementary views of its processes and variables. The models of choice behavior developed by operant psychologists are evidently consonant with models of foraging proposed by animal behaviorists. We believe the two areas have been and will continue to be enhanced by such cross fertilization.

Interestingly, the overwhelming majority of work in the area of foraging and choice is concerned with the allocation of an organism's time, responses, or energy under a system of constraint—the constraint being limitations on time or amount of resources potentially available. The predominant emphasis has been on scarcity of resources. Much less research and theory have been addressed to the other side of the issue, the behavior of an organism during periods of surplus resources. It is this issue which Alan P. Covich addresses in his review.

Covich, a behavioral biologist and ecologist, has previously noted the parallels between economic theory of resource allocation and aspects of ecological theory in his research on seed consumption in two species of mice. He now expands his interest to situations involving abundance of resources in his contribution, entitled "Optimal Use of Space by Neighboring Central Place Foragers: When and Where to Store Surplus Resources." Covich reviews the literature, focusing on two behavioral responses to storage of surplus: centralized, or larder hoarding, versus scatter hoarding. He discusses the adaptive significance of these two responses to abundance, and the determinants giving rise to each response under given situations. The analyses performed incorporate the work from ecology, economics, psychology, and ethology.

On reading the Covich chapter, one might recall Kafka's story "The Burrow," in which the narrator details the building of a burrow where surplus food is hoarded. (Of relevance to the theory of optimal diet selection and foraging, consider the following sentence from the story: "There are times when I am so well provided for that in my indifference to food I never even touch the smaller fry that scuttle about the burrow, which, however, is probably imprudent of me.")[1] "The Burrow" is a story about the human situation, an examination of anxiety, paranoia, and the structure of madness. However, the strategies, decisions, and choices being contemplated or performed by the narrator, including whether to scatter hoard or to centralize the abundant food, can only be constructed under conditions of surplus, similar to those which Covich analyzes.

---

[1] Interestingly, the narrator's behavior of eschewing the "smaller fry" is indeed optimal under conditions of surplus, despite the misgivings expressed.

Chapter 9

Consumer Behavior under Imperfect Information: A Review of Psychological and Marketing Research as It Relates to Economic Theory*

Louis L. Wilde

Division of the Humanities and Social Sciences
California Institute of Technology

1. INTRODUCTION

In recent years, theoretical economists have begun to examine the effects of imperfect information on the existence, uniqueness, and efficiency of market equilibria, both in labor markets (Mortensen, 1976, Wilde, 1977) and in consumer product markets (Butters, 1977; Salop & Stiglitz, 1977; Wilde & Schwartz, 1977). Two significant conclusions can be drawn from this literature: (a) the properties of market equilibria are extremely sensitive to the search strategies used by consumers or workers, and (b) the key to "stabilizing" markets at price or wage distributions which are competitive in an appropriate sense is direct comparison shopping. With direct comparison shopping, consumers, for example, actually compare brands to each other and choose the best from those that they have seen.[1]

Economists commonly assume that consumers search by defining a hypothetical reservation (or cutoff) level against which brands or jobs are compared sequentially. Economic theory, however, is not (or, at least, has not been) very useful in identifying which search strategies are appropriate

---

* This paper is a substantially revised version of CIT SSWP #229 (December 1977). I would like to thank Alan Schwartz for extremely helpful comments on the original draft. Peter Lichtenstein, Charles Plott, and Steve Salop provided additional comments on an earlier revision, and the editors of this volume did the same for the final draft. This research was supported in part by NSF Grant #SES80-03863.

[1] Direct comparison shopping is to be contrasted with "sequential" shopping rules. The difference between the two is discussed in Section 2 below. See also Wilde (1977), and especially Wilde and Schwartz (1979), for a more complete discussion of these points.

to specific informational settings. Moreover, since consumers and workers who face positive information acquisition costs are likely to choose a "satisfactory" alternative rather than an "optimal" one (March & Simon, 1958), the issue of which search strategies people should use may only be resolvable empirically.

This paper concentrates on consumer product markets as opposed to labor markets. This is primarily because the relevant noneconomic literature is dominated by psychologists and marketing specialists.[2] Further, consumer information acquisition problems are currently attracting more attention than the information acquisition problems of workers, because there has been more legislative and regulatory intervention in consumer product and financial markets than labor markets. For example, Day (1976) lists 19 information disclosure requirements related to consumer product and financial markets implemented between 1970 and 1976, and another 29 which he called "probable for the future" (serious proposals under consideration). Moreover, his tabulation is illustrative, not comprehensive. Given the profound impact of some of this legislation, it is crucial that we better understand the process of information acquisition and its implications for market structure.

This paper will also concentrate on the process of information acquisition; its primary purpose is to review experimental and empirical evidence related to individual consumer behavior under imperfect information. Thus I won't say much about market structure. Mainstream economics, of course, has always focused on market outcomes as opposed to individual decision rules, the emphasis being on institutions rather than people.[3] But the literature has now reached a point where some detailed attention must be paid to the latter.

Most of the nontheoretical work reviewed in this paper deals with survey data or experiments. Both of these sources have well-known shortcomings which I will not discuss in detail.[4] My intent is to introduce economists, psychologists, and consumer researchers to literatures which may be new to many. The paper is organized as follows. In the next section an overview of the consumer's information acquisition problem is presented. In Section 3, formal models of information acquisition, primarily as developed by economists, are then reviewed. In Section 4, evidence relevant to these formal models is presented. Sections 5 and 6 are focused on two special topics,

---

[2] For a brief discussion of information and the labor market, see Rees (1966) or Stigler (1962). A more detailed analysis is provided by Yavitz and Morse (1973).

[3] For a further discussion of imperfect information and market structure, see Rothschild's survey (1973). See also Satterthwaite (1977) and Schmalensee (1978) for additional specific examples.

[4] For a comprehensive critique of studies based on survey data, see Newman and Lockeman (1975).

"satisfactory search" and "information overload." In a final section, directions for future research are suggested.

Two generalizations emerge from the discussion which follows. First, it appears that many consumers do little shopping. For example, the surveys discussed in Section 4 typically find that 40% to 60% of the respondents visit only one store prior to purchasing a good, regardless of whether it is durable or nondurable. What this implies is not clear. Certainly it is not altogether surprising, given the large number of purchase decisions the average consumer must make each day, but whether observed levels of search are socially optimal is an unresolved issue.[5] Second, even though most consumers do relatively little shopping, they are sensitive to the costs and benefits of search. Hence, while the specific models of consumer behavior under imperfect information proposed by economists may not always be appropriate, the underlying methodology seems extremely useful.

2. AN OVERVIEW OF THE CONSUMER'S INFORMATION ACQUISITION PROBLEM

In its most general formulation, the consumer's problem is quite complex. It includes deciding when to search and where, how to collect information, how to process it, how to compare different alternatives, and when to stop searching. Several methods for dealing with these problems are available to consumers. Following Hirschleifer (1973), it is useful to distinguish two general classes. The first involves an active adaptation to uncertainty in which the consumer either produces information by direct search or buys information from market sources (consumer magazines, employment services, want-ads, etc.). The second class involves a more passive adaptation to uncertainty in which the consumer monitors and evaluates information exogenously disseminated by firms or other consumers. These distinctions emphasize that information acquisition is a more general process than information search, a point made by Bettman (1977). Bettman also draws a distinction between internal search and retrieval (information sought from memory) and external search (information sought from outside sources). He describes the consumer's search process as follows:

> It is proposed that information search generally begins with internal search, with memory explored for relevant information. As the consumer examines information in memory, that information may prove to be sufficient for the

---

[5] In addition, there is a well-known positive externality associated with shopping activity: an increase in any individual consumer's search efforts results in a better distribution of prices for everyone else. Since this social return is not fully appropriable by the individual, there may be a resultant underinvestment in search (Rothschild, 1973, p. 1289). See Wilde (1977) for a formal demonstration of this externality in the labor market.

purposes at hand, and no further search may be undertaken. However, that information may not be sufficient. Several pieces of information may conflict, information may be lacking, and so forth. . . . Although the consumers' responses to such conflicts or lack of information will vary, one major type of response to insufficient information or conflicting information is external search.[6]

During external search, the consumer examines the environment to see if relevant information is available. The consumer in general uses different detailed search patterns and searches for different amounts of information in different choice situations. Information acquired during external search will lead to further internal search to interpret or elaborate that information. Thus, there is a continual cycling between internal and external search processes. Eventually, of course, the consumer will cease searching for information and make a choice. (1977, pp. 2-3)

The passive mode of information acquisition, monitoring and evaluating exogenously disseminated information, forms a backdrop to the active mode described above; there is a continuous learning process that creates a stock of information which is available to the consumer for internal search and retrieval. If the consumer is able to decide solely on the basis of the stock of stored information, then external search is irrelevant. But (as far as I know) no one has studied this aspect of decisionmaking. Hence this survey will concentrate on the external component of information search.

3. FORMAL MODELS OF EXTERNAL SEARCH BEHAVIOR

The fundamental article in the economics literature on consumer information acquisition is Stigler's "The Economics of Information" (1961). Stigler's theory of consumer behavior under imperfect information advanced the proposition that an individual would invest in information until the marginal cost of further investment is greater than or equal to the marginal gain (in terms of lower expected purchase price). This premise, unsurprisingly, set the tone for most of the subsequent work by economists since it is a natural extension of conventional full-information consumer theory.

Stigler considered an imperfectly informed consumer faced with positive information acquisition costs and interested in purchasing one unit of a homogeneous good. Since the consumer was assumed only to have some general notion of prices, Stigler also assumed the choice method would be to set a fixed number of stores to visit (à priori) and then buy from the store

---

[6] Information is "sufficient" if the expected marginal gain (in utility) from the acquisition of additional information is less than the marginal cost. Operationally, this simply means the consumer can optimally base a decision on stored information. For example, if conflicting information such as disparate reports on durability is present, information in memory may still be "sufficient" if the value of a more precise estimate of durability is not worth its cost.

charging the lowest price of those sampled. The optimal number of stores to visit is determined by a simple cost-benefit calculation.

Stigler's theory, based on the fixed sample size rule, has been criticized by economists on two grounds. McCall (1965, 1970) argued that the best search strategy is a sequential rule in which, after visiting any store, a decision is made whether or not to search further, and Rothschild (1973) criticized both Stigler and McCall for analyzing only one side of the market.[7] That is, he criticized them for taking wage or price dispersion as given and simply analyzing worker or consumer behavior, thus arguing, once again, for a focus on markets as opposed to individuals.

While Rothschild's comments inspired a number of attempts to "close" the search model by explicitly incorporating firms, the resulting work has ultimately led back to the actual search strategies used by consumers; establishing the existence of persistent price dispersion (in equilibrium) turns out to be extremely sensitive to the way consumer information acquisition is modeled.

It now appears that, while the sequential rule is optimal *as a strategy* when consumers know the true distribution of prices, it might not be optimal under less restrictive assumptions regarding consumer expectations. For example, Gastwirth (1976) has shown that, if the consumer's estimate of the distribution of prices is inaccurate, a sequential rule could lead to a significant overinvestment in information. Hence the optimal sample size rule may dominate the sequential rule in such a case (Rothschild, 1973).[8]

Psychologists have used experiments to study both fixed sample size rules (Green, Halbert, & Minas, 1964) and sequential rules (Pitz, 1968).[9] In an especially interesting experiment, Fried and Peterson (1969) directly compared the two. In these experiments, subjects faced a panel consisting of two columns, each containing 24 pairs of red and green bulbs with a button between each pair. Pushing the button caused one member of the pair to light. Which bulb lit up was determined randomly according to some fixed probability. Subjects were not told the true probability, but rather that it was one of two values. The subjects' task was to determine which one, based on their observations.

Two variations of this design were used by Fried and Peterson; in the first, the proportion of red to green lights was either 70:30 or 30:70, and in

---

[7] Stigler, in fact, acknowledged the optimality of a sequential rule (1961, p. 219). He also devoted some attention to the sources of dispersion (1961, pp. 219-220), but never constructed a formal market model.

[8] The optimality of purely sequential search rules is also sensitive to assumptions regarding the nature of search costs and the timing of observations. See, for example, Benhabib and Bull (1982), Gal, Landsberger, and Levykson (1981), or Morgan (1982).

[9] Pitz' paper considers several rules including a sequential one. Related work by Pitz is referenced in Slovic and Lichtenstein (1971).

the second the proportion was either 60:40 or 40:60. In the first design, subjects earned $.30 for a correct decision and were fined $1.70 for an incorrect decision. In the second design, these values took on $.50 and $1.50, respectively. In either case, the cost of observing any pair of bulbs was $0.01. Within each treatment, sequential and fixed sample size rules were used on alternative trials. In the former, the subjects could observe light bulb pairs one-at-a-time and make a decision whenever they liked. In the latter, they had to specify a fixed number of light bulb pairs to observe at the start of the trial and then make a decision based only on the outcome of those observations.

The results of the Fried and Peterson experiment are somewhat surprising. As one might expect, average earnings under the sequential rule were greater than average earnings under the fixed sample size rule. But performance under the fixed sample size rule more closely approximated optimal performance than performance under the sequential rule. In particular, in the first design, a risk neutral subject could expect to earn $3.60 using the optimal sequential rule, as compared to $1.00 using the optimal fixed sample size rule. Mean actual earnings were $2.60 using sequential rules and $1.06 using fixed sample size rules. In the second design, the optimal sequential rule would have yielded expected earnings of $3.38, and the optimal fixed sample size rule would yield expected earnings of − $2.60. Mean actual earnings were $.37 and − $1.85, respectively.

While the theoretical work of Gastwirth and the experiments of Fried and Peterson suggest that it may sometimes be inappropriate to assume that consumers use pure sequential search rules, both sequential and fixed sample size rules share several important features. These include predictions that the amount of information acquired is inversely related to its cost, and that, as prices become more disperse, the expected total cost of purchase decreases (Rothschild, 1974).

The more fundamental of these two predictions is that the amount of information acquired is inversely related to its cost. However, this result is often less useful in application than one might expect. Consider, for example, the effect of education on external search. Some authors have predicted a positive relationship between the two, since education "represents ability and interest in seeking and evaluating information" (Newman & Staelin, 1972, p. 252); that is, they argue that education is inversely related to *direct* search costs for two reasons: (a) educated consumers are more efficient shoppers, and (b) educated consumers may enjoy the information acquisition process. These arguments may or may not be true, but, in any event, *indirect* search costs must also be taken into consideration; one could also argue that an educated consumer will have high opportunity costs associated with time spent shopping, if education increases the value of leisure time. Thus, education may reduce external search. The point of these arguments is that the theoretical relationship between education and external search is ambiguous even if the effect of increased search costs is always to decrease external search.

Similar problems arise with respect to the effect of income on external search. Consumers with high incomes can afford more search than consumers with low incomes, but they also have higher opportunity costs associated with time spent shopping. Hence, as in the case of education, a negative theoretical relationship between search costs and external search does little to help predict the relationship between income and external search.

4. EVIDENCE RESPECTING EXTERNAL SEARCH

The principal aspects of external search are direction and intensity. Direction refers to the sources of information used by consumers and intensity refers to the level of investment in search. Since different sources of information have different costs, the distinction between direction and intensity is not always clear. Nevertheless, consumer researchers have traditionally drawn just such a distinction, and it has begun recently to be recognized by economists as well (e.g., Satterthwaite, 1977). Examples of potential sources of information include shopping at stores, conversations with salespersons or friends, advertisements, and consumer magazines. An additional source of information is direct consumption of goods. This form of information acquisition has been labeled "experience" by Nelson (1970), who was the first contemporary economist to recognize its importance. Experience can be useful when the variance in unobservable qualitative characteristics is high relative to the variance in observable characteristics such as price. It is also likely to be useful for low cost products. An early classification of goods similar to Nelson's was made by Copeland (1923). He divided goods into three classes: shopping goods, convenience goods, and specialty goods. Shopping goods correspond to search goods, while convenience goods and specialty goods correspond roughly to experience goods.[10]

Some work, especially survey research, has considered the direction of external search, Katona and Mueller (1955) providing an early example. The study which most explicitly focuses on direction is Udell (1966). Udell concentrated his survey of shopping behavior on the types of information consumers seek and the sources of information they utilize in shopping for small appliances, concluding that "the typical consumer does *not* go from store to store to gather information and to compare products and prices

---

[10] Nelson never exploited fully the distinction between search goods and experience goods in any formal way. For such an analysis, see Wilde (1981) and Hey and McKenna (1981). The implications of the distinction for advertising are explored in Schmalensee (1978). For a general discussion of all these models, see Wilde (1980b).

when shopping for small electrical appliances. He or she prefers to do much of this searching and shopping in the comfort of the home by using out-of-store sources of information, especially past experience with products and brands, discussions with friends, and printed media advertising.'' Further-more, ''almost two-thirds (65%) of the purchasers believed that they had sufficient information and were ready to buy when they made their first visit to a retail store'' (1966, p. 52).

In a more recent study, Claxton, Fry, and Portis (1974) examined the prepurchase search behavior of furniture and appliance buyers, concentrating on the total number of sources used, number of stores visited, and total deliberation time. This study is somewhat unique in its emphasis on the ''multi-dimensional profile of search activity'' (Bettman, 1977, p. 19); in other words, it considers both the direction of search and the intensity of search. Other studies, such as Katona and Mueller's (1955) or Newman and Staelin's (1972), tend to focus on aggregate measures of information search (see also Engle, Kollat, & Backwell's discussion of external search, 1973, or Newman and Lockeman's critique of measures of information search, 1975).

The Claxton, Fry, and Portis (1974) survey identified three subgroups of buyers. The first, ''thorough/store-intense'' (5% of the furniture buyers and 8% of the appliance buyers) visited a very large number of stores, used many sources, and took a long time to decide. The second, ''thorough/balanced'' (44% of the furniture buyers and 27% of the appliance buyers), visited fewer stores, still used several sources, and took a moderate amount of time to decide. The final subgroup, ''nonthorough'' (34% of the furniture buyers and 65% of the appliance buyers), made few store visits (one or two), used only about one source, and deliberated little.

Regarding the distinction between direction of search and intensity, the interesting comparison in this study is between the thorough/store-intense and the thorough/balanced subgroups for appliance buyers. The former used *fewer* sources of information and made *more* store visits than the latter; that is, there may be a trade-off between direction (in this case in-store sources of information) and intensity—consumers who use fewer sources of information may use them more intensely. If different sources of information are approximately equal in terms of content, this means that total information acquisition may be independent (roughly speaking) of the source/intensity mix. Under these circumstances, the economic approach to information acquisition (which ignores, for the most part, the distinction between the two) might still yield useful predictions. Whether this is true, however, is an open question, since the precise nature of the source/intensity trade-off has not been studied further, either theoretically or empirically.

Existing work provides little help in the effort to unravel these effects, since it provides few clues as to what sort of search strategies consumers commonly use. For example, many of the buyers in Udell's (1966) study of small appliance purchases might have used sequential strategies. He found "a shopper is not likely to examine a small appliance, leave the store without buying it, and return at a later time to make the purchase" (Udell, 1966, p. 52). But Udell did not study the amount of in-store comparison shopping. Similar problems plague other studies. While data is available on number of store visits (Bruce & Dommermuth, 1968; Bucklin, 1966; Dommermuth, 1965; Dommermuth & Cundiff, 1967; Katona & Mueller, 1955; Newman & Staelin, 1972; Udell, 1966), number of shopping trips prior to purchase (Bucklin, 1966), number of prepurchase visits to the store of purchase (Udell, 1966), and number of brands examined (Dommermuth, 1965), no systematic survey is complete enough to support plausible inferences regarding search strategies.

The studies just discussed considered both the intensity of search and the direction. In general, the intensity of external search is a function of its perceived costs and benefits. As Engle, Kollat, and Blackwell put it, "whether external search occurs as well as the extent to which it occurs appear to depend on the consumer's perception of the value of the results of search and the costs involved in engaging in search" (1973, p. 376). This is in accord with the economists' view as outlined in Section 3. The major difference is that psychologists take into account a greater variety of gains and costs associated with external search than do economists.

The value of external search depends, in the psychologists' view, on the amount and appropriateness of stored information and the perceived risk of the purchase decision. Perceived risk encompasses uncertainties associated with "the use of the product and the social consequences inherent in using it" as well as the monetary consequences (Hansen, 1972, p. 89). Thus it is affected by financial risk (involving both price and the expected lifetime of the good), and other social-psychological risk factors (Engle, Kollat, & Blackwell, 1973, pp. 376–82). Additional psychological benefits might include increased satisfaction with the purchase, or feeling that one did a thorough job (Bettman, 1977, p. 20). The psychologists' model predicts that a high degree of perceived risk is associated with more external search. This prediction, along with a more general discussion of perceived risk, can be found in Bauer (1960). Bauer argues that consumers often use other techniques for reducing perceived risk besides external search. These include developing brand loyalty, using advertising, or following opinion leaders. Nelson (1970) discusses, to some extent, the economic incentives for using these various techniques.

The prediction that perceived risk is positively related to external search is consistent with predictions of economic models that greater price dispersion (Rothschild, 1974) and greater durability (Wilde, 1977) imply more search. However, because search increases with perceived risk, the psychologists' model also predicts that higher prices imply more search; economic models, by contrast, consider price alone to be irrelevant. The models discussed in Section 3 typically analyze the behavior of a consumer interested in purchasing a single unit of some good, acting so as to minimize the expected total cost of purchase (final price plus search costs). In this case, a simple shift in the distribution of prices may change some of the parameters which define an optimal strategy (for example, the reservation price associated with a sequential rule), but it will not change the expected amount of search. The scanty evidence available in the economics literature weakly supports the psychologists' position on this issue. Pratt, Wise, and Zeckhauser (1979), for example, sample prices of 50 products by selecting pages at random from the Boston telephone directory. Eliminating products for which the collection of price information was difficult, 39 categories remained. For these, the authors found a "large positive relationship between standard deviation and mean price."[11] Further evidence from the noneconomics literature which supports the psychologists' prediction of a positive relationship between price and external search is discussed later in this section.

Regarding costs of search, the psychological model includes time and money expended, the cost of delaying decisions, and such psychological costs as frustration and the annoyance of dealing with sales personnel. Obviously, the psychological model predicts that higher costs lower external search.

This cost-benefit hypothesis is implicit in the work of Bucklin (1963) and Winter (1975), and is given explicit treatment in Bucklin (1966) and Swan (1972). Bucklin surveyed female heads of household, gathering information about both the number of stores visited per shopping trip and the number of shopping trips taken prior to purchase of a nonfood item worth $5 or more. He used the density of retail establishments as one proxy for search costs, comparing the number of intratrip shopping stops at downtown retail sites with stops at nondowntown sites. In his sample the proportion of products shopped for twice or more in downtown sites was 20.7%, compared with 11.8% for nondowntown sites. This was interpreted as support for the proposition that higher search costs imply less external search.

Swan (1972) devised a simple experiment which included measuring the effect of search costs. He asked subjects to judge the quality of flashlight batteries. The subject who most consistently chose the battery with the longest life won $1. There were five phony brands from which to pick. Choice proceeded sequentially, and, after each choice, a report on the life of one battery of the brands chosen was given to the subject. One group was allowed to switch brands costlessly; the other group had a fixed number of

---

[11] See Thaler (1977) for further discussion of these results.

points subtracted from their scores each time they switched brands. Under the cost treatment, the mean number of brand switches was 2.6 compared to 7.8 under the no-cost treatment.

In a related experiment, Lanzetta and Kanareff (1962) also found that, as the direct cost of information increased, the amount of information demanded by decisionmakers fell. In their experiment, subjects were presented with a series of hypothetical "problems" and asked to make decisions about their solutions. For example, the history of a mental patient would be described and several alternative treatments suggested. In order to receive a payoff, the subject would have to choose the "correct" solution from the offered alternatives, either on the basis of the given information or after obtaining up to five additional pieces of information. Two treatments were used; in the first, the additional information was free and $.05 was awarded for a "correct" answer; in the second, each piece of additional information cost $.05, and $.30 was awarded for a "correct" answer. In fact, there was no "correct" answer, the probability of receiving a payoff being predetermined as a linear function of the number of additional pieces of information the subject accessed (specifically, the probability of receiving a payoff, given the subject used n additional pieces of information, was .2n). Subjects never used on average more than four additional pieces of information, even when it was free. However, they systematically accessed significantly fewer additional pieces of information when it was costly than when it was free ("significantly" here being used in a statistical sense).

Regarding the gains from search, Katona and Mueller (1955), Dommermuth (1965), and Bucklin (1966) all found evidence consistent with the prediction of the psychological model that search increases with product price. Bucklin, for example, reported that the percentage of two-plus-stops shopping increased monotonically from 38.8% in the $5 to $14 category to 64.4% in the $100-plus category (1966, p. 26)—see Table 1.[12] As pointed out above, results such as Bucklin's, that external search is positively related to product price, are not predicted by any existing formal cost-benefit models. Economists have noted this anomaly (e.g., Thaler, 1977—see Footnote 11) but as yet have not resolved it.[13]

---

[12] Bucklin surveyed 506 female heads of household in the area of Oakland, California, in the fall of 1962. Numbers in parenthesis in Table 1 give number of respondents in each category.

[13] This apparent empirical regularity remains as one of the primary challenges to the economic approach to consumer information acquisition. Thaler (1977) suggests an analogy to the Weber-Fedner law of psycho-physics in which the "just noticeable difference in any stimulus is proportional to the stimulus." This is an intriguing possibility, the importance of which is unknown at this time. Stigler (1961), it should be noted, did predict that greater *expenditure* implies more external search. However, he related this to changes in the frequency of purchase, not price changes. Pure shifts in the distribution of prices should have no effect on external search, either with fixed sample size rules or sequential rules (see text, supra note 11).

TABLE 1.   Extent of Shopping as a Function of Produce Price (Bucklin, 1966)*

	$5 to $14	$15 to $49	$50 to $99	$100 +	No Data	Total
One stop	61.2% (314)	55.4% (128)	46.9% (30)	36.6% (21)	33.3% (8)	56.2% (501)
Two-plus stops	38.8% (199)	44.6% (103)	53.1% (34)	64. % (38)	66.7% (16)	43.8% (390)

* Entries give percentages within each price category. Numbers in parameters give total observation for each cell.

A relationship which is clearly predicted by the economics literature is that, other things constant, greater durability implies more search. This is due to two effects. First, greater durability implies that, if a poor purchase is made, it will take longer to correct for it by renewed search for a different (and hopefully better) brand; more care must be taken to select a good brand initially.[14] Second, greater durability implies less frequent purchase. Hence, stored information is less useful and more external search is required. However, there appears to be little external search associated with the purchase of durables. Katona and Mueller reported such a result over 30 years ago (1955). More recently, Newman and Staelin, in a study of prepurchase information seeking for new cars and major household appliances, found that "half the buyers thought mainly of only one brand at the outset of the decision process." Furthermore, "nearly 40% of the buyers who had not used the product before for example, also considered only one brand initially" (1972, p. 256). Although recent research in economics has begun to consider rigorously the question of "how much information is enough" to keep market performance within acceptable bounds (i.e., how many shoppers are needed to keep a market competitive—see Wilde and Schwartz (1979)—current judgments about whether levels of nonshopping by consumers for major durables such as those reported by Newman and Staelin are problematic remain subjective and somewhat impressionistic. The issue is clouded by the argument that internal search (see Section 2) is heavily relied upon in the purchase of consumer durables. As Newman and Staelin point out in the conclusion of their paper, "the findings do not necessarily mean that the buyer is ill-informed. He may have started with what he regarded as sufficient knowledge" (1972, p. 256).

The issue here is by no means a minor one, and it raises yet another conundrum for economists. Economic theory tends to ignore internal search. Yet the available evidence suggests that internal search is an important element in the purchase of consumer durables. This makes intuitive sense, since the purchase of durables may involve more foresight than the purchase

---

[14] This effect is derived formally in Wilde (1977).

of nondurables. Hence, the information acquisition process may take place over an extended period of time. Ideally, one would like to have measures of the *total* amount of search associated with a decision to purchase a good. But accurate measures of total search (internal search at the time the decision to consider a purchase is made, plus any subsequent external search) are likely to be hard to generate. In particular, survey measures will typically understate the actual amount of total search, to the extent that consumers absorb information passively in the early stages of the decision process (or simply forget), and will overstate it to the extent they want to feel like they've been wise shoppers and have made informed choices in post-purchase interviews (Newman & Lockeman, 1975). While it has been suggested that measures of the *total* amount of search are needed (Bettman, 1977), no practical ways of generating such data have yet emerged.

Despite the methodological problems with consumer durables studies, the other evidence cited above strongly suggests that external search is a function of the perceived costs and benefits associated with it. Consumers may vary in their ability to process information (Tversky & Kahneman, 1974; Grether, 1978), but most do act rationally in their response to cost-benefit trade-offs.

Evidence respecting the effects of education and income on external search is both limited and somewhat conflicting. For example, Claxton, Fry, and Portis (1974) found that buyers who used store visits as a major element of their search process had the highest income and education, while Udell (1966) reported the seemingly contradictory result that high income buyers were more likely to make their purchase decisions prior to visiting stores than low income buyers. Consistent with this last observation, Udell also found that buyers with a family income below $5,000 or above $10,000 were *least* likely to examine a product in a store, leave the store without purchasing, and return later to make the purchase.

A similar nonmonotonic relationship between income and external search was reported by Bruce and Dommermuth (1968). These authors divided survey respondents into three classes: *lower class* households were defined as those located in an area with census tract mean household incomes varying from $2,009 to $4,436; *working class* households were defined as those located in an area with census tract mean household incomes varying from $4,299 to $5,941; and *middle class* households were defined as those located in an area with census tract mean household incomes varying from $5,009 to $9,081. The least shopping activity was found in the lower class; 70% of the lower class respondents made a purchase after shopping in one store and considering one brand. The most shopping activity was found in the working class; only 45% made purchases after shopping in one store and considering one brand. Shopping activity in the middle class was less than that in the working class, but not so limited as in the lower class (see Table 2).

TABLE 2.   Shopping Patterns: Percentage of Respondents with Given Brand/Store Activity Patterns (Bruce & Dommermuth, 1968, p. 5)

Number of Brands	1	2	Stores 3	4	5 or More
The Shopping Matric Lower Class (n = 136)					
5 or more	0	1	0	1	0
4	0	0	1	1	0
3	1	0	2	0	0
2	5	8	0	0	0
1	70	1	0	0	0
The Shopping Matrix Working Class (n = 191)					
5 or more	0	0	0	1	4
4	1	2	3	2	1
3	1	2	7	0	0
2	7	8	2	0	0
1	45	4	1	0	0
The Shopping Matrix Middle Class (n = 564)					
5 or more	0	0	1	1	2
4	0	0	2	1	0
3	3	3	5	1	0
2	6	6	2	0	0
1	56	6	1	0	0

Some evidence suggests the relationship between education and external search is also nonmonotonic. Newman and Staelin (1972) found that consumers with advanced degrees (masters, doctorates, or professional degrees) reported about the same amount of external search as consumers with less than high school educations. Consumers with intermediate amounts of education reported substantially more external search. Of course, most surveys of consumer behavior do not control for income when reporting the effects of education, or for education when reporting the effects of income. Since income and education are likely to be correlated, it is not surprising the evidence suggests similar relationships with external search.

5. SATISFACTORY SEARCH AND THE CHOICE PROCESS

In addition to the direct costs and benefits discussed in Section 4, a number of other factors have an indirect influence on the direction and intensity of external search. These include the availability of information, time pressure, and the difficulty of the choice task (Bettman, 1977). The first two of these pose no special problems; the availability of information can be related to search costs while time pressure can be incorporated into the search strategies used by consumers. For example, a modified sequential search rule would require setting a reservation price and a time limit for search. The consumer would then search sequentially until a price which is less than the reservation price is observed or the specified amount of time is exhausted, in which case the good would be purchased at the lowest observed price.

The remaining factor is more problematic. In a market setting the "difficulty of the choice task" is directly related to the complexity of the product. That is, if the product is characterized by a number of attributes, and if these attributes are costly to evaluate (in some appropriate sense), then the choice task (evaluating brands and selecting an acceptable one) is more difficult than the choice task associated with a homogeneous product. Thus, the more difficult the choice task, the more costly it is (by definition) to select the *best* from any given set of alternatives. This suggests that, within a multiattribute choice environment, a consumer is likely to settle for less than the best alternative, since, even if direct search costs are low, evaluation costs may not be. Settling for less than the best is generally referred to as "satisficing" while holding out for the best is called "optimizing."[15]

This section explores the relationship between satisficing and optimizing (as defined above) and external search. Consumer researchers predict a positive relationship between a "concern for optimality" and the degree of external search (Bettman, 1977, p. 28). This is based on the assumption that a consumer concerned with optimality will select a search strategy which yields a large number of observations (a large number of observations being necessary to find the best alternative). In other words, the implicit assumption is that the consumer *first* decides whether to optimize or not, and *then* decides how to search. But how to search and whether to optimize are two aspects of the same decision; an observed positive relationship between external search and a concern for optimality simply reflects the more fundamental link between search and evaluation costs and the degree of external search.

This argument is obvious in choice environments in which there is no cost or uncertainty associated with determining the value of any particular alternative once that alternative has been "observed." If the consumer faces high information acquisition costs in the selection of alternatives for consideration, then the search strategy is likely to be satisfactory with respect to the value of the alternative selected, but it may still be optimal with respect to the net expected value of search.

To see the distinction between optimizing and satisficing when the cost of observing alternatives is positive but the cost of inspecting alternatives (to

---

[15] In their classic discussion of optimal versus satisfactory strategies, March and Simon define an alternative as *"optimal* if: (1) there exists a set of criteria that permits all alternatives to be compared, and (2) the alternative in question is preferred, by these criteria, to all other alternatives. An alternative is *satisfactory* if: (1) there exists a set of criteria that describes minimally satisfactory alternatives, and (2) the alternative in question meets or exceeds all these criteria" (1958, p. 140).

assess their "utility"), once they have been selected for consideration, is zero, consider the fixed sample size rule (Stigler, 1961) versus the sequential rule (McCall, 1965) as described in Section 2 of this paper. Neither requires the consumer to hold out for the very best alternative of those available, but the sequential rule minimizes the net expected cost of purchase (final purchase price minus costs of search). Thus, the latter is optimal *given the costs of observing alternatives,* but both are satisfactory with respect to actual choices.

A more interesting case arises when it is also costly for the consumer to determine the value of alternatives (goods). That is, let goods be described by multiple attributes, with the consumers' having underlying utility functions defined over these attributes. But assume that consumers cannot costlessly observe individual attributes. Then, following Wright, two necessary elements of any choice model can be identified, "a process by which single multiattribute options are evaluated and a rule by which one option is discriminated from the others" (1975, p. 60). The two elements are called the "data combination process" and the "choice rule."

Data combination processes are classified as compensatory or noncompensatory. Compensatory processes "picture a person averaging (or adding) data so that positive and negative data have a balancing impact," while noncompensatory processes "assume a consumer combines data such that the presence (absence) of one attribute may not compensate at all for the absence (presence) of others" (Wright, 1975, pp. 60–61). Standard examples of noncompensatory processes are the well-known lexicographic rule, and the conjunctive and disjunctive rules (Einhorn, 1971). The lexicographic rule requires first that the attributes be ordered according to relative importance. Then *all* options are compared on the single most important dimension. If the consumer cannot discriminate among the options on the basis of the first dimension, then a second is compared, etc. Clearly, this rule requires that all options be compared on at least one dimension. With conjunctive and disjunctive rules, the consumer defines minimum cutoff (reservation) levels for each attribute. The conjunctive rule requires the consumer to reject options with any below-cutoff attributes, and the disjunctive rule requires the consumer to accept options with any above-cutoff attributes. Unlike the lexicographic rule, these rules do not necessarily require all options be inspected. In fact, a number of choice rules besides a "choose the best" can be combined with them. For example, the consumer could select a fixed number of options to inspect, apply a conjunctive rule to inspect each, and then select at random from those which pass the test. Alternatively, the consumer could use a sequential strategy, applying a conjunctive rule to inspect each option and choosing the first option which is acceptable.

Within a multiattribute choice environment, the data combination process and the choice rule are closely related. Assume the consumer attempts to maximize net benefits from purchasing the good. He or she will consider the costs of search, and of evaluating alternative goods, once they are observed, and will then choose a strategy for search *and* for making a final choice. If the choice rule is to satisfice, this is because the consumer has high costs of observing options, or of evaluating specific options, or both, in relation to the expected gains from purchase. If the choice rule exhibits a concern for optimizing, this reflects a different outcome of the cost-benefit calculation. But the same costs and benefits simultaneously effect external search. It is not surprising, therefore, that the observed degree of external search is positively related to a "concern" with the optimality of final choices.

Swan (1969) designed an experiment to test this prediction. It consisted of a series of choice situations, each exposing subjects to four phony brands of shirts. Color slides were shown of the shirts, four shirts per slide. Four ratings of the overall quality of each shirt were available ("good," "acceptable," or "poor") at a cost of $.01 per rating. With all 16 ratings, a subject could identify the correct alternative with certainty.

Each subject was given a budget of $.20 per trial. If a correct alternative was selected, the subject was allowed to keep that portion of the budget not spent on information. In the "optimal choice" treatment, the subject had to identify the one brand with the best set of ratings to receive the payoff (i.e., correct choices yielded the residual budget; incorrect choices had value zero). In the "satisfactory choice" treatment, identifying either of the two best brands was acceptable.

Swan's results clearly confirm the prediction that information seeking is lower with satisfactory choice as compared to optimal choice; the mean number of ratings purchased was 6.63 under optimal choice, as compared to 4.44 under satisfactory choice.

Claxton, Fry, and Portis also found support for the hypothesis that external search is positively related to a concern with optimality in their survey; "nonthorough" buyers were the least concerned about purchasing the "right" product (1974, pp. 39, 41).

Of course, if choice processes derive from more fundamental cost-benefit calculations, then the parameters of particular choice processes (cutoff levels, order of inspection of attributes, etc.) should not be taken as given. As Wright has put it, "consumers are sensitive to simplifying and optimizing differences between the [choice] strategies, and could engage in covert 'cost-benefit' analysis when selecting a decisionmaking procedure" (1975, p. 60). Given this observation, it is clear that researchers should focus on the link between search costs and choice processes. Moreover, the economists' cost-benefit paradigm is likely to be very useful in this effort.[16] Recent theoretical (Wilde, 1982) and experimental (Grether & Wilde, 1984) work has begun to

---

[16] There has been very little formal (i.e., theoretical) analysis of this problem. Shugan (1980, 1981) and Johnson (1979) provide initial attacks on it from a consumer research perspective, but much work remains to be done.

explore these issues. These two papers focus on the conjunctive choice strategy. Wilde develops a theoretical framework in which the conjunctive choice rule can be analyzed. Specifically, his analysis is concerned with the process by which consumers using a conjunctive choice rule determine the minimum cutoff levels for each attribute. He first characterizes the "optimal" cutoff levels using a model based on expected utility maximation, in which information acquisition costs appear explicitly. In particular, he assumes each attribute of the multi-attribute good sought by the consumer has an attribute-specific inspection cost. The consumer's problem is to select a set of cutoff levels, one for each attribute, which maximize expected utility net of inspection costs. The solution to this problem involves a rather complicated set of "first-order-conditions." These are derived by differentiating (mathematically speaking) the expected utility function of the consumer with respect to the various cutoff levels, one for each attribute of the good. While the mathematics are tedious, the resulting set of equations which define the optimal cutoff levels (and hence the optimal conjunctive strategy) have a natural "expected benefit equals expected cost" interpretation. The problem is that they are still quite complicated. Yet the conjunctive rule is generally regarded as a good candidate as a simplifying strategy. In fact, a number of consumer researchers have suggested that conjunctive strategies are commonly used by decisionmakers as initial screening devices in situations where they are contrasted by a large number of choices (Bettman, 1979, p. 215, and the references cited therein—see also Grether & Wilde, 1984).[17] This view suggests that consumers who use the conjunctive rule may not actually set the cutoff levels in an "optimal" fashion (that is, they may use a conjunctive rule, but not set the cutoff levels in a way consistent with the "expected utility net of information acquisition costs" model). The question then arises, how *do* they set the cutoff levels?

One way to approach this question without altogether forsaking the economic approach described above is to preserve the expected benefits equals expected costs interpretation of the so-called optimal solution, but simplify the calculations involved in solving those equations by throwing out or ignoring certain kinds of information. For example, if there are n attributes, then the first-order-conditions involve n "simultaneous" equations which need to be jointly solved to determine the n cutoff levels, one for each attribute. It turns out that there is a natural way to ignore this simultaneity and treat each cutoff level as though it were independent of the other n-1 cutoff levels. Similarly, there is a natural way to ignore the fact that the order in which attributes are inspected matters (if all attributes were equally costly to observe, the consumer should be more choosy on early attributes than later ones, since rejecting a good on the basis of an attribute which is inspected

---

[17] For a critique of this literature, see Lynch (1981).

late in the process means that the consumer has to start all over again with the first attribute—other things equal, it is better to be more discriminating on attributes inspected early in the process than on those inspected late in the process). This effect is referred to as "sequentiality." Ignoring these various kinds of interactions yields a set of "nonoptimal" conjunctive rules. They all have the same form as the optimal conjunctive rule, but the cutoff levels respond differently to changes in attribute-specific inspection costs, depending on whether consumers use the optimal conjunctive strategy or one of the nonoptimal conjunctive strategies. This provides the basis for an empirical test of which conjunctive strategy decisionmakers actually use. Grether and Wilde (1984) report on just such a test, using laboratory experiments.

The experiments run by Grether and Wilde were designed in such a way that subjects were forced to use conjunctive strategies in selecting items from some set of alternatives. Alternatives were described simply by some vector of numbers. For example, a three attribute alternative might be a set of three numbers (x_1, x_2, x_3) where each number x_i was drawn from some distribution $f_i(x_i)$ defined on (x_i^L, x_i^H). Subjects were informed of the distribution f_i and its range (in these experiments f_i was always uniform on some interval (x_i^L, x_i^H)). Each attribute had an attribute specific inspection cost c_i. Utility functions were linear; that is, if the final choice of a subject was (x_1, x_2, x_3), the gross payoff (in dollars) was $x_1 + x_2 + x_3$. Net payoffs were equal to the gross payoff minus any inspection costs incurred in obtaining it. The problem facing the subjects was simple: to pick a set of cutoff levels, one for each attribute, given that final choices would be determined by random draws for each attribute, using the conjunctive rule—i.e., an alternative would be acceptable only if it exceeded the cutoff level selected by the subject on each attribute. The treatment variable in the experiments was inspection costs; holding utility functions and the distributions of attributes constant, inspection costs were varied in such a way as to be able to test whether subjects conformed to the optimal conjunctive rule or to one of the nonoptimal conjunctive rules.

The results of this experiment were rather surprising. It turned out that the subjects did *not* conform to the optimal conjunctive rule. In fact, in two tests, each of four relatively different subject populations, all conformed to the nonoptimal conjunctive rule in which both simultaneity and sequentiality were ignored. What this meant in terms of the response to changes in inspection costs is that an increase in the cost of inspecting attribute i lowered the cutoff level on that attribute, but had no effect on the cutoff levels of other attributes (in the aggregate). Put in economic jargon, "own-effects" responded as in the optimal rule, but "cross-effects" were zero. Given the complexity of the problem subjects were confronted with, this result is relatively surprising. It suggests that subjects picked up on the "first-order" expected benefit-expected cost trade-offs resulting from changes in inspection costs, but in the aggregate they ignored the "second-order" trade-offs which get incorporated into the optimal conjunctive strategy.

6. INFORMATION OVERLOAD

Consumer researchers, and lately policymakers, have been concerned with how much information a consumer needs to make intelligent choices in product markets. In particular, since consumers can only process a limited amount of information in a given time period, the potential danger of "information overload" has attracted a great deal of attention recently. For example, many of the recent debates over revising the Truth in Lending Act, as well as those concerning new disclosure legislation, have relied heavily on this notion. Information overload, at least as used by consumer researchers, generally seems to refer to the proposition that excess information may be dysfunctional. This is a much stronger statement than saying that more information may not be better. It suggests that too much information can lead to confused, irrational choice behavior. The purpose of this section is to review the evidence advanced to support the existence of such a phenomenon.

A recent series of studies conducted by Jacoby and his associates (Jacoby, Speller, & Berning, 1974, 1975; Jacoby, Speller, & Kohn, 1974) concluded that decisionmakers display the greatest accuracy in their choices when "moderate" amounts of information are available. While these studies provide the primary source of supporting evidence for proponents of the overload hypothesis, they have been extensively criticized (Wilkie, 1974; Summers, 1974; Russo, 1974). In fact, in reanalyzing the data generated in the Jacoby experiments, Staelin and Payne (1976) conclude that more information may well be associated with more accuracy in choice, not less.

The experimental design was basically the same in all of the Jacoby experiments. First, each subject was asked to indicate the importance of each attribute associated with the product being used (a "weighting factor"), and to specify an "ideal" brand. These were used to provide a base against which accuracy of choices could be measured. Next, each subject was given x brands to choose from, each brand described by y attributes. The objective was to evaluate the information provided and choose the "best" brand in the set. The best brand was defined as the brand least distant from the ideal brand, where distance was measured linearly using the attribute weights elicited at the outset of the experiment. Across the three experiments, x (the number of brands) ranged from 4 to 16, and y (the number of attributes about which information was provided) ranged from 2 to 6. Using x.y as a measure of the total information available, and plotting the number of correct choices against it, the experimenters concluded that "providing substantial amounts of package information can result in poorer purchase decision" (Jacoby, Speller, & Berning, 1974, p. 40) and that increasing the information load tends to produce "dysfunctional consequences in terms of the consumer's ability to pick the brand which was best for him" (Jacoby, Speller, & Kohn, 1974, p. 67).

The raw data from the Jacoby, Speller, and Kohn (1974) experiment are given in Table 3. Causal inspection of Table 3 is rather interesting in light of the claims of Jacoby et al. First, ignoring chance (the fact that random decisions are *less* likely to yield a "best" choice as the number of brands increases), it appears that, holding the number of brands constant, more "information" per brand is "better" when the number of brands is 4 or 8 and is "neutral" when the number of brands is 12. Similarly, ignoring chance, it appears that, holding "information" per brand constant, more brands to choose from is "better" for two items per brand, "neutral" for four items per brand, and "worse" for six items per brand. It is rather hard to conclude from this interpretation of the data that more information is bad, and it's rather ambiguous whether even more choice is bad: So how did the experimenters reach their conclusions? Consider measuring total "information load" by multiplying items/brand times the number of brands. Plotting the number of correct choices against this variable gives Figure 1. The inverted u-shaped curve in Figure 1 is the source of the rather strong conclusions of Jacoby et al. Plotting the number of "correct" choices against the total number of "bits" of information provided subjects suggests that, as the latter rises, performances increases initially, but, eventually, it peaks, and for increases in the "amount" of information provided beyond that, performance falls!

Taking the basic experimental design as given (this, by itself, requiring a great leap of faith), the transition from Table 3 to Figure 1, a necessary move to be able to conclude that increasing information load tends to produce dysfunctional consequences, requires two implicit assumptions. First, it must be the case that choice accuracy can be compared across the cells of Table 3 with different numbers of brands—the fact that accuracy should

TABLE 3. Number of Subjects (Out of 17 in Each Cell) Correctly Choosing Their "Best" Brand[a]

Number of Items/Brand Revealed	Number of Brands	4	8	12	Total
2		2	3	5	10
4		6	6	5	17
6		11	8	4	23
Total		19	17	14	

[a] From Jacoby, Speller, and Kohn, 1974, p. 65.

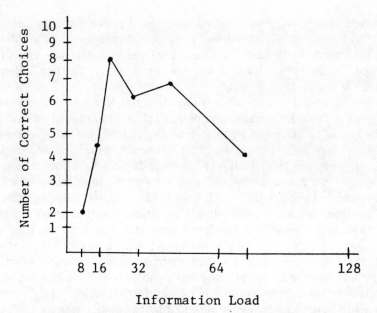

Information Load

FIGURE 1.   **Performance as a Function of Information Load**

fall purely as a matter of chance as the number of brands increases must not matter. Second, there is a one-to-one trade-off between brands and attributes—it is only the total number of "bits" of information confronting the consumer that matters as far as choice accuracy is concerned. These two assumptions are rather problematic, and, in fact, they provide the basis for the critiques of the Jacoby et al. experiments mentioned above. Staelin and Payne (1976) represent the most sophisticated of these.[18]

Staelin and Payne take the basic design of the Jacoby et al. experiments as given. They avoid the first of the two assumptions needed to yield Figure 1 by adjusting Table 3 for random choices. That is, they measure performance by comparing the actual number of correct choices to those based on chance alone for each cell. They then perform a simple regression analysis in which adjusted accuracy is the dependent variable and the independent variables are the product class (one for each of the Jacoby et al. experiments —three in total), the number of brands, and the number of attributes per brand. They conclude that

> as more information is provided the accuracy increases markedly up to and in-
> cluding six pieces of information. However, when the consumer is given eight
> pieces of information per alternative, there seems to be a sharp decrease in ac-

---

[18] Wilkie (1974) also raised the first objection and Russo (1974) suggested both factors cast doubt on the conclusions of Jacoby et al.

curacy, after which more information seems to improve the consumers accuracy...it seems that more information is associated with more accuracy at least within small ranges. (p. 189)

Since Jacoby and his associates also found that their subjects felt more satisfied and less confused with more information, as revealed in a post-experiment questionnaire, the overall conclusion one is led to draw from the project (based on Staelin and Payne) is that increasing consumer information is a good idea whenever it is feasible. This conclusion is polar to that drawn by the original researchers, yet it nevertheless appears to be inescapable.

Perhaps it is not so inescapable, though. After all, it is still based on the presumption that the basic experimental design of the Jacoby et al. experiments was valid. Given the manner in which performance was measured (distance from an "ideal" brand using subjective weights for attributes), there remains some uncertainty as to whether the so-called information overload phenomenon is real or not.

Before continuing, and in light of the above discussion, it will be useful to retreat momentarily and discuss briefly the background of the "information overload" hypothesis. The original notion of information overload, due to psychologists, was related to information acquisition (in particular, external search), not the quality of final choices. As Bettman summarizes the literature, "several researchers have argued that as task difficulty (measured as the total amount of information, or information load) increases, there will first be increases in search, but then eventually decreases as too high an information load is imposed" (1979, p. 126). Studies in the psychology literature which support this conclusion include Sieber and Lanzetta (1964), Streufert, Svedfeld, and Driver (1965) and Schroder, Driver, and Streufert (1967). Information overload, in this case, refers to the fact that information acquisition (i.e., external search) eventually decreases as the total amount of information available to the decisionmaker passes some critical level. Of course, this does *not* imply performance falls as information load increases. In fact, quite the opposite is likely to occur.

Consider the following scenario. Suppose that a decisionmaker has to choose an alternative from some set of multi-attribute items. Suppose further that the decisionmaker only feels strongly about one or two attributes. Now a random sample of, say, two attributes is not likely to provide information about these crucial attributes. Hence, the decisionmaker will be forced to utilize information on both available attributes in order to make a choice. A random sample of, say, four attributes will occasionally include one or both of the crucial attributes. When this is the case, the decisionmaker can base a decision on these and need not utilize the information available on the other two attributes. When it is not the case, however, the decisionmaker might again be forced to utilize information on all four available attributes in order to make a choice. The larger the sample of attributes, the more likely it is that the crucial attributes are included. Thus, on average, as the set of available attributes increases, we would expect the number utilized in making decisions to increase initially, eventually peak, and thereafter fall. But the quality of choices should increase monotonically over the entire range.

The scenario just described seems to be consistent with the observations of psychologists studying information load, although it should be noted that their experiments were designed to focus on information acquisition, not performance. The problem with the way Jacoby and his associates interpret the results of their experiments is that they seem to have assumed that the inverted u-shaped curve which describes the relationship between information load and external search holds also for the relationship between information load and performance. Adjusting Table 3 for chance yields Table 4 and Figure 2. One can interpret Figure 2 as an inverted u-shaped curve, but it is just as plausible to argue that it is rising on the range (0,24) and roughly constant after that. Moreover, as Table 4 indicates, the only time subjects did significantly worse than random behavior would have predicted is in the low information treatments.

TABLE 4.   Number of Correct Choices Out of 17 Minus the Expected Number Given Random Choice

	Number of Brands	4	8	12
	Random Choice	4.25	2.125	1.06
Number of items/brand revealed	2	−2.25	.875	3.94
	4	1.75	3.875	3.94
	6	6.75	5.875	2.93

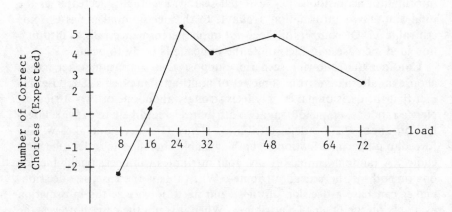

FIGURE 2.   Adjusted Performance as a Function of Information Load

In any case, it is clear that further research is needed on the information overload issue. This research should distinguish between information acquisition and performance, and it should attempt to identify relevant measures of information load—it is not obvious that total "bits" of information (number of brands times items per brand) is very meaningful.

A recent set of experiments by Grether and Wilde (1982) began to explore some of these issues. Their results suggest that individuals are quite good at making certain types of rather complicated choices. While the design included tasks which clearly varied in complexity, the degree of difficulty or "cognitive load" was not well described by simply counting the number of bits of information available. In fact, subjects in these experiments acted as if they were quite capable of ignoring irrelevant information.

The part of the Grether and Wilde experiments most germane to the discussion here involved choices over sets of compound lotteries. For example, Figure 3 displays a problem in which there are two items to choose from (A or B), each described by three binary lotteries. If a subject chose A, then his or her reward would be based on the outcomes of the three simple lotteries, each determined by a separate random draw from a bingo cage containing balls numbered 1–100. In the first simple lottery, the subject would earn $7.60 if 1–35 was drawn and $3.70 if 36–100 was drawn; in the second, he or she would lose $.45 if 1–25 was drawn and earn $.10 if 26–100 was drawn; in the third, a draw of 1–60 would have earned the subject $4.50, while 61–100 would have paid $7.75.

Choice tasks varied in size from 2 items, each consisting of 2 simple lotteries, up to 5 items, each consisting of 5 simple lotteries. Besides varying according to the number of items and the number of simple lotteries, choice tasks varied according to how many of the simple lotteries "mattered." For example, in Figure 3, each item includes one simple lottery which involves very low payoffs compared to the other two. Thus, an "informed" choice for this task would require the subject to consider only two of the three simple lotteries making up each item. The number of such "crucial" simple lotteries in a choice task is called the "difficulty" of the task. Finally, correct choices were defined using the dominance criterion. In other words, for each choice task there existed a unique item which dominated all other items, in

FIGURE 3. **Example of Choice Task in Grether-Wilde Experiments**

	Prospect 1	Prospect 2	Prospect 3
Item A	$7.60 if 1–35 $3.70 if 36–100	−$.45 if 1–25 $.10 if 26–100	$4.50 if 1–60 $7.75 if 61–100
Item B	$.30 if 1–75 −$.25 if 76–10	$8.00 if 1–40 $5.00 if 41–100	$3.50 if 1–65 $7.40 if 66–100

TABLE 5.   Percent Correct Responses

	Number of Items/Number of Simple Lotteries				
Difficulty	2/2	2/3	3/3	4/4	5/5
1	.81	.80	.64	.58	.58
2	.58	.74	.62		
3	.58	.39			
4				.28	

the sense that it placed higher probability on high payoffs than any other item. Table 5 presents the percent of correct responses by task size and difficulty.

Looking down any column in Table 5, it is clear that, whatever determined the degree of difficulty of a task, it was *not* the total number of bits of information available alone. In fact, the table suggests that the most important factor was the number of "crucial" simple lotteries. It also suggests that subjects were generally quite capable of ignoring irrelevant information. In only two of the 11 tasks did the percentage of correct choices fall below approximately 60%, including one with 16 component lotteries and one with 25 component lotteries. Behavior approached random only when the degree of difficulty (the number of crucial simple lotteries) and the number of alternatives increased simultaneously.

7. CONCLUSION

One theme of this survey has been that we can go a long way toward understanding consumer behavior under imperfect information by using variations on the economist's cost-benefit model. Examples of this approach include the basic homogeneous goods models of Stigler and McCall (discussed in Section 3), extensions to heterogenous goods by Nelson and Wilde (discussed in Section 4), and Wilde's formal model of conjuctive choice (discussed in Section 5). While the evidence reviewed provides some support for this position, it also raises some questions. Regarding the former, it seems clear that consumers generally respond as predicted to changes in the perceived benefits and costs of search. Regarding the latter, there are two stylized facts which seem inconsistent with the predictions of the existing search models. First, there appears to be a positive relationship between external search and product price. Second, consumers appear to engage in relatively little shopping for durables. Whether a purely economic model can explain these anomalies is an open question.

The survey also discussed two areas in which much more research is needed, satisfactory search and information overload. The major problem with the former is that it lacks a unifying theoretical foundation. It is here that the cost-benefit paradigm could turn out to be extremely useful. An illustration of how this might be done was discussed briefly in Section 5. Wilde's model of conjunctive choice (1982) was outlined there, and a series of experiments related to it summarized (Grether & Wilde, 1984). While the approach worked well for the conjunctive rule, a useful research effort would be to try applying it to other choice-models.

More work is also needed on information overload. The consumer research literature related to information overload is small, but it has had a large impact—many policymakers are concerned about information overload, and there seems to be a general belief that the phenomenon has been well-documented. Yet Section 6 showed that there is a great deal of confusion on this issue, and that no real evidence exists which links increases in information load to decreases in performance. This is an unfortunate state of affairs, but hopefully one that will be corrected in future research.

REFERENCES

Bauer, R.A. (1960, June). Consumer behavior as risk taking. In R.S. Hancock (Ed.), *Dynamic marketing for a changing world* (Proceedings of the 43rd national conference of the American Marketing Association). Chicago: American Marketing Association.

Benhabib, J., & Bull, C. (1982). *A compound strategy for search in the labor market: A reformulation.* Unpublished manuscript.

Bettman, J.R. (1977). Consumer information acquisition and search strategies. Unpublished manuscript.

Bruce, G.D., & Dommermuth, W.P. (1968). Social class differences in shopping activities. *Marquette Business Review, 12,* 1–7.

Bucklin, L.P. (1963). Retail strategy and the classification of consumer goods. *Journal of Marketing, 27,* 50–54.

Bucklin, L.P. (1966). Testing propensities to shop. *Journal of Marketing, 30,* 22–27.

Butters, G.R. (1977). Equilibrium distribution of sales and advertising prices. *Review of Economic Studies, 44,* 465–492.

Claxton, J.D., Fry, J.N., & Portis, B. (1974). A taxonomy of prepurchase information gathering patterns. *Journal of Consumer Research, 1,* 35–42.

Copeland, M.T. (1923). Relation of consumer buying habits for marketing methods. *Harvard Business Review, 1,* 282–289.

Day, G.S. (1970). Assessing the effects of information disclosure requirements. *Journal of Marketing, 40,* 42–52.

Dommermuth, W.P. (1965). The shopping matrix and marketing strategy. *Journal of Marketing Research, 2,* 128–132.

Dommermuth, W.P., & Cundiff, E.W. (1967). Shopping goods, shopping centers, and selling strategies. *Journal of Marketing, 31,* 32–36.

Einhorn, H.J. (1971). Use of nonlinear, noncompensatory models as a function of task and amount of information. *Organizational Behavior and Human Performance, 6,* 1–27.

Engel, J.F., Kollat, D.T., & Blackwell, R.D. (1973). *Consumer behavior* (2nd ed.). New York: Holt, Rinehart, and Winston.

Fried, L.S., & Peterson, C.R. (1969). Information seeking: Optimal versus fixed stopping. *Journal of Experimental Psychology, 80,* 525–529.

Gal, S., Landsberger, M., & Levykson, B. (1981). A compound strategy for search in the labor market. *International Economic Review, 22,* 597-608.

Gastwirth, J.L. (1976). Probabilistic models of consumer search. *Quarterly Journal of Economics, 90,* 38-50.

Green, P.E., Halbert, M., & Minas, J.S. (1964). An experiment in information buying. *Journal of Advertising Research, 4,* 17-23.

Grether, D.M. (1978). Recent psychological studies of behavior under uncertainty. *American Economic Review, 68,* 70-74.

Grether, D.M., & Wilde, L. (1982). *Consumer choice and information: New experimental evidence on the information overload hypothesis.* California Institute of Technology, SSWP 459.

Grether, D.M., & Wilde, L. (1984). An analysis of conjunctive choice: Theory and experiments. *Journal of Consumer Research, 10,* 373-385.

Hansen, F. (1972). *Consumer choice behavior: A cognitive theory.* New York: Free Press.

Hey, J.D., & McKenna, C. (1981). Consumer search with uncertain product quality. *Journal of Political Economy, 89,* 54-66.

Hirschleifer, J. (1973). Where are we in the theory of information? *American Economic Review, 63,* 31-39.

Jacoby, J., Speller, D.E., & Berning, C.K. (1974). Brand choice behavior as a function of information load: Replication and extension. *Journal of Consumer Research, 1,* 33-42.

Jacoby, J., Speller, D.E., & Berning, C.A.K. (1975). Constructive criticism and programmatic research: Reply to Russo. *Journal of Consumer Research, 2,* 154-156.

Jacoby, J., Speller, D.E., & Kohn, C.A. (1974). Brand choice behavior as a function of information load. *Journal of Marketing Research, 11,* 63-69.

Johnson, E. (1979). *Deciding how to decide: The effort of making a decision.* Unpublished manuscript.

Katona, G., & Mueller, E. (1955). A study of prepurchase decisions in consumer behavior. In L.H. Clark (Ed.), *Consumer behavior: The dynamics of consumer reaction* (Vol. 1) (pp. 30-87). New York: New York University Press.

Lanzetta, J.T., & Kanareff, V.T. (1962). Information cost, amount of payoff, and level of aspiration as determinants of information seeking in decision making. *Behavioral Science, 7,* 459-73.

Lynch, J. (1981). *Looking for confirming evidence: The case of the elusive conjunctive consumer decision process.* Unpublished manuscript.

March, J.G., & Simon, H.A. (1958). *Organizations.* New York: John Wiley and Sons.

McCall, J.T. (1965). The economics of information and optimal stopping rules. *Journal of Business, 38,* 300-317.

McCall, J.T. (1970). Economics of information and job search. *Quarterly Journal of Economics, 84,* 113-176.

Morgan, P. (1982). *Search and optimal sample sizes.* Unpublished manuscript.

Mortensen, D. (1976). Job matching under imperfect information. In O. Ashenfelter (Ed.), *Evaluating the labor market effects of social programs.* Princeton, NJ: Princeton University.

Nelson, P. (1970). Information and consumer behavior. *Journal of Political Economy, 78,* 311-329.

Newman, J.W. (1977). Consumer external search: Amount and determinants. In A.G. Woodside, J.N. Sheth, & P.D. Bennett (Eds.), *Consumer and Industrial Buying Behavior.* New York: North-Holland.

Newman, J.W., & Lockeman, B.D. (1975). Measuring prepurchase information seeking. *Journal of Consumer Research, 2,* 216-222.

Newman, J.W., & Staelin, R. (1972). Prepurchase information seeking for new cars and major household appliances. *Journal of Marketing Research, 9,* 249-257.

Pitz, G.F. (1968). Information seeking when available information is limited. *Journal of Experimental Psychology, 76,* 25–34.

Pratt, J., Wise, D., & Zeckhauser, R. (1979). Price differences in almost competitive markets. *Quarterly Journal of Economics, 93,* 189–212.

Rees, A. (1966). Information networks in labor markets. *American Economic Review, 56,* 559–566.

Rothschild, M. (1973). Models of market organization with imperfect information: A survey. *Journal of Political Economy, 81,* 1283–1308.

Rothschild, M. (1974). Searching for the lowest price when the distribution of prices is unknown. *Journal of Political Economy, 82,* 689–711.

Russo, J. (1974). More information is better: A reevaluation of Jacoby, Speller, and Kohn. *Journal of Consumer Research, 1*(3), 68–72.

Salop, S., & Stiglitz, J. (1977). Bargains and ripoffs: A model of monopolitically competitive price dispersion. *Review of Economics Studies, 44,* 493–510.

Satterthwaite, M. (1977). *The effect of increased supply on equilibrium price: A theory for the strange case of physicians' services.* MEDS Discussion Paper.

Schmalensee, R. (1978). A model of advertising and product quality. *Journal of Political Economy, 86,* 485–504.

Schroder, H.M., Driver, M.J., & Streufert, S. (1967). *Human information processing.* New York: Holt, Rinehart, and Winston.

Shugan, S. (1980). The cost of thinking. *Journal of Consumer Research, 7,* 99–111.

Shugan, S. (1981). *The cost of thinking: Its implications.* Unpublished manuscript.

Sieber, J.E., & Lanzetta, J.T. (1964). Conflict and conceptual structure as determinants of decision making behavior. *Journal of Personality, 32,* 622–641.

Slovic, P., & Lichtenstein, S. (1971). Comparison of Bayesian and regression approaches to the study of information processing in judgement. *Organizational Behavior and Human Performance, 6,* 649–744.

Staelin, R., & Payne, J.W. (1976). Studies of information-seeking behavior of consumers. In J.S. Carroll & J.W. Payne (Eds.), *Cognition and social behavior.* Hillsdale, NJ: Erlbaum.

Stigler, G.J. (1961). The economics of information. *Journal of Political Economy, 69,* 213–225.

Stigler, G.J. (1962). Information in the labor market. *Journal of Political Economy, 70,* 94–105.

Streufert, S., Svedfeld, P., & Driver, M.J. (1965). Conceptual structure, information search, and information utilization. *Journal of Personality and Social Psychology, 2,* 736–740.

Summers, J.O. (1974). Less information is better? *Journal of Marketing Research, 11,* 467–468.

Swan, J.E. (1969). Experimental analysis of predecision information seeking. *Journal of Marketing Research 6,* 192–197.

Swan, J.E. (1972). Search behavior related to expectations concerning brand performance. *Journal of Applied Psychology, 56,* 332–335.

Thaler, R.H. (1977). *Toward a positive theory of consumer behavior.* Unpublished manuscript.

Tversky, A., & Kahneman, D. (1974). Judgment under uncertainty: Heuristics and biases. *Science, 185,* 1124–1131.

Udell, J.G. (1966). Prepurchase behavior of buyers of small electrical appliances. *Journal of Marketing, 30,* 50–52.

Wilde, L.L. (1977). Labor market equilibrium under nonsequential search. *Journal of Economic Theory, 16,* 373–393.

Wilde, L.L., & Schwartz, A. (1979). Equilibrium comparison shopping. *Review of Economic Studies, 46,* 543–553.

Wilde, L.L., & Schwartz, A. (1980a). On the formal theory of inspection and evaluation in product markets. *Econometrica, 48,* 1265–1280.

Wilde, L.L., & Schwartz, A. (1980b). The economics of consumer information acquisition. *Journal of Business, 53,* 5143–5158.

Wilde, L.L., & Schwartz, A. (1981). Information costs, duration of search and turnover: Theory and applications. *Journal of Political Economy, 89,* 1122–1141.

Wilde, L.L., & Schwartz, A. (1982). Optimal and nonoptimal satisficing I: A model of satisfaction choice. California Institute of Technology, SSWP 363.

Wilkie, W.L. (1974). Analysis of effects of information load. *Journal of Marketing Research, 11,* 462–466.

Winter, F.W. (1975). Laboratory measurement of response to consumer information. *Journal of Marketing Research, 12,* 390–401.

Wright, P. (1975). Consumer choice strategies: Simplifying versus optimizing. *Journal of Marketing Research, 12,* 60–67.

Yavitz, B., & Morse, D.W. (1973). *The labor market: An information system.* New York: Praeger.

Chapter 10

Optimal Use of Space by Neighboring Central Place Foragers: When and Where to Store Surplus Resources

Alan P. Covich

Department of Zoology
University of Oklahoma
and
Center for Energy and Environment Research
University of Puerto Rico

I. INTRODUCTION

A. Competition for Scarce Resources

For many years, the analysis of competitive interactions has remained a major focus in both ecology and economics (e.g., Boulding, 1981; Hutchinson, 1978; Nelson & Winter, 1982; Rapport & Turner, 1977). Most ecologists emphasized that competition for scarce resources influenced each consumer's growth and reproduction, so that, over a period of time, the composition of any community or guild of consumers was determined by relative competitiveness. The time scales of these interactions have sometimes been difficult to determine (Altman, 1974; MacArthur, 1972; Wilson, 1975), as have other conditions for realistic models. The search for conditions that either allow for coexistence or result in competitive displacements of one species by another has generated some differences of opinion regarding what factors are important in determining competitive outcomes. One problem is that the definition of *resource availability* must be a dynamic one that includes aspects of uncertainty and proportionality in the timing of supplies of multiple, co-required resources (Covich, 1972; Leon & Tumpson, 1975; Pulliam, 1975; Rapport, 1971; Tilman, 1982). In addition to temporal patterns, the spatial relationships of multiple resources must be simultaneously considered (e.g., Armitage & Harris, 1982; Cormack, 1979; Getty, 1981b, 1981c; Myton, 1974; Paton and Carpenter, 1984).

Currently, ecologists are debating the adequacy of experimental and field observations which assert that competition is a major mechanism regulating community composition (Bowers & Brown, 1982; Connell, 1980, 1983; Schoener, 1982, 1983; Wiens, 1977, 1983). They have broadened the search for regulating mechanisms to include other interactions, such as predation, parasitism, and mutualism (Axelrod, 1984; Anderson & May, 1982; Barnard, 1984; Boucher, James, & Keeler, 1982; Dean, 1983; Levin, 1983; Hazlett, 1983; May, 1982; Paine, 1980; Slatkin & Maynard Smith, 1979; Zaret, 1980). In these deliberations, the importance of very high availability of some resources is often overlooked, because the emphasis typically focuses on *scarcity* of limiting resources. Behavioral adaptations that allow some members of a population to exploit completely the "excess" resources during "good" periods may influence differences in individual success during stressful periods. If some individuals respond quickly to even brief periods of resource superabundance, their behavior may greatly influence predation rates or competitive outcomes. As discussed below, the decision to store some foods during periods of increased availability may protect these resources from consumption by others and also permit the storer to feed on them without exposure to predators.

The importance of different complementary or substitutional qualities of resources relative to competing consumers is now under study, and should provide some important modifications of predictions that consider *all* resources potentially *substitutable* (Covich, 1976; Leon & Tumpson, 1975; Rapport, 1971; Tilman, 1982). Given an array of food resources that differ in their nutritional composition and processing time, some optimal foraging theories predict that consumers will increase their degree of selectivity under conditions of high abundance (Ebersole & Wilson, 1980; Krebs, 1982; Pyke, Pulliam, & Charnov, 1977). A rapid increase in the abundance of one resource, while others remain relatively constant or become scarce, will enhance growth and reproduction of those species capable of substituting the superabundant resource for the others that have been used previously. The prediction will be quite different, however, if the superabundant resource is not a good substitute for the scarce resources (Covich, 1974). One possibility is that the increased abundance of a relatively poor substitute (less preferred, secondary prey) can lead to a "transfer-of-time effect." The high abundance of a subsistence resource may permit the consumer to shift its time budget in such a manner as to save time during moderate levels of consumption of the less preferred, but readily obtained, food. Because of this superabundance of the secondary food, the consumer now has a "surplus" of time and can spend more time than it would otherwise be able to afford in search of the scarce, highly preferred food. By continued searching for, and consumption of, the scarce, highly preferred prey, the consumer eventually could locally eliminate its most preferred food source. Such eliminations of preferred prey species can then lead to instability and increased risk of localized extinctions of the predatory species during periods of scarcity of the less preferred prey.

Another such prediction relates to food storage. High abundance of some resources will allow individuals to spend considerable time and energy in storing food for later consumption. This expenditure of time is economically advantageous in the short run only if: (a) some of the resources are likely to be recovered (i.e., they do not deteriorate) and they can be defended from theft, or (b) the consumers develop other adaptive strategies as discussed below (such as indirect resource interchange: the finding of caches made by neighbors to offset losses to neighbors). The decision to consume a resource now or store it for later consumption may be important in determining long-term competitive interactions of those individuals who store, and those who do not store the resources but find them and use them (Andersson & Krebs, 1978; Roberts, 1979; Sherry, 1982; Shettleworth & Krebs, 1982; Vander Wall & Balda, 1981). Such trade-offs in how time and energy budgets are spent can be viewed as long-term, inter- and intraspecific competition for fluctuating resource availabilities. Food storing can also lead to a type of diffuse, mutualistic interchange of resources. Neighboring individuals, of the same or different species, may enhance the passive access to each others' stored foods by the spatial pattern of their foraging activities: Finding a resource that initially was harvested from outside a consumer's home range but was stored inside the consumer's home range by a neighbor can lead to undirected, mutual interchanges. The adaptive value of any resource interchange will primarily depend on resource qualities, availabilities, dispersions, and the nutritional bases for consumer preferences, as well as the effectiveness of "self-enforcing" interactions (Telser, 1980) in determining when it is beneficial to an individual not to "cheat" its neighbors.

In some cases, competition for scarce resources may be limited to specific cycles, such as seasonal changes in food supply, or to unpredictable, catastrophic events (Wiens, 1977, 1983). In other cases, intermittent periods of superabundance may lead to important interactions among competing consumers that affect reproductive success (Rubenstein, 1982; Schoener, 1982). The shift to feeding on superabundances of lemmings by consumers as diverse as foxes, seabirds, reindeer, trout, and salmon is certainly one of the most dramatic demonstrations of food substitutability ever described (Deevey, 1959). Species adapted for *both* feast and famine will have distinct advantages relative to other species unable to exploit brief periods of superabundance. The total impact of resource uncertainty on consumer interactions is not limited to resource depletion and starvation, but must also include effects of superabundance resulting from resource substitution and complementarity, or from storage and incidental interchange among consumers with overlapping home ranges. A central theme in evaluating the varied responses of consumers during both their storage activities (in times of abundance) and their searching for, and retrieval of, hidden or scattered foods (in terms of scarcity) is how they minimize their exposure to predators while maximizing their probabilities of obtaining nutritionally adequate food.

B. Responses to High Resource Abundances

Some consumers, especially carnivores such as foxes, fishers, and weasels, are known to kill prey and not eat them (Eide & Ballard, 1982; Ewer, 1968, 1973; Kruuk, 1972b; Nunn, Klem, Kimmel, & Merriman, 1976; Oksanen, Oksanen, & Fretwell, 1985; Powell, 1982). Kruuk (1972b) suggested that such "surplus" killing in some cases could be adaptive in the long run and was not wasteful despite a lack of immediate returns for time and energy spent. For example, family or foraging group members may consume prey killed and left by another related member. If young predators are learning how to hunt, they may accrue some long-term benefit from practicing their killing of prey when prey densities are very high and the prey populations not in immediate danger of overexploitation. Another aspect of the cost/ benefit relationship is the total time budget and the demands for other functions. Younger predators may not be feeding offspring or seeking mates, and thus they will have very low "opportunity costs" (alternative values for spending their time).

Typically, observations of large-scale surplus killing are uncommon. The observed excessive predation is on secondary species of prey that do not immediately limit the predator's total consumption. Yet any complete elimination of a secondary, potentially stabilizing source of food from a habitat could be detrimental in the long run during periods of locally severe declines in the primary prey species. In some cases, there is surplus killing of competing species (Eide & Ballard, 1982); such removal could well be advantageous during periods of food scarcity. In other cases, the "surplus" killing is an adaptive mode for opportunistic exploitation of a rare encounter with superabundant prey, and the uneaten prey are stored (Powell, 1982). If the consumer spends a long time in a foraging area during periods of surplus killing, there is an increased risk of encountering either a competitor or, even more costly, a predator capable of eliminating the surplus killer. Thus, the consumer may require another habitat in which to feed safely or to manipulate the prey to kill it. If the forager hides the food, a decision must be made about where to place the "surplus." Storage of food items for later consumption is termed "caching" or "hoarding"; a centralized site for storage is a "nest cache" or "larder hoard." If the consumer encounters a high density of food items in one location, it may carry many of these to different sites for storage; this spreading out of stored items is termed "scatter hoarding" (Ewer, 1968; Glanz, et al., 1982; Macdonald, 1976; Morris, 1962; Smythe, 1970, 1978; Smythe, et al., 1982 and see Figures 1, 2, 3).

To obtain a conceptual perspective on these interactions, I first review several examples from the ecological literature that provide background on the many modes used by various terrestrial vertebrate groups confronting relatively high concentrations of resources. Then I discuss some means of behavioral analyses that are familiar to economists and psychologists who have developed concepts of individual interaction that help to provide a complete analysis of consumer behavior. The connections among ecology, economics, ethology, sociobiology and psychology are increasing rapidly, especially in studies of foraging behavior (Allison, 1983; Battalio, et al., 1981; Baum, 1983; Covich, 1976; Fredlund, 1976; Hainsworth & Wolf, 1979; Kagel, et al., 1981; Kamil, 1983; Lacher, Willig, & Mares, 1982; Lea, 1983; McFarland & Houston, 1981; Noakes & McNicol, 1982; Pulliam, 1981; Pyke, 1978, 1984; Pyke et al., 1977; Rapport & Turner, 1977; Real, 1980). Despite this emerging unity of concepts, there are still several topics that often appear as "special cases" or are interpreted as disproving the generality of optimal foraging. The apparently uneconomic modes of consumption, such as "surplus" killing and hoarding, are potentially adaptive and can be subject to several types of optimal foraging analysis, *if long-term costs and benefits are considered.* In this discussion, I will focus primarily on spatial relationships between multiple centralized locations of food sources and refugia from predators. These types of central-place interactions are frequently analyzed in economic geography (e.g., Colwell, 1982; Eaton & Lipsey, 1982; Greenhut, 1978), and are increasingly of interest to ecologists (e.g., Andersson, 1978; Carlson, 1983; Carlson & Moreno, 1982; Covich, 1976; Don & Rennolls, 1983; Ford, 1983; Hegner, 1982; Houston, 1985; Huntley, Smith, & Ivins, 1986; Lessels & Stephens, 1983; McGinley & Whitham, 1985; Orians & Pearson, 1979; Schoener, 1979). Here I emphasize how the distances travelled between refugia (home or nest sites) and sources of abundant foods influence the optimal location of storage sites. I suggest that many consumers minimize their losses of stored food to thieves and competitors while also minimizing their exposure to predators. The main benefits, regardless of specific advantages to certain spatial patterns of storage, are reduced risks of food deprivation over time, and also reduced risk to predation, resulting from more control over time and location of foraging activities. Simultaneously, there are several associated, but perhaps longer-term, benefits that result from reduced immediate food availability to competitors: future resource scarcity will be less likely for hoarding individuals if nonhoarding competitors have reduced reproductive success. Rapid, intense reductions in the short-term resource supply of specific, nutritious resources can limit population growth of nonhoarding competitors.

II. EVOLUTION OF LARDER AND SCATTER HOARDING

A. Carnivores: Refuge from Thieves and Predators

The origin of larder (centralized) hoarding is thought to be associated with having a safe place to manipulate and consume prey, especially larger food items (Ewer, 1968; Lyons & Mosher, 1982; Nunn et al., 1976; Phelan, 1977; Sherry, in press; Smith & Reichman, 1984). The tendency for foragers to carry food to a secluded location can be experimentally enhanced by placing food in exposed locations and by increasing the size of the food items (Ewer, 1968; Miller & Vick, 1950). As Ewer (1968, p. 57) noted, "the larger the piece of food, the greater is the chance that after an animal has had enough to eat, there will be something left over which can be used later—in fact an incipient hoard..." She added (p. 59) that "the leopard's well known habit of taking remains of its kill up a tree also seems to relate to protecting it from jackals and hyaenas." Kruuk (1972b, p. 240) further pointed out that leopards do not carry their kills up into trees "in areas where there are no competitors." Thus, larder hoarding may have allowed animals to feed over an extended period of time while minimizing their exposure, and the exposure of their surplus food, to other consumers. Scatter hoarding would hide food from competitors, but may expose the hoarder to more risk of predation (during both hiding and retrieving) than would larder hoarding (cf. Figures 1, 2, 3). Is risk of storage loss reduced among scatter hoarders relative to larder hoarders? How do scatter hoarders find their food caches at a later time when they may need them? Before we can attempt to answer these questions, it is necessary to illustrate additional examples of the diversity of hoarding behavior.

One of the best known scatter hoarding systems is that of the canids (Ewer, 1973; Malcolm, 1980). Those who have watched their pet dog pick up one bone after another and hide each in a different location are familiar with the general method used by foxes, wolves, and coyotes. Canids disperse their caches widely by moving out in a series of different directions during each caching sequence. Tinbergen reported on a detailed series of observations on fox predation and scatter hoarding of gull eggs. The different directions and distances that the fox moved while carrying and hiding each egg could be measured from tracks in the sandy dunes. Foxes set up regular trails and had distinct foraging areas. They located their own and other's cached eggs by scent, but some of their cached eggs were lost to hedgehogs "plundering the hoards" (1972, p. 325). Notably, Tinbergen (1972, p. 326) pointed out that "even assuming that in the long run egg losses would differ between the two strategies (i.e., 'clumping' and 'scattering') or assuming that they might even be slightly greater where the hoards were scattered, the danger of occasional *very high* losses, which could readily be critical for the fox, would be greater if he did not...spread out his finds so systematically." Ewer (1968, p. 56) reached the same conclusions: How the losses of caches are distributed in time is what really matters to hoarders.

Shrikes cache rodents, reptiles, and insects in the open, and can relocate them visually (Cade, 1967). They impale their prey in trees or bushes, on thorns or other projections, to hold the prey while eating it. Miller observed that "in American shrikes a potential storing mechanism exists which has arisen secondarily from a method of manipulating food" (Miller, 1931, p. 127). Gray Jays have an even larger variety of cached prey than do the shrikes. Dow (1965, p. 150) reported that they consume insects, and nestling birds, but "that wolf kills form a substantial part of their winter diet. . . . The general foraging of the Gray Jay is probably conducive to the locating of stored food. . . . They tend to store food in the same types of places as those where they are successful through random searching." They form a bolus of meat fragments and stick this round mass to the bark of trees and other structures with saliva.

Larder hoarders store their surplus food at home and thus their cache is readily found (not only by themselves but also by thieves). For example, Kowalski (1976, p. 194) reported that the mole is able to accumulate "stores of earthworms which can amount to several hundred individuals. The earthworms are bitten in such a way that they cannot escape, although they remain alive." Shrews paralyze their prey with a venom and store large numbers of immobilized, comatose prey in larder hoards that do not decay and remain palatable for extended periods of time (Robinson & Brodie, 1982). In some species, discovery and decay may be slowed down by storage underwater, as in larder hoarding by crocodiles and by spotted hyenas (Kruuk, 1972a).

Generally, the prey of carnivores is high in protein and nutritionally similar from one type of prey to another. Exploiting cached foods throughout potentially long periods of scarcity probably does not create the same physiological stress that substituting nutritionally different foods could create for omnivores and herbivores.

B. Omnivores: Resource Diversity and Nutritional Optimization

High variability in food quality may influence the kinds of advantages omnivorous consumers obtain from storing a variety of foods. Their problem then could be gaining access to an *adequate mix of nutritionally distinct foods*. Thus, diversification of hoarded resources from *multiple sources* will also provide a mixed diet that potentially supplies an omnivore's growth requirements more completely than if only one resource was hoarded (Reichman & Fay, 1983).

A few illustrations will serve to demonstrate that naturally available plant and animal foods differ greatly in protein content and other essential nutrients. Sodium is a good example of a required micronutrient, because of the considerable data that suggest sodium availability is a potential limiting factor for consumers in several ecosystems (e.g., Belovsky & Jordan, 1981; Weeks & Kirkpatrick, 1978) although Owen-Smith and Novellie (1982, p. 152) recently questioned the generality of sodium limitation. Specific mineral requirements of most consumers are still incompletely determined, but what is known about micronutrients in natural foodwebs underscores the need to focus on the relative and absolute quantities of *both* macro- and micronutrients, especially sodium.

Squirrels are commonly abundant and known to consume a very wide range of plant and animal foods. In their review of the gray squirrel, Schwartz and Schwartz (1981) reported that, of the perhaps 100 different plant species consumed, there are six major natural sources: hickory, pecan, oak, walnut, elm, and mulberry. These types of trees include many species distributed in widely different habitats. They pointed out (p. 150) that "some woodlands may have one or two staple food items but lack enough variety to maintain sizeable squirrel populations...large river-bottom stands of pure elm, maple or willows...are deficient in suitable foods." With regard to sodium, they further note that "because squirrels select the kernels of acorns to eat and discard the shells, they fail to obtain the salt that is most available in the shells."

Despite a relatively large number of studies on squirrel feeding behavior and nutritional requirements, it is not clear what constitutes the optimal, or even minimal, resource combination. Lewis (1982, p. 254) emphasized that the gray squirrels he studied preferred hickory nuts in relation to their availability "despite yielding a low rate of energy intake." He (p. 256) suggested that the relatively small amount of protein in acorns may be one reason why gray squirrels prefer hickory nuts. He noted that "the relative difference between the protein content of acorns and hickory nuts is exacerbated by the high concentration of tannins in acorns. The tannins may reduce digestible protein to levels below those indicated by measures of crude protein.... Acorns alone may not provide an adequate diet for squirrels." Barnett (1977, p. 326) also noted that squirrels seemed to have disproportionate consumption of hickory nuts relative to acorns because of the relatively high tannin content in acorns: 5.58% for white oak acorns vs. 0.48% for shagbark hickory nuts. In addition to higher levels of available protein in hickory nuts (Havera & Smith, 1979; Lewis, 1980; Smith & Follmer, 1972), they may also be easier for a predator to locate than acorns: they are larger, and their husk and kernel both emit a strong odor.

In their studies of relative food values, Weeks and Kirkpatrick (1978, p. 537) reported that both sodium and potassium differed greatly in acorns and hickory nuts consumed by squirrels: "The sudden and total switch to... nuts...in the late summer and autumn resulted in a considerable reduction in Na intake....Intake of K during this period was not excessive although hickory, the earliest nut eaten in substantial quantities was the highest in K (16,229 ppm)." Furthermore, "the possibility should be considered that limited availability of Na in the environment restricts herbivore productivity and population levels."

C. Herbivores: Nutritional Diversification and Detoxification

Unlike most omnivores that are adapted to consume a wide variety of foods, the more specialized consumers, such as granivores, frugivores and other types of herbivores, may feed much more restrictively on certain species of plant tissues that are spatially clumped and either seasonally or continually of limited nutrient content (Lacher et al., 1982). Moreover, many plants have evolved toxic, distasteful secondary compounds that inhibit consumption by most herbivores and some omnivores (Daly, Rauschenberger, & Behrends, 1982; Freeland & Janzen, 1974; Janzen, 1971, 1979). Herbivores can develop physiological or behavioral adaptations to counteract the toxic substances; generalization of the diet by using multiple food sources is perhaps not only an adaptation to gain required multiple nutrients, but it may also be a means of counteracting toxic substances (Freeland & Janzen, 1974). By widening the selected mix of different antitoxicants over a seasonal sequence of hoarding, those consumers who delay their feeding may lower their exposure to toxic compounds relative to individuals who consume fresh plant foods. As pointed out below, they may also lower their exposure to predators by altering the timing of their foraging activities.

Among the desert rodents, there are several species of kangaroo rats that dry and store foods in order to survive periods of low food production. In so doing, they respond to brief periods of supply following sporadic rainfall. Thus, they may be able to extend the time period during which they mix their food resources in future periods of consumption and thereby avoid toxic compounds. These hoarders may also be selective in determining which seeds to store. Daly et al. (1982, p. 319) state that "whether kangaroo rats sample dangerous food and acquire aversions in nature remains an open question. Novel seeds may be olfactorily classified as food or nonfood without being sampled."

The decision about which food to eat may be less potentially risky if the animal first gathers a wide variety of available foods and then "spreads its risks" by mixing the sequence of feeding on different plant species. For example, two species of kangaroo rat avoided seeds of jojoba (a desert plant now under study for its high rate of waxy oil production), which has seeds containing potentially toxic cyanogenic glucosides. A third species of heteromyid rodent, *Perognathus baileyi,* apparently is adapted somehow to detoxify this glucoside (Daly et al., 1982). Drying of seeds in long-term caches may help to deactivate the toxicity directly or indirectly, and allow for a more mixed diet at a future period of seed consumption. Other species of rodents apparently lack any mechanism for detoxifying simmondsin, the specific glycoside found in jojoba seed (Sherbrooke, 1976).

Reichman (1977, p. 456) reported that many of these desert rodents seem to be "optimizing their diets by ingesting some species of seeds in relatively high proportions which are very low in energy content and availability.... It appears that some of the items ingested provide some essential nutrient which outweighs their energetic deficiencies...or some other undetermined value." These desert rodent communities are thought to be regulated by each species' choice of microhabitat or preference for dispersions of different seeds associated with specific microhabitats (Brown, Reichman, & Davidson, 1979; O'Farrel, 1980; Price, 1978; Wondolleck 1978).

In other harsh environments, such as above timberline near the talus slopes of several high mountain ranges, "rock rabbits" or pikas (*Ochotona*) gather a wide array of plants and "cure" them in the sun (Elliott, 1980; Millar & Zwickel, 1972). These "hay piles" are distributed around (and sometimes under) rock shelters that are used by pikas to avoid predators such as hawks. Pikas were found to include 20 species of plants in their hay piles in central Idaho (Elliott, 1980), and similar populations in Colorado (Conner, 1983; Johnson, 1967; Kawamichi, 1976, 1982) and Montana (Barash, 1973) are also characterized by a high species diversity of plants consumed after haying. Although detoxification of food has not yet been documented, some of these plants probably contain secondary compounds that would be less toxic if they were consumed over extended periods in mixtures of several types after drying than they would be if eaten while fresh and in unmixed diets.

These specialized forms of hoarding and food processing are, as Ewer (1968, p. 61) aptly stated, "at first sight...difficult to explain without attributing to the animals concerned a highly improbable degree of intelligence and foresight....The evolution of the complex behavior shown is actually explicable in very simple terms....Haymaking must have evolved independently" in several taxonomic groups. She speculated that the behavior of a steppe lemming provided a basis for the early development of haymaking. To cut down more grass than is eaten, when abundant food is available, is common among some species: Some species select the most palatable plant tissues for immediate consumption, while leaving behind the more distasteful species for drying. In this manner, Ewer suggested that the evolution of haymaking required only an "intensification of the tendency to cut more food than is immediately required in times of abundances, coupled with postponement of hoarding until later in the season."

The travel patterns and use of space among different species of pikas are quite different in the various mountains they inhabit. Of the four species he studied, Kawamichi (1976, 1982) pointed out that only the North American species, *Ochotona princeps*, maintained active territorial defense of hay piles. Japanese species, in contrast, had no territorial defense, and individuals displayed some degree of mutual food collection. Two Himalayan species on Mt. Everest do not make "typical" hay piles for storage, but actively forage for food during the winter. Thus, different environmental and evolutionary factors appear to result in extremely different adaptive modes within the same group.

In Colorado, Kawamichi (1976, p. 135) studied 31 pikas very intensively near Loveland Pass. He reported that home ranges more or less overlapped. In some of these overlapping areas, hay piles were used by two to four individuals. He recorded 69 instances of "encounters" between neighboring territorial pikas, and only one contest between a resident and "wanderer." Kawamichi (1982, p. 25) noted that "the main function of the territoriality is the protection of hay piles preserved for winter food." The number of hay piles per territory ranged from 0 to 4 in published data of populations from Montana (Barash, 1973), and from 1 to 6 from Colorado (Kawamichi, 1976). A.T. Smith (1974, p. 1375) compared the distances between hay piles of pikas from low and high elevations in California: "low-altitude pikas were characteristically found close to their hay piles and generally foraged only short (20 m) distances..." Territories of hay piles apparently reflect relative locations of rocky shelters, as well as distances to sources of grasses and forbs. Because pikas are diurnal and their home ranges are relatively confined spatially and temporally in open habitat, they are ideal subjects for analysis of foraging activities related to trade-offs between food storage and immediate consumption. The sizes of home ranges and territories of pikas provide considerable information on social dynamics among neighbors. The degree to which spatial distributions of resources influence these dynamics is not yet known, but pika's foraging behavior provides unique opportunities for evaluating the evolution of multiple-resource hoarding strategies.

The previous examples of herbivorous hoarders have mainly illustrated above-ground activities, but many groups actively harvest and store food underwater or in underground burrow systems that spread out in many directions, often from a large, central nest or den. Burrowing animals avoid many predators and thermal stress, but must expend relatively much greater energy in their digging than do foragers travelling above ground. Recent reports by Vleck (1981) and Reichman, Whitham, and Ruffner (1982) provide informative data on burrow structures and adaptive geometry of pocket gophers. Apparently, the location of burrows "play an important role with regard to interactions between neighbors and internal management of resources" (Reichman et al., 1982, p. 688). Other herbivores such as beavers and muskrats cache food underwater: during storage, the food can increase its nutritional value from microbial conditioning. They select particular types of woody vegetation for storage as brush piles under their frozen ponds, and place these caches near their lodges for use during the winter (Aleksiuk, 1970; Jenkins, 1980). They also consume submerged aquatic plants, especially yellow water lilies that apparently provide some of the alkaloids needed for production of scents they use to demarcate their feeding territories (Valenta & Khaleque, 1959).

III. COSTS AND BENEFITS OF DELAYED CONSUMPTION

A. Central Place Foraging and Hoarding
Larder or nest hoarding is conceptually similar to central place foraging (Figure 1) done by birds and small mammals who make many trips out and

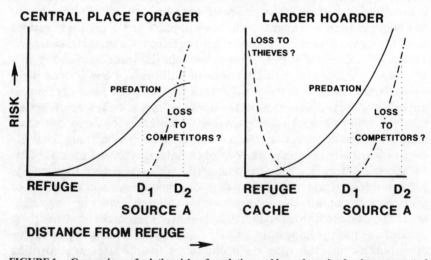

FIGURE 1.   Comparison of relative risks of predation and loss of surplus food among central place foragers and larder hoarders. Both central place foragers and larder hoarders are at increasing risk to predators as they travel farther from their central refuge to find food. Both also risk losing surplus food to competing consumers from under-utilization of a dense food patch (Source A). Each must travel beyond a threshold distance (D_1) to exploit the food source, but will avoid traveling greater distances (e.g., D_2) because of the increasingly high risk of predation associated with the food patch. As more competitors find the source, there will be less food available and potentially greater risk of predation (if nearby predators are attracted to the source by active exploitation among competing prey). The risk of predation will be a function of distance travelled from the refuge, structural complexity of the habitat, evasiveness of the forager relative to its predator, and temporal predictability of food in the surrounding home range (or from the cache in the case of larder hoarders). If the larder hoarder can protect its cache from thieves, it can control the time of day and frequency of foraging trips so as to minimize its risk of predation (compare slopes of predator risk functions—solid lines in graph). The larder hoarder will be at a higher risk of losing previously-stored food (cache) in its refuge, the longer (farther away) it remains away from its refuge. Transient thieves or neighbors can raid its larder hoard if the resident leaves its cache undefended while searching for additional food at distant sources. Thus, the combined higher risk of predation and loss to thieves at greater distances defines boundaries for travel by the larder hoarder, while the central place forager is restricted mainly by the higher risk of predation.

back while feeding nestlings, or by a variety of other consumers (Table 1) who repeatedly return to a site with protective cover in the center of their home range to feed on their gathered resources (Brown & Orians, 1970; Covich, 1976; Hamilton & Watt, 1970; Orians & Pearson, 1979). One main difference is that, once food is centrally stored, it typically is consumed by the hoarder at a later time, rather than fed immediately to young offspring. However, some birds, such as nutcrackers and piñon jays, use their stores of seeds cached in the fall to feed their young (and themselves) in the early spring, before sufficient densities of other foods such as insects are available (Ligon, 1978; Stacey & Jansma, 1977; Tomback, 1977, 1983). Some mammals switch from hoarding hard, dry foods to soft foods when using stored items to feed their litter (Ewer, 1968). Thus, the primary difference between hoarding and foraging is the time between finding food and consuming it. The decision about when to delay consumption will be influenced directly by risks of loss of food to other consumers (Elgmork, 1982; Ewer, 1968; Lanier, Estel, & Dewsbury, 1974; Phelan, 1977) and risk of predation (Figures 1, 2, and 3) as well as degree of satiation (Table 2).

The spatial factors that govern potential net gains from centralized caching were first analyzed quantitively by C.C. Smith (1968) in his thorough study of the tree squirrel, *Tamiasciurus*. He postulated that an individual harvester would be most efficient in locating food for storage if successively larger circular zones were searched during trips back and forth from a single storage site. Because centrally-stored food is subject to loss from fungal decay, or discovery by other consumers, the additional cost of drying the food or protecting it after it is found and carried back to the cache requires a rather large investment of time and energy. Smith concluded that such large investments must be associated with territorial defense that precluded

TABLE 1. **Examples of Studies on Central Place Foragers: Effects of Distances Travelled on Selective Use of Patchy Food Resources**

1. Birds travelling back and forth from nest sites or refugia:
   a. spotted flycatcher *(Muscicapa striata):* Davies, 1976.
   b. Brewer's blackbirds *(Euphagus cyanocephalus):* Orians, 1980.
   c. whinchat *(Saxicola rubetra):* Andersson, 1981.
   d. wheatear *(Oenanthe oenanthe):* Brooke, 1981; Carlson and Moreno, 1981, 1982.
   e. swallows *(Hirundo rustica):* Bryant and Turner, 1982.
   f. house martins *(Delichon urbica):* Bryant and Turner, 1982.
   g. sand martins *(Riparia riparia):* Bryant and Turner, 1982.
   h. starlings *(Sturnus vulgaris):* Tinbergen, 1981; Kacelnik, 1984.
   i. white-fronted bee-eater *(Merops bullockoides):* Hegner, 1982.
   j. red-backed shrikes *(Lanius collurio):* Carlson, 1983.
   k. Lapland longspurs *(Calcarius lapponicus):* McLaughlin and Montgomerie, 1985.
2. Small mammals travelling back and forth from a home site:
   a. beaver *(Castor canadensis):* Jenkins, 1980; McGinley and Whitham, 1985.
   b. eastern chipmunk *(Tamias striatus):* Getty, 1981a; Giraldeau and Kramer, 1982; Kramer and Nowell, 1980.
   c. rat *(Rattus norvegicus):* Killeen, Smith, and Hanson, 1981.

loss to other consumers (for a recent discussion, see Gurnell, 1984). In the case of the tree squirrels, it was apparent that caches of pine cones could be safely stored (without being allowed to dry out) and protected from the few potential competitors because of various aspects of temporal and spatial separation from the competitors. In contrast, later studies on squirrels of the genus *Sciurus* by Stapanian and Smith (1978) suggested that the high costs of defending stored foods from many overlapping competitors would preclude any centralized hoarding of acorns or walnuts. Gray and fox squirrels store their food as individual items and spread these foods out, apparently as a means of reducing loss to co-occurring foragers who can smell buried seeds and nuts. In this genus, scatter-hoarding is the rule. This active dispersal of food is known for other rodents, such as kangaroo rats (Lockard & Lockard, 1971; Reichman, 1981), chipmunks (Elliott, 1978; Kawamichi, 1980; Lockner, 1972), and agoutis (Morris, 1962; Smythe, 1970, 1978), and for a variety of birds, such as marsh tits (Sherry, 1982; Shettleworth, 1983) and piñon jays (Ligon, 1978), black-capped chickadees (Sherry, 1984), and crows (James & Verbeek, 1983).

Scatter-hoarding is essentially the mirror image of central place foraging (cf. Figures 1 and 2). Instead of moving back and forth to find food and returning to a centralized protective area to avoid predators, scatter-hoarders make trips out and back from a centralized source of food to seek cover for their temporary surplus of food. What becomes important when risk of predation is considered is the relative locations and distances between concentrated sources of food and refuge sites, as well as proximity and spacing of caching sites.

The distances and directions of movement by scatter-hoarders may be random or directed. For example, Elliott (1978) observed no apparent patterns for eastern chipmunks in their scatter-hoarding. Some caches were within 3 m of the home burrow, while others were 18 to 24 m from the burrow, close to the periphery of the home range. While minimizing their risk of food loss to thieves, scatter-hoarders may increase their risk to predation (relative to larder hoarders) while hiding and retrieving foods (Figures 2 and 3). In their studies of scatter-hoarding agoutis, Smythe et al. (1982, p. 227) note that, in periods of food scarcity in the tropics, predators are important regulators of agouti populations. The seasonal shortages of food force agoutis to rely on their stored seeds and nuts, and hunger may force them to take greater risks in finding their stored food and in defending their storage sites. No research has yet fully evaluated this potentially high risk to predation among scatter-hoarders. Only a few studies have carefully mapped the actual locations of sources of scatter-hoarded foods and storage sites used by simultaneously active storers. Although risk to predation by hoarders has been almost totally ignored, several interesting hypotheses have been tested recently. Despite relatively small sample sizes, these studies suggest the importance of simultaneous consideration of several alternative hypotheses.

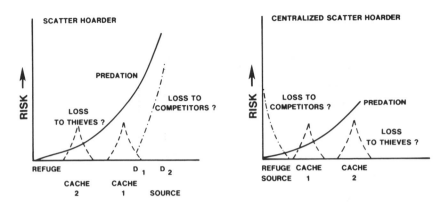

FIGURE 2. **Effects of refuge and source location on scatter-hoarder's losses to competitors and risk of predation.** The scatter hoarder who moves a relatively long distance from a single refuge to obtain food from a remote source is at very high risk to predation, as well as at high risk of losing uncached resources to competitors. In contrast, the centralized scatter hoarder can more readily monopolize a resource and travel closer to its refuge during its hoarding and retrieval if the refuge is located adjacent to the food source. Compared with larder hoarders, it will have less risk of losing its scattered caches to thieves, but it will have higher risk of predation because it travels more frequently and more distance than the larder hoarder for the same amounts of stored food. Also, because caches are not within the confines of a refuge, the centralized and noncentralized scattered hoarders must periodically leave their protective cover and seek food, even if risk of predation is relatively high. Optimal solutions for centralized scatter-hoarders are to: (a) obtain additional refuges, close to the distant source (and to more distant caches); and (b) avoid simultaneous activity with neighbors in zones of home range overlap, so as to minimize attracting predators to caching sites.

Stapanian and Smith (1978) provisioned an open site, 62 m away from the nearest walnut tree, with 375 walnuts. They visually recorded the location of each walnut stored by six focal squirrels, and the sequence of storage sites selected relative to the common central feeding station in the middle of a previously mapped grid. From a cost/benefit model, they predicted that the squirrels would hide their first food close to the feeding station. As the density of cached food reached a critical threshold (the optimal density that precluded discovery by competitors), it was postulated that increased travel costs would only then become worthwhile. The results of their study showed that squirrels *did not place the successive caches farther from the food source.* No food was buried less than 15 m from the source; the average cache was 38.1 m from the feeder. The average inter-cache distance ranged from 8.4 to 16.1 m, with an overall mean inter-cache distance of 9.9 m (for further discussion, see Kraus, 1983). Of considerable interest is their observation that "each squirrel tended to bury its nuts around a den tree" (Stapanian & Smith, 1978, p. 893).

Results were recently reported for similar studies of marsh tits when allowed to feed on high abundances of sunflower seeds that had been indi-

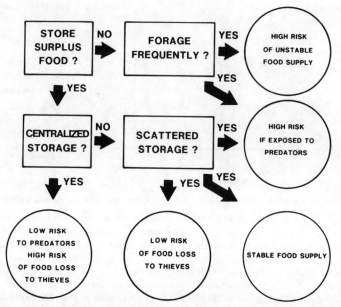

FIGURE 3.   Flow diagram for risk evaluation of food storage and immediate consumption.
The decision to hide food from resident competitors and transient consumers (thieves) results
in relatively low risk of food loss in scatter-hoards and a stable food supply, but can expose the
hoarder to very high risk of predation during storing and retrieving trips if distances from
refugia to scatter-hoards are relatively long. A decision to store all surplus food in a single centralized site avoids highest risk of predation, because travel outside the refuge zone is reduced;
half the number of trips is required to obtain food relative to centralized scatterhoarders, who
must first hide their food and later return to retrieve their caches. However, in larder hoarding,
all stored food can be lost to thieves. In contrast, the decision not to store food leads to a future
need for more frequent foraging, and thereby exposes the consumer to high risk of predation.
A nonhoarding consumer has less flexibility in deciding when and where to search for food,
because it lacks a stable supply of reserves.

vidually numbered and labelled with a low level of radioactive isotope.
Cowie, Krebs, and Sherry (1981, p. 1255) report that "seeds which are
close together in space also tend to be close in the hoarding sequence." They
note that *those seeds stored earlier in the sequence were hidden farther* from
the feeder, *not closer,* as might have been predicted. The birds carried the
sunflower seeds an average of 43.3 m from the source. Cowie et al. (1981,
p. 1255) state that "when both members of a pair stored seeds during the
same experiment, they tended to use slightly different areas...this spatial
segregation of sites would be important if the main advantage of scatter-
hoarding is to reduce predation on seeds by decreasing their density." In a
related study, Sherry, Avery, and Stevens (1982) also found that marsh tits
stored the first seeds taken from a concentrated seed source at greater distances from the source than seeds that were stored later in the sequence of

hoarding. They suggested that the switch from storage at a distance to closer-to-source storage may be influenced by the density of the food source, the total number of previously stored items, and the behavior of others at the source, especially competitors. No precise information is available on the relative locations between each consumer's nest, or home site (refugia from predators), and its caches in any of these three studies on scatter-hoarding of squirrels and marsh tits.

In these detailed studies of scatter-hoarding, it is evident that territorial defense in the strict sense is not associated with travel back and forth from a centralized source of food. What advantage is there to travelling farther from the source to store food than would first seem necessary, if the goal is to merely disperse the food and lower the possible encounters by competitors? What are the major advantages to mutual avoidance of previously-used storage sites among mates or neighboring scatter-hoarders? Previous works (e.g., Rubenstein, 1982; Tinbergen, 1972; Tinbergen, Impekoven, & Franck, 1967) on spacing-out have emphasized the lower risk associated with dispersion. But other advantages, such as obtaining a mixed diet consisting of high-quality nutrients, may also be important for some consumers who locate their protective refugia so as to minimize their exposure to predators and minimize their travel time in storing and retrieving cached food in times of scarcity. One possible explanation is that the first items stored are moved the longer distances from the source, to insure that at least a portion of the high-density resource patch will be less likely encountered by competitors attracted to the patch. Once this initial portion is hidden at maximal distances to insure highest probabilities for future retrieval by the hoarder, then the hoarder is willing to use riskier but less costly caching sites that are close to the source. Sherry et al. (1982, p. 161) note that much of the food stored by marsh tits is recovered within 24 hours after caching, and that "the switch to less costly storage (near the food source) may occur after a sufficient number of items has been stored to provide an adequate supply of stored food for the following day." Alternatively, the more distant cache site can be relatively close to the consumer's nest or refuge, and thus later costs for retrieval are minimized.

B. Indirect Benefits of Overlapping Travel Patterns Among Scatter Hoarders

Some additional hypotheses for the adaptive value of scatter-hoarding are generated by considering an hypothetical example of three individuals, A, B, and C, each with a center of activity (O_A, O_B, O_C in Figure 4) radiating from a home site or nest. The circular home ranges of A and B overlap (distance D_a-D_b in Figure 4), while C has a nonoverlapping home range (for this example, the shapes and sizes of the home ranges are less important than the relative amount of overlapping areas). Each individual has a "core area" of

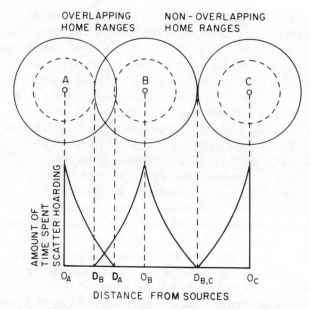

FIGURE 4. Spatial distribution of centralized storage activities. Two centralized scatter hoarders (A and B) make frequent trips from their homes, located at origins O_A and O_B, where there are refugia and sources of high densities of transportable foods. They store food throughout their home ranges (outer, continuous circles), with the initial caches confined to boundaries of their "core" areas (inner, dashed circles). Later caches may be stored even farther away (D_A-D_B). Some of these later caches are in a zone of overlap and are subject to detection and recovery by either the original hoarder, or the neighboring hoarder, or transient thieves. The third hoarder (C) has an isolated, nonoverlapping home range and avoids contact with neighbors, but cannot effectively defend the total home range from intruding thieves.

intensive use during the travel back and forth from the home site. Assume each home is located in a different nut-producing tree, so that each consumer selected both a nest and a dense patch of food associated with the tree when initially establishing its home range. As the three "centralized" scatter-hoarders begin to store their "surplus" food, let us further assume that they follow one general pattern previously observed for fox squirrels and marsh tits; they initially carry their individual food items considerable distances away from the source (the adaptive value of long-distance travel is discussed later), and bury each item before returning home to their food source.

The economic costs and benefits of later searching for, finding, and gathering their scatter-hoarded items depends greatly on the *similarity* of the stored resources and the intensity or timing of food *scarcity*. If A, B, and C all used the *same type of resource* in their hoarding (e.g., each lived in an oak tree and stored acorns), then when food is *simultaneously and uniformly scarce* everywhere it would be likely that individual C will obtain the highest probability of recovering the greatest return on his investment of time and energy by later harvesting a relatively large proportion of the stored items. If food is uniformly scarce, then both A and B are at a high risk of not only losing their stored resources to nonresident consumers, but also to one another. In this case, the neighbors are potentially strong competitors during the period of food scarcity because they have overlapping home ranges.

How will differences in resource quality, abundance, and spatial-temporal distribution influence the relative values of stored foods for these hypothetical consumers? First assume A and B had lived in very different types of trees and stored nutritionally different but essential food resources (e.g., A stored hickory nuts and B stored acorns). Further assume that the densities of stored resources were greater than the quantity required for growth and reproduction at a minimal level. Initially in phase one, both consumers will hide nuts near the boundaries of their *core area,* to minimize loss to thieves (i.e., outside the high "background" density or "seed shadow" produced near the "source tree"). In phase two, they may travel intermediate distances to hide nuts in areas of nonoverlapping home ranges to avoid loss to *both* neighbors and thieves. Finally, in phase three, consumer A may store its nuts at its outer home range boundary that extends into consumer B's home range (area of overlap depicted in Figure 5, with nuts indicated by numbered squares in order of hoarding by A). Consumer B may store its acorns at its home range boundary that extends into consumer A's home range (acorns indicated by numbered circles in order of hoarding by B in Figure 5). Consumers A and B would *both* be nutritionally better fed (e.g., A could gain more potassium, and B could gain more protein) by "losing" some of their originally stored "surplus" items to each other from overlapping areas of their home ranges than if they recovered *only* their own resources. This nutritional advantage of mixed amino acids, minerals, vitamins, etc. could *not* be obtained from eating only their own very abundant, but nutritionally limited, resources. Thus, in this example, consumer C is at a relatively large disadvantage because it gains no mixed dietary advantages and it may lose time and energy, especially if it alone attempts to defend its entire series of caches.

Benefits of passive, indirect interchange of resources (i.e., mutual balancing of "losses" and "gains" among neighbors) would only be realized when nutritionally different resources are spatially clumped and relatively abundant (see Figure 6). When availabilities of spatially clumped resources are low, neither consumer would recover enough of their nearby resource to risk losing any to neighbors in an unreciprocal interchange. At simultaneously very high levels of availability, there will be no mutual advantage to consumers to interchange resources if all resources are spatially and temporally highly dispersed, because under these conditions *all neighbors will have as much of all the resources as they can use.* If all consumers used the

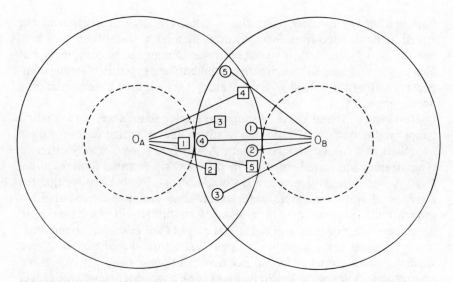

FIGURE 5.   Locations of stored foods scattered in zones of overlap between neighbors. During phase one, neighboring centralized scatter hoarders (A and B) had stored some food initially near the boundaries of their core areas (dashed lines). During phase two they next stored food in the outer sectors of their *nonoverlapping* home range areas. Finally, as depicted here in phase three, they begin to hide "surplus" food in their *zone of overlap*. Each hides a different type of food (denoted by squares for A and circles for B). The sequence of hiding each type of "surplus" food in phase three is indicated by the numbers in each box and circle. At the beginning of phase three, the hoarders move to hide their food (#1 to #5) at relatively farther distances from their refugia to avoid areas already "saturated" with caches. They disperse their caches to avoid detection by nonresident "thieves" in all three phases. They disperse their caches in phase two to avoid loss to neighbors, but, in phase three, loss to neighbors is potentially balanced by future gains as long as some caches (hidden by neighbors) are randomly found and harvested by each neighbor over the long run. Frequent losses in overlap zones to neighbors ("cheaters") who do not cache in overlapping areas leads to avoidance of these areas as future caching sites. Overlapping areas of home ranges containing "novel" caches of nutritionally different resources (hidden by neighbors) will be favored as choice sites for future caching, even if some of the superabundant "local" resources are lost to neighbors.

same resources but the timing of resource supply varied significantly from one source to another, there may be some temporal advantages to passive, incidental interchange of resources among neighbors whose total supply would be more uniform than if no interchange occurred. Resource quality, quantity, and spatial/temporal dispersion, as well as consumer mobility and preference, all interact to determine when home ranges of hoarders will overlap, and indirect interchange will be mutually advantageous (Figure 6).

Resource dispersion must be considered relative to mobility and travel patterns of the consumers, and the intruding "thieves" and predators. A "cheater" strategy of storing *all* resources close to the core area, and searching for the neighbors' caches in overlapping areas, would not be as advan-

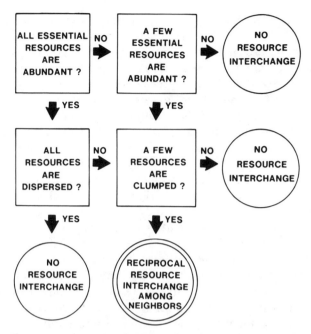

FIGURE 6. **Flow diagram for evaluating conditions leading to mutual interchange of re-sources among neighbors.** If *essential resources are scarce* (top arrows from left to right), the risks of losing the minimally required resources to neighbors and thieves are greater than potential benefits obtainable from resource interchange among neighbors, and *no interchange is predicted*. If *essential resources are abundant* but evenly dispersed spatially (arrows from top to bottom on left side), then all neighbors have a high probability of storing ample supplies of identical resources, and *no interchange is predicted*. Likewise, no interchange is predicted if none of the abundant resources are spatially clumped, and isolated in only some neighboring home ranges. Thus, *resource interchange among neighbors is predicted only if a few required resources are abundant and spatially clumped in different neighbor's home ranges* (arrows from top to bottom on right side), so that each neighbor obtains additional diversity in nutrient content of its diet by storing and "losing" some of its abundant resource in exchange for "finding" abundant, stored resources hidden by neighbors. This indirect redistribution of cached resources will continue to occur over time only if relatively long-lived individuals remain in the same local neighborhoods and continue to gain individual benefits (increased dietary diversity and/or increased uniformity of supply) that exceed individual costs (transportation and storage during periods of superabundance).

tageous in the long run as a reciprocal interchange, because the cheater's centralized caches would have a higher risk of loss to thieves. Mutual interchanges are only potentially "self-enforcing" (*sensu* Telser, 1980) over the long run, because areas of overlap with cheaters would not continue to be used for caches, and mutualistic neighbors would learn to avoid locations with high risk of loss after a series of losses to resident cheaters. In such instances, nonreciprocating neighbors who cheat would be considered analogous to transient "thieves." In a self-enforcing process, each individual decides unilaterally whether or not to continue a given relationship with others. The decision to stop participating in any activity that results in potential gain for each individual is made only if the current gain from stopping exceeds the expected present value of gains from continuation (Telser, 1980). A party to a self-enforcing process frequently determines if the gains from cheating ("free rider" behavior) are greater than the loss of future net benefits that would accrue if the cheating resulted in exclusion from continued access to potential future gains associated with a given relationship. If a cheater gains more than he or she loses then he or she will decide to risk ending the relationship. Thus, several individuals will only continue to share a location for storing their surplus foods if they find sufficient food in the area they share over an extended period of time. If cheaters deplete the caches, then their neighbors will avoid using the areas that overlap in the cheater's home range, and both parties will lose any future potential gains. For scatter-hoarders, this process of resource redistribution is not a bilateral, intentional exchange. It is an indirect consequence of different resource supplies being spatially and temporally restricted in such a way that expanded access to some restricted resources is only feasible through the multiple use of overlapping areas for storing those localized resources that are seasonally abundant. The present and future value of these locally available resources is potentially less than the future value of other distant resources that can be obtained only through this indirect means of shared storage areas, and the result is resource redistribution. For self-enforcing relationships to occur, there must be sufficient time for neighbors to become familiar with the behavior of each other. The absolute amount of time required will be a function of the number of storing events and the lengths of time between storing and retrieving cached resources. Such relationships might well be limited to relatively long-lived animals that maintain stable "neighborhoods" composed of small groups of interacting hoarders. As group size increases, the information on losses associated with more overlap from larger numbers of neighbors could be insufficient for self-enforcing relationships to occur. In these larger groups, cheaters could destabilize the interchange.

C. Ownership of Stored Foods in Overlapping Areas

Once food has been hidden in areas of overlapping home ranges, do the original hoarders recognize their own caches? Apparently, in some species there is a marked preference for eating food stored by other individuals of the same species. Food "envy," or taking food being eaten by others, is widespread among animals (Ewer, 1968, 1973) and could lead to reduced fitness of the "robbed" individuals if they themselves are not also reciprocal "robbers." Wrazen and Wrazen (1982, p. 70) stated that "chipmunks strongly preferred eating food from a conspecific's cache when it was available.'' Chipmunks can determine cache "ownership" probably on the basis of olfactory-gustatory cues. Other species maintain exclusive rights to their own caches by strong territorial defense of storage sites (e.g., the American kestrels studied by Balgooyen, 1976).

In some groups, there may be passive interchange determined by neighborhood proximity as well as total group size. A neighborhood social structure of the type proposed by Healey (1967) for deer mice may be a general way not only to reduce aggression, as he proposed, but also to allow for resource interchange. Healey (1967, p. 388) suggested that "established animals resist the settling of strangers....However, a high level of interaction among established animals would waste energy. The social unit then comprises an animal and its neighbors, among whom mutual aggression is reduced, and whose range boundaries are maintained by habit and mutual avoidance.'' Several other recent studies on small mammals from adjacent home ranges have also found interesting social effects of this neighborhood grouping pattern (Madison, 1977; Melemis & Falls, 1982; Myton, 1974; Vestal and Hellack, 1978).

In terms of seed hoarders, Schwartz and Schwartz (1981) suggest that squirrels in Missouri appear to have no individual defense of scatter-hoarded acorns. They note (p. 151) that "stored seeds have no particular ownership, and the members of a squirrel community share each other's efforts.'' Kawamichi (1980, p. 218) noted that "the hoarding places were scattered within the home ranges, which were widely overlapped with those of other individuals, and the scattered hoards were used in common by two or more individuals'' among the Siberian chipmunks she studied. Unfortunately, in these studies the persistence of neighborhoods or kin relationships among neighbors are not known.

D. Distance Travelled to Storage Sites

As a consumer spends more time carrying and hiding food in different locations, the shift from surplus killing to larder and scatter hoarding is influenced by risks of exposure to predation and loss to thieves. The actual distances over which a scatter-hoarder carries food before hiding it varies greatly among different species (Yahner, 1975). For example, Smythe (1978) noted that agoutis on Barro Colorado Island in Gatun Lake, Panama, carry fruits and seeds for distances up to 50 m in various directions from the source. Buried food items may be found and carried to another location by neighbors, so that, if a single item is sequentially hidden and relocated, it will be moved over considerable distances in a serial transfer of resources. Smythe (1978) reported that agoutis transport seeds from neighboring home ranges as much as 150 m in a series of caches.

Scatter-hoarding is primarily a response to minimizing loss of food, but can result in additional benefits such as resource interchange. The hypothesis just described for mutual advantage resulting from scatter hoarding in overlapping home ranges is dependent upon the·lengths and directions of each neighbor's total of storing trips, but is independent of the sequential order. If only some of the trips are relatively long and reach the boundary areas of overlap, then the advantages of resource interchange are possible, given the constraints already discussed (Figure 7). The mutual interchange hypothesis suggests that there is an advantage to carrying foods farther than a principle of least effort would suggest (Figures 7, 8) or a minimization of exposure to predation risk would predict (Figure 3). Why then are scatter hoarders observed to move farther distances in some trips than others? What is the general importance of the timing of relatively long trips? Is there a predictable pattern of the travel, or is scatter-hoarding a random process? These are the questions raised by results obtained by Stapanian and Smith (1978), and by Cowie et al. (1981) and Sherry et al. (1982) in their field tests.

Scatter hoarders cannot maximize their long-term benefits by ignoring their neighbors or their more unfamiliar competitors and predators. The first goal is to prevent detection of the initially highly concentrated, exposed food patch by other consumers; the second goal is to prevent detection of caches. Thus, if resource abundances initially are high and spatially clumped, any scatter hoarder will obtain the *most individual benefit and least loss* by:

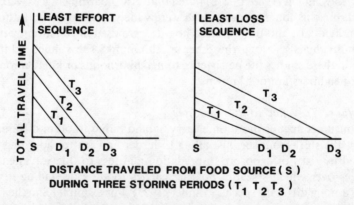

FIGURE 7.   **Comparison of distances traveled from food sources by scatter hoarders minimizing effort or minimizing loss of stored food.** During the first phase (T_1) of transporting food from a centralized source (S), the scatter hoarder will initially hide food close (S to D_1) to its refuge and food source. Only after "saturating" this inner zone will it make additional trips to carry and hide food in outer zones (S to D_2 and D_3) during later phases (T_2, T_3). In contrast, a scatter hoarder that first hides food at intermediate distances (S to D_1) will avoid loss to transient thieves by lowering cache density and avoiding the attraction of thieves and competing consumers to its source area. It will balance its losses to neighbors by finding and exploiting caches hidden by neighbors in its outer zones (S to D_3) during its later (T_3) stages of caching. In the "least-loss" sequence more "surplus" food is transported farther distances than is typical in the previously proposed "least effort" sequence.

(a) first maximizing the initial storing distances from the main concentration at the source of food, to *insure that at least a portion of its stored reserve is undetected* by nonresidents and neighbors but still within its own home range, and, if possible, outside an area of overlapping home ranges of neighbors (e.g., Case I, Fig. 8); (b) frequently changing directions of travel during the earlier long-distance storing trips, so as *to further spread out reserves;* and (c) selecting different directions and distances of travel that maximize storage in overlapping areas of as many neighbors as possible only during the latter series (e.g., phase three of Figure 7) of long trips to further spread risks *and to diversify potential resource interchanges* and *to minimize losses to neighbors who do not store their surplus resources in*

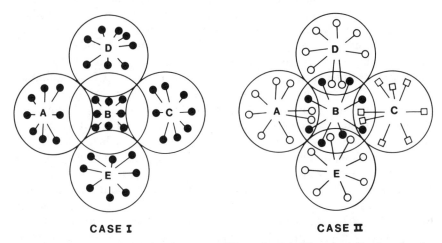

CASE I   CASE II

FIGURE 8.   Contrasts of storing the same or different foods inside and outside of overlapping zones of neighboring home ranges. In case I, *all* centralized scatter-hoarding *consumers store the same type of resource.* Centrally-located consumer B first stores its surplus resource within its home range, but avoids zones of overlap with neighbors and avoids the most centralized core of its home range *to maximize dispersal of its stored food and to minimize loss to neighbors and intruders,* as in phases one and two in Figure 7. In case I, because all consumers have access to and store the same abundant resources, *there are no advantages to resource interchange.* But in case II, several consumers have different abundant resources to store in their own home ranges. In case II, consumer B moves farther from its home source of surplus food (dark circles: for example, pecans), and stores in areas of overlap during its third phase of food storage. Neighbors also store resources in overlapping areas, but of nutritionally different types from those stored by B. Consumers A, D, and E each store a second type of food (open circles: for example, acorns), while consumer C stores a third resource (open squares: for example, hickory nuts). In case II, *all consumers benefit from increased maximization of dispersal of their stored food and from increased nutrient diversity in their future diets if each finds and uses some of the surplus foods stored by neighbors.* The highest dietary diversity and potential nutritional value is obtained by individual B. In this example, individual B would be a dominant member of this neighborhood and have lowest potential loss to transient thieves if A, C, D, E serve as "buffers" (assuming all cache densities are sufficiently dispersed to avoid area intensive searching by thieves).

zones of overlap but who nonetheless search for and find caches of their neighbors (Case II, Figure 8). These criteria for long-term optimization of nutrition are opposite to those suggested by principles of least effort, and very different from those suggested by previous workers (Cowie et al., 1981; Kraus, 1983; Lockner, 1972; Miller & Vick, 1950; Sherry et al., 1981; Sherry et al., 1982; Stapanian & Smith, 1978, 1984; Waddel, 1951).

E. Cost Minimization: Spatial Memory and Resource Monopolies

If hoarders relied completely on trial and error to search for and to find their own randomly placed caches, they would need to spend considerable time to obtain their required food from stored supplies unless the cache densities were quite high. If cache densities were high, then trial-and-error searching by hoarders would likely increase competition with intruding thieves for stored food, because both the thieves and hoarders would have the same chance of finding the caches. On the advantageous side, however, these hoarders could potentially benefit from resource interchange with neighbors. An intermediate solution of using some feature of the habitat or landmark as a directional guide to finding caches would give the hoarders an obvious advantage over intruding thieves but still provide occasional opportunity for interchange with those neighbors using similar habitat guides. A third possibility is for the hoarder to remember the location of each cache. Over time, imperfect memory of all cache locations might well lead to errors in recovery and thus provide a means for passive resource interchange. A perfect memory of each individual cache would lead to a high degree of recovery of stored resources and a monopolization of patches of high quality resources. Thus, we might expect hoarders to gain significant advantages by developing a large capacity for spatial memory only when they specialize on nutrient-rich resources that are only seasonally available or clumped in space, and readily transported and stored (see Table 2). A few well-studied examples of hoarders with exceptionally accurate, long-term spatial memory tend to support this hypothesis.

Several species of birds are thought to have high percentages of cache recovery based on various forms of spatial memory. The previously mentioned Clark's nutcracker is an excellent example. Tomback (1977, 1982) estimated that an individual nutcracker in the eastern Sierra Nevada buries about 7,000 whitebark pine seed caches each year (with about 4 seeds per average cache). These stored resources represent up to three times the bird's energetic needs during spring and summer (unless, as breeding adults, they use some stored seeds to feed their young). Although some seeds are lost to thieves, nutcrackers recover a high percentage of the pine seeds from where they apparently remembered they had hidden them. Nutcrackers make distinctive prod marks in the soil or snow where they dig up their buried seeds. It is possible to count the number of successful and unsuccessful seed recoveries, because the birds generally eat the seeds and leave behind the hulls adjacent to the excavated cache. In some instances, however, they are known to simply move the seeds from one cache site to another, and thus leave no sign of their own successful finding and relocation of the cache. In field studies, then, only conservative estimates of recovery are possible and it cannot be determined if the same individual finds its own cached seeds. In laboratory studies with controlled access to a hoarding site, Vander Wall (1982) demonstrated that Clark's nutcrackers use larger objects such as rocks as guides for finding their caches, and only secondarily rely on smaller objects or soil microtopography as visual cues. Intruders into the controlled cache site also used soil features, typically disturbed areas, as visual cues for finding caches made by another nutcracker. The rates of successful recovery ranged from 52% to 78% for those individuals who had cached seeds, and was only 8% to 12% for noncaching intruders. Vander Wall further demonstrated that nutcrackers do not use olfactory cues or random search to find their caches.

Shettleworth and Krebs (1982) provide additional experimental data that support the idea that at least some birds do not rely on random searching to relocate their seed caches. They studied captive marsh tits by watching the birds in a large aviary supplied with many tree branches that could be used by the birds for seed storage. Numerous holes were drilled into each branch, and each hole had been covered with a flap of cloth which the birds learned to lift in order to store their seeds or to search for the presence of a previously-stored seed. The birds were provided with a surplus of seeds and allowed to store seeds in the branches. Then the birds (and the unstored seeds) were removed from the aviary for approximately 2.5 hrs. The birds were later observed, upon their return to the aviary, to determine success rates of seed finding for those seeds just previously stored. The birds made very few errors in recovering their stored seeds, and thus did not rely on random searching. Errors per seed relocation did increase with successive finds. Shettleworth and Krebs interpreted this result to be consistent with a model of active spatial memory. The decline in successful relocations could also be influenced by decreased motivation to find seeds as hunger levels declined. The birds avoided revisitation of previously searched locations, which is consistent with laboratory tests of spatial memory of rats and chimpanzees (Menzel, 1973, 1978; Olton, Handelman, & Walker, 1981; Yoerg & Kamil, 1982). Ability to remember precisely where previously hidden food was located allows, first, for efficient relocation for delayed use in times of scarcity. Secondly, the ability to avoid already searched areas allows the hoarder to maximizes the rate of successful relocations, and to minimize the time of exposure to risk of predation.

F. Multiple Central Places: Optimal Diet and Low Risk of Predation

Because a consumer is familiar with its own home range and refugia, the risk of being exposed to predators is minimized relative to the risk of predation on intruders. In central place foraging, the consumer can occupy a single home range with multiple refugia (Covich, 1976), and thereby have several "central" places where it enjoys an expanded relative advantage, by harvesting resources from a larger area than if only a single refuge were used. A similar advantage could exist for a scatter hoarder who can hide more stored food and lower risks of cache detection by intruders. In both cases, multiple refugia potentially give access to a greater diversity of resources. Moreover, multiple refugia allow the scatter hoarder at a future time of need to search for stored food near the boundaries of its home range and still be relatively close to one of its refugia to avoid predators.

The number and location of multiple central refugia can be adjusted seasonally to include new food sources as they become available. For example, Layne (1954, p. 258) suggested that, for the red squirrel, "a particular food source may influence the shape and size of the home range and might even induce some individuals to actually shift their home range." Schwartz and Schwartz (1981, p. 149) observed that "gray squirrels usually live most of their lives in and around one nest tree and seldom travel farther than 200 yards from home in any one season. . . . However, as different sources of food become available during the growing season, they may shift their home one or more times."

In his research on prairie deer mice, Terman (1962, p. 222) found that "each mouse maintained an average of 4.4 refuges or nest sites." Brown (1966, p. 118), in studies of natural populations of field mice and bank voles, noted that they have "several home sites, usually four or five, that are used at one time for each individual. . . in the autumn several of the holes will be used as food stores and will be visited regularly." The actual distances travelled among multiple nest or home sites and scattered caches vary considerably among different species. For example, all species of deer-mice cache food resources to various degrees (Eisenberg, 1968; Tadlock & Klein, 1979) but some have several highly concentrated caches (Howard & Evans, 1961) very close to their nest chamber, while others have a higher number of less concentrated and more dispersed scatter hoards. Criddle (1950, p. 175) reported that deermice "travel long distances for choice seeds, carry fully loaded cheeks back to their stores. . . . Some went to cherry bushes, 238 yards away, occasionally 312 yards to a granary." The distances between multiple sources of food, caching sites, and refugia probably all shift seasonally and in relation to risk of predation.

For many consumers, the choice between making multiple caches in a few "larder hoards" or many "scatter hoards" will be responsive to changing conditions of risk to predators and thieves. For example, in her detailed study of the Siberian chipmunk, Kawamichi (1980) observed 1,596 instances of hoarding behavior; 775 were scatter hoarding, and 821 were nest or larder hoarding. Both types were frequently observed in October and in May. She observed seven cases of stealing from nest hoards by other chipmunks during spring and fall. Elliott (1978, p. 81) observed pilfering of larder-hoarded beech nuts by Eastern chipmunks. Shaffer (1980) reported that the Eastern chipmunk moves stored maple seeds from scatter hoards to a central larder hoard following periods of theft by neighbors in spring and summer, when food is relatively scarce. In such instances, it requires much more time and is riskier to forage for new food than to replenish the main larder hoard from the nearby scatter hoards. If *both* theft and predation are frequent, the best strategy will be to use both types of hoarding and thereby reduce exposure to predators (during exploitation of a restricted number of larder hoards) and loss to thieves (by having reserves spread out in a larger number of scatter-hoards). By altering the time of day consumers hide or retrieve their stores relative to peak activities of predators and thieves, these dual risks of predation and theft can be further reduced. Previously, Lockner (1972) suggested that food-deprived, hungry rodents (red-tailed chipmunks) stored surplus food in larder hoards, while sated individuals scatter-hoarded, but his laboratory studies did not evaluate risks of predation on the hoarder. When risk of predation is high, a satiated consumer may well accept the relatively low risk of losing some larder-cached supplies to thieves and continue to larder hoard if an abundant source of food is very near the home refuge. As distance to the source increases, a risk-averse behavior of minimizing losses to thieves would be potentially more adaptive, and nocturnal scatter-hoarding would be expected.

G. Territorial Defense of Resources

Several workers have explicitly modeled the net gains of foraging and hoarding resources (Andersson & Krebs, 1978; Roberts, 1979). Generally, it is expected that, if consumers spend a significant amount of time and energy storing food in a cache, they are more likely to defend it from exploitation by others than are consumers who spend less time and energy storing food. Roberts (1979) proposed a model for the evolution of avian food-storage. He postulated that the many species of birds which store food (typically small, durable seeds, but also insects and other prey in some cases) "developed the trait in accord with the principle of economic defendability" (p. 435). This concept, first developed by J.L. Brown (1964), emphasizes that relative costs and benefits of defending and exploiting a territory have distinct thresholds of profitability (see Davies, 1980): An individual will not spend more effort in defending an area larger than that required for supplying the food required for successful reproduction. Roberts (1979) concluded from his review that defense of the cache and some degree of seasonal resource scarcity are both important influences in raising expected benefits from recovering caches over the costs of hiding and defending them.

Andersson and Krebs (1978) also proposed a generalized cost/benefit analysis to measure the net benefit to a solitary consumer for hoarding a single resource within an exclusive feeding area. In their analysis, they considered variables such as the cost of hoarding, the probability that non-hoarded items would remain available (i.e., potential for loss to fungal decay, competitors or thieves), and the multiplication factor of nonhoarded food items within a cycle of high and low resource densities (i.e., potential overall gain due to regrowth). They also examined the effects on hoarding efficiency if nonhoarding "cheaters" were actively exploiting caches. Andersson and Krebs (1978, p. 708) concluded that "if a given hoarded item is sufficiently more likely to be found by the hoarder than by other individuals, hoarding may be adaptive even in the presence of non-hoarding group mates." This increased probability of a hoarder finding its own cache (rather than losing it to a cheater) could be achieved by territorial defense or spatial memory of the cache locations.

As Andersson and Krebs point out (p. 707): "it is easy to envisage that hoarding might be of advantage in preserving excess food for a future period of hardship. There are, however, instances in which hoarders apparently have no specific memory of their storage sites..." and in some species "they do not hoard only within an exclusive territory." Would an undefended or forgotten cache ever be cost effective? Both Roberts (1979) and Andersson and Krebs (1978) note that, if genetically related conspecifics find foods stored by other relatives, there can be additional advantages to storing foods among group-living hoarders; this kin selection can be especially significant for longer-lived species and those that share communal storage areas. As previously discussed, resource interchange among neighbors may also be mutually advantageous.

The actual values for the multiplication factor of the cost/benefit analysis proposed by Andersson and Krebs can be very difficult to measure. In certain species, the hoarder prevents germination by placing the seeds above ground in holes or crevices of trees (Ewer, 1968; Kowalski, 1976). Some hoarders manipulate the seeds to insure short-term benefits by minimizing loss from seed germination. For example, mature gray squirrels remove the growing point of white oak acorns before burying them, to prevent germination in autumn (Barnett, 1977; Fox, 1982), while red oak acorns, which are dormant over winter, are not treated in this manner. Younger, inexperienced gray squirrels cache undamaged white oak acorns which typically germinate in autumn and produce a seedling with a taproot that takes up the food reserves from the acorn, making the acorn unusable by the squirrels.

H. Benefits of Communal Storage

The reduction of costs for defending and retrieving communally-stored food appears to be very important in groups of Clark's nutcrackers (Balda, 1980; Vander Wall & Balda, 1977, 1981) and pinòn jays (Bossema, 1979; Ligon, 1978), as well as for acorn woodpeckers (MacRoberts, 1970; MacRoberts & MacRoberts, 1975; Stacey & Jansma, 1977; Trail, 1980). Vander Wall and

Balda (1981) proposed a model to examine variables such as time required for seed harvesting and distance required for seed transport to the caching site. Losses to other corvids and rodents are minimized by locating the cache site at considerable distance (> 20 km) from the seed source. Costs of finding the seeds and recovering them are also reduced by sharing the best locations for caches (where soil thickness is adequate for hiding seeds and where the topography and wind are such that snow depth is minimal and does not require great expenditures of energy for seed recovery during winter). The balance between energy and time expended in transporting the seeds and recovering them later in winter is favorable to those groups with morphological adaptations for carrying relatively large loads of seeds in a single trip from source to cache, and for those with good spatial memory of the cache site. The importance of avoiding risks to predation by selecting communal caching sites relatively free of predators has not yet been considered in models of long-distance, communal storage. The choice of caching sites may well involve trade-offs between transportation costs to the storage areas with multiple source areas, transportation costs to protected nest sites during food retrieval, and travel costs associated with avoiding high risks to predators. The most preferred caching sites will provide southern exposures, wind-swept areas with little snow cover, *and* yet still have adequate protective cover to avoid exposure to predators and also be relatively close to the nest site (that may be located in very dense cover). Some birds may select clear areas for seed storage to increase their visual perceptive field and lower risk to ambush predators (J.A. Grzybowski, 1985, personal communication).

Vander Wall and Balda (1977) suggest that communal cooperation allows young birds to learn where the best sites are for seed storage, and that this multi-generational use of a restricted area increases the likelihood for reharvesting at least some of the stored seeds. The ultimate expression of communal storing occurs consistently among the acorn woodpeckers, who eat acorns throughout the year. Members of distinct groups defend "granaries" and maintain definite dominance hierarchies based on age and sex (MacRoberts & MacRoberts, 1975). They store food in a variety of locations, but mostly in dead trees that they have riddled with holes. Some storage trees have as many as 50,000 holes of just the right size to firmly hold a single acorn. These woodpeckers use acorns from several available species of oaks, and also store insects in their storage trees during seasonal peaks of insect abundance. At various times they also tap trees for sap. Actual costs and benefits of this intensive storage and defense of communal foods are very difficult to measure, because of the complexity of acorn woodpecker social organization. One interesting aspect that has been recently analyzed is the spacing between territories of neighboring groups of acorn woodpeckers (Mumme, Koenig, & Pitelka, 1983; Brewer & McCann,

1985). In central coastal California, MacRoberts and MacRoberts (1975) found that no overlap existed between neighboring territories, and that the area defended by each group was larger than that used in any one year. The smaller groups of woodpeckers were able to defend relatively large areas. These disproportionately larger territories apparently were held because individuals in the smaller groups gained some advantages from decreasing costs of defense once a critical group-size threshold had been reached. Beyond this threshold of group-size, the advantages of adding additional group members declined in terms of costs and benefits of food gathering, storing, and defending. Within the territories, woodpeckers appeared to rotate from using one subsection to another during different years. The relative competitive advantages of periodically defending more area than is used in any given time period are under study for a wide variety of species, and the overall significance of this type of "super territory" remains an active topic of debate (MacLean & Seastedt, 1979; Parker & Knowlton, 1980; Robertson & Gibbs, 1982; Tullock, 1983; Verner, 1977). The pattern of sequential use shown by acorn woodpeckers, and of nonterritorial serial use of distinct sectors by marsh tits (Cowie et al., 1981) and squirrels (Stapanian and Smith, 1978), may complicate the analysis of how much space is eventually used during any short-term study.

I. Balancing Needs for Immediate and Delayed Consumption

Spatial location, risk of exposure to predation, probability of loss to thieves, and potential for reciprocal interchange all interact to determine when and where a consumer will decide to locate "surplus" food. But how is a given level of resource determined to be "adequate" for immediate needs relative to that level likely to be required for future needs? Economists have considered several aspects of this general problem of adequate "savings" (e.g., Hahn, 1970; Hey, 1979; Karni, 1982; Somermeyer & Bannink, 1973). A consumption function and a hoarding function can simultaneously be considered to predict optimal proportions of savings and consumption that satisfy individual needs and that are still within acceptable levels of uncertainty. Hirshleifer and Riley (1979) and Zeckhauser (1974) review the general importance of considering uncertainty in economic analyses. Ecologists are also generating models of uncertainty and risk-taking with regard to adaptive responses to various environmental stresses (Caraco, 1981; Cerri & Fraser, 1983; Lima, Valone, & Caraco, 1985; Palmer, 1981; Real, 1980; Rubenstein, 1982; Sih, 1980). Temporal uncertainty in rewards has been studied by psychologists interested in size-selective, optimal foraging (Green, Fisher, Perlow, & Sherman, 1981; Kagel, Green, & Caraco, 1986; Snyderman, 1983); the relationships between uncertainty of availability of differently sized prey and hoarding behavior remain unexplored.

Dornbusch and Mussa (1975) and Quirk (1976) describe a graphical analysis for studying intertemporal optimization of present and future consumption. In order to evaluate the various ways in which individuals allocate their income in these types of graphical models, it is necessary to use relatively ranked levels of consumer satisfaction. These levels can be iso-contours of equally-valued combinations of goods, the frequently used "indifference curves" (Battalio et al., 1981; Covich, 1972; Rapport, 1971). The main focus here is on the choice of parameters for analysis. For example, if all of a consumer's time and energy budget were spent to consume all the resources obtainable at a given level of availability, none would be stored for future consumption. This level can be depicted graphically (C_2 in Figure 9) as the x intercept, and compared to the amount of resources that could be stored using this same time and energy budget (S_2 in Figure 9) on the y axis. The budget constraint boundary for all possible combinations of immediate consumption and levels of storage is depicted as a line (C_2-S_2). Any combination of partial storage and partial consumption is possible that falls

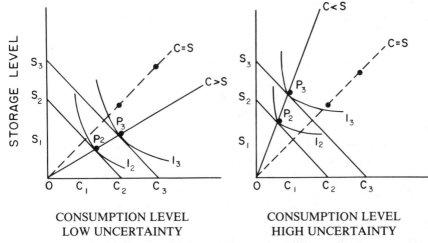

CONSUMPTION LEVEL
LOW UNCERTAINTY

CONSUMPTION LEVEL
HIGH UNCERTAINTY

FIGURE 9. An indifference curve analysis of the choices between immediate consumption and future consumption of stored resources. The iso-utility curves (I_2, I_3) are tangent to the budget lines (C_2S_2 and C_3S_3) at equilibrial points (P_2 and P_3) that denote an individual consumer's choice to store a proportion of the total resources available for immediate consumption. At an initial level of resource abundance, the consumer can use all of the resources immediately (C_2) and store none. Or the consumer can delay all immediate consumption and store all the available resources (S_2). A combination (P_2) of some reduced level of immediate consumption and some reduced storage level is a hypothetical equilibrial choice that optimizes the highest possible level attainable within the given budget limitation and the highest level of satisfaction (depicted by the iso-utility or indifference curve I_2). The slope of the line that connects the optimal points gives an indication of the relationship between storage and immediate consumption as the level of resource abundance increases. The shapes of indifference curves reflect individual consumer evaluations at immediate and delayed consumption. If the supply of resources is relatively certain, a lower proportion of resources is expected to be stored than if supply is highly uncertain. If the risk of losing stored resources increases, then the slope of the budget lines (CS) will decrease (i.e., flatten out).

along or below this boundary. Any point on the graph below this boundary does not completely use the available time and energy budget for resource allocation. Any point above this line (e.g., P_3 in Figure 9) is beyond the attainable level unless resource availabilities increase or the budget increases. Given the limited budget and resource levels, the optimal allocation in this first example is a point (P_2 in Figure 9) that represents complete use of the available budget and highest attainment of utility or satisfaction that can be afforded. The tangential intercept of the budget line (C_2S_2) and the iso-utility curve or indifference curve (I_2) at point P_2 in Figure 9 is thus the optimal choice. This point represents maximal budgetary allocation at the highest level of satisfaction affordable. All such optimal choices fall along an "optimal path" that allow for a measure of the consumer's response to changing budgets and resource availabilities.

This type of graphical analysis can be tested experimentally, just as other types of consumer theory are now being tested (Battalio et al., 1981; Kagel et al., 1981), and should lead to some useful predictions for a wide range of natural consumers whose hoarding functions are perhaps easier to measure than are human hoarding functions. For example, if consumers consistently encountered highly *certain* supplies of spatially evenly distributed food, over a long series of consumption, they would be expected to store a lower proportion of their food at all food densities and at all levels of time and energy budgets (Figure 9, left). In contrast, if food supplies were consistently highly *uncertain,* consumers would be expected to store higher proportions of their food (Figure 9, right). Failure of experimental observations to verify these predictions would suggest some other set of parameters must be included in the analysis. Even with long exposures to highly certain, predictably abundant resources, some consumers may continue to gather and to store more than they consume each day, if daily trips to obtain food are limited by their diet time/energy budgets and stressful weather conditions. In some cases the mere "convenience" of avoiding travel on certain days may be sufficient to stimulate food storage even when supplies are stable. Some species show a very predictable temporal pattern of food storing. For example, Jaeger (1982) showed that seasonality per se was not important in determining when the prairie deermouse stored food: the daily feeding cycle has a dusk peak in feeding activity that represents maintenance intake to allow for foraging, while the later dawn peak represents compensatory and anticipatory food intake associated with caching. The daily balance between these two phases of feeding activity either increases or decreases the amount of stored food regardless of time of year.

J. Length of Storage
Once a consumer decides to delay consumption and to store a portion of currently available resources, further questions remain regarding the relationship between immediate and delayed consumption. For how long are

the resources stored? Are some reserves carried over longer than others? As already mentioned, some species, such as the marsh tits, store their food for relatively short periods of time (24 hours or less), while others typically hoard food for several months. Wrazen and Wrazen (1982) point out that eastern chipmunks periodically sample their cached food even when adding additional stores to their larder hoards. Such behavior is thought to be adaptive in that the condition of the stored food can be periodically evaluated while determining how much additional food to store. Economists analyze how expected values of stored resources are maximized in terms of optimal stockpiling models. Given an objective function of resource values, costs of storage, and adequate information on currently existing supplies, an optimal solution to determine times and amounts of "carry over" for different resources is obtained using dynamic linear programming techniques that incorporate the stochastic uncertainty of future production and resource availability (Gardner, 1979; Wright & Williams, 1982). One of the major points that emerges from these types of economic studies is that optimal solutions are very much influenced by the number and similarity of resources available throughout the time frame of analysis. The more similar an alternative resource is to the stored resource in terms of palatability, and the more dissimilar it is in terms of supply variability, the smaller is the optimal carry over of the stored resource. Furthermore, the impact of alternative resources increases. In ecological and behavioral studies of caching, the need for joint analysis of multiple types of resources is often ignored.

Current economic models of storage suggest several testable hypotheses for ecologists to consider: (a) the amount and length of storage time for any single type of food resource (e.g., acorns) will be highest in the absence of any close substitutes (e.g., hickory nuts) that have similar seasonal supply functions and in the absence of any other dissimilar substitutes (e.g., insects) that have different seasonal supply functions; (b) the number of items stored and the length of storage time will decrease as the marginal cost of storage associated with deterioration and theft increase; (c) the number of items stored, but not the length of storage time, will increase as the marginal costs of finding (or constructing) storage sites decrease.

IV. SUMMARY AND CONCLUSIONS

Many species have adapted their foraging behavior to avoid periods of scarcity. Relatively small, short-lived species often restrict their growth and reproduction to those seasons with the most abundant resources. They do not defend specific areas of resource supply. In contrast, larger, longer-lived species may be more active throughout different seasons and occupy distinct home ranges. They sometimes defend their core areas of intensive use from nonresident conspecifics. If population densities are high and food supplies unpredictable, these resident consumers may have important advantages over nonresidents and resident neighbors only if the resident consumers choose to locate their nest areas and refugia next to relatively stable sources of foods. Where a resident consumer decides to locate its refugia during times of resource superabundance may well influence its later competitive abilities if foods become scarce. By storing a proportion of very abundant, locally available foods, resident, centralized foragers may stabilize their food supply and lower their exposure to predators (Table 2). The ability to spread out these caches (scatter-hoarding) and later to retrieve them provides foragers, not only with increased uniformity in food supply, but also with increased flexibility in travel time that can reduce exposure to predators, while simultaneously lowering risks of losing stored foods to thieves and of losing unstored foods to competitors. For those foragers who store their food for only a few hours, the main advantages will be a reduction in exposure to predation (relative to continuous feeding at a concentrated food source) and reduced access of competitors to a readily-found and efficiently-exploited food source.

As a somewhat paradoxical consequence of this competition for food, I postulate that a potential exists for diffuse mutualism that results in indirect interchange of nutritionally complementary food resources. The proposed incidental resource interchange hypothesis predicts that continued access to spatially remote sources of complementary foods will occur only if neigh-

TABLE 2.   Contrasts in Timing of Consumption

	Responses	
A. Consumer Attributes	**(1) Immediate consumption**	**(2) Store for future**
Metabolic energy level	negative or neutral	positive
Body size	small	large
Longevity	short	long
Age	old	middle-aged
Spatial memory	poor	good
Residency	transient	permanent
Olfactory food detection	highly localized	long-range
Visual food detection	localized	long-range
Population density	sparce	crowded
Predator escape tactics	fast, evasive or freeze	slow, noctural
B. Resource Attributes		
Size of food	small	large
Abundance	scarce	abundant
Supply availability	predictable	unpredictable
Perishability	high	low
Substitutability	high	low
Proximity to storate site	remote	close
Proximity to refugia	close	remote
Number of refugia	low	high

boring consumers have: (a) restricted access to nutritionally unbalanced food sources that occur in very high abundances during short periods; (b) an ability to remember at least the general location of surplus, nonperishable foods that were previously stored during periods of high abundance; (c) information about probabilities of retrieving some foods from a specific caching site over a series of scatter-hoarding cycles.

This hypothesis provides the basis for a series of laboratory and field tests that require consideration of multiple interactive factors, such as distributions of alternative substitutable resources, alternative ways of spending foraging and nonforaging time, intensity and timing of risks to predation, and the group size and predictability of foraging behavior by neighbors. Currently, interest among ecologists, economists, psychologists, and behaviorists is growing and beginning to focus on the importance of consumer uncertainty. As methods are developed to consider multiple alternative choices that are quantitatively influenced by different types of uncertainty, the solutions to optimal foraging questions will become increasingly realistic and useful.

REFERENCES

Abbott, H.G., & Quink, T.F. (1970). Ecology of eastern white pine seed caches made by small forest mammals. *Ecology, 51,* 271–278.

Aleksiuk, M. (1970). The seasonal food regime of arctic beavers. *Ecology, 51,* 264–270.

Allison, J. (1983). Behavioral substitutes and complements. In R.L. Mellgren (Ed.), *Animal cognition and behavior* (pp. 1–30). Amsterdam: North Holland Press.

Altman, S.A. (1974). Baboons, space, time and energy. *American Zoologist, 14,* 221–248.

Anderson, R.M., & May, R.M. (1982). Coevolution of hosts and parasites. *Parasitology, 85,* 411–426.

Andersson, M. (1978). Optimal foraging area: Size and allocation of search effort. *Theoretical Population Biology, 13,* 397–409.

Andersson, M. (1981). Central place foraging in the whinchat, *Saxicola rubetra. Ecology, 62,* 538–544.

Andersson, M., & Krebs, J. (1978). On the evolution of hoarding behaviour. *Animal Behaviour, 26,* 707–711.

Armitage, K.B., & Harris, K.S. (1982). Spatial patterning in sympatric populations of fox and gray squirrels. *American Midland Naturalist, 108,* 389–397.

Aronson, R.B., & Givnish, T.J. (1983). Optimal central-place foragers: A comparison with null hypotheses. *Ecology, 64,* 385–399.

Axelrod, R. (1984). *The evolution of cooperation.* New York: Basic Books.

Balda, R.P. (1980). Recovery of cached seeds by a captive *Nucifraga caryocatactes. Zeitschrift fur Tierpsychologie, 52,* 331–346.

Balgooyen, T.G. (1976). Behavior and ecology of the American kestral (*Falco spaverius* L.) in the Sierra Nevada of California. *University of California Publications in Zoology, 103,* 1–83.

Barash, D.P. (1973). Territorial foraging behavior of pikas (*Ochotona princeps*) in Montana. *American Midland Naturalist, 89,* 202–207.

Barnard, C.J. (1984). When cheats may prosper. In C.J. Barnard (Ed.), *Producers and scroungers: Strategies of exploitation and parasitism.* New York: Chapman and Hall.

Barnett, R.J. (1977). The effect of burial by squirrels on germination and survival of oak and hickory nuts. *American Midland Naturalist, 98,* 319–330.

Battalio, R.C., Kagel, J.H., Rachlin, H., & Green, L. (1981). Commodity-choice behavior with pigeons as subjects. *Journal of Political Economy, 89,* 67–91.

Baum, W.M. (1983). Studying foraging in the psychological laboratory. In R.L. Mellgren (Ed.), *Animal cognition and behavior* (pp. 253–283). Amsterdam: North-Holland Press.

Belovsky, G.E., & Jordan, P.A. (1981). Sodium dynamics and adaptations of a moose population. *Journal of Mammalogy, 62,* 613–621.

Boucher, D.H., James, S., & Keeler, K.H. (1982). The ecology of mutualism. *Annual Review of Ecology and Systematics, 13,* 315–347.

Boulding, K.E. (1981). *Evolutionary economics.* Beverly Hills, CA: Sage Press.

Bowers, M.A., & Brown, J.H. (1982). Body size and coexistence in desert rodents: chance of community structure? *Ecology, 63,* 391–400.

Brewer, R., & McCann, M.T. (1985). Spacing in acord woodpeckers. *Ecology, 66,* 307–308.

Brooke, M. de L. (1981). How an adult wheatear *(Oenanthe oenanthe)* uses its territory when feeding nestlings. *Journal of Animal Ecology, 50,* 683–696.

Brown, J.H., Reichman, O.J., & Davidson, D.W. (1979). Granivory in desert ecosystems. *Annual Review of Ecology and Systematics, 10,* 201–227.

Brown, J.L. (1964). The evolution of diversity in avian territorial systems. *Wilson Bulletin, 76,* 160–169.

Brown, J.L., & Orians, G.H. (1970). Spacing patterns in mobile animals. *Annual Review of Ecology and Systematics, 1,* 239–262.

Brown, L.E. (1966). Home range and movement of small mammals. *Symposium of the Zoological Society of London, 18,* 111–142.

Bryant, D.M., & Turner, A.K. (1982). Central place foraging by swallows *(Hirundinidae):* The question of load size. *Animal Behaviour, 30,* 845–856.

Cade, T.J. (1967). Ecological and behavioral aspects of predation by the northern shrike. *Living Bird, 6,* 43–86.

Caraco, T. (1981). Risk-sensitivity and foraging groups. *Ecology, 62,* 527–531.

Carlson, A. (1983). Maximizing energy delivery to dependent young: A field experiment with red-backed shrikes *(Lanius collurio). Journal of Animal Ecology, 52,* 697–704.

Carlson, A., & Moreno, J. (1982). The loading effect in central place foraging wheatears *(Oenanthe oenanthe* L.) *Behavioural Ecology and Sociobiology, 11,* 173–185.

Carlson, A., & Moreno, J. (1981). Central place foraging in the wheatear *Oenanthe oenanthe:* An experimental test. *Journal of Animal Ecology, 50,* 917–924.

Cerri, R.D., & Fraser, D.F. (1983). Predation and risk in foraging minnows: Balancing conflicting demands. *American Naturalist, 121,* 552–561.

Colwell, P.F. (1982). Central place theory and the simple economic foundations of the gravity model. *Journal of Regional Science, 22,* 541–546.

Connell, J.H. (1980). Diversity and the coevolution of competitors, or the ghost of competition past. *Oikos, 35,* 131–138.

Connell, J.H. (1983). On the prevalence and relative importance of interspecific competition: Evidence from field experiments. *American Naturalist, 122,* 661–696.

Conner, D.A. (1983). Seasonal changes in activity patterns and the adaptive value of haying in pikas *(Ochotona princeps). Canadian Journal of Zoology, 61,* 411–436.

Cormack, R.M. (1979). Spatial aspects of competition between individuals. In R.M. Cormack & J.K. Ord, (Eds.), *Spatial and temporal analysis in ecology* (pp. 151–212). Fairland, MD: International Co-operative Publications House.

Covich, A.P. (1972). Ecological economics of seed consumption by *Peromyscus:* A graphical model of resource substitution. In E.S. Deevey, (Ed.), *Growth by intussusception* (pp. 69–94). New Haven: Connecticut Academy of Arts and Sciences.

Covich, A.P. (1974). Ecological economics of foraging among coevolving animals and plants. *Annals of Missouri Botanical Garden, 61,* 794–805.

Covich, A.P. (1976). Analyzing shapes of foraging areas: Some ecological and economic theories. *Annual Review of Ecology and Systematics, 7,* 235–257.

Cowie, R.J., Krebs, J.R., & Sherry, D.F. (1981). Food storing in marsh tits. *Animal Behaviour, 29,* 1252–1259.

Criddle, S. (1950). The *Peromyscus maniculatus bairdii* complex in Manitoba. *Canadian Field-Naturalist, 64,* 169–177.

Daly, M., Rauschenberger, J., & Behrends, P. (1982). Food aversion learning in kangaroo rats: A specialist-generalist comparison. *Animal Learning and Behavior, 10,* 314–320.

Davies, N.B. (1976). Parental care and the transition to independent feeding in the young spotted flycatcher *Muscicapa striata. Behaviour, 59,* 280–295.

Davies, N.B. (1980). The economics of territorial behaviour in birds. *Ardea, 68,* 63–74.

Davies, N.B., & Houston, A.I. (1981). Owners and satellites: The economics of territory defense in the pied wagtail, *Motacilla alba. Journal of Animal Ecology, 50,* 157–180.

Dean, A.M. (1983). A simple model of mutualism. *American Naturalist, 121,* 409–417.

Deevey, E.S. (1959). The hare and haruspex: A cautionary tale. *Yale Review, 49,* 161–179.

Don, B.A.C., & Rennolls, K. (1983). A home range model incorporating biological attraction points. *Journal of Animal Ecology, 52,* 69–81.

Dornbusch, R., & Mussa, M. (1975). Consumption, real balance and the hoarding function. *International Economic Review, 16,* 415–421.

Down, D.D. (1965). The role of saliva in food storage by the gray jay. *Auk, 82,* 139–154.

Eaton, B.C., & Lipsey, R.G. (1982). An economic theory of central places. *Economic Journal, 92,* 56–72.

Ebersole, J.P., & Wilson, J.D. (1980). Optimal foraging: The responses of *Peromyscus leucopus* to experimental changes in processing time and hunger. *Oecologia, 46,* 80–85.

Eide, S.H., & Ballard, W.B. (1982). Apparent case of surplus killing of caribou by gray wolves. *Canadian Field Naturalist, 96,* 87.

Eisenberg, J.F. (1968). Behavior patterns. In J.A. King (Ed.), *Biology of Peromyscus (Rodentia)* (pp. 451–495). Stillwater, OK: American Society of Mammalogists.

Elgmork, K. (1982). Caching behavior of brown bears *(Ursus arctos). Journal of Mammalogy, 63,* 607–612.

Elliott, C.L. (1980). Quantitative analysis of pika *(Ochotona princeps)* hay piles in central Idaho. *Northwest Science, 54,* 207–209.

Elliott, L. (1978). Social behavior and foraging ecology of the eastern chipmunk *(Tamias striatus)* in the Adirondack Mountains. *Smithsonian Contributions to Zoology, 265,* 1–107.

Ewer, R.F. (1968). *Ethology of mammals.* New York: Plenum Press.

Ewer, R.F. (1973). *The carnivores.* Ithaca, NY: Cornell University Press.

Ford, R.G. (1983). Home range in a patchy environment: Optimal foraging predictions. *American Zoologist, 23,* 315–326.

Fox, J.F. (1982). Adaptation of gray squirrel behavior to autumn germination by white oak acorns. *Evolution, 36,* 800–809.

Fredlund, M.C. (1976). Economics of animal systems. In *Frontiers of economics* (pp. 11–25). Blacksburg, VA: University Publications.

Freeland, W.J., & Janzen, D.H. (1974). Strategies in herbivory by mammals: The role of plant secondary compounds. *American Naturalist, 108,* 269–289.

Gardner, B.L. (1979). *Optimal stockpiling of grain.* Lexington, MA: Heath.

Getty, T. (1981a). Analysis of central-place space-use patterns: The elastic disc revisited. *Ecology, 62,* 907–914.

Getty, T. (1981b). Territorial behavior of eastern chipmunks *(Tamias striatus):* Encounter avoidance and spatial time-sharing. *Ecology, 62,* 915–921.

Getty, T. (1981c). Structure and dynamics of chipmunk home range. *Journal of Mammalogy,* 62, 726–737.

Giraldeau, L.A., & Kramer, D.L. (1982). The marginal value theorem: A quantitative test using load size variation in a central place forager, the eastern chipmunk, *Tamias striatus. Animal Behaviour, 30,* 1036–1042.

Glanz, W.E., Thorington, R.W., Jr., Giacalone-Madden, J., & Heaney, L.R. (1982). Seasonal food use and demographic trends in *Sciurus granatensis.* In E.G. Leigh, Jr., A.S. Rand, & D.M. Windsor (Eds.), *The ecology of a tropical forest* (pp. 239–252). Washington, DC: Smithsonian Institution Press.

Green, L., Fisher, E.B., Jr., Perlow, S., & Sherman, L. (1981). Preference reversal and self control: Choice as a function of reward amount and delay. *Behaviour Analysis Letters, 1,* 43–51.

Greenhut, M.L. (1978). Impacts of distance on microeconomic theory. *Manchester School of Economic and Social Studies, 46,* 17–40.

Gurnell, J. (1984). Home range, territoriality, caching behaviour and food supply of the red squirrel. *(Tamiasciurus hudsonicus fremonti)* in a subalpine lodgepole pine forest. *Animal Behaviour, 32,* 1119–1131.

Hahn, F.H. (1970). Savings under uncertainty. *Review of Economic Studies, 37,* 21–24.

Hainsworth, F.R., & Wolf, L.L. (1979). Feeding: An ecological approach. *Advances in the Study of Behavior, 9,* 53–96.

Hamilton, W.J., III, & Watt. K.E.F. (1970). Refuging. *Annual Review of Ecology and Systematics, 1,* 263–286.

Havera, S.P., & Smith, K.E. (1979). A nutritional comparison of selected fox squirrel foods. *Journal of Wildlife Management, 43,* 691–704.

Hazlett, B.A. (1983). Interspecific negotiations: Mutual gain in exchanges of a limiting resource. *Animal Behaviour, 31,* 160–163.

Healey, M.C. (1967). Aggression and self-regulation of population size in deer mice. *Ecology, 48,* 375–392.

Hegner, R.E. (1982). Central place foraging in the white-fronted bee-eater. *Animal Behaviour, 30,* 953–963.

Hey, J.D. (1979). *Uncertainty in microeconomics.* New York: New York University Press.

Hirschleifer, J., & Riley, J.G. (1979). The analytics of uncertainty and information—an expository survey. *Journal of Economic Literature, 17,* 1375–1421.

Houston, A. (1985). Central-place foraging: some aspects of prey choice for multiple-prey loaders. *American Naturalist, 125,* 811–826.

Howard, W.E., & Evans, F.C. (1961). Seeds stored by prairie deer mice. *Journal of Mammalogy, 42,* 260–263.

Huntley, N.J., Smith, A.T., & Ivins, B.L. (1986). Foraging behavior of the pika *(Ochotona princeps),* with comparisons of grazing versus haying. *Journal of Mammalogy, 67,* 139–148.

Hutchinson, G.E. (1978). *An introduction to population ecology.* New Haven, CT: Yale University Press.

Jaeger, M.M. (1982). Feeding pattern in *Peromyscus maniculatus:* The response to periodic food deprivation. *Physiology and Behaviour, 28,* 83–88.

James, P.C., & Verbeek, N.A.M. (1983). The food storage behaviour of the northwestern crow. *Behaviour, 85,* 276–291.

Janzen, D.H. (1971). Seed predation by animals. *Annual Review of Ecology and Systematics, 2,* 465–492.

Janzen, D.H. (1979). New horizons in the biology of plant defenses. In G.A. Rosenthal & D.H. Janzen (Eds.), *Herbivores: Their interaction with secondary plant metabolites* (pp. 331–350). New York: Academic Press.

Jenkins, S.H. (1980). A size-distance relation in food selection by beavers. *Ecology, 61,* 740–746.

Johnson, D.R. (1967). Diet and reproduction of Colorado pikas. *Journal of Mammalogy, 48,* 311–318.

Kacelnik, A. (1984). Central place foraging in starlings *(Sturnus vulgaris).* I. Patch residence time. *Journal of animal ecology, 53,* 283–299.

Kagel, J.H., Battalio, R.C., Rachlin, H., & Green, L. (1981). Demand curves for animal consumers. *Quarterly Review of Economics, 96,* 1–15.

Kagel, J.H., Green, L., & Caraco, T. (1986). When foragers discount the future: constraint or adaptation? *Animal Behaviour, 34,* 271–283.

Kamil, A.C. (1983). Optimal foraging theory and the psychology of learning. *American Zoologist, 23,* 291–302.

Karni, E. (1982). Risk aversion and saving behavior: Summary and extension. *International Economic Review, 23,* 35–42.

Kawamichi, M. (1980). Food, food hoarding and seasonal changes of the Siberian chipmunks. *Japanese Journal of Ecology, 30,* 211–220.

Kawamichi, T. (1976). Hay territory and dominance rank of pikas *(Ochotona princeps). Journal of Mammalogy, 57,* 133–148.

Kawamichi, T. (1982). Factors affecting sizes of home range and territory in pikas. *Japanese Journal of Ecology, 32,* 21–27.

Killeen, P.R., Smith, J.P., & Hanson, S.J. (1981). Central place foraging in *Rattus norvegicus. Animal Behaviour, 29,* 64–70.

Kowalski, K. (1976). *Mammals, An outline of theriology* (Translated from Polish). Warsaw: Poland: Panstwowe Wydawnictwo Naukowe.

Kramer, D.L., & Nowell, W. (1980). Central place foraging in the eastern chipmunk, *Tamias striatus. Animal Behaviour, 28,* 772–778.

Kraus, B. (1983). A test of the optimal density model for seed scatter hoarding. *Ecology, 64,* 608–610.

Krebs, J.R. (1982). Optimal foraging: Decision rules for predators. In J.R. Krebs & N.B. Davies (Eds.), *Behavioural ecology: an evolutionary approach* (pp. 26–63). Sunderland, MA: Sinauer.

Kruuk, H. (1972a). *The spotted hyena: A study of predation and social behavior.* Chicago: University of Chicago Press.

Kruuk, H. (1972b). Surplus killing by carnivores. *Journal of Zoology, London, 166,* 233–244.

Lacher, T.E., Willig, M.R., & Mares, M.A. (1982). Food preference as a function of resource abundance with multiple prey types: An experimental analysis of optimal foraging theory. *American Naturalist, 120,* 297–316.

Lanier, D.L., Estep, D.Q., & Dewsbury, D.A. (1974). Food hoarding in muroid rodents. *Behavioral Biology, 11,* 177–187.

Layne, J.N. (1954). The biology of the red squirrel, *Tamiasciurus hudsonicus logaux* (Bangs), in central New York. *Ecological Monographs, 24,* 227–267.

Lea, S.E.G. (1983). The analysis of need. In R.L. Mellgren (Ed.), *Animal cognition and behavior* (pp. 31–63). Amsterdam: North-Holland Press.

Leon, J., & Tumpson, D. (1975). Competition between two species for two complementary or substitutable resources. *Journal of Theoretical Biology, 50,* 185–201.

Lessels, C.M., & Stephens, D.W. (1983). Central place foraging: Single-prey loaders again. *Animal Behaviour, 31,* 238–243.

Levin, S.A. (1983). Some approaches to the modelling of coevolutionary interactions. In M.H. Nitecki (Ed.), *Coevolution* (pp. 21–65). Chicago: University of Chicago Press.

Lewis, A.R. (1980). Patch use by gray squirrels and optimal foraging. *Ecology, 61,* 1371–1379.

Lewis, A.R. (1982). Selection of nuts by gray squirrels and optimal foraging theory. *American*

Midland Naturalist, 107, 250–257.

Ligon, J.D. (1978). Reproductive interdependence of piñon jays and piñon pines. *Ecological Monographs, 48,* 111–126.

Lima, S.L., Valone, T.J., & Caraco, T. (1985). Foraging-efficiency-predation-risk trade-off in the gray squirrel. *Animal Behaviour, 33,* 155–165.

Lockard, R.B., & Lockard, J.S. (1971). Seed preference and buried seed retrieval of *Dipodomys deserti. Journal of Mammalogy, 52,* 219–221.

Lockner, F.R. (1972). Experimental study of food hoarding in the red-tailed chipmunk, *Eutamias ruficaudus. Zeitschrift für Tierpsychologie, 31,* 410–418.

Lyons, D., & Mosher, J.A. (1982). Food caching by raptors and caching of a nestling by the broad-winged hawk. *Ardea, 70,* 217–219.

MacArthur, R.H. (1972). *Geographical ecology.* New York: Harper and Row.

Macdonald, D.W. (1976). Food caching by red foxes and some other carnivores. *Zeitschrift für Tierpsychologie, 42,* 170–185.

MacLean, S.F., & Seastedt, T.R. (1979). Avian territoriality: Sufficient resources or interference competition? *American Naturalist, 114,* 304–308.

MacRoberts, M.H. (1970). Notes on the food habits and food defense of the acorn woodpecker. *Condor, 72,* 196–204.

MacRoberts, M.H., & MacRoberts, B.R. (1975). Social organization and behavior of the acorn woodpecker in central coastal California. *Ornithological Monographs, 21,* 1–115.

Madison, D. (1977). Movement and habitat use among interacting *Peromyscus leucopus* as revealed by radiotelemetry. *Canadian Field Naturalist, 91,* 273–281.

Malcolm, J.R. (1980). Food caching by African wild dogs *(Lycaon pictus). Journal of Mammalogy, 61,* 743–744.

Martindale, S. (1983). Foraging patterns of nesting Gila woodpeckers. *Ecology, 64,* 888–898.

May, R.M. (1982). Mutualistic interactions among species. *Nature, 296,* 803–804.

McFarland, D., & Houston, A. (1981). *Quantitative ethology: The state space approach.* Boston: Pitman.

McGinley, M.A., & Whitham, T.G. (1985). Central place foraging by beavers *(Castor canadensis):* A test of foraging predictions and the impact of selective feeding on the growth form of cottonwoods *(Populus fremontii). Oecologia, 66,* 558–562.

McLaughlin, R.L., & Montgomerie, R.D. (1985). Flight speeds of central place foragers: Female Lapland longspurs feeding nestlings. *Animal Behaviour, 33,* 810–816.

Melemis, S.M., & Falls, J.B. (1982). The defense function: a measure of territorial behavior. *Canadian Journal of Zoology, 60,* 495–501.

Menzel, E.W. (1973). Chimpanzee spatial memory organization. *Science, 182,* 943–945.

Menzel, E.W. (1978). Cognitive mapping in chimpanzees. In S.H. Hulse, H. Fowler, & W.K. Honig (Eds.), *Cognitive processes in animal behavior* (pp. 375–422). Hillsdale, NJ: Erlbaum.

Millar, J.S., & Zwickel, F.C. (1972). Characteristics and ecological significance of hay piles of pika. *Mammalia, 36,* 58–68.

Miller, A.H. (1931). Systematic revision and natural history of the American shrikes *(Lanius). University of California Publication in Zoology, 38,* 11–242.

Miller, G.A., & Vick, P. (1950). Hoarding in the rat as a function of the length of the path. *Journal of Comparative Physiology and Psychology, 43,* 66–69.

Morris, D. (1962). Behaviour of the green acouchi *(Myoprocta pratti)* with special reference to scatter hoarding. *Proceedings of the Zoological Society of London, 139,* 701–732.

Mumme, R.L., Koenig, W.D., & Pitelka, F.A. (1983). Are acorn woodpecker territories aggregated? *Ecology, 64,* 1305–1307.

Myton, B. (1974). Utilization of space by *Peromyscus leucopus* and other small mammals. *Ecology, 55,* 277–290.

Nelson, R.R., & Winter, S.G. (1982). *An evolutionary theory of economic change.* Cambridge,

MA: Belknap-Harvard University Press.

Noakes, D.L.G., & McNicol, R.E. (1982). Geometry for the eccentric territory. *Canadian Journal of Zoology, 60*, 1776-1779.

Nunn, G.L., Klem, D., Kimmel, T., & Merriman, T. (1976). Surplus killing and caching by American kestrels. *Animal Behaviour, 24*, 759-763.

O'Farrel, M.J. (1980). Spatial relationships of rodents in a sagebrush community. *Journal of Mammalogy, 61*, 589-605.

Oksanen, T., Oksanen, L., & Fretwell, S.D. (1985). Surplus killing in the hunting strategy of small predators. *American Naturalist, 126*, 328-346.

Olton, D.S., Handelman, G.E., & Walker, J.A. (1981). Spatial memory and food searching strategies. In A.C. Kamil & T.D. Sargent (Eds.), *Foraging behavior: Ecological, ethological and psychological approaches* (pp. 333-354). New York: Garland Press.

Orians, G.H. (1980). *Some adaptations of marsh-nesting black birds.* Princeton, NJ: Princeton University Press.

Orians, G.H., & Pearson, N.E. (1979). On the theory of central place foraging. In D.J. Horn, R.D. Mitchell, & G.E. Stairs (Eds.), *Analysis of ecological systems* (pp. 154-177). Columbus, OH: Ohio State University Press.

Owen-Smith, N., & Novellie, P. (1982). What should a clever ungulate eat? *American Naturalist, 119*, 151-177.

Paine, R.T. (1980). Food webs: Linkage, interaction strength and community intrastructure. *Journal of Animal Ecology, 49*, 667-685.

Palmer, A.R. (1981). Predator errors, foraging in unpredictable environments and risk: The consequences of prey variation in handling time versus net energy. *American Naturalist, 118*, 908-915.

Parker, G.A., & Knowlton, N. (1980). The evolution of territory size—Some ESS models. *Journal of Theoretical Biology, 84*, 445-476.

Paton, D.C., & Carpenter, F.L. (1984). Peripheral foraging by territorial rufous hummingbirds: defense by exploitation. *Ecology, 65*, 1808-1819.

Phelan, F.J.S. (1977). Food caching in the screech owl. *Condor, 79*, 127.

Powell, R.A. (1982). *The fisher: Life history, ecology, and behavior.* Minneapolis, MN: University of Minnesota Press.

Price, M.V. (1978). Seed dispersion preferences of coexisting desert rodent species. *Journal of Mammalogy, 59*, 624-626.

Pulliam, H.R. (1975). Diet optimization with nutrient constraints. *American Naturalist, 109*, 765-768.

Pulliam, H.R. (1981). Learning to forage optimally. In A.C. Kamil & T.D. Sargent (Eds.), *Foraging behavior: Ecological, ethological and psychological approaches* (pp. 379-388). New York: Garland Press.

Pyke, G.H. (1978). Are animals efficient harvesters? *Animal Behaviour, 26*, 241-250.

Pyke, G.H. (1984). Optimal foraging theory: A central review. *Annual Review of Ecology and Systematics, 15*, 523-575.

Pyke, G.H., Pulliam, H.R., & Charnov, E.L. (1977). Optimal foraging: a selective review of theory and tests. *Quarterly Review of Biology, 52*, 137-154.

Quirk, J.P. (1976). Intertemporal decision making and the market for assets. In *Intermediate microeconomics* (pp. 182-202). Chicago: Science Research Associates.

Rapport, D.J. (1971). An optimization model of food selection. *American Naturalist, 105*, 575-587.

Rapport, D.J., & Turner, J.E. (1977). Economic models in ecology. *Science, 195*, 367-373.

Real, L.A. (1980). On uncertainty and the law of diminishing returns in evolution and behavior. In J.E.R. Staddon (Ed.), *Limits to action: The allocation of individual behavior* (pp. 37-64). New York: Academic Press.

Reichman, O.J. (1977). Optimization of diets through food preferences by heteromyid rodents.

Ecology, 58, 454–457.

Reichman, O.J. (1981). Factors influencing foraging in desert rodents. In A.C. Kamil & T.D. Sargent (Eds.), *Foraging behavior: Ecological, ethological and psychological approaches* (pp. 195–213). New York: Garland Press.

Reichman, O.J., Whitham, T.G., & Ruffner, G.A. (1982). Adaptive geometry of burrow spacing in two pocket gopher populations. *Ecology, 63,* 687–695.

Reichman, O.J., & Fay, P. (1983). Comparison of the diets of a caching and noncaching rodent. *American Naturalist, 122,* 576–581.

Roberts, R.C. (1979). The evolution of avian food storing behavior. *American Naturalist, 114,* 418–438.

Robertson, R.J., & Gibbs, H.L. (1982). Superterritoriality in tree swallows: A reexamination. *Condor, 84,* 313–316.

Robinson, D.E., & Brodie, E.D. (1982). Food hoarding behavior in the short-tailed shrew *Blarina brevicauda. American Midland Naturalist, 108,* 369–375.

Rubenstein, D.I. (1982). Risk, uncertainty and evolutionary strategies. In B.C.R. Bertram, T.H. Clutton-Brock, R.I.M. Dunbar, D.I. Rubenstein, & R. Wrangham (Eds.), *Current problems in sociobiology* (pp. 91–111). Cambridge, England: Cambridge University Press.

Schoener, T.W. (1979). Generality of the size-distance relation in models of optimal feeding. *American Naturalist, 114,* 902–914.

Schoener, T.W. (1982). The controversy over interspecific competition. *American Scientist, 70,* 586–595.

Schoener, T.W. (1983). Field experiments on interspecific competition. *American Naturalist, 122,* 240–285.

Schwartz, C.W., & Schwartz, E.R. (1981). *The wild mammals of Missouri.* Columbia, MI: University of Missouri Press.

Shaffer, L. (1980). Use of scatter hoards by eastern chipmunks to replace stolen food. *Journal of Mammalogy, 61,* 733–734.

Sherbrooke, W.C. (1976). Differential acceptance of toxic jojoba seed *(Simmondsia chinensis)* by four Sonoran Desert heteromyid rodents. *Ecology, 57,* 596–602.

Sherry, D.F. (in press). Foraging for stored food. In M.L. Commons, A. Kacelnik, & S.J. Shettleworth (Eds.), *Quantitative analyses of behavior. (Vol. 6): Foraging.* Hillsdale, NJ: Erlbaum.

Sherry, D.F. (1982). Food storage, memory and marsh tits. *Animal Behaviour, 30,* 631–633.

Sherry, D.F. (1984). Food storage by black-capped chickadees: Memory for the location and contents of caches. *Animal Behaviour, 32,* 451–464.

Sherry, D.F., Avery, M., & Stevens, A. (1982). The spacing of stored food by marsh tits. *Zeitschrift für Tierpsychologie, 58,* 153–162.

Shettleworth, S.J. (1983). Memory in food-hoarding birds. *Scientific American, 248,* 102–110.

Shettleworth, S.J., & Krebs, J.R. (1982). How marsh tits find their hoards: The roles of site preference and spatial memory. *Journal of Experimental Psychology: Animal Behavior Processes, 8,* 354–375.

Sih, A. (1980). Optimal behavior: Can foragers balance two conflicting demands? *Science, 210,* 1041–1043.

Slatkin, M., & Maynard Smith, J. (1979). Models of coevolution. *Quarterly Review of Biology, 54,* 233–263.

Smith, A.T. (1974). The distribution and dispersal of pikas: influences of behavior and climate. *Ecology, 55,* 1368–1376.

Smith, C.C. (1968). The adaptive nature of social organization in the genus of tree squirrels *Tamiasciurus. Ecological Monographs, 38,* 31–63.

Smith, C.C., & Follmer, D. (1972). Food preferences of squirrels. *Ecology, 53,* 82–91.

Smith, C.C., & Reichman, O.J. (1984). Evolution of food caching by birds and mammals. *Annual Review of Ecology and Systematics, 15*, 329–351.

Smythe, N. (1970). Relationships between fruiting seasons and seed dispersal methods in a neotropical forest. *American Naturalist, 104*, 25–36.

Smythe, N. (1978). The natural history of the Central American agouti *(Dasyprocta punctata)*. *Smithsonian Contributions in Zoology, 257*, 1–52.

Smythe, N., Glantz, W.E., & Leigh, E.G., Jr. (1982). Population regulation in some terrestrial frugivores. In E.G. Leigh, Jr., A.S. Rand, & D.M. Windsor (Eds.), *The ecology of a tropical forest* (pp. 227–238). Washington, DC: Smithsonian Institution Press.

Snyderman, M. (1983). Optimal prey selection, delay of reinforcement and self-control. *Behaviour Analysis Letters, 3*, 131–147.

Somermeyer, W.H., & Bannink, R. (1973). *A consumption-savings model and its application.* New York: American Elsevier.

Sork, V.L. (1983). Mast fruiting in hickories and availabilities of nuts. *American Midland Naturalist, 109*, 81–88.

Stacey, P.B., & Jansma, R. (1977). Storage of pinon nuts by the acorn woodpeckers in ponderosa pine forests in Colorado. *Ecology, 49*, 831–843.

Stapanian, M.A., & Smith, C.C. (1978). A model for seed scatter hoarding: Coevolution of fox squirrels and black walnuts. *Ecology, 59*, 884–896.

Stapanian, M.A., & Smith, C.C. (1984). Density-dependent survival of scatterhoarded nuts: An experimental approach. *Ecology, 65*, 1387–1396.

Tadlock, C.C., & Klein, H.G. (1979). Nesting and food-storage behavior of *Peromyscus maniculatus gracilis* and *P. leucopus noveboracensis. Canadian Field-Naturalist, 93*, 239–242.

Telser, L.G. (1980). A theory of self-enforcing agreements. *Journal of Business, 53*, 27–44.

Terman, C.R. (1962). Spatial and homing consequences of the introductions of aliens into semi-natural populations of prairie deer mice. *Ecology, 43*, 216–223.

Tilman, D. (1982). *Resource competition and community structure.* Princeton, NJ: Princeton University Press.

Tinbergen, M.J. (1981). Foraging decisions in starlings *(Sturnus vulgaris* L.) *Ardea, 69*, 1–67.

Tinbergen, N. (1972). Food hoarding by foxes *(Vulpes vulpes* L.) In *The animal and its world* (pp. 315–328). Cambridge, MA: Harvard University Press.

Tinbergen, N., Impekoven, N., & Franck, D. (1967). An experiment on spacing-out as a defense against predation. *Behaviour, 28*, 307–321.

Tomback, D.F. (1977). Foraging strategies of Clark's nutcrackers. *Living Bird, 16*, 123–161.

Tomback, D.F. (1982). Dispersal of whitebark pine seeds by Clark's nutcrackers: A mutualism hypothesis. *Journal of Animal Ecology, 51*, 451–467.

Tomback, D.F. (1983). Nutcrackers and pines: Coevolution or coadaptation? In M.H. Nitecki (Ed.), *Coevolution* (pp. 179–223). Chicago: University of Chicago Press.

Trail, P.W. (1980). Ecological correlates of social organization in a communally breeding bird, the acorn woodpecker, *Melanerpes formicivorus. Behavioral Ecology and Sociobiology, 7*, 83–92.

Tullock, G. (1983). Territorial boundaries: An economic view. *American Naturalist, 121*, 440–442.

Valenta, Z., & Khaleque, A. (1959). The structure of castoramine. *Tetrahedron Letters, 12*, 1–5.

Vander Wall, S.B. (1982). An experimental analysis of cache recovery in Clark's nutcracker. *Animal Behaviour, 30*, 84–94.

Vander Wall, S.B., & Balda, R.P. (1977). Coadaptations of the Clark's nutcracker and the piñon pine for efficient seed harvest and dispersal. *Ecological Monographs, 47*, 89–111.

Vander Wall, S.B., & Balda, R.P. (1981). Ecology and evolution of food-storage behavior in conifer-seed-caching Corvids. *Zeitschrift für Tierpsychologie, 56,* 217–242.

Verner, J. (1977). On the adaptive significance of territoriality. *American Naturalist, 111,* 769–775.

Vestal, B.M., & Hellack, J.J. (1978). Comparison of neighbor recognition in two species of deer mice *(Peromyscus). Journal of Mammalogy, 59,* 339–346.

Vleck, D. (1981). Burrow structure and foraging costs in the fossorial rodent, *Thomomys bottae. Oecologia, 49,* 391–396.

Waddel, D. (1951). Hoarding behavior in the golden hamster. *Journal of Comparative and Physiological Psychology, 44,* 383–388.

Weeks, H.P., Jr., & Kirkpatrick, C.M. (1978). Salt preferences and sodium drive phenology in fox squirrels and woodchucks. *Journal of Mammalogy, 59,* 531–542.

Wiens, J.A. (1977). On competition and variable environments. *American Scientist, 65,* 590–597.

Wiens, J.A. (1983). Competition or peaceful coexistence? *Natural History, 92*(3), 30–34.

Wilson, E.O. (1975). *Sociobiology: The new synthesis.* Cambridge, MA: Belknap Press of Harvard University Press.

Wondolleck, J.T. (1978). Forage-area separation and overlap in heteromyid rodents. *Journal of Mammalogy, 59,* 510–518.

Wrazen, J.A., & Wrazen, L.A. (1982). Hoarding, body mass dynamics and torpor as components of the survival strategy of the eastern chipmunk. *Journal of Mammalogy, 63,* 63–72.

Wright, B.D., & Williams, J.C. (1982). The economic role of commodity storage. *Economic Journal, 92,* 596–614.

Yahner, R.H. (1975). The adaptive significance of scatter hoarding in the eastern chipmunk. *Ohio Journal of Science, 75,* 176–177.

Yoerg, S.I., & Kamil, A.C. (1982). Response strategies in the radial arm maze: Running around in circles. *Animal Learning and Behavior, 10,* 530–534.

Zaret, T.M. (1980). *Predation and freshwater communities.* New Haven, CT: Yale University Press.

Zeckhauser, R. (1974). Risk spreading and distribution. In H.M. Hochman & G.E. Peterson (Eds.), *Redistribution through public choice* (pp. 206–228). New York: Columbia University Press.

Author Index

Subject Index